# ENERGY POLICY
# AND LAND-USE PLANNING

An International Perspective

# ENERGY POLICY AND LAND-USE PLANNING

## An International Perspective

*Edited by*

David R. Cope, Peter Hills
and Peter James

PERGAMON PRESS

OXFORD · NEW YORK · TORONTO · SYDNEY · PARIS · FRANKFURT

| U.K. | Pergamon Press Ltd., Headington Hill Hall, Oxford OX3 0BW, England |
| --- | --- |
| USA | Pergamon Press Inc., Maxwell House, Fairview Park, Elmsford, New York 10523, USA |
| CANADA | Pergamon Press Canada Ltd., Suite 104, 150 Consumers Road, Willowdale, Ontario M2J 1P9, Canada |
| AUSTRALIA | Pergamon Press (Aust.) Pty. Ltd., P.O. Box 544, Potts Point, N.S.W. 2011, Australia |
| FRANCE | Pergamon Press SARL, 24 rue des Ecoles, 75240 Paris, Cedex 05, France |
| FEDERAL REPUBLIC OF GERMANY | Pergamon Press GmbH, Hammerweg 6, D-6242 Kronberg-Taunus, Federal Republic of Germany |

First edition 1984

**Library of Congress Cataloging in Publication Data**
Main entry under title:
Energy policy and land-use planning.
(Urban and regional planning series; v. 32)
Includes index.
1. Land use—Planning. 2. Energy policy.
3. Environmental policy. 4. Space in economics.
I. Cope, David R. II. Hills, Peter J. III. James, Peter. IV. Series.
HD108.6.E53   1983      333.73'17      83-13236

**British Library Cataloguing in Publication Data**
Energy policy and land-use planning.—(Urban and regional planning).
1. Land   2. Regional   planning—Economic aspects
I. Cope, David R.      II. Hills, Peter
III. James, Peter      IV. Series
333.7      HD111

ISBN 0-08-026757-2 (Hardcover)
     0-08-031323-X (Flexicover)

311055

*Printed in Great Britain by A. Wheaton & Co. Ltd., Exeter*

To Sharon
   Maria
   Susan

# About the Authors

DAVID R. COPE

David R. Cope is a Lecturer in Environmental Planning at Nottingham University. During the period 1981–84 he took leave of absence from the university to work as Environmental Team Leader of the Economic Assessment Service of the International Energy Agency's Coal Research Service in London. While at Nottingham he collaborated closely with Peter Hills on several research projects related to coal, environment and planning issues in Britain, the USA and the Federal Republic of Germany, organised by the Energy and Planning Group.


JOHN GLASSON

John Glasson is now Acting Head of the Department of Town Planning, Oxford Polytechnic. He is also the Project Investigator for the Power Station Impacts Research Project which is based at Oxford. His recent publications include 'An Introduction to Regional Planning', 'The Socio-Economic Effects of Power Stations on their Localities' and 'Environmental Impact Analysis: From Theory to Practice'.


MICHAEL GOUGH

Michael Gough is a Senior Planner with Dublin Corporation and is currently President of the Irish Planning Institute. Formerly a planner with Waterford Corporation, he has written a number of papers and reports on energy and planning matters in Ireland.


PETER HILLS

Peter Hills is now Senior Lecturer in Urban Planning in the Centre of Urban Studies and Urban Planning, University of Hong Kong. He was formerly a Lecturer in Planning Studies at Nottingham University, where he worked closely with David Cope on a number of research projects concerning energy/environment issues. His primary interests are in the field of environmental assessment procedures and techniques and energy resource development.

## PETER JAMES

Peter James is now a freelance journalist covering energy and environmental matters for the press, radio and television. He was formerly a research assistant with the Energy and Planning Group at the University of Nottingham. He is the author of 'The Future of Coal' (Macmillan, 1982).

## ANTOINE H. M. JANSSEN

Antoine H. M. Janssen has a degree in Law and has been employed in various functions by the Netherlands Ministry of Economic Affairs since 1974. During this period he has been involved in questions related to European integration, multinational enterprises and cartel policy. At present he is attached to the Directorate for Electricity and Nuclear Energy of the Directorate-General of the Ministry and has worked on the Memorandum on Power Generation Fuels, published in July, 1980, which served as a starting point for the Public Discussion on energy problems held in the Netherlands in 1981–82.

## J. OWEN LEWIS

Owen Lewis qualified as an architect at University College Dublin and has been Research Architect at the Institute for Industrial Research and Standards in Dublin. He joined the staff of the School of Architecture in University College Dublin in 1974 and is now College Lecturer in Building Technology at the school.

He is active in the European solar energy research programme, particularly in performance monitoring of solar-heated dwellings and passive solar energy. He is a founder member of the Solar Energy Society of Ireland and was its secretary from 1976–79 and Chairman from 1979–81.

## G. A. MACKAY

G. A. (Tony) Mackay is a partner with PEIDA, a firm of economic consultants based in Edinburgh. He spent 13 years on the staff of the University of Aberdeen and has written various books and articles on North Sea oil, energy and regional economics.

## JON O'RIORDAN

A graduate of the Geography Department of the University of Edinburgh, Jon O'Riordan completed his Ph.D on water resource management in

British Columbia, Canada. After working on a federal/provincial study on comprehensive river basin planning, he joined the provincial government in 1973 as a member of the Secretariat of the Provincial Cabinet's Environment and Land Use Committee.

He is now Director of Planning in the British Columbia Ministry of Environment, responsible for developing long term environmental management plans for the province.

SUSAN OWENS

Susan Owens graduated in Environmental Sciences at the University of East Anglia, where she subsequently completed her Ph.D in the field of energy demand and planning. She compiled the 'Register of Energy Research in the Social Sciences' for the Social Science Research Council's Energy Panel and subsequently worked for 2 years with the Energy and Planning Group at the University of Nottingham. She is now University Assistant Lecturer in Geography and Fellow of Newnham College, Cambridge.

PETER ROBERTS AND TIM SHAW

Peter Roberts and Tim Shaw were previously Senior Lecturers in the Department of Town and Country Planning, Liverpool Polytechnic and were responsible for starting the Celtic and Irish Sea Oil and Gas Research Unit. They have collaborated on various papers dealing with the development of oil and gas resources. Peter Roberts is currently Principal Lecturer in Regional Planning at Coventry (Lanchester) Polytechnic. Tim Shaw is a Lecturer in Planning in the Department of Town and Country Planning at the University of Newcastle-upon-Tyne.

# Preface

FEW issues have captured public and political attention to quite the same extent as energy over the period since the early 1970s. Academics too have shown increasing interest in the technical, economic, social and environmental aspects of energy supply and demand systems. The literature on energy issues has increased dramatically since the first 'oil crisis' of 1973–4.

Despite this undoubted interest in energy, certain aspects of the relationships between energy systems and policy making and regulatory systems have remained relatively neglected. One such important area is the relation between energy and land-use planning. This field of planning activity relates to the issues, procedures and methods used to determine the use of land, the linkages between different land uses and the implications of choices in the use of land for such important factors as employment generation and environmental impacts. Although a growing number of commentators have emphasised the potential significance of land-use planning systems, both as a positive factor in managing and controlling energy-related impacts and achieving more energy efficient societies, or as a negative factor in constraining much-needed energy supply projects, relatively little literature is available which attempts to investigate the linkages between energy and planning in a systematic fashion. It is towards filling this particular gap that the present book is directed.

The central concerns of this book relate to two main groups of issues. Firstly, it has become increasingly clear that public discussion and evaluation of energy investment decisions usually arise in their most open and intense form during the course of the land-use planning development control, or permitting, process which is pursued in response to plans to construct individual energy developments. This has meant that land-use planning systems have been a primary vehicle in the evaluation of national energy plans and quite often, as a result, have been put under considerable strain as they have usually not been specifically designed for such a task. This has certainly been the case in the United Kingdom but is also evident elsewhere.

Secondly, there has been growing recognition that as a result of the point made above and because of the increased demand for exhaustive and open evaluation of energy development proposals, the land-use planning process is being seen more and more as a constraint on the achievement of certain goals laid down by, or for, energy utility developers. This constraint arises from the time required to progress through the various stages of the process. The outcome has variously been demands for the streamlining of the process, proposals for exempting developments from the normal processes of law, or attempts by energy facility developers to come to terms with the demands imposed upon them by adopting particular procedures to ensure greater conformity with the requirements of the planning process. One excellent example of this adaptive response has been the increasingly widespread use of Environmental Impact Assessment (EIA) in the project appraisal process. These, then, are the broad categories of issues addressed in the various chapters of this book.

The book is not, at least primarily, concerned with the energy aspects of economic planning, such as relations between energy growth and GDP growth, capital supply, investment decisions and so on. Nor is it primarily concerned with relationships between energy supply and consumption and resulting physical environmental pollution effects except as far as these are considered by land-use planning systems. In other words, it is not intended to be yet another book on 'energy and the environment' of which there are already a large number. Obviously, it is not possible to divorce land-use planning considerations completely from either national economic planning or environmental pollution interactions, but as the reader will find, these are not the central concerns of the chapters in this book.

As with any book there are numerous individuals and organisations whose help and co-operation has contributed in no small measure to the realisation of the project.

The editors, in particular, would like to express their appreciation to the Geography and Planning Committee and the Energy Panel of the Social Science Research Council (SSRC) which provided funding during the period 1977–82 to support research projects and research students associated with the Energy and Planning Group at Nottingham University. Although none of the chapters in this book is based specifically on SSRC-funded projects we do nonetheless wish to acknowledge the considerable contribution which the SSRC has made to the development of social science energy research in the United Kingdom.

On behalf of all the contributors to this book we would like to thank the many individuals in the energy industries, government departments and planning agencies, who have made available information on which the various chapters draw.

The editors would also like to express their gratitude to the contributing authors to this book. The task of organising their contributions was made much easier by the way in which they responded to our deadlines and requests for amendments. Contacts for the two chapters on Ireland and the Netherlands were made in June, 1979 when David Cope attended session 191 of the Salzburg Seminar, Schloss Leopoldskron, Salzburg, Austria, and we are grateful for the opportunities provided by the Seminar and the Faculty of session 191.

Finally, we would like to thank Renata Loj and Sue Pinkett for typing the manuscript and Gill Thomas for her excellent work on the maps and diagrams.

*Nottingham*                                   DAVID R. COPE
                                               PETER HILLS
                                               PETER JAMES

# Acknowledgements

The editors wish to express their thanks to the following for permission to use certain maps, diagrams and tables which appear in this book:

The National Coal Board—Figures 2.1 and 2.2.

The North East of Scotland Development Agency—Figure 3.1

The British Gas Corporation—Figure 4.1.

The National Radiological Protection Board—Figure 10.2

The Radioactive Waste Management Advisory Committee—Figure 10.5

and Table 10.1.

The Commission of the European Communities, DG XII. Science, Research and Development—Figure 10.4.

# Contents

*Units*

All the units used in this book are metric. To convert to British Imperial and US units the following approximate conversion factors can be used.

| To convert from | to | multiply by |
|---|---|---|
| metre | foot | 3.281 |
| kilometre | mile | 0.621 |
| square metre | square foot | 10.765 |
| hectare | acre | 2.471 |
| hectare | square mile | $3.861 \times 10^{-3}$ |
| cubic metre | cubic foot | 35.315 |
| tonne | US (short) ton (2000 lb) | 1.102 |
| tonne | long ton (2240 lb) | 0.984 |
| $N/m^2$ | standard atmosphere | $9.870 \times 10^{-6}$ |
| $Wh/m^2$ | Btu/square foot | 0.317 |
| $J/m^2$ | Btu/square foot | $88.07 \times 10^{-6}$ |

One million tonnes of coal equivalent (assuming 1 tonne of coal to be $25.64 \times 10^9 J$) is approximately equal to:

$25.64 \times 10^{15} J$

$600 \times 10^3$ tonnes petroleum

$24.5 \times 10^9$ cubic feet of natural gas

$700 \times 10^6$ cubic metres of natural gas

$2.1 \times 10^{12}$ watt hours of electrical energy produced at an operating thermal efficiency of 32%.

# Abbreviations and Acronyms

ACC          Association of County Councils
AFR          away-from-reactor
AGR          advanced gas-cooled reactor
ASEC         Area Surface Environmental Committee (National Coal Board)
AVM          Atelier Vitrification Marcoule (France)
AWRE         Atomic Weapons Research Establishment, Aldermaston
BC           British Columbia/Borough Council
BGC          British Gas Corporation
BMD          Brede Maatschappelijke Discussie over Energie (Broad National Debate on Energy) (Netherlands)
BNFL         British Nuclear Fuels Ltd
BNOC         British National Oil Corporation
BP           British Petroleum PLC
BSC          British Steel Corporation
CC           County Council
CEC          Commission of the European Communities
CEGB         Central Electricity Generating Board (England and Wales)
CENE         Commission on Energy and the Environment, 1978–81 (UK)
CHP          combined heat and power
CHP/DH       combined heat and power (with the heat used for) district heating
DC           District Council/direct current
DEn          Department of Energy (UK)
DH           district heating
DoE          Department of Environment (England and Wales)
EC           European Community
EEF          European Energy Fund
EIA          environmental impact assessment
ESB          Electricity Supply Board (Eire)
FFr          French franc
GB           Great Britain (England and Wales and Scotland)
GW(e)        gigawatt of electrical output, from thermal electricity generating stations
ha           hectare
HEP          hydro-electric power

| | |
|---|---|
| HEPC | Headquarters Environmental Planning Committee (National Coal Board) |
| HIDB | Highlands and Islands Development Board |
| HLW | high-level (radioactive) waste |
| Hz | Hertz |
| IAEA | International Atomic Energy Authority |
| ICC | Industrial Credit Corporation (Eire) |
| IDA | Industrial Development Authority (Eire) |
| IEA | International Energy Agency |
| IGS | Institute of Geological Sciences (UK) |
| ILW | intermediate level (radioactive) waste |
| JWP | joint working party |
| km | kilometre |
| $kN/m^2$ | kilonewton per square meter (pressure) |
| kV | kilovolt |
| LLW | low-level (radioactive) waste |
| m | metre |
| M | mega ($10^6$) |
| MAFF | Ministry of Agriculture, Fisheries and Food |
| MBC | Metropolitan Borough Council |
| MW | megawatt |
| MW(e) | megawatt of electrical output, from thermally generated power stations |
| Mtce | million tonnes of coal equivalent (see section on units) |
| NCB | National Coal Board (Great Britain) |
| NEB | National Energy Board (Canada) |
| NEPA | National Environmental Policy Act, 1969 (USA) |
| NESDA | North East Scotland Development Authority |
| NGL | natural gas liquids |
| NIREX | Nuclear Industry Radioactive Waste Executive (UK) |
| NRPB | National Radiological Protection Board (UK) |
| NUM | National Union of Mineworkers (Great Britain) |
| OSO | Offshore Supplies Office (UK) |
| OTA | Office of Technology Assessment of the US Congress |
| p | pence |
| PADC | Project Appraisal for Development Control (University of Aberdeen) |
| PSI | Power Stations Impact study (Oxford Polytechnic) |
| PWR | pressurised water reactor |
| RCEP | Royal Commission on Environmental Pollution (UK) |
| R, D & D | research, development and demonstration |
| RDO | Regional Development Organisation (Eire) |
| RF | recovery factor (proportion of a mineral resource in place that can be extracted) |

| | |
|---|---|
| RTPI | Royal Town Planning Institute (UK) |
| RW | radioactive waste |
| RWM | radioactive waste management |
| RWMAC | Radioactive Waste Management Advisory Committee (UK) |
| SCLSERP | Standing Conference on London and South-East Regional Planning |
| SDD | Scottish Development Department |
| SEPD | Scottish Economic Planning Department |
| SESI | Solar Energy Society of Ireland |
| SNG | synthetic natural gas |
| SO | Scottish Office |
| $SO_2$ | sulphur dioxide |
| SPF | site population factor |
| SRF | short rotation forestry |
| SSRC | Social Science Research Council (Great Britain) |
| THORP | Thermal Oxide Reprocessing Plant, Sellafield (Windscale), Cumbria |
| UK | United Kingdom (England and Wales, Scotland and Northern Ireland) |
| UKAEA | United Kingdom Atomic Energy Authority |
| USA | United States of America |
| V | volt |

# CHAPTER 1

# Introduction and Overview

DAVID R. COPE, PETER HILLS and PETER JAMES

Since the dramatic oil price rises which followed the 1973 Arab-Israeli War and which were repeated after the Iranian Revolution in 1979, the 'energy crisis' has dominated national and international politics. Although the early stridency of this debate, reflected in President Carter's identification of energy security as 'the moral equivalent of war' (Carter, 1977), has now abated there has been a permanent, qualitative shift in awareness of the centrality of energy issues, in a direction taken formerly only by a few prescient commentators (Kirk, 1982).

The way in which the modern world, particularly its highly-industrialised areas, has been shaped by the availability of cheap energy supplies is widely recognised. Industrial growth, spreading outwards from the UK was based on the economic and other advantages of coal compared to alternative fuels. The latter part of the twentieth century saw the development of new industries and economic regions and the decentralisation of residential and economic patterns, based on the growing use of cheap oil for road and air transport, heat-raising and feedstocks. If the era of cheap energy is indeed over, it is clear that major economic and social adjustments will be necessary in the industrialised world.

For many, the 1970s have also demonstrated that the world is faced not merely with an adjustment to higher energy prices but a period of absolute shortages of energy and other vital materials. The spectre of international tension as stagnant economies struggle for access to resources, with the weakest going to the wall, the strongest rent with social tensions, and a marked shift in global power from energy-consuming to energy-producing nations has haunted the contemporary imagination.

Such pessimistic views have been supported by the obvious effects of energy price discontinuities on the world economy. Although other factors have also been at work, the deep economic recessions of 1973–74 and from 1979 were closely related to the 1973 and 1979 oil price rises and the industrialised world enjoyed a much lower rate of growth in the 1970s than had been customary in the 1960s and 1950s. This was accompanied by, and helped cause, higher rates of inflation and unemployment, with consequent

1

social and political tension in many countries. In the future, continued instability in the Middle East and the prospect of oil prices rising whenever growth and increased energy demand resume, thus choking recovery before it has barely begun, seem to many to cast a blight over economic prospects to the year 2000 (Goodman *et al.*, 1981).

The most common response to the energy crisis in many countries has been massive investment, and plans for more, in energy resources to open up new supplies and reduce dependence on imported oil. These are clearly of great economic importance, with considerable effects on society, politics and the environment and likely to be a determining influence on the economic geography of the twenty-first century. It is about these plans, their feasibility, desirability, possible alternatives in whole or in part and, in particular the possibilities for conflict and reconciliation between them and the many other social, economic and environmental goals set by groups in advanced industrial economies that the interrelationship between land-use planning and energy—the focus of this book—is concerned.

This sudden need for large new energy developments partially caused, and partially coincided with, an increasing awareness of the environmental and social impacts of modern economic activity. There has been a growing concern about the environmental pollution which accompanied the economic growth of the post-war years. Much of this has been directed at the energy industries, which are collectively major users and polluters of land, water, air and other resources. Associated with this trend has been increasing apprehension over the risks to life associated with modern industrial activities. Although this was given a great impetus in the UK by the Flixborough explosion of 1974, its main focus soon became the energy industries. Nuclear developments in particular have been confronted with growing opposition, based on a mixture of fears, including the dangers of radiation exposures from plant operation and waste disposal, the possibility of a catastrophic accident and the prospects of nuclear proliferation or sabotage.

In recent years the techniques of risk assessment have been applied to all energy technologies and there is now a recognition that any energy option— including energy conservation has potential health and environmental risks, although the question of which are the most risky remains controversial (Cohen and Pritchard, 1980). This awareness has presented particular problems to densely populated countries with little scope for spatial segregation of hazardous developments, as the chapter on gas in the UK and that on nuclear power in the Netherlands demonstrate.

These questions of risk and environmental impact have coincided with other intellectual developments which also focused on the role of energy in Western society. Huge energy developments became for many the symbol of a centralised, authoritarian and technocratic world, imposing unacceptable hardships on the population as a whole or particular areas and depriving citizens of chances to influence the decisions which determined their lives. With currents within and outside planning running towards physical environments on a 'human scale' and technologies which are 'appropriate'—and preferably 'small and beautiful'—such huge developments as nuclear power stations or new coalfields are bound to be extremely controversial

## The Energy Debate in the 1980s

The intense discussion of energy in the 1970s has been replaced by a different, perhaps more sophisticated, perhaps more complacent, view of the problem. In the USA President Carter's 'moral equivalent of war' has given way to the Reagan administration's view that government responses to the events of the 1970s 'demonstrated the shortcomings of trying to treat energy as an issue separate from the many others that influence our economy and of trying to isolate energy from the forces of the marketplace' (International Communication Agency, 1982). Similar, though less extreme, changes in emphasis have taken place in other countries.

Such rapid changes in the perceived significance of energy issues and the downward revision of energy demand forecasts in almost all western countries form the backcloth to this book. Much thinking on the relationship between planning and energy has been in response to the very high expectations of future energy requirements made in the mid-1970s. The reduced forecasts of recent years may suggest that problems have been overemphasised. Certainly, expectations of large numbers of energy developments piling on top of each other (Watt Committee, 1979) have declined but the procedural issues which concern large parts of the chapters in this book are not likely to diminish in intensity while the environmental and other impacts of developments which *do* go ahead are unlikely to be less problematic.

One striking feature of the evolution of the energy debate over the past decade has been the recognition of the many obstacles which inevitably hinder the rapid implementation of energy supply or demand management programmes—especially those on the 'fast track' (priority developments, intended to be implemented rapidly) because of the multitude of interests affected by energy concerns. Early attempts to develop coherent programmes of energy supply and demand management, whether general programmes such as the 1977 Carter proposals (*Congressional Quarterly Weekly Report*, 1977) and the Energy Policy Consultative Document (Department of Energy, 1978) or technical scenarios such as those developed by the UK Department of Energy (1979) did not go far beyond recognising the traditional financial investment constraints which might inhibit achievement of desired goals. The interlinkages with employment and environment policy, let alone wider considerations of economic growth and overall lifestyles, were either ignored or seen as peripheral to the achievement of the supply and demand goals, about which consensus was assumed. The concern of land-use planning to identify interrelationships between one policy area and others must take considerable credit for a subsequent broadening of the base of energy policy.

The past decade has also seen a shift in focus from a dominant concern with energy *supply* strategies, to strategies which, at least to an extent, consider the options which demand management and conservation may offer. Alvin Weinberg's contention that energy policy ought to concentrate on the supply side because this was so much more tractable to policy manipulation than the individual decisions of millions of consumers has been undermined by the realisation that it has been demand-side changes, albeit many of them unwilling (and some undesirable), which have led to the position of 'energy glut' in the early 1980s (Weinberg, 1980).

The shift in focus to a greater recognition of the role of demand-side management presents some dilemmas to the land-use planning system, as discussed in Chapter 9. This is because, at least as currently constituted, the land-use planning systems of most countries have a limited ability to manage the spatial aspects of conservation, even where there is reliable information on just what it can achieve. Nevertheless, even though the part which could be played by land-use planning in energy demand management is less clear-cut than its obvious involvement in siting decisions and impact assessment of energy supply facilities, the concerns of planning have contributed to the emerging recognition of demand management issues and the arenas for debate provided by planning procedures have often led to influential statements on the importance of conservation.

## Energy and the Planning System

The provision of energy and its related problems have had a major effect on the practice of land-use planning, at a general level. The simultaneous assumption and objective of planning in the UK and elsewhere—a prosperous and expanding local and national economy, within a context of relatively abundant resources to apply to policy goals (slum clearance, improved communications and so on) and the need for strict land-use regulation to minimise the costs and optimise the benefits of growth, has been undermined.

Today the containment or reduction of national and local government expenditures has become a policy objective for governments in the UK and most other western countries, imposing many constraints on planning activities. As the external environment has changed, planners have become aware how much their past activities were conditioned by energy patterns which are now seen as one of the main determinants of land uses and spatial structures. At the heart of this process was the new mobility offered by oil-fuelled road and air transport leading to faster growth in outer suburbs and small/medium-sized towns than other areas—to the detriment of the inner cities—as well as new patterns of housing, employment and leisure.

The land-use planning systems of the UK, and other urbanised and industrialised societies, have been essentially based on the need to achieve the optimum use of a scarce resource whose quantity was fixed—land—compared to the more elastic nature of the other factors of production, capital and labour.

However, from 1973, it appeared that energy represented another 'hidden' factor, which was even more scarce than land and therefore took priority. Thus with many of the major energy developments of the 1970s—such as North Sea oil installations, the Selby coalfield, the Windscale reprocessing plant in the UK—it appeared that the over-riding national need for their output outweighed normal planning considerations, whatever their effects might be.

This new emphasis on energy as a fundamental determinant of economic and social activities and their spatial form also seemed to offer a new opportunity to planners and the planning system. The hopes of improved built environments and planning-based social transformation which accompanied the 1947 Town and Country Planning Act in the UK, and similar legislation in other countries had, over the years, given way to disillusionment and considerable hostility to planners and their activities by the general public. During the 1970s many planners were searching for a new role and a large number agreed with the view of Amory Lovins (1977) that 'energy—pervasive, symbolic and strategically central . . . offers the best integrating principle for the wider shifts of policy to which we are groping'.

Some commentators implied that only by addressing energy-related issues could planning incontrovertibly establish itself as an integral part of modern social organisation (Hall, 1978) while others suggested that only through the emergence and application of particular perspectives and processes based on principles derived from urban and regional planning could an 'efficient and equitable' resolution of energy problems be achieved (Paget and Lloyd, 1980). The outburst of research, analysis and comment to which this enthusiasm for energy has given rise, although sometimes unstructured and ill-considered, has undoubtedly been a great stimulus to the development of land-use planning.

This involvement of land-use planning with energy issues has been accentuated in some countries by the specific requirement by central or other levels of government that some part of the national effort in resolving energy supply problems should be met by the co-ordinated development of local energy plans. In the Netherlands, where the particular geographical circumstances place a high premium on integrated physical planning, it is inevitable that spatial planning should be expected to play such a role. In Denmark, municipal and regional heat supply plans are a critical part of the national energy supply planning and systematic local plans have been required to be developed since 1979. In Sweden there is even more demanding local planning. Local authorities have to develop total energy system plans for their areas, dealing with the supply, distribution and use of energy *and* the environmental impacts of discharges. This mandatory energy planning was introduced in 1977 and by mid-1982 all municipalities were expected to have detailed energy management plans prepared (International Energy Agency, 1981; Ministry of Industry, 1981).

In the UK the expectations placed by central government on local administrations have been less clear-cut. As noted in Chapter 9, a Parliamentary Committee recommended as long ago as 1975 that regional and transport plans, as well as structure plans, should pay particular attention to energy management and the energy implications of their proposals but the government's response was to play down the specific significance of energy considerations in such planning. Consequently, the initiative has been left very much with individual authorities facing energy developments or particular energy management needs.

**Changes in Planning**

Alongside the pressures for change created by various energy developments, other changes in planning's emphases and organisation have occurred in most western countries in the past decade. These changes and their consequences will continue to affect the ability of planning systems to handle the issues raised by future energy developments. They have involved the ways in which the tasks of planning are identified and acted upon, the ways that planners equip themselves for these tasks, the remits of the organisations in which planning is carried out and the relationship between planning and those sectors of society—the general public, developers of particular proposals and others—with an interest in how planning handles the problems presented it.

The early 1970s saw planning under the strong influence of a systems analysis approach, with a marked presumption towards a purely rational, technocratic activity. This was considered necessary to manage the consequences of the growth, mentioned earlier in the case of energy, but expectations of which permeated all sectors of activity with which planning was concerned. A decade later, the emphasis is far more on the preservation of vulnerable economic security and the mitigation of relative or even absolute economic decline.

The emergence of structure planning, with its emphasis on long-term strategic questions and interactions between various areas of public policy at the local and regional levels, obliged a move away from planning's preoccupation with land-use and built form to a much broader perspective. It is this perspective which permeates the chapters of this book, despite the use, for convenience, of the term 'land-use' in its title. There was a parallel trend in this strengthening of a broad policy perspective in the move towards corporate management, stimulated by the Bains Report (1972).

Within the discipline of planning, there was a response to the inexorable widening and deepening of its remit through the strengthening of social science perspectives in planning education and an increasing emphasis on policy-orientated research in local planning authorities, academia and consultancies. However, the parallel increase in demand for a technical competence on the part of planners, occasioned by the growth of energy-related and many other complex technological considerations has been less successfully met. The long-standing stale dominance of design and dogma-orientated conceptions of planning within planning education have combined to produce a situation where many other disciplines—the natural and applied sciences, economics and the law in particular—have provided the personnel with the competence to handle authoritatively the detailed technical and procedural issues created by complex technological developments.

The division of responsibilities for various fields of planning between different levels of local government has been another area where considerable change has occurred with important consequences for energy-related developments. In the UK, as in most western countries, there has been a trend towards amalgamation and rationalisation of historically-inappropriate small authorities. However, the creation of multi-tier authorities, as with the county and district system in England and Wales in 1974 (regions and districts in Scotland) and similar systems in other countries, has opened the way for conflicts of interest between strategic policy developed at regional levels and the desires of local administrations.

In the UK, although not in most other western industrial countries, there has been a decline in the formal recognition given to regional scale planning (at least in England and Wales), especially after 1979 with the advent of a determinedly centralising government. However, at the same time, the exigencies of energy-related and other environmental and economic policies have suggested the need for regionally-oriented agencies to handle the cumulative impact of incremental developments. This theme, especially regional identity and equity conflicts, may be an emerging characteristic of the relation between energy policy and planning in the last part of the twentieth century, as discussed in the concluding chapter of this book.

The most significant change in planning during the 1970s has been in its external relationships—with the general public (increasingly represented by specific interest groups) and those on whom the activities of planning are brought to bear, especially project developers. Although some intense controversies occurred in the 1960s (Gregory, 1971), there has been a change in the 1970s in the *expectation* on the part of the public to be informed widely and consulted, if not actively involved, in the decision-making process. This trend has been notably illustrated by the experience of several energy developments as shown by the subsequent chapters of this book. In some cases, public hostility has resulted in so great an impasse that a very wide remit indeed has been adopted before governments or public authorities have felt confident enough to advance particular proposals. The best example is probably the Dutch 'Broad Public Debate' discussed in the chapter on nuclear power in the Netherlands.

Some persuasions are hopeful that this process has reached a conclusion or can even be reversed towards greater public compliance with large developments. However, recent experience, as with the case of radioactive waste disposal discussed in Chapter 10 shows that in the UK at least, implacable public opposition, augmented by the overlap of energy and planning issues with other sensitive political considerations which are expressed through locally-active public groupings, can force fairly substantial and precipitate changes in government policy.

The relationship between planning and developers has evolved under the influence of this wider setting of public participation. Initially, many developers, frustrated by the delays to proposals because of the need to prepare wide-ranging descriptive and analytical documentation and to engage in consultation exercises, attributed the origination of this process to planners, instead of recognising that the planning system was merely responding to the development of a sufficient head of political steam which necessitated some response if the planning system was to retain any basis of legitimacy. Increasingly however, there has been an acceptance of the need at least to inform affected or interested members of the public on the consequences of developments on as wide a basis as possible. In some cases, developers' recognition of this need has run ahead of its political acceptability, as with the widely reported wish of the Central Electricity Generating Board to finance the presentation of opponents' cases at the public inquiry into the proposed pressurised water reactor at Sizewell being overridden by the Secretary of State for Energy.

## The Distinctiveness of Energy Developments for Planning

The energy debate of the last decade has also made it clear that for land-use planning and indeed any other policy-oriented discipline, the simple, physical, definition of energy as the capacity to do work does not encapsulate all the connotations that the word carries. Discussion of 'energy' in planning and policy-related literature is a discussion of a complex, usually difficult-to-define set of interactions between the forms of *supply* of energy, the ways in which it is *consumed*, the *end purposes* for which this consumption occurs and all the *organisational, economic, regulatory and attitudinal considerations* which attach to these interactions. At the very least, the critical distinction between energy supply and demand should underlie any examination of the relation between planning and energy. Approaches which adopt a unitary conception of 'energy' tend to be almost mystical in their treatment of the relations between energy issues and planning.

TABLE 1.1 *Characteristics of Energy Supply and Demand Relevant to Planning.*

| Physical and Locational Impacts | Organisational Characteristics | 'Interrelational' Characteristics |
|---|---|---|
| Size of developments, including land requirements, usually large | Lead times for bringing developments onstream or for achieving major changes in use patterns tend to be very long | Competition between different energy producers and between energy producers and others for a limited number of sites |
| Environmental impact of supply developments and energy use are great | Capital requirements for development are large | Indispensibility of energy for achievement of social goals |
| Limited number of suitable sites for accommodating developments | Risk of rapid obsolescence of developments due to economic and technical change | Impacts of energy extend from the local to the global and cannot be considered independently |
| Potential hazards associated with many developments and with the use of energy | Great diversity of ways of achieving a specified pattern of end-use consumption | A global system of energy supply means that distant, uncontrollable events can have profound local consequences |
| Energy supply developments have a marked division into constructional and operational phases | Involves highly technical activities | Energy policy is intertwined with a great many other policy areas, many with their own relevance to planning |
| Employment characteristics—in some cases, e.g. deep mined coal, considerable levels of employment; in others relatively little employment given the level of capital investment | Production, distribution and consumption tend to be subject to tightly controlled ownership or scrutiny | The diversity of 'actors' involved in formulating energy policy brings many external pressures to bear on it |
| | Energy supply developments have a marked division into constructional and operational phases | Energy consumption involves the depletion of irreplaceable resources and implies a particular perspective regarding temporal equity |
| | A very diverse set of 'actors' is involved in decision-taking over energy developments | Energy supply and distribution systems represent major parts of nations' and regions' total economies |

Table 1.1 classifies features of the energy system into three categories:

Physical and Locational—the external impacts which supply and consumption of energy may have on the physical environment and on the physical, economic and social circumstances of individual localities

Organisational—characteristics which stem from the ways in which societies go about organising the supply and consumption of energy

'Interrelational'—characteristics which arise from the dynamism of energy supply and demand systems, especially in their interlinkages with other sectors in the organisation and operation of economies and societies, over space and time

A systematic examination of the literature on energy and planning shows that commentators have justified claims about the distinctiveness of energy in its relationship to planning by pointing to particular characteristics of energy supply and demand arrangements. These range from the very general to specific features of individual developments. Some characteristics identified in the literature have been drawn together in Table 1.1. It can be seen immediately that not one of them is in any way unique to the energy system or to its interrelationships with the concerns of planning. Parallel examples occur in many other areas of economic and social organisation besides energy. If, therefore, there is any basis for singling out energy supply and demand for special attention in terms of their relationship with the operation of urban and regional planning, this can be justified only on the grounds that the *combination* of characteristics which the energy system displays is such that it can usefully be examined in isolation, outside of a more comprehensive, thematic consideration of the nature of planning.

Obviously, any classification will inevitably be arbitrary to a degree. Some characteristics are highly interrelated with others; some can be classified under more than one of the three categories identified. The characteristics which originate from social and economic considerations will be related to the ways in which individual countries organise their energy systems and to the nature of their planning systems. They are therefore inherently more variable in their significance than purely physical characteristics.

Despite these inevitable deficiencies, the classification presented can help to structure any examination of the relationships between energy and planning. There is a sequence in the three categories which moves from characteristics historically and indisputably located at the centre of concern of urban and regional planning—physical and locational features—to much broader, aspatial considerations formerly considered to lie outside the remit of spatial planning but which have progressively come to impinge upon it. This last point is a major theme in every chapter in this book, although a critical reading will show that there is no consensus among the authors on the extent to which this is a desirable (or completed) process.

## Procedural and Substantive Issues

In addressing different aspects of energy and planning, each of the chapters in this book invariably considers both *substantive* and *procedural* issues. Recognition of the distinction between these two classes of planning concern is so fundamental that it is often taken for granted. At the same time there are complex interlinkages between them—for example, the emergence of a particular substantive area of concern may generate pressure for a specific procedure, or modification of an existing procedure, the better to address particular features of the area. The substantive aspects of energy/ planning interactions which feature frequently in the pages of the chapters which follow include the host of physical environmental, economic and social consequences which flow from particular developments, some of which are identified, in a general way, under the heading 'Physical and Locational Impacts' in Table 1.1. The *organisational* characteristics of energy supply and consumption also presented in Table 1.1 also give rise to many issues of substance but, especially to the extent that they are important in determining the number and nature of actors in the decision-making processes related to energy, they can have considerable significance for procedural issues as well. The *interrelational* characteristics have a similar dual role giving rise to many of the most intense issues of substance, such as the concern about very long-lived environmental impacts of nuclear power and some other energy options, but also to procedural dilemmas. These stem from uncertainties about how and where to draw the boundaries between what is considered relevant to decision-making about a particular development or policy and what is not. Such procedural concerns are an inevitable consequence of the struggle to identify complex substantive issues. If an issue defies analysis, or exhaustive analysis, it may be down-graded in any assessment procedure or, adopting a fail-safe perspective, the very uncertainty attached to it may guarantee it a crucial role in the procedure. The way in which this and many other dilemmas are handled is a reflection of the procedural propensity of the planning system concerned.

### Planning and Energy: Substantive Issues

The substantive aspects of energy/planning interactions which feature frequently in the pages of the chapters which follow include the host of physical environmental, economic and social consequences which flow from particular developments. Some consequences are superficially straightfor-ward and uncontroversial—the amount of land required by a development or its total employment generation but such uncontested impacts are remarkably few. What seems initially to be a straightforward impact often turns out to have many areas of controversy or unforeseen consequences. Energy impacts tend inexorably towards the 'transcientific' (Weinberg, 1972). Even where, in theory, there should be little difficulty in objectively establishing the nature and planning consequences of energy developments, obstacles may arise because important data are not available. This is particularly well illustrated by Susan Owens in Chapter 9, who notes the lack of information on spatial patterns of energy consumption.

As well as these 'simple' substantive impacts, other substantive considera-tions of a more complex character tend to recur in the discussions about energy policy and its relation with spatial planning. These 'second level' issues have had considerable attention devoted to them by planners although their successful analysis and resolution often remain elusive. It is issues of this kind which tend to be identified by commentators and regulators who approach particular energy-related developments from a 'planning perspective' as opposed to a specific concern with, for example, the physical environmental or employment generation aspects of such developments.

Some of these complex substantive issues are identified in Table 1.2. The listing there is not intended to present any order of priority and there is considerable overlap between many of the issues identified. Table 1.2 is not by any means exhaustive, but anyone who has examined a particular energy development, or the general policy framework on which the development is based will recognise that these issues have had an increasingly powerful influence in formulating attitudes to the development or policy.

TABLE 1.2 *'Complex' substantive issues in the relation between energy and planning.*

---

(a) spatial aggregational characteristics, especially the synergistic effects of individual developments

(b) 'chain' effects, including the occurrence of 'downstream' developments, subsequent to an individual development.

(c) assessment of complete 'energy cycle' impacts, rather than consideration of discrete stages in the cycle

(d) multiple choice decision making, especially siting optimisation, and the dilemmas presented

(e) option foreclosure, including the economic opportunity costs, and spatial opportunity costs, incurred by developments

(f) the long-term nature of impacts, necessitating the need to forecast circumstances enduring over long periods of time and also specific events occurring at distant, and often unspecified points in the future

(g) uncertainty—given the difficulty of (f)—and the need to accommodate it

(h) the balancing of a search for scientific replicability in evaluation (coupled with the desire to 'take out' issues from dispute by establishing a consensus on what their impacts are and the ways of mitigating them) with the ability to recognise the 'unique', especially the site-specific, characteristics which individual developments occasion

---

## Planning and Energy: Procedural Issues

Table 1.3 identifies some of the *procedural* themes discussed in the contributed chapters of this book. Again, the listing is neither exhaustive nor intended to suggest any order of priorities among the issues identified.

It is not difficult to see that most of these procedural issues involve addressing one or more aspects of the trade-off between efficiency and representation equity. Behind the great amount of attention paid to procedural issues in the treatment of energy/planning interrelations tends to lie the assumption that it should be possible to achieve agreement over energy policy, especially in societies with high levels of consensus. Even the undoubtedly adverse local impacts which may arise should, it is felt, be relatively uncontroversial, if the appropriate compensatory mechanisms can be developed. To the extent that this is not the case, inadequate procedures are held to be the fault and while research on substantive issues cannot be

TABLE 1.3 *Procedural issues frequently occasioned by planning aspects of energy projects and policies*

---

(a) identification of those parties with a 'legitimate' right to be consulted, or directly involved in, decision-making over projects or policies and ways of making it possible for them to do so

(b) identification of issues of agreement, especially enduring issues, thereby to set them aside from dispute over a development or policy

(c) acceleration of the decision-making process, while guaranteeing adequate representation of divergent views on the project or policy. Included here can be the development of project/policy evaluation schedules.

(d) determination of the relative balance between local versus regional versus national (versus international) interests in evaluation of a project or policy

(e) identification of the boundaries of relevant analysis—the limits to the evaluation of impacts over space and time (and therefore to the number and centrality of those who can claim legitimate interest in the project or policy under discussion)

(f) methods of guaranteeing the impartiality of the decision-making process, its openness to the widest range of information and opinions and the greatest deference to its decisions

(g) methods of guaranteeing equal access to the widest range of information and to resources for organising its interpretation

(h) identification and resolution of disfunctional divisions of responsibility between different agencies charged with assessment or regulation of different aspects of a project's or policy's impacts

(i) methods of establishing the entitlement to and adequacy of compensation mechanisms for adverse impacts from developments, especially unforeseen impacts

(j) determination of whether the land-use planning system is adequate to and appropriate for, evaluation of *all* the diverse range of energy policy consequences

---

ignored, the thrust of attention has been devoted to the search for procedural mechanisms which would 'take out' energy policy from the arena of intractable public controversy.

While each of these procedural issues has been the subject of considerable attention from within and outside the planning profession, two particular considerations stand out as having been the focus of especial concern. One can be identified as *project appraisal*—how to develop comprehensive but manageable methods of identifying all the consequences of a proposal before its implementation. The second is *project monitoring* because the goal of identification of *all* of a project's consequences remains very much an ideal.

## Project Appraisal

At the procedural level, one of the questions most frequently discussed in the following pages is the need for standardised and comprehensive project appraisal techniques to ensure that all significant outcomes of a development are identified, and all the information necessary to understand these outcomes is available. Central to this debate in many countries has been the issue of environmental impact assessment (EIA) and whether or not this systematic, comprehensive approach to the assessment of the environmental implications of development proposals should be introduced as a statutory requirement within the UK and other planning systems. Energy supply projects have proved to be probably the single most significant reference point in the debate about the merits of EIA and much of the experience gained in the UK and elsewhere in relation to the development and application of EIA methods has been associated with the energy sector (Petts and Hills, 1982).

Such an approach was first institutionalised in the United States, where the preparation of environmental impact statements for major new federal projects having a significant impact on the environment had been made a statutory requirement under the terms of the National Environmental Policy Act (NEPA) of 1969. Not surprisingly, the concept of EIA was picked up in many other countries and the American experience was closely scrutinised in the early to mid-1970s.

It is generally accepted that this debate was initiated in the UK by the Roskill Commission's attempt to broaden the basis of conventional cost-benefit analysis in its appraisal of alternative sites for a third London airport. Although the Commission's report was poorly received in some quarters (Self, 1975) it nonetheless directed attention to the need for a novel approach for appraising large-scale, complex development proposals. The debate was given further impetus by the growing number of North Sea oil and gas related projects for which planning permission was sought from the early 1970s onwards. These projects were generally associated with green-field sites in some of the most attractive and environmentally sensitive coastal areas of Scotland. The projects were typically large-scale, complex and, in terms of the planning system's experience, 'unusual' (Scottish Development Department, 1974). From the outset the Scottish Development Department (SDD) recognised that they must be rigorously and comprehensively appraised 'if the UK planning procedures were to meet the demands of both developers and those concerned with the quality of the environment' (Clark, et al, 1981a, p.128). The SDD did, in fact, play a prominent role in launching the first series of EIAs carried out in the UK, funding as it did four of the five oil platform construction site assessments that were prepared between 1973 and 1974 (House of Lords, 1981).

Although the SDD has always adopted a far more positive line on the use of EIA, the Department of the Environment (DoE), the ministry responsible for planning matters in England and Wales, also showed some interest in the mid-1970s. The DoE commissioned two studies to explore firstly, the need for and feasibility of introducing a formal EIA requirement into the UK planning system (Catlow and Thirlwall, 1976) and, secondly, an appropriate procedure and methodology for local planning authorities to follow (Clark, et al., 1976). Catlow and Thirlwall supported the introduction of EIA, indicating that it might be required for between 30 and 50 development projects per year. Clark and his colleagues produced a manual for the assessment of major industrial applications which set out 'a systematic assessment procedure for the appraisal of projects'. The manual was commended to local planning authorities by the DoE and a revised version (Clark *et al.*, 1981b) was subsequently published incorporating the experience gained from the application of the earlier version.

The debate on EIA has not been fuelled only by domestic events and activities. The European Commission has been attempting to introduce some form of EIA procedure in all member states of the European Communities (EEC) since the late 1970s. Although not alone in its opposition to a large number of draft preliminary directives, the UK has nonetheless appeared to be in the vanguard of hostility to the Commission's proposals. During 1982 the likelihood of the proposed directive being introduced receded again and substantial revisions seem to be required before it is acceptable to the UK and certain other member states. The UK's opposition to the proposed system has mainly hinged on the Commission's proposals to list certain categories of development for which a mandatory assessment would be required. The DoE with the support of most other UK government departments has wished to retain the maximum flexibility possible in implementing any environmental assessment directive.

Although central government and representatives of many industries view the prospect of a mandatory EIA with some considerable concern because they fear that it will lead to even longer planning delays and thereby increase development costs, a growing number of both private and public sector organisations do nonetheless prepare EIAs for new projects. This has certainly been the case in the energy sector, where the British Gas Corporation (as examined in Chapter 4) and British Petroleum (BP) have taken a strong lead. The National Coal Board and the Central Electricity Generating Board are also now active in this field (see Chapters 2 and 5) and the preparation of impact assessments has become an almost routine component of project appraisals carried out by these organisations.

British official reluctance contrasts with many other countries, as several chapters in this book make clear. Chapter 6 demonstrates that Canada has a comprehensive EIA system which operates both at the federal and provincial level. The Netherlands has also made substantial progress towards the implementation of a quite sophisticated EIA system. As Gough and Lewis indicate in Chapter 7 a provision for EIA has also existed in Irish planning legislation since 1977 although it has been little used.

## Monitoring

The interest in EIA as a means of predicting the impacts of developments has been paralleled by a new emphasis on procedures for monitoring actual outcomes after approval has been given by the relevant authorities. One of the main reasons for this is the apparent divergences between the anticipated impacts of major new energy supply projects (and, indeed, projects in other sectors) and their actual effects on physical, economic and social systems. In some cases, previously unforeseen adverse consequences have occurred. In other situations, anticipated beneficial impacts have not arisen at all or have to a lesser extent or less frequently than originally envisaged.

This past under-emphasis on monitoring can be related to statutory requirements—the need to prepare structure plans in the UK and similar strategic plans elsewhere—and is an interesting example of the way in which such requirements determine methodological preoccupations within the profession. Only after the implementation of such plans following government approval did planners start to turn their attention to monitoring plan implementation and the impact of new considerations on the plan itself. It is now increasingly clear that planners' considerable attention needs to be directed to monitoring procedures during both the construction and operation phases—as, for example, John Glasson points out in Chapter 5 for power station developments. Firstly, monitoring the implementation of specific projects is required to determine whether planning or other conditions imposed on the project are being met. Secondly, during both construction and operation planning authorities and other relevant regulatory agencies need to ensure that the project's effects, both short- and long-term, do not conflict with existing plans or policies and do not prejudice the requirements or operations of other developments. Thirdly, continuous monitoring of major developments represents an important source of data to improve assessment methodology. 'Post-auditing', the post-implementation monitoring of developments to compare predicted with observed outcomes, has yet to be extensively developed, but is likely to become a major requirement in the future.

**The Contributed Chapters**

As noted earlier, most of the attention given to energy issues by planners has concerned supply matters. This is reflected in the following pages, most of which address specific primary or secondary energy sources. Of course, in the real world, energy supply sources are not discrete, independent options but are linked in a complex process of decision-taking, where current prices and expectations of future supply security and price levels interact to influence policy choices.

The chapters on coal, natural gas, petroleum, renewable energy sources and conventional and nuclear electricity generation each explore some of these interactions with other energy supply packages. A common theme of these chapters is that the spatial planning and environmental characteristics of different energy choices need to be given as much attention as price and strategic security considerations. These chapters explore the links between energy policy and other, equally important matters such as employment generation, regional development policy, housing provision and housing location, transport infrastructure and policies towards agricultural and recreational countryside. In particular, the authors have been invited to examine cases where the failure adequately to take these linkages into account when specific energy supply or management targets were set, has resulted, through the operation of the planning system, in constraint on the realisation of these targets.

Much of the discussion of the relation between energy supply development and land-use planning, especially that emanating from supply-oriented institutions, has described such constraints as undesirable and needing to be diminished in their frequency or their compass, either by a reduction in the 'competence' of planning, or by developing mechanisms to streamline the planning and public consultation process, a term which is often a euphemism for emasculate. The contributed chapters do not share this viewpoint but attempt to demonstrate that the land-use planning process has been a healthy counter-balance to an energy-supply myopia which developed out of the energy traumas of the last decade and which at times threatened to overwhelm other, equally important, social goals.

However, in discussing the procedural issues covered earlier in this introduction, the chapters also explore the extent that the land-use planning system can resolve disputes over the wider directions in which economies may move and which are frequently held to be symbolised by different energy options. At a more specific level, several instances are advanced where the early and comprehensive application of a land-use planning perspective in the preparation of plans for energy developments has led to the speedy passage of proposals, often modified to accommodate environmental goals, through the planning system to the satisfaction of all parties with an interest in their fate.

Most of the chapters are based on the energy circumstances of the United Kingdom. At present, this country has a diverse and abundant energy resource base. Consequently, the choices *between* different energy sources are to some extent made more tractable by their indigenous availability. However, in other cases, the choices are more difficult because of the existence of interest lobbies, including regionally-based lobbies, associated with competing supply sources (and, to a lesser extent, with management options as well).

There is no chapter specifically concerned with nuclear power generation in the United Kingdom. Some aspects of this energy source are considered in Chapter 5, where nuclear power stations are covered alongside fossil-fuelled stations. This approach serves to emphasise that, in terms of their land-use planning aspects, there are many similarities between these forms of electricity generation. The planning aspects of nuclear power stations and reprocessing operations in the UK have been extensively discussed in other sources, as listed in Chapter 10. However, at present there is no single, comprehensive source on the relation between land-use planning and the final stage of the nuclear fuel cycle—radioactive waste management. Chapter 10 is intended to provide such a source.

There are three chapters on overseas situations—in Ireland, the Netherlands and Canada. In each case, the contribution to a comprehensive perspective on energy and land-use relations made by these chapters is varied. Ireland and the Netherlands have been chosen to illustrate the problems which may arise in countries without as diverse an energy resource base as the UK. The chapter on Canada, drawing especially on the situation in British Columbia, differs from the other chapters in this book in that it develops its arguments not from examination of a single energy source or management theme but rather from the diversity of potential energy sources within a large, sparsely-populated province. In so doing, it evaluates the efficacy of the interesting procedural developments which have emerged in Canada to handle the conflicts over energy impacts on relatively undeveloped, high-quality territories. These have provided examples which have been urged for wider application, not least in the UK.

Information on land-use problems and procedural issues attached to nuclear power in countries outside the UK and North America is not readily available but Chapter 8 on the Netherlands illustrates the particularly acute demands which the unique geography of that country places on the land-use planning system's treatment of energy supply dilemmas. It also gives details of a procedural response to these dilemmas which is probably the most complex national debate and public consultation exercise carried out on energy policy in any western country to date.

Chapter 7 on Ireland illustrates how intently a country without a strong fossil-fuel supply base needs to consider renewable energy sources, which are particularly demanding in their requirements for anticipatory planning. They will necessitate complex new infrastructure provision which will have to be reconciled simultaneously with other development goals. The special problems which the predominantly rural environment and economy create are discussed in detail in this chapter and are relevant to similar regions in many other countries.

Finally, a major new area of concern to planning is handled in Chapter 9, on the role of demand management and conservation through modification of the built environment and the transport infrastructure. An important theme of this chapter—the recognition of the limitations as well as the capabilities of land-use planning, is taken up in the concluding chapter of this book and is one which planners must accommodate if inflated claims for the competence of land-use planning in the energy field are not to lead to frustration and disillusionment. Above all, this chapter points to the need for coherent, stable, incremental long-term planning policies because of the slow speed of change in the built environment.

If there is one theme which runs through all the chapters of this book it is that the place of land-use planning in the formulation of energy policies is no different from, and is interrelated with, the place of planning in the formulation of many other policies. The central recognition of planning in development of energy policy depends on a similar recognition being accorded it in addressing problems such as employment generation, housing renewal, regional decline, transport infrastructure provision or amenity protection. The problems of energy supply provision and demand management may have accentuated the need for coherent, comprehensive, anticipatory planning and made this need manifest to interests which formerly may not have appreciated it but a planning response cannot be applied in isolation to the energy sector alone. All the policy review mechanisms, participation vehicles and anticipatory techniques which have been urged for application to energy problems, require for their successful implementation a parallel application to the other, interlinked, economic and social dilemmas of the closing decades of the twentieth century.

## References

Bains, M. A. (1972) *New Local Authorities,* Department of the Environment, London.

Carter, J. (1977) *Congressional Quarterly Weekly Report,* April 23, 753.

Catlow, J. and Thirlwall, C. (1976) *Environmental Impact Analysis,* Department of the Environment, London.

Clark, B., Chapman, K., Bisset, K. and Wathern, P. (1976) *Assessment of Major Industrial Applications: A Manual,* Department of the Environment, London.

Clark, B., Bisset, R. and Wathern, P. (1981a) The British Experience, in O'Riordan, T. and Sewell, D. (eds.) (1981) *Project Appraisal and Policy Review,* John Wiley, Chichester.

Clark, B., Chapman, K., Bisset, R., Wathern, P. and Barrett, M. (1981b) *A Manual for the Assessment of Major Development Projects,* HMSO, London.

Cohen, A. V. and Pritchard, D. K. (1980) *Comparative risks of electricity production systems: a critical survey of the literature,* Health and Safety Executive, London.

*Congressional Quarterly Weekly Report* (1977), April 23, 727–732.

Department of Energy (1978), *Energy Policy Consultative Document,* HMSO, London.

Department of Energy (1979), *Energy Projections, 1979,* Department of Energy, London.

Goodman, G., Kristoferson, L. and Hollander, J. (eds.) (1981) *The European Transition from Oil,* Academic Press, London.

Gregory, R. (1971) *The Price of Amenity,* Macmillan, London.

Hall, D. (1978) Energy options and planning, Report of Proceedings: Town and Country Planning Summer School, Royal Town Planning Institute, London.

House of Lords (1981) *Environmental Assessment of Projects* Eleventh Report of the Select Committee on the European Communities, HMSO, London.

International Communication Agency (1982) Reagan Administration commentary on disbandment of US Department of Energy, May 24.

International Energy Agency (1981) *District Heating in IEA Countries,* Organisation for Economic Cooperation and Development, Paris.

Kirk, G. (1982) *Schumacher on Energy,* Jonathan Cape, London.

Lovins, A. (1977) *Soft Energy Paths,* Pelican, London.

Ministry of Industry (1981) *Guidelines for Energy Policy: Summary of the Government Bill on Energy Policy,* Ministry of Industry, Stockholm.

Paget, G. and Lloyd, G. (1980) Energetic future in store for planning system. *Planning,* November 7, 6–7.

Petts, J. and Hills, P. (1982) *Environmental Assessment in the United Kingdom: A Preliminary Guide.* University of Nottingham, Nottingham.

Scottish Development Department (1974) *Appraisal of the Impact of Oil-Related Development,* Scottish Development Department, Edinburgh.

Self, P. (1975) *Econocrats and the Policy Process,* Macmillan, London.

Watt Committee (1979) *Energy and Land Use in the UK,* Report no. 4, Watt Committee on Energy, London.

Weinberg, A. M. (1972) Science and Trans-Science, *Minerva* **10**, 209–222.

Weinberg, A. M. (1980) Energy: the need for technical fixes, *Nature,* January 31, 425.

CHAPTER 2

# Planning for Coal: Issues and Responses

PETER HILLS

## Introduction

Coal mining in the United Kingdom is a large industry by any standards. The National Coal Board (NCB), the publicly-owned corporation responsible for almost all coal production, employs approximately 250,000 people. In 1981 there were almost 300 operational deep mines and opencast sites producing 125 million tonnes of coal. Coal accounts for 40 per cent of the UK's primary energy consumption. Its major markets are power stations, the steel industry and other secondary fuel producers (Table 2.1). It is the oldest and most well-established industry in the energy sector. In contrast to oil and gas it is wholly land-based. The environmental impacts of coal production and use are very evident over large areas of the country and generate a diverse and complex mix of planning issues.

Coal's prospects have been potentially transformed since the mid-1970s. The industry is currently pursuing an ambitious expansion programme to increase production significantly by the end of the century. Its future is however surrounded by many uncertainties and it has many problems to overcome if it is to achieve a guaranteed place in the long term development of the UK energy economy. Irrespective of its fortunes over the next two decades, the nature and intensity of the interactions between the coal industry and the planning system seem set to undergo some important changes.

## Coal in the United Kingdom

### Organisational Features

Coal was the first UK energy industry to be taken into public ownership by the Labour government of the immediate post-war period. The Coal Industry Nationalisation Act (1946) paved the way for the creation of the NCB, thus bringing to an end the fragmented pattern of ownership and the

TABLE 2.1 *Inland Consumption of Coal in the United Kingdom in 1980.*

| MARKET | Million tonnes | % Total Consumption |
|---|---|---|
| SECONDARY FUEL PRODUCERS: | | |
| Electricity Supply Industry | 89.57 | 72.5 |
| Coke Ovens | 11.61 | 9.4 |
| Manufactured Fuel Plants[1] | 3.02 | 2.4 |
| TOTAL INPUT TO SECONDARY FUEL PRODUCERS | 104.20 | 84.4 |
| DIRECT FUEL CONSUMPTION: | | |
| Industry | 7.84 | 6.4 |
| Domestic[2] | 8.95 | 7.2 |
| Transport | 0.06 | $\phi$ |
| Public Administration & Miscellaneous | 1.75 | 1.4 |
| TOTAL DIRECT FINAL CONSUMPTION | 18.60 | 15.1 |
| CONSUMED AT COLLIERIES | 0.66 | 0.5 |
| TOTAL INLAND CONSUMPTION | 123.46 | 100.0 |

Source: HMSO (1981b, p. 44).

[1] Low temperature carbonisation plants and patent fuel plants.
[2] Includes consumption of house coal, anthracite and dry steam coal and miners' concessionary coal.

unplanned and uncoordinated mining activity that had characterised the industry since the beginning of the Industrial Revolution. The Board assumed responsibility for coal production on January 1, 1947.

The NCB's coal-producing activities are currently organised in 12 Mining Areas and 6 Opencast Executive Regions (as listed in Table 2.5). These Areas and Regions provide the organisational framework for a wide range of management functions, for performance monitoring and financial accounting. Although deep mining and opencast activities are currently treated as a single accounting unit, it is widely recognised that they represent two quite different operations (HMSO, 1981a). The Commission on Energy and the Environment, established in 1978 to advise government on the interaction between energy and the environment, considered in the context of their Coal Study whether the Opencast Executive should be established as a separate Corporation. They rejected this idea but recommended that the Executive be treated in the NCB Annual Report and Accounts as a separate accounting unit. The Commission argued (HMSO, 1981a, p.91) that:

> This would permit a much more informed assessment of the appropriate balance between the economic effects of opencast production and its environmental costs.

Although many management functions are devolved to the Areas and Regions, and indeed down to individual mine and opencast site managers, strategic planning and decision making are the responsibility of staff and Board members based at the NCB's London headquarters. Long term strategic planning issues generally fall within the remit of the Board's Central Planning Unit, which also deals with much of the forward planning for new mining projects. Responsibility for the implementation of new projects would however devolve to the appropriate Area or Region.

The industry's activities, both in the short and long term, have also been influenced by the workings of the Coal Industry Tripartite Group. This Group, consisting of representatives of the NCB, government and mining unions, meets from time to time to discuss specific issues as well as general relations between government and the industry. The Group was, for example, responsible for drafting the document entitled 'Coal for the Future' (Department of Energy, 1977), which revised upwards the coal production targets set initially in the NCB's own 'Plan for Coal' (NCB, 1974). In February, 1981 the Group convened to discuss and subsequently to resolve the immediate problems that had arisen as a result of the Board's proposed programme of accelerated mine closures necessitated by the financial targets embodied in the 1980 Coal Industry Act.

The NCB's organisational arrangements for dealing with environmental and planning policy issues relating to existing and new mining projects are particularly relevant to this chapter. In contrast to the gas and electricity industries, the NCB has been somewhat slow in establishing what might be regarded as an appropriate organisational structure for dealing with such issues. To a large extent, this may be seen as a legacy of the past and the fact that 'concern about environmental issues does not come naturally to the industry' (HMSO, 1981a, p.95).

Until 1980/81 non-workplace environmental matters were regarded as the responsibility of line management (NCB, 1980a). A Headquarters Environmental Planning Committee (HEPC) had been established but its activities were limited to assessing the implications of new and potential legislation and updating the Board's practices in the environmental field. In keeping with the general pattern of devolved responsibility, the coordination of environmental policy issues was a matter to be dealt with by the Deputy Director (Administration) in each Area. During 1980/81 the Board introduced a number of important changes to extend and strengthen arrangements for handling environmental matters. The HEPC continues to operate but since April, 1981 it has been supplemented by Area Surface Environmental Committees (ASEC). The ASECs are expected to liaise with the HEPC and are responsible for:

> . . . the various existing arrangements for dealing with such matters as disposal of colliery waste, subsidence and the general environmental impact of the Board's activities. (NCB, 1981, p.31)

In addition, these Committees are expected to 'liaise closely with local authorities'. The Opencast Executive is represented on both the Area and Headquarters Committees.

While endorsing these new arrangements and accepting that environmental impact is a matter of considerable concern at all levels in the NCB, the

Commission on Energy and the Environment has expressed a number of important reservations regarding the Board's ability to deal effectively with environmental issues. The Commission generally support devolved responsibility but point out that the system is susceptible 'to the vagaries of the individual' (HMSO, 1981a, p.95). They also express doubts about the availability of skilled and experienced staff within the Board capable of translating environmental concern into action. The Commission suggest a strengthening of Headquarters resources in the field to enhance policy making and the quality of advice available to Areas. They also consider it 'essential' that responsibility for environmental matters be assigned to a senior person, preferably a full or part-time Board member, a suggestion that has subsequently been taken up by the NCB.

Again in contrast to the situation that prevails in the gas and electricity industries, planning procedures and related issues associated with new mining projects have not, to date, been handled by a specific specialist department or unit within the NCB. As noted above, although strategic planning decisions concerning the selection, timing and financing of new projects are taken centrally, the responsibility for the preparation of feasibility studies, environmental assessments and liaison with local planning authorities lies with the appropriate Area or Region. Headquarters staff will however often join Area personnel in presenting the Board's case at public inquiries into new projects. The NCB do not therefore rely on in-house expertise and facilities to carry out the required studies and in recent cases (North East Leicestershire, Park and South Warwickshire) the Board has been heavily dependent on the services of specialist consultancies. The Board's position regarding Environmental Impact Assessment (EIA) is somewhat ambiguous. Although a quite detailed form of impact analysis has become an almost standard component of project feasibility studies, the NCB has consistently expressed its opposition to any formal statutory EIA system of the type proposed by the EEC (HMSO, 1981a; NCB, 1980c).

### Coal Resources and Reserves

Coal is widely distributed throughout much of mainland Britain and massive deposits are also known to exist under extensive areas of the North Sea (Figure 2.1). Coal is mined in 23 counties in England and Wales and four Scottish Regions (HMSO, 1981c). It was also mined on a small scale in Northern Ireland until the mid-1960s, although the NCB's statutory responsibility for coal production does not extend there.

The situation regarding UK coal resources and reserves in the early 1980s has been usefully summarised by Moses (1981). Total 'coal-in-place' is estimated on the basis of two criteria: firstly, that the deposits be located at a depth of less than 1.2 km, since greater working depths generally give rise to problems of strata behaviour and ventilation and cooling difficulties, and,

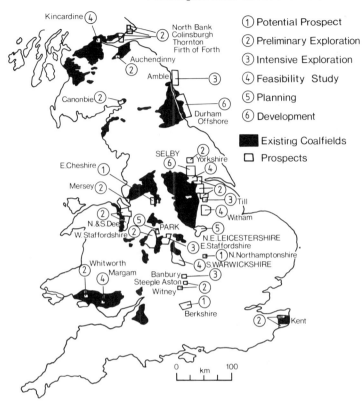

Kincardine ④

North Bank
② Colinsburgh
Thornton
Firth of Forth

Auchendinny
②

Amble ③

Canonbie ②

⑥
Durham
Offshore

① Potential Prospect

② Preliminary Exploration

③ Intensive Exploration

④ Feasibility Study

⑤ Planning

⑥ Development

■ Existing Coalfields

□ Prospects

E.Cheshire ①

SELBY ②
⑥ Yorkshire
④

Mersey ②

②
③ Till
② ④ Witham

②
N.&S.Dee ⑤
W.Staffordshire ②

PARK ⑤

⑤

N.E.LEICESTERSHIRE
③ E.Staffordshire
① N.Northamptonshire
④ S.WARWICKSHIRE

Whitworth ②
Margam ④

Banbury □
Steeple Aston □ ③
Witney □ ②

① 

Berkshire

② Kent

0    km    100

FIG 2.1 *National Coal Board Exploration Programme*

secondly, that coal seams should be greater than 60 cm in thickness since it is not a viable proposition to work thinner seams. Applying these criteria, total 'coal-in-place' in 1976 was estimated at 190 bn tonnes ($190 \times 10^9$ tonnes), a figure that as yet has not been significantly revised even though the NCB has been engaged in an extensive exploration programme since the mid-1970s.

Total 'coal-in-place' is however only part of the picture. A more relevant measure of national reserves is provided by estimates of the quantity of coal that is 'economically recoverable' on the basis of current economic conditions and current mining technology. Economically accessible reserves are estimated to total 100 bn tonnes. Some 45 per cent of this total is deemed to be recoverable after applying factors representing the effects of barriers and pillars and the average national rate of extraction—the latter being termed the 'Recovery Factor'. 'Economically recoverable' reserves of coal in the UK therefore total 45 bn tonnes ($45 \times 10^9$ tonnes), an estimate that has given rise to the often quoted figure of 300 years supply of coal at present rates of use (for example, Ezra, 1978).

The Recovery Factor (RF) is a very important and, in certain respects, controversial topic. In 1974 the average national RF was 45 per cent. By the beginning of the 1980s it had risen to 52 per cent. As Moses (1981) points out, there are enormous regional and local variations in the RF, which ranges from below 30 per cent at some mines to over 70 per cent at others. Overall however, Moses suggests that the RF has been 'remarkably stable'. It has been suggested (Tregelles, 1976) that the RF may improve significantly by the end of the century, possibly to an average figure approaching 70 per cent or even more. The proposed North East Leicestershire project would however only achieve an anticipated RF of 41 per cent (Stocks, 1980). Some critics of the NCB's expansion programme have repeatedly drawn attention to the RF figures, arguing that if a marked improvement could be achieved then the case for capital investment in new capacity would be significantly weakened as existing capacity could be used to meet projected increases in output (see Manners, 1981).

The final element in the reserves equation is represented by what the NCB term 'operating reserves'. These reserves are estimated to total approximately 7 bn tonnes ($7 \times 10^9$ tonnes). They are calculated by annual local assessments at each mine and are also governed by such factors as the availability and allocation of capital for investment. These reserves 'will reflect the fortunes of nature at the mines' and, consequently, 'will always be a variable figure' (Moses, 1981, p.44). They will be reduced each year by the amount of coal extracted and may be supplemented by any further information that becomes available concerning seam viability.

### The UK Coal Industry: Plans and Prospects

Since 1973 the role of coal in the UK energy economy has come under increasing scrutiny from politicians, the public and a growing number of academic commentators. The arguments for and against a sustained expansion of coal production have been advanced on numerous occasions, one of the more recent and notable examples being the context provided by the public inquiry into the NCB's application for planning permission to develop the North East Leicestershire Coalfield. A detailed overview of the evolution of UK energy policy and the role of coal lies outside the scope of the present chapter. The following discussion identifies the main themes in the arguments of both the NCB and its critics since the future path of the industry will obviously strongly influence the nature and scale of interactions with the planning system.

1974 was a turning point in the fortunes of coal. The NCB's 'Plan for Coal' (NCB, 1974), agreed with government and the mining unions, set out to end 60 years of decline and contraction in the industry. The Plan established a

TABLE 2.2 *Production from Different Types of Mine to Meet Projected 1985 Output (million tonnes).*

|  | Date of Review | | |
| --- | --- | --- | --- |
|  | 1974 | 1976 | 1978 |
| New Mines | 20 | 10 | 7 |
| Existing Mines with Major Projects | 63 | 89 | 82 |
| Other Collieries | 37 | 21 | 31 |
|  | 120 | 120 | 120 |

Source: Dunn (1979, p.390).

target of 120 million tonnes of deep mined output in 1985 plus 15 million tonnes of opencast production, although it also provided for the possibility of future production increases to meet a potential demand of 150 million tonnes. Its immediate objective was however to stabilise output from deep mining. The Plan provided for three things to achieve this objective (Dunn, 1979):

1. Expanding the capacity of selected long life collieries with sufficient reserves to justify large scale investment;
2. Extending the life of certain other collieries by providing access to new reserves;
3. Constructing completely new collieries.

Table 2.2 shows how projected 1985 output levels were to be achieved and how the contributions of different elements have been revised subsequently. The contribution from new deep mine capacity has been progressively revised downwards from the original forecasts presented in 'Plan for Coal'. The NCB argue that this is because it has been taking longer than expected to obtain planning approval for new projects and carry them through to the operational phase. In contrast, the contribution from existing mines with major projects has been increased and so too has the contribution from other collieries, at least in the 1978 review. This is because collieries have not been exhausting at the anticipated rate and because more opportunities to modernise and improve existing mines have been identified. Despite these revisions the NCB was confident that the target capacity of 120 million tonnes of deep mined coal in 1985 would be achieved. The opencast target of 15 million tonnes was met in 1980/81, well ahead of schedule.

The planned capacity revisions for 1976 appeared in 'Coal for the Future' (Department of Energy, 1977), which was a review of progress with the 1974 Plan. This document also included revised forecasts of demand for coal in 1985 and forecasts for the year 2000. These data are presented in Table 2.3, together with other recent coal demand forecasts. Official forecasts of total coal demand in 2000 have been revised downwards quite significantly and Department of Energy forecasts compiled in 1982 showed a continuing

TABLE 2.3 *Coal Demand Forecasts for the UK, 1985, 1990 and 2000 (million tonnes).*

| Forecast | 1985 range | 1985 mid-point | 1990 range | 1990 mid-point | 2000 range | 2000 mid-point |
|---|---|---|---|---|---|---|
| Plan for Coal 1974 | 125–150 | 138 | — | — | — | — |
| Coal for the Future 1977 | 125–135 | 130 | — | — | 135–200 | 168 |
| Energy Policy Consultative Document 1978 | — | 129.5 | — | — | — | — |
| Energy Projections 1979 | — | — | 124–132 | 128 | 128–165 | 147 |
| Energy Projections 1979 (revised version) | — | — | 105–126 | 116 | 110–159 | 135 |

TABLE 2.4 *Deep Mine Capacity in 1985, 1990 and 2000 without New Mines*

| | Million tonnes | | |
|---|---|---|---|
| | 1985 | 1990 | 2000 |
| Total, given no further major investment | 120 | 105 | 80 |
| Incremental output available from unapproved projects at existing mines | — | 9 | 15 |
| Total capacity in absence of further new mines | 120 | 114 | 95 |

Source: Moses (1979, p.3).

downward trend in both aggregate energy demand and the demand for coal in 2000.

'Plan for Coal' has provided a mechanism for stabilising deep mine output but the NCB argue that in itself it does not guarantee either long term stability in the industry or the possibility of significantly expanding coal production. Moses (1979), in evidence presented on behalf of the NCB to the North East Leicestershire public inquiry, argued that further investment in new mining capacity was necessary to enable the industry to avoid slipping into a rapid decline in the 1990s. Unless further investment was undertaken the total deep mine capacity of the industry could drop to 95 million tonnes by the year 2000 (Table 2.4).

Both the NCB and government have produced various forecasts of the future demand for coal which have seemed over-optimistic to various commentators. Shortly after publication of 'Plan for Coal', Berkovitch (1977) and Cook and Surrey (1977) drew attention to possible problems regarding the size of future markets for UK coal. Manners (1981, p.21) has succinctly summarised the nature of the problem in the following way:

> The present coal question, therefore, is not how much coal can be produced, and for how long, but how much can be (profitably) sold over the next 20 years.

Manners presents a powerful critique of the NCB's investment programme and future plans. He argues (1981, p.91) that:

> . . . a number of fundamental qualifications must surround . . . future NCB production capabilities, particularly as they relate to existing mines. All of these qualifications suggest that the capacity figures quoted by the Board in its plans and public statements if anything underestimate the production potential of the industry in its existing and modernised facilities in the 1980s and 1990s. In consequence . . . they throw serious doubts upon the necessity for the industry to open as many new mines as the Board have proposed. They also raise questions about the size of the industry's capital requirements over the next 20 years.

Manners questions whether the NCB have properly accounted for any possible future increases in productivity at existing mines. He also argues that improvements in the Recovery Factor could 'increase substantially the output potential of existing facilities' (1981, p.92). Furthermore, Manners believes that the output of the Selby field could be higher than anticipated.

It also appears that figures for future capacity at existing mines are rather higher than originally thought. Manners argues that 'new and profitable mining opportunities may be recognised in existing mines' as real energy prices increase. He also draws attention to the colliery closure issue, pointing out that the NCB will encounter very strong opposition from the National Union of Mineworkers (NUM) when attempting to close older, uneconomic mines. This means that the Board's projected exhaustion rate may well prove to be lower than expected. Manners also calls into question the economics of new coalfield developments, arguing that the direct costs of North East Leicestershire coal would almost certainly be greater than Selby coal and possibly higher than coal extracted from modernised and improved mines in the East Midlands and Yorkshire areas. The indirect costs, in terms of pollution and loss of amenity, should he argues, also be added to the overall costing of North East Leicestershire coal.

Robinson and Marshall (1981) also question the credibility and viability of the NCB's planned expansion programme. They launch a fierce attack on the NCB's monopoly position and suggest that even if the global prospects for coal appear generally favourable, the outlook for the UK industry is not so bright due to its cost structure and uncertainties about the future size of certain key markets. They argue the case for an end to the NCB's monopoly by lifting restrictions on the import of low cost foreign coal, which they suggest, would pressurise the Board into operating more efficiently and offer UK consumers greater choice and security of supply.

Coal's prospects for the remainder of this century will undoubtedly be strongly influenced by the size of the power station coal burn. This is an extremely sensitive issue involving not only the question of coal imports but also the more fundamental issue of the Central Electricity Generating Board's (CEGB) commitment to coal-fired capacity. The NCB argues (1980b, p.11) that:

> To maintain the coal burn at around the present level, it is important that sufficient modern power stations exist to ensure that future coal supplies produce electricity efficiently and with the minimum environmental impact.

This is a somewhat contentious statement for a number of reasons. Firstly, it reflects a totally supply-orientated view of the role of coal in relation to its principal market. Secondly, it begs the question of the CEGB's power station ordering programme and whether this should be geared to nuclear plants, as at present, or to coal. Thirdly, there are those who would contest the Board's assertions regarding the efficiency of coal-fired plant and, more significantly in planning terms, the levels of environmental impact involved, especially if the effects of the entire coal cycle are taken into account.

James (1982), Manners (1980; 1981), Robinson (1980), Robinson and Marshall (1981) and Spooner (1981) have all argued that the size of the power station coal burn will affect the viability of the coal industry and the credibility of its expansion programme. The NCB has been preoccupied since the mid-1970s with defending this particular market, especially against cheap coal imports. Government has provided some support for this policy, a notable example being the previous Labour government's support to subsidise the power station coal burn in 1978/9. In October, 1979 the NCB and CEGB signed a Joint Understanding which provided for the supply of 75 million tonnes a year of NCB coal to the generating Board for 5 years with the proviso that increases in the cost of the coal to the CEGB did not exceed the annual rate of inflation (NCB, 1981). This Understanding provides a suitable measure of short term protection for this vital market.

In the longer term however many uncertainties surround the CEGB's fuel base. The CEGB have not ordered any new coal-fired plant since the Drax B station in 1974. Although the CEGB's Medium Term Development Plan (Electricity Council, 1981) makes a clear commitment to a major new nuclear power programme it now seems that even this is subject to considerable uncertainty. Until early 1982 the government supported a programme which would have entailed ordering one new nuclear station a year from 1982. It now appears that the government will only authorise new nuclear stations as and when each is justified in terms of the growth in demand for electricity. Between 1979 and early 1982 electricity demand actually fell by 5 per cent. The CEGB has apparently decided in principle to refurbish some existing coal-fired plant and may eventually convert some other existing stations to coal or dual firing. Considerable pressures are undoubtedly building up against a large-scale expansion of nuclear power in the UK. The Report of the Commons Select Committee on Energy (HMSO, 1981e) expresses many reservations about the cost, safety and other implications of the nuclear programme. Nonetheless, the CEGB is pressing forward, with government support, with its plans for a PWR station at Sizewell in Suffolk, which went to a public inquiry in 1983. The politics of coal and electricity generation seem set to remain critically intertwined for many decades to come.

## Planning for Coal: Issues

### General Features

From the planning viewpoint coal is perhaps the most fascinating and complex of energy industries. Its impacts are probably more diverse and pronounced than those of the other primary energy industries. This arises from a number of important factors. In contrast to oil and gas extraction which have to date been primarily off-shore activities, all stages of the coal fuel cycle are land-based. Furthermore, oil and gas have, in planning terms, become closely associated with a number of major developments located at coastal sites often in areas with a low population. Coal mining is however far more widely dispersed and is largely an inland activity which frequently takes place close to, or even within, major centres of population. Coal-related impacts are further intensified by the locational characteristics of major coal consumers, especially thermal power stations.

Coal is also a very old and well-established industry. Although there have certainly been local and sub-regional shifts in the centre of mining activity in various parts of the country, the overall geography of the industry has changed relatively little over the past 100 years and is only now beginning to show signs of any significant change. Many of the industry's most pronounced and deleterious impacts arise from the fact that for much of its history mining took place in a haphazard and uncoordinated fashion, free from any form of environmental or planning control. In fact, many operational collieries pre-date the emergence of the statutory planning system by many decades. Only 23 collieries are less than 40 years old and the average age of all operational collieries is over 80 years (Moses, 1979). The life expectancy of collieries generally far exceeds that of almost any other form of energy sector development and certainly extends well beyond the forecasting and assessment capabilities of the planning system. Its age and character as an extractive industry has also meant that coal mining has declined and terminated in many areas, leaving a legacy of industrial dereliction, severely weakened local economies and demographically unbalanced communities. Decline in the coal industry has also often been associated with contraction in other industries, the most notable example being the steel industry. Overall, the conventional environmental image of coal is distinctly unfavourable.

Underground mining of coal, the dominant method of production in the UK, remains a labour intensive activity, a feature which again serves to distinguish coal from the other energy industries and which inevitably accentuates its overall pattern of environmental impact. The economic fortunes of many areas continue to be closely linked to those of the industry. Coal mining has led to the creation of settlements which are widely accepted to have a distinctive, if not unique, character (Bulmer, 1975; Denis, Henriques and Slaughter, 1956). The industry and its workforce have been at the centre of the British political stage for much of the twentieth century and coal, perhaps more than any other industry, brings sharply into focus the crucial interplay between politics and planning at both the national and local levels.

Until the mid-1970s coal had been in decline for 60 years. Production reached an all-time peak of 292 million tonnes in 1913. The UK was then the world's largest coal producer. The industry went into a slow but steady decline for the next 50 years. This decline was inevitable in many ways given the problems identified by the Reid Committee in 1945 (HMSO, 1945). The Committee found the industry to be fragmented, unplanned, under-mechanised, lacking in technical development and only achieving productivity levels that had improved little over the previous 30 years (HMSO, 1981a).

The slow decline continued after nationalisation but even so by the end of 1959 total production was still comfortably above 200 million tonnes, more than 700 mines were operational and the total mine workforce exceeded 650,000. The rate of decline and contraction accelerated rapidly during the 1960s and early 1970s. It was then that the changes in the international energy economy initiated in 1973 impacted on the UK coal industry. In fact, a combination of international and domestic pressures, the latter arising from within the industry itself, resulted in a major shift of government policy towards coal. A commitment to expand coal production and use made initially in 1974 and subsequently reiterated on numerous occasions by both Labour and Conservative governments resulted in a recovery in production levels by the late 1970s. In the early 1980s total annual output from deep mining and opencast activities has stabilised at around 125 million tonnes. This however is being achieved with only just over 200 operational mines and a mine workforce of just under 230,000. The industry paid a very heavy price in terms of closures and job losses during the relatively short period of rapid decline between 1960 and 1974. That experience still exerts a very strong influence on contemporary relations between the mining unions and the NCB and between the industry, its workforce and government.

Furthermore, it is not surprising that the industry now faces a major problem in breaking away from the image and reality of decline with which it has been associated for so long. This problem regarding the image of coal is in a sense compounded by the fact that the UK coal industry cannot really be viewed as a unitary entity. There are various 'coal industries'. The differences between deep mining and opencasting have already been mentioned but these differences go beyond simple operational characteristics. NCB opencast activities generate very large operating profits in contrast to many of the Board's deep mining operations. Within the deep mining side of the Board's activities there are enormous variations in the performance and profitability of different mining areas. The peripheral areas of Scotland and South Wales and indeed the majority of the Board's twelve areas are consistently unprofitable but losses are particularly high in the aforementioned areas and in the North East, Western, Doncaster and North Yorkshire coalfields (Table 2.5). (Table 2.5).

These major loss making areas will inevitably bear the brunt of future colliery closures and regional decline in the mining industry. In marked contrast, the prospects for the central mining region based on parts of the Yorkshire field and the East Midlands coalfields appear much brighter and any future expansion of mining activity seems likely to be concentrated there, as evidenced by Selby and North East Leicestershire.

Stabilising the coal industry became a major political and energy policy priority in the mid to late 1970s. However, the basic commitment was actually to expand coal production and use and in effect, therefore, to re-establish coal as a long term cornerstone of the UK energy economy. The industry is currently working to ambitious plans which, if successfully

TABLE 2.5 *Summary of Operating Results of NCB Mining Activities 1981.*

| | Saleable Output (million tonnes) | Colliery output per manshift (tonnes) | Colliery average manpower (thousands) | Profit/(loss) (£ million) | Costs (£ per tonne) |
|---|---|---|---|---|---|
| **Mining areas** | | | | | |
| Scottish | 7.7 | 1.92 | 20.5 | (28.9) | 37.20 |
| North East | 14.1 | 2.07 | 32.9 | (34.5) | 36.97 |
| North Yorkshire | 8.5 | 2.68 | 15.4 | (16.8) | 33.29 |
| Doncaster | 7.2 | 2.18 | 16.7 | (21.4) | 36.37 |
| Barnsley | 8.3 | 2.62 | 15.6 | (10.7) | 33.49 |
| South Yorkshire | 7.4 | 2.17 | 16.9 | (9.5) | 36.03 |
| North Derbyshire | 8.2 | 3.21 | 12.3 | 26.5 | 28.29 |
| North Nottinghamshire | 12.0 | 3.04 | 18.4 | 60.7 | 27.94 |
| South Nottinghamshire | 8.8 | 2.68 | 15.8 | 1.2 | 30.97 |
| South Midlands | 8.5 | 2.36 | 16.8 | (11.4) | 33.32 |
| Western | 11.2 | 2.35 | 22.7 | (17.6) | 36.45 |
| South Wales | 7.7 | 1.46 | 25.8 | (72.5) | 51.40 |
| **Total mining areas** | 109.6 | 2.32 | 229.8 | (134.9) | 34.88 |
| **Opencast Regions** | | | | | |
| Scottish | 2.9 | | | 29.6 | 21.31 |
| North East | 3.0 | | | 32.7 | 25.74 |
| North West | 1.2 | | | 8.0 | 26.92 |
| Central West | 2.4 | | | 35.0 | 15.18 |
| Central East | 3.6 | | | 40.2 | 21.22 |
| South Western | 2.2 | | | 11.0 | 37.50 |
| **Total opencast regions** | 15.3 | | | 156.5 | 24.02 |

Source: NCB (1981, pp. 64–65).

implemented with continuing government support, could significantly transform its productive capability and enhance its economic viability. Although the NCB now looks to the future with a considerable degree of confidence there remains, as previously noted, much doubt and uncertainty outside the industry about its long term position in the UK energy economy.

Many of the issues surrounding the future of coal, including the industry's interactions with the planning system and the whole question of the environmental implications of increased coal production and use, came under unprecedented public scrutiny in the late 1970s and early 1980s. Although few of the many uncertainties surrounding coal's future have actually been resolved there can be no doubt that the debate on the nature, implications and desirability of alternative UK coal futures is proceeding on a more informed basis. This is certainly the case with its environmental and planning policy implications. The attention given to these issues increased markedly in the late 1970s largely as a result of two key factors: the controversy surrounding the NCB's proposed development of the North East Leicestershire Coalfield and the 6 month long public inquiry into these proposals which took place between October 1979 and May 1980; and, in a non-project-specific context, the Commission on Energy and the Environment's (CENE) Coal Study. The CENE Study, published in September 1981, has been labelled 'a companion volume' (Jones, 1982) to the Sixth Report of the Royal Commission on Environmental Pollution on 'Nuclear Power and the Environment' (HMSO, 1976), and represents a comprehensive and authoritive assessment of the environmental implications of increased coal production and use in the UK.

Other dimensions of coal potentially impacting on planning also attracted considerable attention in 1980/81, a period which also amply demonstrated the highly-charged political context of the industry. In 1980 Parliament passed one of a series of regular Coal Industry Acts. This particular Act set out what soon proved to be extremely contentious new financial targets for the NCB. The most damaging implications of these targets, from the workforce's viewpoint, became apparent in February 1981 in the form of NCB proposals for the accelerated closure of up to 50 'uneconomic' mines. The NUM eventually threatened national strike action if the closure programme went ahead. Seemingly anxious to avoid a major confrontation with the miners the government relaxed the cash limits within which the NCB would be expected to operate. The Coal Industry Bill (1982) reinforced this trend towards a more moderate government line on NCB finances and went some way to resolving one area of uncertainty concerning its immediate and medium term prospects. As 1981 drew to a close, attention centred on the contest for the Presidency of the NUM and its possible implication for future relations between the union, NCB and government. Arthur Scargill, a radical left wing candidate, was subsequently elected by an overwhelming majority of miners. In the following years, however, the miners rejected the advice of the NUM National Executive and followed a far more moderate line in accepting modest annual pay increases and a relatively high rate of pit closures.

These examples of labour problems in the coal industry illustrate the dynamic, uncertain and highly-politicised context within which planning for coal-related developments takes place. Despite the many problems that coal undoubtedly faces, the CENE Coal Study report reflects a widely held, though admittedly conventional, view when it observes (HMSO, 1981a, p.8) that:

> . . . the UK coal industry now faces a fundamental change in its long term prospects, notwithstanding the short term difficulties posed by the depth of the current recession. The value of the UK's substantial coal reserves has been transformed. To seize the opportunities opened by these potential prospects constitutes a massive challenge to the industry.

It is not only the coal industry itself that must respond to this challenge. A significant expansion of coal production and use on the scale envisaged by the NCB and endorsed by successive governments would inevitably increase the level of interaction between the industry and the planning system. Perhaps more importantly, it could imply a significant reorientation on the part of both the industry and planners away from a preoccupation with day-to-day operational issues and the problems associated with local and regional decline to a much more diverse perspective in which planning for new or improved capacity, the environmental implications of technological change and the diversification of coal markets would also figure prominently. Indeed, there are already some signs of such a shift of emphasis. If, on the other hand, as some commentators suggest, the industry should be forced to contract once again in the face of a major shortfall in demand and what they see as its inherent economic vulnerability, then the planning system would clearly have to respond to some particularly demanding problems. It is however important to note that there would be differential contraction in the industry in such a situation, this being a reflection of the varying long term potential of NCB Mining Areas. Indeed, even in a situation of aggregate contraction in the industry it is still possible that there could be localised growth in mining activity where suitable and profitable opportunities existed. Nonetheless, irrespective of coal's fortunes over the period up to the end of the century, it is virtually inevitable that it will impose a variety of pressures on the planning system.

### Planning Control of Coal Mining and Related Activities

Figure 2.2 summarises the way in which planning permission is currently granted for different types of coal-related development. This is a complex topic, detailed coverage of which lies outside the scope of this chapter. The following discussion will overview the main features of the current situation.

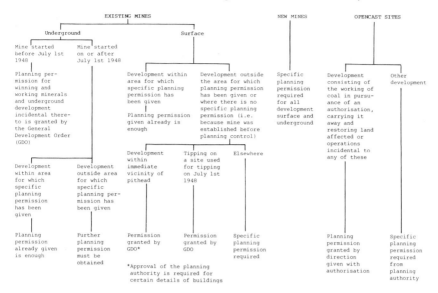

FIG 2.2 *Planning Control of Coal Mining and Related Activities (as at July, 1981)*

For a more detailed exposition on this topic the reader is referred to reports by the Royal Town Planning Institute (1979), NCB (1980c) and the Commission on Energy and the Environment (HMSO, 1981a).

Briefly, all underground and surface operations by the NCB, licencees or lessees, workings exempted from nationalisation and small opencast sites (where the tonnage of coal in the area does not greatly exceed 25,000 tonnes) operated under licence from the NCB are subject to planning control and are the ultimate responsibility of the Secretary of State for the Environment. The one notable exception is opencast mining by the NCB or its contractors which is subject to the provisions of the Opencast Coal Act 1958, as amended by the Coal Industry Act 1975. The Act requires the NCB to obtain authorisation from the Secretary of State for Energy, who, in granting such an authorisation, can direct that deemed planning permission be granted subject to appropriate conditions. As the RTPI (1979, p.117) observes:

> Thus in these cases the local planning authorities are solely consultees in the authorisation process but remain responsible for the enforcement of conditions attached to the deemed planning permission.

With the exception of the small licenced sites, control over opencast mining is similar in some respects to the procedures applicable to power stations (see Chapter 5). The prevailing situation regarding planning control over opencasting is anachronistic. It apparently has its origins in the war-time need to gain access to private land to mine coal. It is however a source of some concern to planners and various other groups and this concern has intensified since the mid-1970s as opencast mining has expanded and as the developments themselves have become more contentious. The RTPI (1979, p.122) has argued that:

> There is a strong case for normal planning procedures to be applied to all forms of mineral extraction to include opencast coal operations presently authorised by the Secretary of State for Energy.

This view has been endorsed by the Commission on Energy and the Environment, which recommends that planning applications for opencast mining should be dealt with under the normal minerals planning machinery (HMSO, 1981a).

### The Environmental Impact of Coal Mining

A useful starting point for the identification of coal-related planning issues is provided by the concept of the energy cycle (Figure 2.3). Planning responses to coal have been dominated by issues associated with the extraction, beneficiation (i.e. coal preparation), waste disposal and decommissioning (i.e. colliery closure, termination of opencast working) phases of the cycle. These are the phases which give rise to activities occurring underground and at or adjacent to the pithead or opencast site which impact, physically, economically and socially on the surrounding area. In a broader sense all phases of the cycle generate planning-related concerns but for the purposes of the present chapter discussion will be confined for the most part to the phases referred to above. The local impacts of the conversion phase are also dealt with in Chapter 5, which examines some of the issues associated with power station planning.

The two quite distinct types of mining—deep (underground) and opencast—give rise to rather different patterns of environmental impact and related planning issues (James, 1982). Deep mining involves the sinking of vertical or inclined shafts (called drifts) through the rock strata to the coal measures which are usually located at depths of 100 m–1000 m (NCB, 1979b). Opencast, or strip, mining involves stripping off the overburden concealing the coal and then working the seams by means of excavating plant. Opencast working depths have progressively increased: from 10–15 m in the early post-war years to around a maximum of 200 m today. This trend has also been associated with dramatic increases in the ratio of overburden to coal: from 5:1 to figures approaching 25:1 (HMSO, 1981a; RTPI, 1979), a factor that has increased the overall environmental impact of the activity.

Of the two methods, deep mining is by far the most important in volume terms in the UK, accounting for approximately 88 per cent of total production in 1980. Although opencasting generates highly contentious impacts its overall range of effects does not match those of deep mining. This reflects the operational characteristics and requirements of the latter, especially its very long-term nature and the size of the associated workforce.

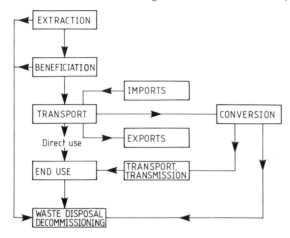

FIG 2.3 *The Coal Energy Cycle (after Cope, Hills and Winward, 1981)*

### *Deep Mining*

The conventional image of coal in the UK is dominated by deep mining. Its major physical impacts are land take, subsidence, visual intrusion of pithead facilities and spoil tips, and air, water and noise pollution (HMSO, 1981a; NCB, 1979b; RTPI, 1979). It also has significant economic and social effects on surrounding areas in terms of employment and demographic impacts and demands on infrastructure provision. This last effect, especially housing provision for the mine workforce associated with new projects, has become a sensitive issue, as the experience at Selby indicates (Arnold and Cole, 1981). The problem for local authorities does however extend beyond housing provision to include, for example, highways, education and social service provision.

The beneficiation phase of the cycle is closely related both operationally and locationally to the extraction process. Coal preparation plants are usually located adjacent to the pithead and are used to separate coal from waste material and to sort, grade and wash the product. This creates significant demands for process water. Up to 1939 only approximately 20–30 per cent of the run-of-mine, that is, coal and associated waste material, was treated by water-based processes. This proportion has now increased to 90 per cent (NCB, 1979b). Although most of the water used is recirculated in the plant a certain amount is associated with mine tailings—suspensions of shales and sandstones and waste coal separated from the saleable coal. These tailings must either be filtered or stored in lagoons so that they can settle out by gravity. Lagoons represent part of the overall waste disposal problem associated with deep mining. This problem has become a matter of increasing concern to the NCB and planners since the mid-1960s. The catastrophic collapse of the spoil tip at Aberfan in 1966 (Whittow, 1980) directed attention to one particular dimension of the problem, although it should be noted that tip safety falls within the remit of HM Inspector of Mines rather than planning agencies. Waste disposal involves major land take and visual impacts as well as loss of agricultural production in many areas. The scale of the waste problem is enormous. In 1978/9 deep mines produced 105.2 million tonnes of saleable coal and 54.5 million tonnes of waste, a ratio of 1.9:1. To set these waste production figures in perspective it is interesting to note that in 1978/9 waste disposal authorities in England, which are the metropolitan and non-metropolitan counties and the Greater London Council, accepted a total of 25.2 million tonnes of domestic, industrial and commercial waste for disposal (HMSO, 1980). Of the 54.5 million tonnes of waste produced by deep mines in 1978/9, 49.5 million tonnes were disposed of on 345 active tips. A further 757 tips were either closed or disused, making a total of 1102 tips in existence in that year. In 1969 the figure had been 2024 (NCB, 1979b). It has been suggested (RTPI, 1979) that the total amount of waste in tips exceeds 3 bn ($3 \times 10^9$) tonnes, and that these tips occupy some 12,200 ha. of land.

Surface tipping of waste material adjacent to the pithead is, from the NCB's viewpoint, a cheap and efficient means of disposal but it is not the only option available. Some waste is currently dumped into the sea or on to the foreshore but this is proving to be increasingly environmentally contentious. Some have argued that the NCB could store sizeable amounts of waste underground. This could mitigate the surface impacts of tips and possibly help to reduce subsidence impacts by filling the void left by the removal of coal. The NCB dispute the feasibility of underground stowage of waste on the basis of cost, productivity and safety considerations. Another waste disposal option that arose in connection with the proposed North East Leicestershire development has been the disposal of waste to a location some considerable distance from the originally proposed mine sites. Detailed research by a joint NCB–local authorities study group (Leicestershire CC, 1978) showed that the Board would incur significant cost penalties if such an option were to be pursued. The experience of the NCB at North East Leicestershire, which is dealt with in a later section, confirms the view of a growing number of commentators who suggest that the waste disposal problem is likely to present the Board with considerable difficulties in the future and may well represent a significant constraint on the industry's ability to achieve projected output targets. These difficulties will almost certainly intensify if, as seems inevitable, the industry moves increasingly towards a very pronounced pattern of regional concentration based on the central mining areas of the Midlands and Yorkshire.

It is not only the original disposal problem that generates tensions between the NCB, local authorities, residents and amenity groups. The reworking of old spoil tips frequently gives rise to local conflicts (RTPI, 1979). Probably the most significant area of concern is however the reclamation and rehabilitation of tips. Dereliction resulting from mining activity and waste disposal is widespread and severe in many parts of the country. In part, this legacy of the industry should be seen as a component of the closure problem discussed in a later section. The NCB is however coming under increasing pressure to undertake progressive restoration of tips and to restore them to alternative uses, particularly agriculture, as soon as possible. The Board is naturally keen to publicise its successes in tip rehabilitation but so far these have only been on a relatively small scale. Land reclamation is also a field in which local authorities play a direct and prominent role, although financial stringencies will probably limit future reclamation initiatives. NCB practices will continue to receive close scrutiny. The Board will undoubtedly be expected to prepare long-term waste tipping and rehabilitation programmes for any new mining projects. In the North East Leicestershire case a 50 year tipping and restoration programme was prepared in relation to the originally proposed spoil tip sites although the affected local authorities expressed concern that this did not extend over the total life expectancy period of the proposed mines, which was in excess of 70 years (Cope and Hills, 1979; Sabey, 1980).

### Opencast Mining

In 1980/81 opencast production totalled 15.3 million tonnes, a figure slightly exceeding the maximum target of 15 million tonnes per year by 1985 set in 'Coal for the Future' (Department of Energy, 1977). At this time the NCB had 67 authorised and working sites distributed over the 6 Opencast Executive Regions. Opencasting is highly profitable in marked contrast to so much of the NCB's deep mining activities. In fact it plays a vital role in off-setting deep mining losses as well as making an important contribution to overall coal production. It provides good quality coal which is in part used to meet the demands of specialist markets and for blending purposes (HMSO, 1981a). Despite these advantages, opencasting is however an environmentally disruptive operation and one which almost invariably provokes a hostile response from those actually or potentially affected by it.

Opencast operations give rise to very obvious and often severely damaging environmental impacts, the most important of which are land take, noise, dust and dirt and visual effects. The NCB, while accepting that these impacts are adverse, has long maintained that they are partly off-set by the temporary nature of the activity. This argument has come under increasing attack however and it has been pointed out that far from being a short-lived activity opencasting may take place within the same localised area for anything up to 40 years (HMSO, 1981a; Opencast Mining Intelligence Group, 1979) although individual sites may themselves be short-lived.

The physical impacts mentioned above are often intensified for local residents because opencast operations are frequently undertaken close to existing residential properties. In some cases they may extend to within less than 50 m of occupied houses. It is widely felt that site boundaries should be drawn up to ensure a greater degree of protection for local residents. The CENE Coal Study report recommends that the Opencast Executive, local authority associations and the Departments of Environment and Energy should consult with a view to establishing a minimum limit in excess of the current 50 yard figure which has been applied for some time. The Commission also recommend that the Executive should make full use of its powers to make discretionary property purchases—with the owner's agreement—to reduce hardship to property owners (HMSO, 1981a). The Commission would like to see a decline in the level of opencast production in the longer term as more efficient and profitable deep mines come into operation replacing the older, unprofitable and often environmentally unacceptable mines. In the interim, the Commission would like to see the adoption of a set of guidelines which 'define more strictly the sites where opencast coal might be mined' (HMSO, 1981a, p.212), a suggestion made by the RTPI in their evidence to the Coal Study (RTPI, 1979). The guidelines suggested by the Commission would limit opencasting to those sites meeting the following criteria:

1. Built development would sterilise workable coal deposits;
2. Coal working or restoration would produce environmental improvements or other environmental benefits e.g. waste disposal sites;
3. Where deep mining cannot meet the need for certain special types of coal for particular needs for blending;
4. Where short term demand increases cannot be met by deep mining.

Opencasting is a contentious activity that gives rise to severe adverse environmental impacts. It has blighted large parts of certain regions of the country and has created major land restoration problems. Its impacts have created an increasing amount of public and planning concern, a situation which is reflected in the growing number of opencast applications that are having to go to public inquiry. In the period up to 1973 only 19 inquiries were held on a total of 215 applications. Between January, 1974 and May, 1981 140 applications to work sites were made to the Secretary of State for Energy. Although the majority of these were subsequently approved without an inquiry (93 cases), some 25 applications did go to inquiry.

### Colliery Closures

Given the long history and fluctuating fortunes of the coal industry many local planning authorities have inevitably experienced at first hand the problems associated with colliery closures. The scale of closures since the creation of the NCB has been enormous. Between 1947 and 1981 over 750 collieries were closed. During the same period, the mine workforce declined from 700,000 to less than 230,000. Many mines have closed in coalfields which are still extensively worked but in some cases—for example, Somerset and Shropshire—they have disappeared entirely from previously established mining areas. The closure of mines is one of the most significant dimensions of change in the coal industry. It is an extremely emotive topic where the mining unions are concerned and one which is central to the contemporary politics of coal. Closures also impact heavily on local planning authorities who in many cases find themselves confronted with severe dereliction problems as well as various adverse economic and social consequences.

The exhaustion of workable reserves is an inevitable concomitant of mining activity. Collieries and coalfields will eventually exhaust in relation to the prevailing operational criteria. Exhaustion of workable reserves is however only one of a number of factors which may determine the life expectancy of individual collieries. Closures may result from geological difficulties which impede access to and working of the coal seams or they may be necessary for safety reasons. Although the mining unions have generally accepted the case for recent closures stemming from geological or safety reasons they have shown themselves far less willing to accept those closures that may be attributed purely to the economic performance of individual collieries. This attitude was clearly displayed in the events of February, 1981.

The continued existence of some collieries, especially in South Wales, has also been increasingly linked to the fortunes of certain key industrial users of coal, foremost among which is the British Steel Corporation (BSC). Reduced demand for coking coal resulting from contraction of BSC's South Wales activities was another contributing factor to the situation that developed early in 1981. The geographical and economic linkages and interdependencies that have developed between coal mining and various other industries, but especially steel, will almost certainly exert a strong influence on the future pattern of closures in some areas, assuming that the NCB can actually close mines in the face of fierce opposition from the mining unions. Any such closures will have major local employment consequences and will intensify the economic, social and physical environmental problems of regions already hit by long term structural change in the UK economy (see, for example, Islwyn BC, 1980). Coal mining does in any case tend to be associated with areas having above average levels of unemployment and many of the areas which have been the focus of the regional policies of successive Governments are characterised by the more vulnerable elements of the contemporary coal industry.

The intensification of the economic pressures on the NCB has, since 1978, brought the colliery closure issue into much sharper focus. The predicament of the South Wales field has received special attention from a sub-committee of the Coal Industry Tripartite Group. This sub-committee concluded (Department of Energy, 1979b) that there existed 3 main areas for decision and action if financial viability for the coalfield were to be achieved:

1. A programme of investment;
2. A programme to deal with losses on current operations;
3. A willingness by the Government to provide a measure of financial support to help sustain the coalfield in the period during which financial viability is to be achieved.

The sub-committee recognised that 'there may be special difficulties in areas with heavy loss-making collieries, particularly where there is no neighbouring replacement capacity' (Department of Energy, 1979b, p.16). While it might have been expected that the then Labour Government would have taken a reasonably sympathetic view of the sub-committee's conclusions, the overall political context was to change within weeks of the publication of the report.

From May, 1979 until February, 1981 the Conservative Government took a rather harder line with the NCB than did its predecessor, especially regarding the Board's finances. The 1980 Coal Industry Act progressively eliminated grants to the Board to cover its operating deficits and it was expected to break even by 1983/4. The events that followed have already been described. The Government's change of attitude in February, 1981 undoubtedly produced a solution to the immediate crisis but the high cost element of the industry is certain to be an enduring problem for which short term palliatives, politically pragmatic as they may be, may well prove inappropriate.

Between June, 1978 and April, 1980 the NCB closed 15 collieries. All but three were closed due to the exhaustion of 'realistically workable reserves' (NCB, 1980b, p.2). Two were closed for geological reasons and the remaining one for safety reasons. At the time of closure these collieries employed 5800 men. Of these, almost 3900 were subsequently redeployed at other locations. Redeployment is however only offered to workers under the age of 55. For older men made redundant the NCB operates a compensation scheme. The Board maintain that where closures occur adjacent to operational collieries employment impacts should be small, especially if closures can be geared to the 'absorption capability of continuing collieries' (NCB, 1980b, p.4). Opportunities for redeployment may also be provided by new capacity. Transfers between closing and new or continuing collieries may be funded under the provisions of the 1980 Coal Industry Act. Where such opportunities do not exist in close proximity to closing collieries then impacts are potentially far more severe, even allowing for longer distance transfers among the younger elements of the mine workforce. Indeed, there may be situations in which the movement away of younger miners and their dependents exacerbates the impact of closure.

The dereliction problems associated with closures are keenly felt over large areas of the country. The Barnsley area provides a graphic illustration of the overall physical impact of mining (Barnsley MBC, 1979). Dereliction not only represents a form of unacceptable environmental degradation (HMSO, 1981a) but also intensifies the problem of economic and social regeneration in declining mining areas. In South Wales there are additional problems stemming from the topography of the area which limits the amount of land suitable for development. This means that an even greater premium is attached to bringing derelict land back into productive use. Between 1976–81 the Welsh Development Authority constructed more than 50 per cent of its new factory space on reclaimed land (HMSO, 1981a). The costs of new industrial and commercial developments may however also be significantly higher in currently or recently worked mining areas in view of the additional precautions that must be taken to avoid subsidence damage. These additional costs may represent a deterrent to new investment (RTPI, 1979).

The CENE Coal Study Report examines various aspects of the dereliction problem in some detail. The Commission recommend, firstly, that the NCB continue to develop its approach to the management and use of land not required for operational purposes and, secondly, that the Government should exempt from capital expenditure allocations expenditure by local authorities on derelict land clearance. The dereliction problem in Yorkshire receives special attention from the Commission, who recognise that steps must also be taken to deal with the potential impact of the planned increase in mining in the area over the period up to the end of the century. The Commission recommend that the Government assess the feasibility of setting up 'an independent regional development agency with its own budget to deal with problems such as derelict land clearance' (HMSO, 1981a, p.211).

As noted above, colliery closures may have profound employment consequences as well as various other adverse social consequences. In County Durham, for example, over 38,000 mining jobs were lost over the 20 years between 1951–71. Although the rate of closures has slackened considerably since 1974, impacts may still be severe at the local level. These include not only the obvious loss of employment opportunities and, since 1974, relatively high wages, but also the attendant increases in unemployment, the development of demographic inbalances with implications for the demands made on social service facilities and on the financial resources of both central and local government and implications for housing provision. Declining mining areas may become locked into a downward spiral of economic and social circumstances and may experience a general loss of confidence on the part of existing residential and commercial property owners which further intensifies the overall pattern of decline and blight (RTPI, 1979).

A major difficulty encountered by local authorities faced with colliery closures has been the NCB's unwillingness to give reasonable advance notice of their intentions. Unless adequately forewarned of impending closures local authorities can at best respond in only a limited reactive manner rather than by framing long term planning policies to cope with the problem. The RTPI (1979, p.50) has argued that:

> There is clearly a case for more co-ordination on colliery closures between the NCB and central government on the one hand and local government on the other hand. This would greatly assist in preparing for the problems caused by closures and increase the possibility of re-using the sites involved.

Given the sensitive nature of the closure issue it is perhaps not surprising that the NCB is unwilling to publicise its future plans unless of course it suits its own purposes at a particular point in time. For example, although the NCB made available information on possible closures for the Nottingham-shire Structure Plan Topic Report on Mining, it did not wish this to be circulated to County Councillors and had not apparently consulted with the National Union of Mineworkers (Coates, 1979). However, shortly after-wards the Board did provide detailed information on the likely future pattern of colliery closures in Nottinghamshire and Leicestershire to advance its case at the public inquiry into its plans to develop the North East Leicestershire Coalfield, a case which in part rested on the argument that the new project provided regional replacement capacity.

The problem of colliery closures will remain prominent in the context of political and planning responses to coal. The planning system has had a considerable amount of experience in dealing with the problem but it still finds it difficult to cope with, especially when it further intensifies the economic, social and environmental problems endemic to some areas. Despite the important role of local authorities in formulating responses to the problem the involvement of planners in consultations regarding NCB closure plans has been disappointingly limited. There is a very strong case for much greater involvement of planners in such a consultative process, a view firmly expressed by the RTPI (1979, p.50):

> The Institute has stressed the need for quadripartite consultations between the NCB, central government, mining unions and local authorities and it is particularly crucial in the case of colliery closures in view of the serious social and economic consequences.

In an otherwise comprehensive perspective on the relationship between coal and the environment, the CENE Coal Study Report has surprisingly little to say about the economic and social impacts of colliery closures. Whereas the Commission's recommendations on many topics are very specific, even to the point of suggesting possible institutional/organisational arrangements, they go no further than stating the following (HMSO, 1981a, p. 211):

> We conclude that there is an important linkage between pit closures, clearance of derelict land, and the generation of alternative employment opportunities. Forward planning based on early warning and the closest cooperation between all interested parties is required.

This rather non-commital position may well reflect the acute political sensitivity of the closure issue and the Commission's own preoccupation with physical effects at the expense of socio-economic considerations.

## Technological Change

Future prospects for coal will, as noted, be strongly influenced by such factors as the size of the power station market and the industry's own cost structure. Changes in mining and coal utilisation technologies may however also be of significance in shaping the industry's future (James, 1982). Diversification of markets may reduce the NCB's long term dependence on the size of the coal burn in power stations. New mining methods and techniques may help the industry to improve productivity levels and its cost profile.

Technological change has already dramatically altered the nature and scale of some coal-related planning problems. Perhaps the most notable example is the colliery waste disposal problem which has intensified with the progressive increases in the proportion of coal power-loaded in collieries (Rosborough, 1982). This trend of a decline in the quality of the run-of-mine is unlikely to be reversed (NCB, 1977).

There are a whole series of potential technological changes that could have implications for planning responses to coal. These can be grouped under four main headings (RTPI, 1979):

1. Developments in conventional mining;
2. Developments in conversion and end use technologies;
3. New methods of conversion to gaseous and liquid fuels;
4. Unconventional exploitation of coal, especially *in-situ* conversion to gas or liquids.

The most significant development in conventional mining will be the already evident trend towards larger mines. The typical mine in 2000 is likely to have a capacity of 3–5 million tonnes per year (Tregelles, 1976). Such a trend may produce both gains and losses in environmental terms. A reduced number of larger production units could lessen the overall impact of the extractive phase of the coal cycle but could also result in more severe local problems regarding the disposal of waste and the transport of men and materials. Large-scale, high productivity capacity is most likely to be effectively utilised in Yorkshire and the Midlands, and this will also serve to intensify the pattern of concentration of mining activity in the central region. It is also anticipated that manpower levels in new colliery developments of the future will show a significant reduction on those in existing operations, with consequent implications for local planning authorities.

Other types of technological change falling under this broad heading may also impact on planning. For example, changes which permit increases in the underground distances over which men and coal can be moved economically may permit existing collieries to be extended. This could ensure greater continuity of employment for the workforce and might even reduce the need for some new mining developments.

Developments in conversion and end use technologies include:
1. Environmentally benign methods of coal burning, probably the best known of which is fluidised bed combustion;
2. Methods encouraging the substitution of coal for natural gas and oil products as an industrial and domestic heat source and chemical feedstock;
3. Methods of wide application designed to extract a greater amount of useful heat from the burnt fuel.

The major planning implications of these developments are likely to arise in relation to coal transport and distribution, especially in urban areas, and the land use patterns arising from the possible introduction of Combined Heat and Power (CHP) schemes (see Chapter 9).

Coal conversion technologies have become the focus of a major international research effort since the mid-1970s. The basic technologies are in fact well known and have been used in some countries (for example, South Africa) for many years. Descriptions of various technologies for liquefaction and gasification are readily available (Department of Energy, 1978; HMSO, 1981a; NCB, 1978; 1979) and some preliminary assessments have been made of their potential contribution in the UK (HMSO, 1979). Their environmental and planning policy implications have however received relatively little attention so far.

Liquefaction and gasification technologies are both under development in the UK. In 1981 the government agreed to provide some financial support to establish a pilot liquefaction plant at Point of Ayr colliery in North Wales. The necessary supplementary financial backing from the private sector has not however materialised. The main emphasis appears to be on the gasification technologies, especially the British Gas Corporation Lurgi slagging gasifier. The 1978 Energy Policy Consultative Document foresaw a sizeable market for Substitute Natural Gas (SNG) produced from coal by the end of the century. Energy Paper 39 (HMSO, 1979) presented a rather more cautious view in which a significant level of SNG production would not be required or achieved until the second quarter of the next century.

The nature of SNG producing facilities and their environmental implications have been examined in some detail by the Commission on Energy and the Environment (HMSO, 1981a). Site requirements will be determined by 5 major considerations:
1. Land requirements of between 80–120 hectares;
2. Access to up to 15,000 tonnes of coal per day;
3. Access to large quantities of cooling water, possibly as much as 50,000 cubic metres per day;

4. Access to solid waste disposal facilities;
5. Safety considerations.

In terms of physical characteristics and patterns of socio-economic impact SNG installations would strongly resemble existing petro-chemical complexes. Siting these installations could however present the gas industry and the planning system with certain problems and this particular topic attracted considerable attention in the CENE Coal Study Report. The Commission observe that there is no conclusive evidence of a shortage of new sites but by the same token there are not a great number of feasible sites available either. Some plants could be located on existing operational land held by the BGC, which has already identified 25 sites, mainly in urban areas, that should be held for SNG purposes. Of these sites only 12 appear suitable for gasification plants—the others could be used for oil gasification or feed-stock storage—and these would provide only enough capacity to meet approximately 25 per cent of a possible ultimate gasification requirement (HMSO, 1981a).

The Commission recommend (HMSO, 1981a, p.214) that:

> . . . long term contingency planning for site identification, and for project and process appraisal, should proceed on the basis of forecast need for up to 10 sites for SNG plants in the first decade of the next century.

and conclude that:

> . . . there is some urgency in assessing siting requirements for SNG plants, despite uncertainty about how in detail the build-up of demand will take place.

The consideration of unconventional methods of coal exploitation is a far more speculative venture, although there are several plausible reasons why such methods might appear attractive, including the occupational risks of conventional mining, the need to exploit reserves which are currently inaccessible to conventional mining for operational and economic reasons, and possible environmental benefits, especially a reduction in the scale of the waste disposal problem. The most significant of these methods is the *in-situ* conversion of coal to gaseous or liquid fuels. The NCB has been investigating the feasibility of underground coal gasification, which could prove economically viable, but further developments in this field appear some way off.

Many of the new coal technologies currently being researched are long-term prospects and their uptake will clearly be determined by their cost-competitiveness. For the period up to the end of the century the UK coal industry will continue to be heavily dependent on conventional mining methods and existing markets, although some changes in both mining and conversion/end-use technologies appear likely. Patterns of environmental impact and related trade offs are however unlikely to change significantly over this period. The planning system will probably encounter some difficulties in coping with the technical issues involved in the short term but there should be a progressive build up of the necessary expertise in local authorities.

**New Coal Developments**

*The Ladder of Exploration and Project Development*

The North East Leicestershire public inquiry and the publication of the CENE Coal Study Report have greatly increased the amount of publicly available information concerning the nature and extent of the NCB's exploration programme and the way in which possible future mining projects are identified.

The NCB refers to this programme in terms of a 'ladder' or hierarchy of exploration knowledge (Moses, 1981), indicating the status of different mining prospects. There are 6 levels in the hierarchy:

1. Potential Prospects: areas where coal is known to exist (through geological or gravity surveying data, for example);
2. Preliminary Exploration: areas where an attempt is made to define the boundaries of the deposit;
3. Significant Exploration Stage: areas where detailed analyses of coal seams, coal chemistry and mineability are undertaken;
4. Feasibility Study: if the previous stage produces 'encouraging results' the prospect will be upgraded to this stage, which will involve determination of output levels, mine sites and the economics of the operation;
5. Planning Stage: represented by the status of the North East Leicestershire Prospect;
6. Development Stage: represented by the status of the Selby project.

The existence of 'coal in place' does not by any means guarantee that the NCB will seek to develop the deposits involved. As Moses (1981, p.44) observes:

> . . . the early steps in the ladder involve constant sieving techniques in order to concentrate scarce resources on the more attractive prospects for promotion to the Planning Stage. The sieving is always against criteria of 'relative attractiveness now', given knowledge being gained elsewhere and also of market changes, and so on.

Figure 2.1 shows the distribution of existing coalfields and the location of mining prospects existing in the Ladder of Exploration as at March, 1981.

Until late 1980 it appeared that Park in Staffordshire would be the next new mining development to proceed to the Planning Stage following North East Leicestershire. The CEGB then however expressed serious concern at the high chlorine content of the Park coal and indicated that it would not be prepared to accept it for the power station market. It is surprising that Park had proceeded to such an advanced stage in the 'Ladder' given this problem. It is possible that the CEGB's posture is more a reflection of its sensitive relationship with the NCB on the power station coal burn issue. The NCB has now dropped its proposal to construct a single 3 million tonne per year colliery at Park.

The NCB now appears to be concentrating on the South Warwickshire Prospect, which is at the Feasibility Study Stage. A preliminary appraisal of the planning issues involved has already been undertaken by the county council (Warwickshire CC, 1980). Other future mining areas could include Canonbie in Scotland (Preliminary Exploration Stage) and Banbury in Oxfordshire (Significant Exploration Stage). The Oxfordshire Coalfield is especially interesting as it points to the possibility of the industry moving well away from established mining areas, although it is unlikely that any development would take place before the end of the 1980s. Furthermore, given that developments involving extensions to existing fields are proving increasingly contentious the likelihood of anything other than a long, hard struggle to develop the Oxfordshire field seems remote. Other potentially workable coal deposits have been located in Lincolnshire (Kesteven and Witham Prospects) and in the area to the south of the Selby field in Yorkshire, but again the NCB is unlikely to be seeking approval to develop these until the late 1980s.

The identification of these mining prospects reflect the successes of the NCB's intensive exploration programme initiated after 1974. In the late 1970s the Board was drilling about 100 deep boreholes a year and expenditure on boreholes and seismic work was in the order of £20 million per year. The geographical pattern of future new coal mining projects is now becoming increasingly clear:

> While much of the new capacity programme still depends on future exploration and appraisal, it is clear that the great concentration of new developments in the foreseeable future will be on the extensions to existing coalfields, principally in Yorkshire and the Midlands. (NCB, 1980b, p.10)

This emphasises still further the trend towards a concentration of mining activity in the central region. New developments here will also reflect the strong geographical relationship between the coal and its power station market. The majority of major coal-fired power stations (i.e. those with an annual output exceeding 2.0 TWh) are located in the CEGB's Midlands and North Eastern Regions. In 1979/80 these two Regions accounted for 67 per cent of the total coal consumed in power stations in mainland Britain. The major constraint on the realisation of the Board's plans for new projects is likely to be the future size of this market, a factor which is surrounded by considerable uncertainty in the early 1980s.

The NCB has enjoyed considerable success with its post-1974 exploration programme and a whole series of potential new mining projects may be in prospect. The information now at the Board's disposal has important implications for the planning system. The Board is coming under increasing pressure to weigh environmental factors more heavily in its assessment of the feasibility of new projects and to consider these factors at an earlier stage than in the past (HMSO, 1981a). The CENE Coal Study Report also recommends that the 'Ladder of Exploration and Project Development' be more widely publicised and that the NCB consult with local authority associations and other interested parties before investment decisions have proceeded too far. There are indications therefore that the environmental trade offs associated with alternative coalfield development options will be dealt with more explicitly in the future and that in the longer term a more acceptable balance between coal mining and the maintenance of environmental quality may be achieved.

### Planning Responses to New Deep Mine Developments

Since its inception in 1947 the statutory planning system has had relatively little experience of dealing with the requirements and implications of new deep mine projects. For most of this period coal was, of course, in decline and only a very few new mines were actually constructed in the period up to 1974. Since then, a number of new projects have been initiated and are now at various stages in the 'Ladder of Exploration and Project Development' outlined in the previous section. Selby in North Yorkshire is at the development stage and produced its first saleable coal in 1981. The North East Leicestershire (Belvoir) project remains at the planning stage following a ministerial decision in March, 1982 necessitating changes in the project as originally proposed. Selby and Belvoir provide various insights into the planning issues involved and the pattern of response of local planning authorities dealing with new deep mine projects.

### Selby

The Selby Coalfield lies to the south of York in the County of North Yorkshire. Coal was discovered in the area in 1972. In August, 1974 the NCB submitted a formal planning application to North Yorkshire County Council seeking permission to sink drifts at Gascoigne Wood and a shaft at Wistow. Plans for the construction of four additional satellite shafts to transport men and materials and to ventilate the workings were also outlined. The application related to an area of approximately 285 km$^2$ (110 sq m) and the NCB sought permission to extract 600 million tonnes of coal from the Barnsley seam at an annual rate of 10 million tonnes. The coal was to be transported out of the area by rail. The total manpower requirements of the project were estimated at 3000 men (Arnold and Cole, 1981).

The Secretary of State for the Environment 'called in' the application for his own determination in November, 1974. A public inquiry into the Board's application took place between April 2 and June 7, 1975. On March 31, 1976 the Secretary of State announced that he would be granting planning permission to develop the field subject to various planning conditions.

The events surrounding the Selby project have been extensively researched by a team based at the University of York and their findings and conclusions have been presented in a report published in 1981 (Arnold and

Cole, 1981). The following discussion, which draws largely on this published material, summarises some of the main themes that have arisen in connection with the Selby project.

Although the NCB initiated contacts with local authorities prior to the submission of the planning application, a notable feature of the early stages in the relationship between the Board and those authorities was the county and district councils' surprise at the scale of the application. The picture presented by the Board in early discussions with the two councils was of a much smaller project. The County Planning Officer's response was to request more details and more time to consider the formal application, while Selby District Council submitted a formal holding objection to the project. The NCB's initial response seems to have been to apply pressure for an early decision, hopefully with the minimum of rigid conditions, but it did subsequently agree to an extension to the normal 2 month determination period. The local authorities were clearly at a disadvantage since they, and indeed the planning system generally, had no previous experience in dealing with a major application to develop an entire coalfield. Local councillors and officers of the two councils were thrown back very much on their own resources. Furthermore, little was yet known about the attitudes of the local community to the project and, if the councils did agree to press ahead as rapidly as the NCB wished, local residents would have little chance of keeping up with events surrounding the application, let alone influencing the outcome. This preliminary skirmishing between the NCB and local authorities was however brought to an abrupt halt by the Secretary of State's decision to 'call in' the application and convene a local planning inquiry.

The inquiry lasted for 37 days, followed by 12 days during which a tour of inspection took place. More than 100 witnesses were heard and over 300 letters were received and put before the Inspector. Arnold and Cole (1981) identify seven substantive issues that emerged at the inquiry. The four that provoked the greatest argument were subsidence, land drainage and flooding, visual intrusion and road and rail movements. The three other issues proved to be just as contentious but were dealt with in less detail. These were: the diversion of the East Coast Main Line; manpower and housing; and, the effect of the new coalfield on other areas in West and South Yorkshire.

The subsidence, land drainage and flooding issues were interlinked. Selby is a low lying area and, as events in the winter of 1981/2 showed, is susceptible to flooding. Subsidence could increase its vulnerability in that respect. The NCB however maintained that subsidence impacts could be controlled to produce a maximum effect of 0.99 m at the surface. The NCB also undertook to compensate for surface damage that occurred and to leave pillars of supporting coal to prevent subsidence in and around Selby itself and along the River Ouse. As Arnold and Cole (1981, p.34) note:

. . . the conclusive nature of the NCB's technical evidence carried the day. Furthermore, the Board showed a definite determination to handle this issue convincingly, not the least because in the future its record on subsidence control might have a direct influence on any forthcoming planning application.

The visual impact of the project generated the 'most bitter' response from local residents largely because it appears they felt they had been misled by the NCB in the early public meetings that took place prior to the inquiry. They generally assumed that pithead facilities would not exceed about 13 m (40 ft) in height, although it subsequently transpired that for safety reasons heights would have to be closer to 30 m (100 ft). Similarly, concern about transport-related impacts increased significantly when the true scale of the project became known. Particular concern was expressed at the road movements generated during the construction phase and the long term impact of greatly increased rail movements.

The need to reroute the main eastern rail link to Scotland to avoid sterilising a large amount of coal in the area was aired for the first time only at the public inquiry. It implied major adverse effects to Selby itself including the possible loss of a mainline station, increased journey times and the loss of more agricultural land. British Rail did not appear particularly concerned about this matter, primarily because they stood to gain valuable extra revenue from shipping out Selby coal to its markets.

The whole issue of the size of the proposed workforce and associated housing requirements was a major matter of concern to the local authorities and one which subsequently led to considerable friction between the NCB and the two affected councils. The county council had always maintained that it wanted to know much more about these aspects of the project. At the inquiry the NCB presented revised estimates of its manpower requirements, which now totalled 4000 men. The actual mechanics of obtaining miners did not appear to present the NCB with any major problems. Housing received relatively little attention from the NCB. A total of 2400 dwellings was mentioned, of which 2000 would be for rental, but the NCB placed the responsibility for housing provision firmly on the shoulders of the local authorities. As subsequent events were to show however this was to prove a

dangerous and sensitive political issue, liable to divide communities . . . As events took their course, integration through housing and the cost of housing provision were to become the most intractable problems for the local authority. (Arnold and Cole, 1981, p.38)

The regional impact of the project was a matter of particular concern to neighbouring West Yorkshire County Council, which was at that time preparing its structure plan. West Yorkshire was concerned about the possible adverse economic aspects that might result in some areas as miners moved away to work at the new Selby pits, the impact of Selby on investment and spending in West Yorkshire, its impact on migration and commuting patterns, and transport-related impacts and the colliery waste disposal problem. The NCB attempted to set West Yorkshire's mind at rest by indicating that no mines in that area would be prematurely closed to man the new Selby pits.

Other issues did arise at the inquiry, including the waste disposal problem (which was not a major difficulty due to the high quality of the coal seams), the cost of the scheme and the CEGB's position regarding the market for Selby coal.

The Inspector's Report to the Secretary of State recommended the granting of planning permission for the project subject to specified conditions. It is important to note, especially in the light of events at subsequent energy related inquiries, that the issue of national need for Selby coal was never disputed. Indeed, the local authorities and many local residents appear to have had no doubts about this aspect of the development. The Inspector certainly shared this view and observed in his Report that:

> I have come to the conclusion that the production of this valuable coal during the lifetime of the mine is of such importance to override all other considerations which have come before the inquiry. (quoted in Arnold and Cole, 1981, p.42)

As Selby followed so closely in the wake of the 1973/4 oil price rises at a time when the UK was still deeply traumatised by these events, it is not surprising that Selby was viewed as nothing other than a tremendous national asset that had to be exploited as soon as possible.

The Secretary of State endorsed the conclusions of the Inspector and announced his decision in March, 1976. The time taken by the Minister to reach a decision on the application apparently triggered off some resentment among the local planning authorities that had come under such intense pressure in the early stages to determine the NCB's application as quickly as possible. The most significant of the conditions attached to the permission related to subsidence, which was to be limited to 0.99 m unless prior consent was obtained from the county council and Yorkshire Water Authority, and the height of the shift headgear, which was not to exceed 30 m. The Secretary of State also stipulated that working parties should be established to examine flooding, subsidence and drainage problems and that review arrangements should be made for dust, noise and other environmental pollution.

The Selby experience, which has only been briefly outlined here, raises a number of significant points concerning the relationship between the NCB and the planning system. The affected local authorities clearly came under intense pressure from the NCB for an early decision on the application, a pattern which has subsequently been repeated elsewhere. There were clearly major problems concerning the flow of information between the NCB and affected parties regarding the nature, scale and implications of the project. In this context, it is important to note that no form of detailed environmental assessment of the implications of the project was prepared by either the NCB or the affected local authorities. The local authorities appear to have felt that they required a considerable amount of additional information at all stages in the process but this does not always seem to have been forthcoming from the NCB, who evidently produced several major surprises at the public inquiry.

There are some other important questions surrounding the nature of the planning conditions imposed on the permission. For example, it is far from clear what would happen if the subsidence condition were to be breached. Given the area's vulnerability to poor drainage and flooding this is a matter of considerable importance. The NCB may encounter similar planning conditions elsewhere in the future and the Selby experience will doubtless be closely scrutinised by both the Board and various local planning authorities. Although arrangements were to be made for dealing with various pollution issues, construction site noise impacts have been a major problem from time to time and at one point the NCB faced the possibility of 'stop notices' being served by the local authority.

The issue which has generated the most concern for the affected local authorities at Selby has however been housing and service provision. These received totally inadequate attention in the Inspector's Report and the Secretary of State's decision letter. The NCB were always opposed to providing miners' housing since this would inhibit the process of integration they wished to foster between the mine workforce and local residents. The burden, in their view, should fall on the local authorities, especially Selby DC. From the council's viewpoint the costs of building 2000 additional new homes was a totally unreasonable and unrealistic proposition. Despite continuing negotiations with the NCB in 1976/77, by the end of the latter year the situation had deteriorated to such an extent that Selby DC decided to cut its housebuilding programme by 25 per cent and told the Department of the Environment that due to financial uncertainties its plans included no provision for miners' housing. Eventually, in April, 1978, a housing subsidy agreement was finalised between the NCB and Selby DC. The housing problem still however remained partially unresolved in the early 1980s due to various outstanding issues and uncertainties, including the siting and phasing of new housing development, land availability, the actual level of demand for housing by incoming miners, central government finance for public housing and council house sales policy and the impact on housing supply and demand of any delays in developing the coalfield.

Selby has become an important reference point in the analysis of the relationship between the NCB and the planning system. Clearly, its timing and certain of its characteristics set it apart from other possible deep mine projects of the future. Nonetheless it provided several important lessons which were reflected in the events surrounding the proposed development of the North East Leicestershire coalfield, described below.

*North East Leicestershire*

Almost exactly 4 years after it submitted the application to develop Selby, the NCB formally applied for planning permission for its next major coalfield project in North East Leicestershire. This project, which is also widely known as the Belvoir coalfield, achieved the status of a national controversy in the late 1970s and early 1980s. It was associated with the longest, most wide-ranging and expensive public inquiry that has ever been held into an NCB deep mining application. It focused attention on many of the uncertainties surrounding the coal industry as it entered the 1980s and, like Selby, revealed many of the difficulties confronting local planning authorities when formulating responses to such large scale and complex development proposals.

Although coal had been known to exist in the area for many decades it was not until 1974 that the NCB carried out detailed exploration work in North East Leicestershire. This subsequently led to the identification of a very large coalfield containing more than 1400 million tonnes of reserves, underlying an area of about 234 km$^2$ of mainly agricultural land in Nottinghamshire, Leicestershire and Lincolnshire. In June, 1977 a feasibility study prepared by consultants to the NCB was published (Thyssen UK/Leonard and Partners, 1977). This described how the field could be exploited and also included an 'impact analysis' of some of the potential environmental implications of the proposed project. The NCB submitted formal planning applications for the project in August, 1978. These applications related to the construction of three new deep mines, pithead facilities and spoil tips at Hose (in the Vale of Belvoir), Asfordby and Saltby. The mines would produce 7.2 million tonnes of coal and 2.5 million tonnes of colliery waste a year and would exploit recoverable reserves estimated at 510 million tonnes. They would have a total life of 70–80 years and would employ 3800 miners plus a further 300 administrative and clerical staff (Cope and Hills, 1979; Lewis, 1978). The Secretary of State for the Environment 'called in' the applications in January, 1979. A preliminary meeting prior to the public inquiry took place in early May, 1979. The inquiry itself commenced on October 30, 1979. It sat until May 2, 1980, during which time there were 84 days of formal proceedings and a number of site visits. Over 100 witnesses presented evidence. The Inspector submitted his report to the Secretary of State in late 1980. The Secretary of State did not however announce his decision on the NCB's planning applications until March 25, 1982, arguing that the proposed development 'raised a number of complex issues which it was important to explore fully before any decision was taken' (Department of the Environment, 1982). The Minister decided to refuse the NCB's original planning applications for the Belvoir development but has left the door open for the Board to amend its proposals and submit revised applications. In mid-1982 the NCB, Department of the Environment and affected local authorities were involved in discussions intended to resolve the nature and extent of these revised plans for the development of the coalfield, which, as the Secretary of State observed in his decision letter represents a 'massive national resource'. Unlike Selby therefore, Belvoir has not, at the time of writing, been resolved and many uncertainties surround the ultimate scale and timing of any development that may subsequently be approved. The following discussion will therefore focus on the inquiry proceedings and the ways in which the affected local planning authorities responded to the original planning applications submitted by the NCB in 1978.

The NCB and local planning authorities did liaise prior to the inquiry through the mechanism of the Joint Working Party. This comprised the six affected local authorities (Leics. CC, Notts. CC, Lincs. CC, Melton DC, Rushcliffe BC, S. Kesteven DC), represented by County and District Planning Officers, and the NCB, represented by officers of the South Midlands and South Nottinghamshire Areas). The JWP first met in September, 1977, some 3 months after the publication of the NCB's consultants' report. Its purpose was:

> To examine and cost the infrastructure and other factors likely to be associated with or to flow from a planning application by the National Coal Board to mine coal in North East Leicestershire and adjoining areas of Nottinghamshire and Lincolnshire.

The parties involved tackled this task:

> Without accepting that the need for 'Belvoir Coal' has been proved and without prejudice to or pre-emption of any decisions of the local authorities concerned or the National Coal Board. (Leicestershire CC, 1978, p.1)

Subsidiary working groups were set up to investigate three topics: infrastructure implications and costs with respect to housing, employment, transport and ancillary requirements (shopping, education, social services etc); colliery waste disposal, including the comparative costs of surface, underground and off-site disposal methods; and, subsidence and drainage issues.

These three topics were selected because of their intrinsic importance and because they had not been dealt with in any detail in the NCB's consultants' report. Although this report had incorporated an environmental impact analysis this had dealt with only six issues: visual effects, loss of landscape value, loss of agricultural production, noise effects, road capacity limitations, and, the impact of increased traffic flows. The nature of this analysis has been reviewed by Williams, Hills and Cope (1978). Certain socio-economic impacts were specifically excluded from the consultants' brief as they were regarded as issues requiring consultation between the NCB and local authorities. Housing, infrastructure and manpower implications fell into this category of excluded impacts. So too did subsidence and, to some extent, waste disposal, two of the most controversial impacts of the proposed project. The NCB maintained, in late 1977, that additional work was required to establish the scale of potential subsidence impacts and the operational and economic feasibility of alternative waste disposal options, the latter again in consultation with the local authorities.

The JWP published an Interim Report in April, 1978 (Leicestershire CC, 1978). The infrastructure group findings indicated that the major capital costs associated with Belvoir would be for housing, water services, highways and education. Interestingly, it also revealed that unit costs of development could be higher for options involving the construction of two or three new mines than for a single mine. The Report concluded that the development needs arising from the NCB's proposals would require considerable capital investment by affected local authorities, over and above existing commitments. Costs (assuming 90 per cent public housing and at 1977 prices) were estimated to range from almost £49 million for the three mine option to just over £12 million for the lowest cost single mine option.

The waste disposal group examined the environmental and engineering feasibility of local, underground and off-site (remote) disposal options. Having identified feasible options, cost comparisons were undertaken and an attempt made to assess the effects of factors regarded as uncostable. The group established that there would be a high cost penalty associated with remote disposal, although this could provide a means for overcoming one of the most deleterious local environmental impacts of the proposed mines.

The subsidence and drainage group focused primarily on impacts on surface structures, services and drainage. Few firm conclusions were reached on these topics in the Interim Report as further investigations were required. The NCB carried out an extensive subsidence survey programme during 1978/9 (NCB, 1979a), providing estimates of impacts and possible damage to existing buildings. About 30 per cent of the 3500 conventional houses in the coalfield might be affected by subsidence. In addition, 1.5 per cent of the 207 km$^2$ of agricultural land in the area could be adversely affected.

The JWP continued to function after the publication of the Interim Report. While the original terms of reference were retained it was agreed after submission of the NCB's planning applications that the JWP would continue with the additional objective of reaching agreement on facts, defining issues for debate at the public inquiry and reaching agreement on those issues where possible. Five meetings took place between December, 1978 and April, 1979. In the meantime, a Transportation Joint Working Party was also established, its Interim Report being published in August, 1979 (Leicestershire CC, 1979b). Leicestershire CC also produced its own impact assessment of the project during this period (Leicestershire CC, 1979a).

JWP activities involving the NCB and local planning authorities spanned a two-year period and only terminated a matter of weeks before the inquiry itself commenced in late October, 1979. This liaison process attracted a certain amount of attention, not least from the then Secretary of State for the

Environment, Peter Shore, who referred to the activities of the JWP in his much publicised speech on Major Public Inquiries (Shore, 1978).

These contacts were undoubtedly valuable, a view echoed by the inquiry Inspector himself (Mann, 1981), but they could not and did not resolve many of the crucial points at issue between the NCB and local authorities, particularly the central issue of need for the development (Sabey, 1979).

Belvoir was by any standards 'a big inquiry'. In many ways, it was to coal what Windscale had, to that time anyway, been for nuclear power in the UK. It provided an opportunity for detailed public scrutiny of the NCB's future plans and prospects in the context of a highly controversial new mining project. It also attracted attention in a more general sense as it was widely seen as a significant test of the traditional public inquiry's ability to cope with strategic policy issues, especially the need for the project itself, as well as the more conventional local and regional planning concerns that were expected to arise. Belvoir therefore became an important reference point in the debates concerning the future of coal and the appropriateness and effectiveness of planning inquiry procedures.

All the previously mentioned issues were fiercely debated at the public inquiry into the Board's applications. The NCB faced a large number of objectors including the three affected County Councils, Melton Borough Council, the Countryside Commission, the Council for the Protection of Rural England and the so-called 'Alliance', a grouping of the National Farmers' Union, the Vale of Belvoir Protection Group and the Vale of Belvoir Parish Councils.

Two groups of issues were dealt with at the inquiry. The first concerned the need for the coal, the proposed timing of the development and alternative ways of achieving Government policy without developing the field. The second group concerned local and regional impacts of the project, particularly colliery waste disposal, visual effects, subsidence, the loss of agricultural land and production and the impact of increased traffic flows.

The NCB argued that Belvoir was essential to the achievement of its future plans, which had been accepted by successive Governments. Furthermore, as Moses (1979) pointed out:

> In the national context, there is no other prospect currently at the stage of development which could create a viable alternative at this time or within the next few years.

The project, which would provide replacement capacity in the East Midlands needed to offset losses resulting from the exhaustion of existing mines in South Nottinghamshire and Leicestershire, was required to maintain the NCB's deep-mining capacity in the 1990s.

Objectors presented a very strong case against the NCB's assertions regarding coal's future prospects and the need for Belvoir coal. This case was most powerfully presented by Manners (1980) and Robinson (1980), who represented the Alliance and Leicestershire County Council respectively.

Both questioned the NCB's demand projections and emphasised the uncertainties surrounding the size of the power station coal market in the 1990s and beyond. They supported this main line of attack with arguments relating to the future capacity of existing mines, the economics of investment in new capacity, anticipated productivity levels and the potential role of coal imports in the UK energy economy. It is quite clear, from both the report of the Inspector (HMSO, 1982) and the Secretary of State's decision letter (Department of the Environment, 1982), that the NCB's case regarding the need for Belvoir coal was by no means totally convincing and that the witnesses appearing for various objectors revealed many of its inherent weaknesses. As the decision letter observes (Department of the Environment, 1982, p.3):

> The Inspector's view on need was that it is somewhat more likely than not that there will be a need for a supplement to indigenous deep-mine capacity at about the time the Belvoir coalfield could become fully operational . . . he was unable to refine his opinion by suggesting the year in which the need would arise or the exact extent of that need. The Secretary of State accepts that the coal will be needed at some time in the future, but he is not convinced on the information at present before him that the degree of need demonstrated outweighs the adverse environmental effects . . .

The local impacts of the proposed development that commanded the greatest attention at the inquiry were waste disposal, visual effects and subsidence. Due to the character of the seams, Belvoir coal is relatively dirty, having a coal to waste ratio of 3:1. Large amounts of waste would therefore be extracted with the product and would have to be disposed of. This could be done in various ways and the precise nature of the waste disposal option that should be pursued at Belvoir has always been one of the most controversial aspects of the development. The favoured NCB option of local tipping would have involved considerable land-take. Over a fifty-year period of tipping it was estimated that 682 ha of land would be used. Tipping would also give rise to visual impacts, especially in relation to the sites at Hose and Saltby. Both the Inspector's report and the decision letter of the Secretary of State deal at some length with the spoil tip issue and the visual impact of the pit head installations associated with the mines. The winding towers, which would be approximately 60 m high—almost twice as high as those at Selby—would intensify the overall visual impact of the development. The Secretary of State has indicated that the original proposals regarding tipping at Hose and Saltby are unacceptable and it is quite clear that the waste disposal issue played a major part in his decision to refuse the NCB's planning applications. Even in the case of the Asfordby site, which has never been as contentious as either Hose or Saltby, the Secretary of State expressed concern about the impact of spoil tipping on agricultural production, an issue also very relevant in the context of other two proposed mine sites. Subsidence impacts, though not as sensitive an issue as at Selby, did nonetheless receive considerable attention at the inquiry. The available evidence—from the NCB—suggested that a considerable number of houses in the area might be affected if mining were to take place. Drainage of farmland might also be affected. Although an emotive local issue, subsidence appears to have had little bearing on the ministerial decision and indeed it is not mentioned in the decision letter.

The housing requirements generated by the proposed development were also quite extensively debated at the inquiry. There is no doubt that the earlier events at Selby did much to sharpen the awareness of the issue on the part of the local authorities at Belvoir. Additional housing requirements attributable to the development were estimated at 5000 dwellings. The long delay in announcing the ministerial decision on the NCB's applications has seriously disrupted the formulation of housing policies in Leicestershire and in the Melton District Council area.

It is impossible to do justice to the complexities of Belvoir in the present chapter. The inquiry did after all last for 84 days, generated several million words of transcripts, proofs of evidence and inquiry documents, and cost in excess of £2 million. As a 'big inquiry', Belvoir proved well able to cope with the enormous pressures that were imposed upon it. The local inquiry mechanism proved robust enough to provide an effective and efficient forum within which the need for a major project could be extensively debated. The Inspector's ability to handle the proceedings in a businesslike and perceptive manner was widely praised and the overall success of the inquiry was due in no small measure to this factor.

Compared with Selby, Belvoir was a totally different proposition for both the NCB and objectors, although the latter group seem to have appreciated this rather more than the Board. Belvoir was fought largely on the issue of need and on this point the NCB case certainly lacked credibility. In terms of local impacts, the major distinguishing feature of the two projects was the nature and scale of the potential waste disposal problem at Belvoir. In that sense, Belvoir will be a crucial reference point with respect to one of coal's most dramatic, contentious and enduring environmental impacts.

### Forward Planning for Coal

At various points in this Chapter attention has been drawn to the problems faced by local planning authorities when responding to the issues raised by both growth and decline in the coal industry. Experience suggests that for the most part planners have been obliged to adopt a reactive rather than an anticipatory role. This reflects a number of factors. As far as closures are concerned the NCB will, given the prevailing situation, proceed very cautiously and its ability and willingness to provide adequate advance notice of closures must remain in doubt. Planners in the more vulnerable mining areas probably do have a clear idea of the mines most at risk, although supposition is no substitute for hard information. The generation of alternative employment opportunities may take years whereas advance notice of closures is often measured in months. Until a comprehensive and realistic policy on high cost mines is agreed between the NCB, Government and unions it seems unlikely that planners will find their own position in the matter significantly improved.

In the case of new mining projects the situation may prove to be rather different. If the NCB responds positively to CENE's recommendations concerning the 'Ladder of Exploration' and the wider consultation process, then planners will have an opportunity to make significant inputs at a far earlier stage in the project planning process. Other problems will however remain as the CENE report acknowledges (HMSO, 1981a). A key difficulty is that the planning procedures, timescales and decision making processes of organisations like the NCB do not mesh effectively with the planning activities of local authorities. It has proved very difficult to accommodate the future requirements of the coal industry in most structure planning exercises. Plans tend simply 'to confirm the existing use of land by statutory undertakers' and 'tend to be retrospective whereas they ought to be prospective' (HMSO, 1981a, p.199). Energy developers only take final investment decisions at a relatively late stage in the project planning process and planning authorities are consequently unwilling to make advance provision for major schemes so as to avoid blight and possible problems in justifying these at a Structure Plan Examination in Public. The fact that planning permission is not automatically granted to projects included in the Structure Plan may deter developers themselves from publicising their future plans. In fact, intending developers could find themselves having to argue the case for a new project at both the Examination in Public and at a subsequent local planning inquiry (HMSO, 1981a).

The need for forward planning to meet the requirements of existing coal mining activity has also been increasingly recognised. In the case of deep mining a major focus of attention has been the waste disposal problem and this again was a topic addressed by the CENE report. The possibility of strategic planning for opencast mining has also attracted attention and this approach has, in fact, been developed with some success in Durham.

### Conclusions

Coal dominated the UK energy economy for 200 years from the beginning of the Industrial Revolution until the 1960s. For most of this period it was unconstrained by almost any form of environmental or planning control. Unlike the UK's natural gas and oil industries, which first appeared and then rapidly developed during the 1960s and 1970s, the coal industry's patterns of interaction with the planning system have been profoundly influenced by the long term impacts of investment decisions made by independent mining entrepreneurs up to 100 years ago or more.

Coal's fortunes have fluctuated markedly over the period since 1945. In the early 1980s the industry stands at the crossroads. The NCB will continue to argue that coal is an essential form of energy insurance that can be depended upon to provide a significant (and growing) proportion of the UK's primary energy requirements for many decades after the exhaustion of North Sea oil and gas. If it is to fulfil that role then, the Board maintains, continuing investment in new and improved capacity is essential. This will serve to increase the industry's overall productive capability and significantly improve its cost profile.

The NCB's public optimism about coal's future prospects is not however shared by a number of informed commentators, who have fundamental doubts about the nature and scale of future coal markets, particularly the level of the power station coal burn. These critics also express reservations about the ability of the NCB to improve its cost structure and point to its potential vulnerability to lower cost coal imports.

It is difficult to determine just where the coal industry will stand in the 1990s. A decline on the scale experienced during the 1960s seems unlikely in view of the NUM's determined opposition to colliery closures. The acute sensitivity of this particular issue became clearly apparent in 1982 with the controversy surrounding the NCB's supposed 'hit-list' of uneconomic pits and the specific case of the Snowdown Colliery in Kent, which the Board wished to close down on a temporary basis. Further closures do however appear inevitable as situations will arise where mines exhaust or must be closed for safety reasons.

Existing mines will almost certainly exhaust at a lower rate than the NCB previously anticipated and it may well be that the industry's existing capacity will be more than adequate to meet market demands for the foreseeable future. There is certainly no shortage of coal in the early 1980s and the NCB faces the prospect of steadily growing stockpiles as supply continues to outstrip demand. Given this situation, the NCB will have some difficulty in presenting a credible case for investment in new deep-mine capacity. Even allowing for the fact that new capacity would probably not come on-stream until the 1990s there are major uncertainties surrounding the size of the power station coal burn, industrial demand for coal and possible demand generated by SNG production during that decade and thereafter.

This chapter has sought to demonstrate that the contemporary coal industry poses a variety of problems for the planning system. Evidence suggests that the planning system often encounters major problems of information availability in relation to the NCB's activities. This information problem has two basic dimensions. Firstly, there is the availability of technical and other information concerning the nature, scale and implications of NCB activities, both existing and proposed. The Board very often has this information but on many occasions seems unwilling or unable to make it available to local planning authorities. It is perhaps a reflection of the

NCB's relative lack of experience in dealing with the planning system, as well as its own organisational structure, that it does not seem fully to appreciate either the role of local planning authorities or their legitimate information requirements. Indeed, the Board seems at times to view the planning system simply as an obstacle to be overcome and one which is totally irrelevant to the achievement of its own objectives. At both Selby and North East Leicestershire the NCB applied considerable pressure on the planning authorities to give a rapid decision on the planning applications and then seemed somewhat surprised when those authorities requested more time to evaluate what were obviously complex, large-scale development proposals with far-reaching implications for the affected areas.

The other dimension of the information problem relates to local planning authorities' own lack of experience and expertise in dealing with new coal-related developments. Coal is certainly an under-researched area in terms of socio-economic factors (Cope, Hills and Winward, 1981). Even where the conventional planning impacts of both existing and new developments are concerned (e.g. demographic effects, housing, multiplier effects) surprisingly little information is currently available. This obviously intensifies the problems faced by local planning authorities when formulating acceptable and appropriate policies for coal and coal-related developments.

As the coal industry moves towards the 1990s existing variations in productivity, output and profitability are likely to become even more striking. Planning responses to the industry's requirements and to its problems are likely to vary markedly between different regions. For many planning authorities the problems of decline in the coal industry seem destined to become a major pre-occupation. For some others, there may be the prospect of major new mining projects or other types of coal-related development, such as SNG production plants.

Coal in the UK is a fascinating and complex industry. It generates a wider range of planning issues and problems than probably any other form of major industrial development. The industry's relationship with the planning system has certainly been tense at times, but there are indications that this situation may improve in the future. The future path of the coal industry and the pattern of its relationship with the planning system will however be determined as much by political considerations as by the activities of the NCB and local planning authorities.

### References

Arnold, P. and Cole, I. (1981) *The Development of the Selby Coalfield: A Study in Planning,* Selby Research Paper 1, HMSO, London.
Barnsley Metropolitan Borough Council (1979) *Coal Study: Evidence of Barnsley Metropolitan Borough Council to the Commission on Energy and the Environment,* Barnsley MBC, Barnsley.

66    Peter Hills

Berkovitch, I. (1977) *Coal on the Switchback: The Coal Industry Since Nationalisation*, George Allen and Unwin, London.
Bulmer, M. (1975) Sociological models of the mining community, *Sociological Review*, **23**, 61–92.
Coates, K. (1979) The National Coal Board: what price consultation?, in *Jobs and Community Action* (eds. G. Craig, M. Mayo and N. Sharman), Routledge & Kegan Paul, London.
Cook, P. L. and Surrey, A. J. (1977) *Energy Policy: Strategies for Uncertainty*, Martin Robertson, London.
Cope, D. R., Hills, P. and Winward, J., (1981) *Social Science Research Requirements for Alternative Coal Energy Futures*, A Report to the Energy Panel of the Social Science Research Council, Nottingham University, Energy and Planning Group.
Cope, D. R. and Hills, P. (1979) Coal takes its turn in the dock, *New Scientist*, **84**, 1178, October 25, 1979, pp.258–63.
Council for Environmental Conservation (1979) *Scar on the Landscape? A Report on Opencast Coal Mining and the Environment*, Council for Environmental Conservation (CoEnCo), London.
Dennis, N., Henriques, F., and Slaughter, C. (1956) *Coal is Our Life*, Tavistock Press, London.
Department of Energy (1979a) *Energy Projections 1979* (original and revised versions), Department of Energy, London.
Department of Energy (1979b) *Report of the Coal Industry Tripartitie Group Sub-Committee on the South Wales Coalfield*, Department of Energy, London.
Department of Energy (1978) *Coal Technology: Future Developments in Conversion, Utilisation and Unconventional Mining in the United Kingdom*, Department of Energy, London.
Department of Energy (1977) *Coal for the Future: Progress with 'Plan for Coal' and Prospects to the Year 2000*, Department of Energy, London.
Department of the Environment (1982) Secretary of State's Decision Letter on the National Coal Board's planning applications to mine coal in North East Leicestershire.
Dunn, R. B. (1979) Coal in the UK, *The Mining Engineer*, February, 1979, 527–533.
Electricity Council (1981) *The Electricity Supply Industry in England and Wales: Medium Term Development Plan 1981–88*, The Electricity Council, London.
Ezra, D. (1978) *Coal and Energy*, Ernest Benn Ltd., London.
HMSO (1982) *Inspector's Report on the Vale of Belvoir Public Inquiry*, HMSO, London.
HMSO (1981a) *Coal and the Environment*, Report of the Commission on Energy and the Environment, HMSO, London.
HMSO (1981b) *Digest of United Kingdom Energy Statistics 1981*, HMSO, London.
HMSO (1981c) *Digest of United Kingdom Mineral Statistics 1981*, HMSO, London.
HMSO (1981d) *Environmental Assessment of Projects*, 11th Report of the House of Lords Select Committee on the European Communities, Session 1980–81, HMSO, London.
HMSO (1981e) *The Government's Statement on the New Nuclear Power Programme*, 1st Report of the House of Commons Select Committee on Energy, Session 1980–81, 4 Volumes, HMSO, London.
HMSO (1980) *Digest of Environmental Pollution and Water Statistics*, HMSO, London.
HMSO (1979) *Energy Technologies for the United Kingdom*, Energy Paper 39 (2 Volumes), HMSO, London.
HMSO (1978) *Energy Policy: A Consultative Document*, Cmnd 7101, HMSO, London.
HMSO (1976) *Nuclear Power and the Environment*, 6th Report of the Royal Commission on Environmental Pollution, HMSO, London.
HMSO (1945) *Coal Mining: Report of the Technical Advisory Committee* (Chairman: C. Reid), Cmd 6610, HMSO, London.
Islwyn Borough Council (1980) *Coal and Steel Cutbacks: The Impact on Islwyn*, Report by the Chief Development Officer, Islwyn, Gwent, Development and Planning Department.
James, P. (1982) *The Future of Coal*, Macmillan, London.
Jones, P. M. (1982) Review of Coal and the Environment: Report of the Commission on Energy and the Environment, *Atom*, **303**, January, 1982, 11–13.
Leicestershire County Council (1979a) *North East Leicestershire Coalfield: Impact Assessment*, Report of the County Planning Officer, Leicester County Planning Department, Leicester.
Leicestershire County Council (1979b) *North East Leicestershire Coalfield: Interim Report on Transportation Issues*, Local Authorities–National Coal Board Transportation Working Party, Leicestershire County Planning Department, Leicester.

Leicestershire County Council (1978) *North East Leicestershire Coalfield: Local Authorities–National Coal Board Working Party Interim Report*, Leicestershire County Planning Department, Leicester.

Lewis, J. J. (1978) Progress in the development of the North East Leicestershire coalfield, *Colliery Guardian*, August, 1978, 501–521.

Mann, M. (1981) Problems of the local planning inquiry, in Salter, J. and P. Thomas (eds) *Proceedings of the Seminar on 'Planning Law for Industry'*, Churchill College, Cambridge, March 29th–April 2nd, 1981, International Bar Association, London.

Manners, G. (1981) *Coal in Britain: An Uncertain Future*, George Allen and Unwin, London.

Manners, G. (1980) *North East Leicestershire Coalfield Public Inquiry: Proof of Evidence No. 115*.

Moses, K. (1981) Britain's coal resources and reserves—the current position, in *Assessment of Energy Resources*, The Watt Committee on Energy, Report No. 9, 40–49, The Watt Committee on Energy Ltd., London.

Moses, K. (1979) *North East Leicestershire Coalfield Public Inquiry: Proof of Evidence No.11*.

National Coal Board (1981) *Reports and Accounts 1980/81*, National Coal Board, London.

National Coal Board (1980a) *Report and Accounts 1979/80*, National Coal Board, London.

National Coal Board (1980b) *Commission on Energy and the Environment Coal Study—Topic Five: Patterns of Environment Impact*, National Coal Board, London.

National Coal Board (1980c) *Commission on Energy and the Environment Coal Study—Topic Six: Policy and Planning Procedures*, National Coal Board, London.

National Coal Board (1979a) *North East Leicestershire Prospect: Mining Subsidence (Abridged Report)*, National Coal Board, South Nottinghamshire Area, Bestwood, Nottinghamshire.

National Coal Board (1979b) *Commission on Energy and the Environment Coal Study—Topic One: Land Use Aspects of Mining-Deep Mines*, National Coal Board, London.

National Coal Board (1979c) *Commission on Energy and the Environment Coal Study—Topic Three: Environmental Implications of the Markets for Coal and its Use, Part II: Conversion of Coal to other Fuels and Chemicals*, National Coal Board, London.

National Coal Board (1978) *Liquid Fuels from Coal: A National Coal Board Report prepared by the Planning, Assessment and Development Branch of the Coal Research Establishment*, Coal Research Establishment, National Coal Board, Stoke Orchard.

National Coal Board (1977) *Mining Beyond 2000 AD: A Consideration of Possible Devices and Techniques and Related Matters for the New Century*, National Coal Board, London.

National Coal Board (1974) *Plan for Coal*, National Coal Board, London.

Opencast Mining Intelligence Group (1979) *A Reassessment of Opencast Coalmining*, Opencast Mining Intelligence Group, Leeds.

Robinson, C. (1980) *North East Leicestershire Coalfield Public Inquiry: Proof of Evidence No.50*.

Robinson, C. and Marshall, E. (1981) *What Future for British Coal?: Optimism or Realism on the Prospects to the Year 2000*, Institute of Economic Affairs, Hobart Paper 89, Institute of Economic Affairs, London.

Rosborough, L. (1982) *Assessing the Impact and Planning Implications of Colliery Waste*, Unpublished Ph.D thesis, Nottingham University.

Royal Town Planning Institute (1979) *Coal and the Environment—a Submission to the Commission on Energy and the Environment Coal Study*, Royal Town Planning Institute, London.

Sabey, D. (1980) *North East Leicestershire Coalfield Public Inquiry: Proof of Evidence No. 53*.

Sabey, D. (1979) Belvoir coal, in *Energy Policy and Local Planning*, Council for the Protection of Rural England, Symposium Proceedings, Council for the Protection of Rural England, London.

Shore, P. (1978) *Major Public Inquiries*, A Speech by the Secretary of State for the Environment, Manchester, September 1978, Department of the Environment Press Release, London.

Stocks, J. (1980) *North East Leicestershire Coalfield Public Inquiry: Proof of Evidence No. 92*.

Spooner D. J. (1981) The geography of coal's second coming, *Geography*, January, 1981, 29–41.

Thyssen UK/Leonard and Partners (1977) *The Belvoir Prospect: Surface Works Report to the National Coal Board, South Nottinghamshire and South Midlands Areas*, National Coal Board, South Nottinghamshire and South Midlands Areas.

Tregelles, P. G. (1976) A typical colliery in the year 2000, *Colliery Guardian Annual Review*, August 1976, 411–16.

Warwickshire County Council (1980) *Coal in Central Warwickshire: A Report by the County Planning Officer*, County Planning Department, Warwick, Warwickshire.

Whittow, J. (1980) *Disasters: The Anatomy of Environmental Hazards*, Penguin Books, Harmondsworth.

Williams, K., Hills, P. and Cope, D. R. (1978) EIA and the Vale of Belvoir coalfield, *Built Environment*, June, 1978, 142–151.

CHAPTER 3

# North Sea Oil: The British Experience*

G. A. MACKAY

## Introduction

The scope of this chapter requires some definition and explanation. It is primarily concerned with experience in Scotland, because that is where most of the onshore impacts generated by the North Sea oil developments have occurred, and therefore the chapter deals only incidentally with oil-related developments in other parts of Britain. It also covers some gas developments in Scotland although the gas industry is the separate concern of Chapter 4.

There are two main reasons for this apparent overlap. The first is that in many cases it is impossible to isolate the separate effects of the North Sea oil and gas developments—they use the same supply bases, the production platform yards build both oil and gas platforms, and some fields produce both oil and gas. The second is that the Scottish planning system differs from that in England and Wales and therefore there are useful comparisons which can be drawn with the English experience discussed in Chapter 4, in particular the planning of the Morecambe Bay and St. Fergus landfall terminals.

As far as the oil industry is concerned, the concentration on Scotland is only a minor limitation. The great bulk of activity has occurred in Scotland. For legal purposes latitude 55°55'N is taken as the dividing line between English and Scottish waters. The two areas are usually referred to as the Southern and Northern North Seas. At the end of 1981 there were 25 oil fields in production in the UK sector of the North Sea; all of these are north of 55°55'N. Southern North Sea production is entirely gas at present and there have been no signs to date of commerical oil fields in that area.

There are some non-Scottish oil developments, however, which merit attention. There is onshore oil production (albeit on a very small scale compared with the North Sea) in two areas—the East Midlands and

* I am very grateful for comments on an earlier draft made by Peter Cockhead, David Cope, Roger Crofts, Peter Hills, Ronnie Nicoll, Stan Pickett and Trevor Sprott. Any remaining errors are my own, as are the views expressed which are not necessarily shared by the above.

Dorset—and there is active exploration elsewhere in the country. Offshore blocks have been licensed all round the coast of the UK and outside the North Sea there is active exploration in the English Channel, the South-West Approaches, the Celtic Sea, Morecambe Bay and off the west coast of Scotland. To date the only commercial discovery has been the Morecambe Bay gas field, discussed in Chapter 4, but the exploration activity has led to the establishment of onshore supply bases (harbours and airports) in these areas.

Oil from the Ekofisk field in Norwegian waters is landed by pipeline at a terminal at Teesside in north-east England where there are treatment and processing facilities. Also quite a few firms in England, particularly in the North East and East Anglia, produce equipment for the North Sea and some of these developments have substantial planning implications, notably the production platform and module yards. Nevertheless, similar developments exist in Scotland, and are discussed in this chapter, so it is not felt that the concentration on the Scottish experience is a limitation.

In the wake of the large oil price rises during the 1970s there has been renewed interest in indigenous supplies of oil and other fuels and a massive growth in exploration throughout the world. Most countries are seeking their own domestic supplies of oil and natural gas and the Scottish and UK experience is of international interest in that context. Furthermore, geological and geographical conditions have meant that many such resources lie offshore and therefore the North Sea experience is particularly relevant. Often, as in Scotland, it is the more rural regions of the countries which are involved. This is the case in Canada, for example, where the main offshore discoveries have been close to Labrador, Newfoundland and Nova Scotia. An attempt is made in this chapter to relate the UK experience to developments, actual or potential, in these other countries.

This introductory section is followed by a brief review of the North Sea oil industry to date. The next sections deal with the locus of control, the regional distribution of oil-related activity within Scotland and the legislative framework. The final part of the chapter examines in detail the issues in the main areas affected—Aberdeen, St. Fergus/Peterhead, Easter Ross and Shetland—and the conclusions attempt to identify more general issues and implications.


**A Brief History of North Sea Oil Developments**

In terms of the offshore oil and gas industries the North Sea has a relatively long history in that exploration drilling first began in 1965, the first gas field came into production in 1967 and the first oil field in 1975. Interest stemmed originally from the discovery onshore in the Netherlands of the Slochteren gas field, near Groningen. The reservoir rock was of a type which extended under the North Sea and into Yorkshire, where some small gas discoveries had also been made, suggesting that there may have been opportunities for similar discoveries in the North Sea itself. Exploration had to await international agreement on boundaries in the North Sea, which came with the Geneva Convention of 1958 and the subsequent implementation of that agreement in the UK in the Continental Shelf Act 1964.

Throughout the 1960s interest was concentrated on the shallow waters of the Southern North Sea, particularly off the coasts of East Anglia and Yorkshire. Up until the end of 1969, 146 exploration wells were drilled in the UK sector, of which 130 were in the southern part and only 16 in Scottish waters. There were a few gas discoveries during this period, some of which have proved fairly substantial, but given the oil companies' predominant interest in oil, rather than gas, the level of interest in the Southern North Sea was relatively small and declined sharply after 1969.

Exploration activity gradually moved northwards as improvements in technology allowed the rigs to operate in deeper and deeper waters. The major stimulus to and redirection of effort came in December 1969 with the discovery in Norwegian waters of the large Ekofisk oil field. This led to a great increase in drilling activity off the east coast of Scotland and subsequently in the East Shetland basin.

There is obviously a close link between the level of exploration activity and the success/discovery rate. Interest has remained high in the Northern North Sea because of the large number of commercial discoveries, of which the biggest have been Forties, Brent, Frigg and Ninian. These are shown in Figure 3.1, together with the other significant discoveries, and the concentration in the area east of Aberdeen and in the East of Shetland basin are clearly evident. In contrast, in other areas such as Eastern Canada, exploration activity fell sharply when no commerical discoveries were made.

It is misleading to regard the oil industry as a single entity. A simple disaggregation into three phases—exploration, development and production—is useful because each has distinct planning implications. The exploration phase comprises seismic surveying, hydrographic work and actual drilling; the main onshore facilities needed are marine supply bases and airports for both fixed-wing and helicopter traffic. The development phase covers the construction of all the necessary facilities—production platforms, pipelines, terminals and so on. Once a discovery has been deemed commercial it normally takes 3 to 6 years to construct the facilities and bring the field into production.

The production phase usually lasts for 15 to 20 years although some fields in the North Sea have an expected lifespan of 25 years and others as short as 6 years. For oil fields the normal production profile is 3 year build-up to peak production, a plateau of 4 to 5 years and then a slow decline at about 25 per cent a year. Gas fields usually have a flatter production profile. In some instances it is useful to divide the production phase into two to take account

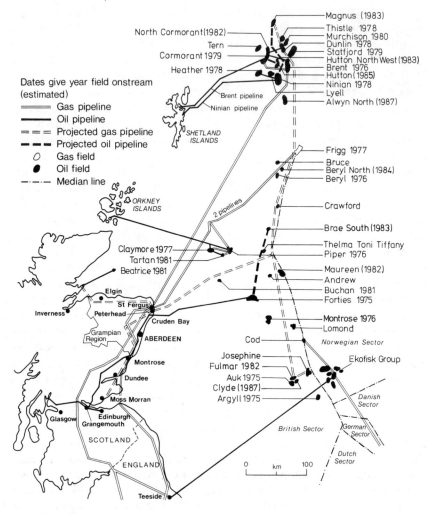

FIG 3.1 *North Sea Oil Fields and Pipelines*

of downstream refining and petrochemical developments, which may have different planning and locational implications from landfall terminals.

To date Scotland has been relatively little involved in downstream developments although the picture has changed significantly in the last years, as discussed below.

Briefly, the main interest of this chapter is with the development and production phases because these generate the important onshore developments. The exploration activity requires relatively few facilities and can usually be accommodated easily, although in the early years in Scotland there were problems with harbours being used as supply bases. In contrast many of the subsequent activities are both land and labour intensive. For example, a production platform yard can require upwards of 200 ha of flat land, adjacent to water, and the Scottish yards have had peak labour forces of up to 3500. A pipecoating yard requires a waterfront site of 12 to 40 ha with the ideal site having no more than a 3 per cent slope, a low water table and a high load bearing capacity. Landfall terminals, refineries and petrochemical plants have similarly substantial physical needs and in addition raise environmental questions. These locational characteristics are discussed in more detail below. Their main relevance here is the point that they differ substantially from phase to phase and therefore over time.

Another important aspect in the present context is the effect these characteristics have had on the geographical distribution of oil-related activity in Scotland. This is the subject of the section following the next. The second map shows the main onshore developments in Scotland; most, but not all, are located on the east coast and in the Orkney and Shetland islands.

Finally, in this section, a few words on the macroeconomic impact may help to set the scene for the following discussion. An indication of the importance of North Sea oil and gas production for the UK is the fact that in 1981 indigenous production (largely offshore) accounted for just under 60 per cent of total fuel consumption, compared with 5 per cent in 1970.

The UK is now self-sufficient in oil (in other words is a net exporter) which is markedly different from the early and mid-1970s when oil imports created major problems for the balance of payments and indirectly the level of national economic activity. North Sea oil production began in 1975, in which year it totalled 1.1 million tonnes and by 1980 it had risen to 78.7 million tonnes, about which level it should be maintained for at least a decade.

In 1980 North Sea oil and gas production accounted for just under 3 per cent of gross national product (GNP). Sales of oil were estimated at £8.9 $\times 10^9$ (1980 prices) and of gas £0.6 $\times 10^9$. The Government's revenue from royalties, petroleum revenue tax and Corporation tax were an estimated £3.8 $\times 10^9$ in the 1980–81 financial year, compared with only £0.08 $\times 10^9$ in 1976–7 and £0.2 $\times 10^9$ in 1977–8. There can be little doubt, therefore, that the North Sea oil and gas developments have had a substantial impact on the UK economy.

### The Locus of Control

The offshore oil industry falls under the responsibility of a number of government departments. The main control is exercised by the Department of Energy who are responsible for, among other things, exploration and production licences and the approval of development plans. However, the Treasury have prime responsibility for fiscal matters, such as Petroleum Revenue Tax, and they have an interest in the level of offshore activity, particularly on decisions as to whether or not to develop discoveries. Labour matters, such as training, come under the Manpower Services Commission and the Department of Employment; health, safety and environmental matters under the Department of the Environment (and the Scottish Development Department in Scotland), and the Health and Safety Executive, although the Department of Trade, because of its responsibility for marine shipping, exercises some of these, and other relevant, functions.

Similarly, a number of other central government departments is involved, which makes coordination and integrated planning difficult.

It is important to remember that the key North Sea policies are developed at central government level. These include the number and location of licences, the taxation regime, production levels and the activities of the British National Oil Corporation (BNOC). Since 1965 the basic policy of all the governments has been that of rapid exploration and development. The objective has been to reduce the country's dependence on imported oil as quickly as possible by maximising indigenous oil and gas production. More recently, in the light of constraints on public expenditure, the government has been trying to increase its own income from royalties and taxes, which has had some implications for the level of production. These objectives have been met to the extent that the UK is now a net exporter of oil.

This policy has had significant implications for planning at the regional and local levels. In general the 'national need' has been determined as paramount and other considerations of secondary importance. This is in marked contrast to experience in Norway where local and sectoral interests, such as those of the fishing industry, have brought about a significantly slower rate of exploration and development (Lind and Mackay, 1980), although it should be remembered that Norway is not a major consumer of oil.

The system of government in the United Kingdom results in some special arrangements in Scotland. Although not a federal system akin to that in Canada or West Germany, for example, there is some devolution of responsibility to Scotland (and also to Northern Ireland and Wales). Some central government functions are devolved and administered by the Scottish Office, such as schools, agriculture and fisheries, local authority expenditure, housing, roads and planning.

In the field of industrial development the Scottish Economic Planning Department (SEPD), and more recently the Locate in Scotland office, carry out a promotional role and provide grant aid for manufacturing industry. In some instances there appears to be a blurring of roles—for example, the Department of Energy occasionally acts on its own in Scotland but normally leaves Scottish energy issues to SEPD.

In the context of this chapter the key government body at the Scottish level is the Scottish Development Department. However, the implicit division within the Scottish Office of economic and physical planning creates problems in the sphere of planning, although in practice the two bodies work well together. Regional and local planning fall under the auspices of SDD. Legislation has changed markedly since local government reorganisation in 1975. The key legislation in force at present is the Local Government (Scotland) Act 1973 which introduced a two-tier system, with a few exceptions (minor in the overall Scottish context but important in relation to the oil developments). Most powers are vested in the nine regional authorities, with the 53 districts' main functions being local planning, housing, leisure and recreation and environmental health. The peculiar circumstances of the three island groups—Orkney, Shetland and the Western Isles—resulted in their being designated all-purpose authorities; the first two are very important in the context of North Sea oil, although the significance of their status should be seen in the light of their small populations. Similarly, in the Highland Region (in Figure 3.2, the northern part of Scotland, to the west and north of the Grampian Region boundary line) the division of functions between region and district differs slightly from that in most of the rest of the country. For example, it was thought that the districts were too small to handle planning satisfactorily and that is therefore a regional function.

Thus the planning of the North Sea developments occurs at four levels of government: the UK, Scotland, region/islands authority and district. Each has fairly well-defined areas of responsibility but inevitably some overlap occurs. Also, there is no reason why the interests of the four levels should coincide and it is not surprising that conflicts have arisen. Two merit specific mention. The first is simply that the national policy for rapid development and a high level of production have made it more difficult for the local authorities to plan the developments occurring in their areas. The second is that within Scotland there have been differences of opinion between the Scottish Office and some of the regional authorities over the distribution of oil-related activity. This latter aspect is the focus of the next section.

### Regional Distribution within Scotland

Economic activity is not spread evenly over geographic space and this manifests itself in Scotland in the different structures and scales of the economies of the Scottish regions. Similarly, the onshore developments generated by North Sea oil and gas are themselves highly concentrated, with noted locational biases and the inevitable result of these two facts is that the developments have had differing impacts on different parts of the country.

A good starting point is the present geographical distribution of oil-related employment in Scotland. Employment is undoubtedly the best single indicator of onshore impact and the distributions of output, capital investment, etc. normally mirror closely the employment pattern. Although some differences may be important, they can be ignored in the present context. Similarly, there are problems in the precise measurement of oil-related employment but they can also be largely ignored here.

TABLE 3.1 *Regional differences within Scotland, end 1980.*

| Region | Oil employment (no.) | Oil employment (%) | Total employment (%) | Unemployed (%) | Population (%) |
|---|---|---|---|---|---|
| Grampian | 39200 | 57.6 | 8.5 | 4.7 | 9.0 |
| Shetland | 7800 | 11.5 | 0.5 | 0.1 | 0.4 |
| Strathclyde | 6800 | 10.0 | 49.5 | 57.8 | 47.2 |
| Highlands | 5300 | 7.8 | 3.3 | 4.1 | 3.6 |
| Tayside | 2800 | 4.1 | 7.4 | 7.1 | 7.8 |
| Fife | 2300 | 3.4 | 6.2 | 5.6 | 6.6 |
| Lothians | 1800 | 2.6 | 16.3 | 12.2 | 14.5 |
| Western Isles | 1300 | 1.9 | 0.2 | 0.6 | 0.6 |
| Orkney | 500 | 0.7 | 0.3 | 0.2 | 0.4 |
| Others | 300 | 0.4 | 7.8 | 7.6 | 10.0 |
| | 68100 | (100) | (100) | (100) | (100) |

The December, 1980 distribution of oil-related employment is given in Table 3.1, together with the percentage distributions of total employment, the unemployed and the population. Over 55 per cent of oil employment is in the Grampian region, almost all in the Aberdeen area (although much of this is actually located offshore); this contrasts sharply with the Grampian region's 8.5 per cent of total employment, 4.7 per cent of the Scottish unemployed and 9.0 per cent of the Scottish population. The other regions with higher-than-proportionate shares of oil employment are the Shetland Islands, with a total population of about 28,000 at present, of whom 7800 are employed in oil-related work (mainly temporary construction work at the Sullum Voe oil terminal), the Highlands (7.8 per cent of oil employment and 3.3 per cent of total employment), the Western Isles (1.9 per cent and 0.2 per cent) and Orkney (0.7 per cent and 0.3 per cent). Coincidentally, these five regions and islands areas comprise the North of Scotland, as shown by the figures.

It is worth commenting briefly on the figures for the Strathclyde and Tayside regions. As Table 3.1 shows, the worst of Scotland's economic problems are concentrated in Strathclyde which includes Glasgow, where 57.8 per cent of the Scottish unemployed live (the region's unemployment rate is currently 15.1 per cent). The 6800 oil jobs are very small when compared with the unemployed total of 105,000. Also, Tayside has a similarly small share of oil-related employment, despite its geographical proximity to some of the oil fields, particularly those discovered in the early 1970s at the beginning of the northward move in activity. Table 3.1 shows clearly the marked geographic concentration of oil-related activity in Scotland and the figures give more detail of the types of activity involved.

In any analysis it is essential to consider the separate phases of activity. As mentioned, earlier, there are three main phases—exploration, development and production—and each has distinct locational requirements which affect the regional distribution of activity.

It is impossible in a short chapter to discuss all these locational factors so an example is given from each of the three phases: supply bases, production platform yards and landfall terminals. All these three activities account for significant proportions of activity and employment in their respective phases. Each has important physical manifestations and each to a greater or lesser degree attracts other activities. All aspects of offshore activity in the North Sea require support bases for the supply of materials and services. An exploration rig or a production platform, whilst drilling, requires 2000–3000 tonnes of pipe, drilling mud, food, water and so on, each month, as well as maintenance and other services. There is an overriding need for quick and regular access, to avoid costly delays and to redress the lack of storage space at sea. It is not surprising that support bases have been established in eastern and northern Scotland, near the main offshore areas, either by adapting existing harbours or by constructing new facilities. At the present time, there are 17 bases in operation, of which eight are in Aberdeen, two each in Peterhead and Lerwick, and one in each of Dundee, Montrose, Sandwick (Shetland), Leith and Invergordon. Leith handles mainly coated pipe for offshore laying and indeed there are other variations of scale and function among the support bases.

With platform fabrication, nearness to the offshore fields is not a decisive factor, though it has weight if other locational factors permit. The main considerations affecting the location of platform yards are the demanding physical requirements, particularly for level land alongside moderately deep water. In the case of steel platforms, which are built and floated out on their sides, the required water depth is up to 10 m: since sites offering this are available on the east coast nearness to the offshores fields has in fact steered the steel platform units to eastern Scotland and (in one case) north-east England.

The three in operation in Scotland are at Nigg and Ardersier on the Cromarty and Moray Firths, and at Methil, Fife. For concrete platforms, much deeper, sheltered water is necessary, especially in the second and third stages of construction when the platform is progressively sunk in the vertical position as the superstructure is added. There are at present four concrete platform sites, all of them in western Scotland where the necessary depths of sheltered water are to be found. These are at Ardyne Point, Loch Kishorn, Portavadie and Hunterston, although the Ardyne site is now closed and Portavadie has never received an order, partly as a result of the swing away from concrete structures. Recently both Kishorn and Hunterston have become involved in steel work. These sites are shown in Figure 3.2.

The third of the more specialised facilities required by the offshore industry is the landfall terminal. The existing production alternatives for offshore oilfields are the use of offshore tanker loading facilities or transport by pipeline. Where a pipeline is used, the preferred landfall will generally be the nearest possible suitable site to the field in order to minimise costly underwater pipelines. Thus oil from the Forties field is now flowing to the landfall terminal at Cruden Bay in the Grampian region; that from Piper and Claymore (later joined by the Tartan production) is being landed at Flotta in Orkney. Beatrice oil is being piped to Nigg near Invergordon. For the fields in the East Shetland basin two separate pipeline systems have now been completed, each delivering to the terminal recently completed at Sullom Voe, in Shetland. The oil from Forties is transported onward from Cruden Bay, by a land pipeline, to BP's Grangemouth refinery and to a loading terminal at Hound Point on the Forth. In the case of the two island terminals and that at Nigg, all onward movement is by tanker, so that tanker loading and storage facilities are essential elements, with the related needs for suitably deep water for tanker access.

The offshore loading of gas is at present not feasible in the North Sea, so all the gas for commercial consumption is being piped to the mainland (as

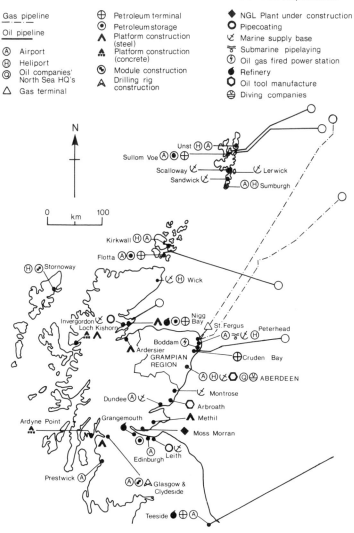

| | | | | | | | |
|---|---|---|---|---|---|---|---|
| Gas pipeline | ⊕ | Petroleum terminal | | ◆ | NGL Plant under construction | | |
| Oil pipeline | ⊙ | Petroleum storage | | O | Pipecoating | | |
| Ⓐ Airport | ∧ | Platform construction (steel) | | Ⓒ | Marine supply base | | |
| Ⓗ Heliport | ⏶ | Platform construction (concrete) | | ⩫ | Submarine pipelaying | | |
| ◎ Oil companies' North Sea HQ's | Ⓢ | Module construction | | ∅ | Oil gas fired power station | | |
| △ Gas terminal | Ⓐ | Drilling rig construction | | ✦ | Refinery | | |
| | | | | O | Oil tool manufacture | | |
| | | | | ⊜ | Diving companies | | |

FIG 3.2 *Onshore Oil-related Developments and Facilities*

distinct from Orkney or Shetland, where there are only tiny domestic markets). Figure 3.2 shows the two pipeline system from the Anglo-Norwegian Frigg field to the St. Fergus terminal, just north of Aberdeen, and there is also a gas pipeline from the Brent field (which has substantial reserves of both oil and gas) to St. Fergus. For some time there have been detailed discussions about a proposed new gas gathering line, linking a number of small fields, but towards the end of 1981 the scheme was proven to be unviable in the form proposed. The eventual outcome will probably be a series of small linking lines to the two main pipeline systems. At St. Fergus the gas is stripped of any liquids, stabilised, pressurised and transferred to British Gas for injection into the national gas grid. The liquids can be used as feedstocks for petrochemical production and one such plant is under construction at Moss Morran in Fife, with the possibility of an adjacent ethylene cracker. At the oil terminals some remaining gas liquids are separated but at the present time the volumes appear insufficient to justify major processing plants in Orkney and Shetland.

Physical and geographical factors do not provide a complete explanation of the pattern of oil-related activity now to be observed. They do not, for example, offer a satisfactory account of the emergence of Aberdeen as the dominant centre of offshore servicing and administration; as will be seen later in examining the city's offshore role, this has been due in no small measure to the cumulative and self-reinforcing advantages of a concentration of activities, which the economist calls 'external economies of scale'.

**Government Policy and Planning Controls**

An influence that calls for especial note is that exerted by government policy and the operation of physical planning. Central government has not had a comprehensive 'strategy' for North Sea oil but a number of its policies have had geographical implications or dimensions and have further influenced specific locational decisions. As has been made clear, the overriding objective of official policy has been to encourage a fast rate of development, to get a substantial volume of oil and gas flowing as soon as possible, in order to relieve the balance of payments of the burden of imported energy and generate substantial government revenue. Thus the Offshore Petroleum Development (Scotland) Act, 1975, gave the government powers of compulsory purchase of land for oil-related developments, as well as power to provide supporting financial assistance. These powers have been used to support the construction of the Hunterston and Portavadie platform yards, as well as to control operations (the final stage, completion operations for concrete platform jackets) in Loch Fyne and the Sound of Raasay.

Apart from legislation, and the laying down of planning guidelines—for example, in a series of discussion papers—official influence on the location of major oil-related activities has been exercised through decisions of the Secretary of State for Scotland on specific planning applications, taken after the reference to him of the proposals (under Part III of the Town and Country Planning (Scotland) Act 1972) and sometimes after a public inquiry. Almost all major development proposals are dealt with under this procedure: the establishment, and hence location, of all the platform fabrication sites, for example, were subject to it and the latest example is the Moss Morran petrochemical complex in Fife.

Three discussion papers were issued by the Scottish Development Department in the early 1970s: *Production platform towers: construction sites* (1974), *Pipeline landfalls* (1974) and *Coastal planning guidelines* (1974). The first two identified possible sites and discussed the general issues surrounding them. The third paper set out guidelines for local authorities and identified 'preferred development zones' and 'preferred conservation zones'. These were followed by *National planning guidelines* and associated *Land use summary sheets on petrochemicals* issued by the SDD to local authorities in 1977. More recently new *National planning guidelines 1981* were issued to replace the 1977 ones.

The preface to the 1981 guidelines states that their purpose 'is an attempt to define the land based resources or potential for development which are of national significance; to suggest the safe-guarding policies to be incorporated in regional reports, structure or local plans; and where appropriate, to specify those development proposals which because they might impinge unacceptably on a resource or potential, should be notified to the Secretary of State so that he might consider whether he should take the decision. In addition, this approach has been used as a means of disengagement from local decisions. As policies for safeguarding certain national resources have been adopted by planning authorities, reference to the Secretary of State has been dropped.'

Specifically regarding petrochemical developments, the new guidelines list six sites which have been identified in structure and local plans, and for these sites and any that the Secretary of State may later add, it is stated that:

(i) the land should be reserved in the national interest for petrochemical development;

(ii) a site should be incorporated in a Local Plan if this has not already been done, to allow the environmental and safety issues to be fully considered in advance of development;

(iii) the Local Plan should be accompanied by a development control brief for the site and its environs which takes account of the range of developments in prospect, safeguards the points of access or egress for pipelines, and sets out the environmental standards that developers will be required to meet;

(iv) planning authorities should consult the Health and Safety Executive in the preparation of siting policies which take into account existing and anticipated developments in the vicinity of possible petrochemical sites as well as setting the safeguarding criteria for new development;

(v) where an authority intend to grant permission to develop on or outwith the sites which could prejudice the petrochemical development potential of any of the sites including their associated pipelines and terminals as identified in approved Structure Plans and adopted Local Plans the Secretary of State and the Regional Council should be notified.

The main implications of the guidelines and the Scottish Office/SDD policies are discussed in the next section.

Of course, development proposals are a matter in the first place for local authorities and their attitudes can decisively influence the direction in which such developments go. Although generalisations are hazardous, it is the case that virtually all local authorities have welcomed the oil and gas developments because of the new income and employment they bring, subject to being able to impose certain safeguards on environmental and social impacts. Indeed, the number of serious applications for oil-related developments which have been rejected has been very small.

In this context, however, it is worth noting that two local authorities—the old Zetland and Orkney County Councils—obtained special legislation (Zetland County Council, 1974, and Orkney County Council Act, 1975) to enable them to deal more efficiently with oil-related developments. The legislation gave harbour authority powers to the two Councils, including powers of compulsory purchase over key areas of land, and this enabled them to exercise the control of landlord over these areas in addition to their normal control as planning authorities. The two acts were in a sense forerunners of the Offshore Petroleum Development (Scotland) Act and within the islands have been major influences on locational patterns.

They have also attracted a great deal of attention from overseas and, for example, were used as a model for the legislation introduced by the provincial government of Newfoundland to control offshore oil developments there. As with many such proposals, however, actual practice in Shetland and Orkney has differed significantly from original intentions and what has happened is discussed in the relevant section below.

One other act of official policy which had a distributional purpose was the decision to locate the headquarters of the Offshore Supplies Office (OSO) in Glasgow. Once it had been decided, on a mixture of political and industrial policy grounds, to move the OSO to Scotland, a Glasgow location was selected as placing the Office at the heart of the traditional manufacturing industry of central Scotland. It has always been official policy to try to involve this industry to the maximum degree in the business of offshore supply and this policy has met with some success. Similarly the headquarters of the BNOC were located in Glasgow, although they maintain offices in both Aberdeen and London.

Although the Strathclyde share shown in Table 3.1 is small, the region has managed to attract some of the more footloose activities such as module manufacture and rig construction, although unfortunately with the downturn in development activity over the period 1977–9 a few of the facilities have closed down. Nevertheless, it is important to remember that about 60 per cent of the equipment for the North Sea fields is imported into Scotland, mainly from England, but also from the United States, West Germany and other overseas countries.

This level of imports sets substantial constraints on what the planning authorities can do, because the imposition of controls on developments in Scotland could easily lead to oil companies or their subcontractors deciding to place orders outwith Scotland. In other words, the desire to attract oil-related developments and create local employment has usually outweighed other planning considerations. When faced with an oil-related planning application, the local authority has frequently had at the back of its mind the thought that if the application were not handled quickly and positively, the company involved would find an alternative location within Scotland or find a foreign supplier of the goods or services in question. This danger or threat has varied with the locational requirements of particular developments but has certainly been important on the Scottish mainland and in those regions which did not have the attractions of Aberdeen. It is important to remember that many local authorities have joint planning and development committees or, if not, many of the councillors (local politicians) are on both committees and well aware of the political pressures on them to attract new jobs. This is not intended to imply that wrong decisions have been taken in every or many cases but there are certainly a few examples of where short-term political pressures have led to bad planning decisions. These examples are discussed in the geographical sections later in this chapter.

The dilemma or conflict between employment creation and 'good' planning is probably most evident in the Grampian Region, which includes Aberdeen. Since local government reorganisation in 1975 the Grampian Regional Council's Department of Physical Planning has built up an excellent and justified reputation for its knowledge of and handling of North Sea Oil developments. Many other authorities in Scotland, Norway, the United States and elsewhere have looked to them for advice. Unfortunately, with the downturn—or levelling out—in offshore activity, there has been growing pressure locally to find additional oil-related employment, particularly in the petrochemical sector, and these policies have been adopted by the Regional Council. Recently, the Department's oil-related employment forecasts have been increased and although they continue to take an objective approach, there is a feeling in some circles that they have become more employment targets than forecasts (see, for example, Grampian Regional Council, 1981).

In many cases these objectives of maximising production and employment could lead to conflicts at the local and regional levels. Problems have occurred inevitably but the conflicts have been surprisingly minor, the main reason for this is that virtually all the local authorities have shared the Scottish Office's objective of employment creation. Shetland is the outstanding exception and is discussed below. Virtually all the other authorities have welcomed oil-related development proposals, although it should be pointed out there have been local interest groups, particularly environmental, who have not shared the authorities' eagerness.

The 'jobs first' approach must be seen in the context of the poor state of the Scottish economy. Although regional policy has had a marked beneficial effect over the last 10 to 15 years, most of Scotland remains designated as a Development Area and much of Strathclyde in particular is a Special Development area, including the Clydebank Enterprise Zone.

In these areas regional policy assistance is available for investment. High unemployment, low incomes, net emigration and a rapidly shrinking manufacturing sector (comprised largely of declining industries such as steel, coal mining, shipbuilding and, more recently, motor vehicle manufacture) exemplify the depressed state. It cannot be surprising that North Sea oil was welcomed as an opportunity to remedy some of these problems and provide the country with a broader and more secure economic base.

Success can be judged by a few indicators. There are the 70,000 jobs listed in Table 3.1, but these represent only 3 per cent of the total employed Scottish population of 2.1 million. The ratio of Scottish unemployment to the UK average improved steadily throughout the 1970s, although there has been a recent deterioration as a consequence of the national economic recession. According to the New Earnings Survey average weekly earnings of manual males (aged 21 and over) in Scotland in 1971 were 96.6 per cent of the GB average; for non-manual males the figure was 95.1 per cent. By 1976 these had risen to 101.7 per cent and 99.0 per cent respectively and in 1980 the figures were 100.4 per cent and 98.8 per cent respectively. Similarly, net emigration from Scotland totalled 20,100 in 1970, 21,700 in 1971 and 27,600 in 1972. This last figure was 50 per cent above the level of natural increase so the country's population actually fell. Over the 5 years 1973–77 the average level of net emigration was only 9300 (in 1974 it was as low as 2000) but there has been a renewed increase since then, coinciding with the levelling out of offshore oil and gas activity.

Where there has been less success is in the attempts to redistribute oil-related activity in order to match up geographically, demand and supply. The severe problems of Strathclyde and Tayside were mentioned earlier; their shares of oil-related activity are tiny in comparison, as is evident from Table 3.1. However, the efforts of these regions to increase their involvement, and the support of the Scottish Office, have not been shared by the other areas, at least to the extent that the attempts were directed towards a spatial reallocation of activity, as distinct from the creation of new activity. Grampian Region in particular has been unhappy about the threat to activity within their region, for example in relation to petrochemical developments.

Planning within the different oil-affected areas provides a different perspective from these interregional issues. As it is impossible to cover all areas and aspects of interest, this chapter concentrates on four which illustrate certain general policies and principles—Aberdeen, St. Fergus, Easter Ross and Shetland. First, however, it may be useful to discuss in more detail the implications of the Scottish Office's innovatory legislation.

*The Offshore Petroleum Development (Scotland) Act*

The legislation came on the statute books in 1975. Prior to that there had been concern in some government circles that there were insufficient production platform sites in Scotland and that consequently important orders were being lost abroad, notably to Norway and France. A major factor had been the success of some groups in preventing or delaying planning permission being given for platform sites in rural areas, the outstanding example being Drúmbuie on the west coast. Because of the physical requirements of the sites, most of the suitable ones were to be found in the more rural parts of the country and planning applications attracted a good deal of opposition on the grounds of the likely detrimental impact (social, economic and environmental) on the local areas. Most of the major applications were 'called in' by the Scottish Office, subjected to public inquiries and a subsequent decision by the Secretary of State having received the inquiry reporter's conclusions and recommendations. This turned out to be a lengthy process and in the case of the famous Drúmbuie inquiry (Drúmbuie being a site on Loch Carron) led to a refusal of planning permission.

One purpose of the 1975 Act was to circumvent this procedure. Initially the main proponents were the Department of Energy and the Offshore Supplies Office. Their forecasts of future production platform demand eventually convinced the Scottish Office that there was a need for special legislation. At the time there was some opposition on the grounds that the Department of Energy's forecasts were exceedingly optimistic and that also the benefits of platform construction in Scotland were not clear cut (Mackay, 1974) but these arguments were largely ignored. In the event the opposition proved well-founded. Using the Act's powers of compulsory purchase of land, the Scottish Office bought and constructed two platform yards at Portavadie in Argyll and Hunterston in Ayrshire; these are shown in Figure 3.2. The estimated costs in 1976 were £16 million and £5 million respectively.

The former was leased to a potential builder, Sea Platform Contractors Ltd., along with an adjacent labour camp for 450 people, also built with government money. Sea Platform Contractors never received an order and gave up the lease on the yard eventually but unfortunately the yard had been built with their particular design in mind and the Scottish Office were unable to find another company to take over the lease. Thus the Portavadie yard has never been used and for some years now a working group, plus consultants, have been attempting to find an alternative use. A complication is that an error or oversight in the agreement with Sea Platform Constructors means that they continue, at least nominally, the owners of the labour camp and they have been reluctant to give that up, seeing it as an opportunity to recoup some of their own expenditure. To date the cost to the Government has been about £40 million (in 1981 prices).

Hunterston has had a similarly embarrassing history, although in 1980 the lessee of the yard, Ayrshire Marine Fabricators, obtained an order—ironically for part of a steel platform (the yard had been built for concrete platforms needing the deeper water of the west coast). Two other yards, one steel and one concrete, have gone out of business through lack of orders and activity and employment in the others have fluctuated substantially. Also, the established builders have claimed that Ayrshire Marine have had an unfair advantage over them by having access to a subsidised yard.

Other provisions to the 1975 Act have been used to control platform construction activity offshore—specifically in two designated areas in the Sound of Raasay and Loch Fyne. Concrete platforms are built vertically and the final stage of operations requires deep water offshore. This means inevitable interference with fishing and other marine activities and the Act has reduced these problems to a minimum.

Certainly the unique nature of concrete platform construction necessitated special planning measures. However, with hindsight, the onshore provisions of the Act have proved both unnecessary and costly. They have raised questions in Scotland about the advisability and ability of central government 'interfering' or intervening in the oil industry, and have cast unnecessary doubts on the suitability of the existing planning system. Regarding the latter, it is probably fair to conclude that the established system would have resulted in a better outcome than that generated by the 1975 Act, in terms of the supply and demand of sites, but prior to its introduction there was a great deal of confusing speculation about platform sites and no apparent means of controlling their number. The oil companies' own forecasts of platform demand were also optimistic.

Regarding the former criticism, the evidence tends to support the view that the Scottish Office did not have the in-house abilities to understand adequately and control the platform sector of the industry. Indeed, given the complex nature of the oil industry and its vast size, it would have been most surprising if they had had such expertise. Therefore the real mistake was probably to rely on the advice of other government bodies—the Offshore Supplies Office and the Department of Energy—who were in reality in a similar position and also were biased parties in the sense of wanting to see a large number of platform sites in Scotland.

One unfortunate consequence of the criticisms of the 1975 Act and the waste of money at Portavadie has been a marked reluctance on the part of the Scottish Office to take innovatory measures in other aspects of the North Sea oil industry. Since 1978 the Scottish Office has taken a largely passive stance, reacting to proposed developments rather than promoting or encouraging. This is in contrast to the active period of the early 1970s, exemplified by the planning guidelines and discussion papers referred to above. Of course, the change in attitude is also partly attributable to the steady move from the development phase to production, which reduces the uncertainties involved.

**Local Issues**

With the exception of the 1975 Act and various public inquiries North Sea oil has been dealt with at the local level by the planning authorities. In that regard it is the same as any other industry, although it has peculiar features. From the local planning perspective three key aspects have been speed, scale and uncertainty.

The oil industry is one in which time is very important. The sums of money involved are such that closing down a rig or platform, for example, for any period would be extremely expensive. Developments occur very quickly, labour forces are built up rapidly over short periods (and on occasions dispersed with the same speed) and a great emphasis is placed on good communications. Speed is a distinctive feature of the industry and has placed unusual obligations on the local authorities and local communities, including pressure to provide housing, schools, roads and other infrastructure over the same timescale as the oil developments themselves. Not surprisingly, there have been problems in providing such infrastructure in line with the rate of growth in employment.

Scale is the second distinct feature. Largely by an accident of geography, the onshore developments have occurred in the more sparsely populated parts of the country. This is particularly true of the production yards and the landfall terminals. For example, prior to North Sea oil the population of the Shetland islands was about 19,000; the peak labour force on the construction of the Sullum Voe terminal there was about 7,000, so planning and other problems were unavoidable given the sheer scale of the impact. As a general rule, the impact of any development is a function of its size and the size of the local area; the smaller the area, the greater the relative impact—and the obverse.

Thirdly, uncertainty has been one of the industry's dominant characteristics in the north of Scotland. Again this is inevitable: commercial discoveries of oil and gas cannot be guaranteed and energy prices have changed dramatically during the last decade. Initially the uncertainty centred on the possible nature and scale of activities proposed but later the emphasis moved to the potential locations for certain developments, not least when there was a number of competing sites.

The planners in many of the areas had little experience of manufacturing industry of any type. Most economic activities were traditionally on a small scale and in the primary and service sectors. Looking back to the early days of North Sea oil, the planners jocularly maintain that their main concerns were planning applications for shop signs, holiday homes and dormer windows. Oil terminals and ethylene crackers are very different!

Solutions to the difficulties created have come in two main ways, through the use of specialist consultants and through the acquisition of the relevant knowledge and experience. The former has been particularly important in the areas of hazard and risk analysis and potential pollution dangers. The latter has inevitably been a slow process but was helped by the new system of regional reports and structure plans which encouraged a flow of information from one planning authority to another. In that respect, as mentioned earlier, Grampian regional Council's Department of Physical Planning has been particularly prominent and helpful. With hindsight, the Scottish Office could probably have played a more active role in the dissemination of information, although they have funded a number of external research studies, particularly regarding the economic impacts of the North Sea developments, which have been widely used by the local authorities.

*Aberdeen*

In terms of these factors, Aberdeen has undoubtedly been the best placed to respond to the various pressures. Although not a large city by UK or European standards, the area's population is over 250,000 and the city has had a fair manufacturing base (food processing, shipbuilding, textiles and paper), with a number of large firms.

The 40,000 jobs listed in Table 3.1 represent nearly 60 per cent of oil-related employment in Scotland and this proportion has increased steadily throughout the decade: it was 32 per cent in 1970 and 43 per cent in 1976 and will possibly reach 75 per cent by the mid-1980s, when the rundown in the development phase (particularly terminal and production platform construction) is well underway.

It is not necessary to discuss in detail the reasons for the emergence of the existing locational pattern. Proximity to the fields has been a major factor, particularly the fields discovered in the period 1969–72 when the main companies were choosing their bases. Transport facilities have been very important: obviously a good harbour but also a good airport, the absence of which has been a major deterrent to the growth of Dundee. Size has been another factor, explaining the attractiveness of Aberdeen and Dundee, for example, compared with Montrose and the Northern Isles.

Aberdeen's dominance needs some further explanation, however. A crucial reason has been the existence or creation of agglomeration economies. Agglomeration is the logical pattern for units of an output-orientated industry whose markets are concentrated at one or a few locations. For some firms, such concentration or clustering is attractive, despite the fact that they may be competing with each other. The common feature of such complexes is that each individual firm finds the location beneficial because of the presence of the others. Under these circumstances, the demand is not so much for one particular product but for a wide range of goods and services, and the greater the range provided at the particular location, the greater the demand that location will attract. Aberdeen fits well into this classification, as does Houston in the US and Calgary and Edmonton in Canada.

Both the operating companies and the supply/servicing companies have clustered in Aberdeen. Once Amoco, BP and Shell chose Aberdeen as their exploration headquarters, other firms followed and moved there to take advantage of the external economies being created. Improvements in infrastructure, particularly at the harbour and the airport, widened the nature of the external benefits.

This pattern was reinforced by the uncertainty of the North Sea developments. By its very nature the North Sea market is volatile in that a large proportion of the demand for equipment depends on successful commercial discoveries which cannot be guaranteed. Rigs, boats and barges are mobile and hence can and do move about in the North Sea and to other offshore areas. For individual suppliers, therefore, the market, although large, is very uncertain. In such a situation it is understandable that firms, recognising the unpredictability of costs and prices, and even the difficulties in measuring external economies, have not gone to great lengths to find the most profitable location for their operations, but instead have opted for a location that seems viable in the long run and have relied on efficiency in other respects to demonstrate their competitiveness. Uncertainty explains to a large extent the industry's reluctance to locate facilities in the Northern Isles, Caithness and mainland ports such as Peterhead and Montrose. Recent expansions by Norscot and Ocean Inchcape in Lerwick are a good indication of changing attitudes as uncertainty is reduced, because a sufficient number of fields have now been established in the East Shetland Basin to make investment there an acceptable risk since the potential market is now much clearer.

Another important factor has been the initiatives of the local authorities, the Aberdeen Harbour Board and the airport authorities (Mackay and Moir, 1980b). Here it is only necessary to point out that, on the whole, the local authorities in the Aberdeen area have been willing and able to provide the necessary infrastructure and support to attract oil-related companies and to keep them there. This has been particularly important in relation to industrial estates and offices, the ease and speed in obtaining planning permission for such developments and the improvement of transport facilities at the harbour and the airport. The development arm of the local authority, the North East of Scotland Development Authority (NESDA), has been very active in promoting Aberdeen both in the UK and in the United States. In all these aspects, timing and the speed of provision have been very important.

This point, and especially the significance of transport facilities, may appear to be obvious but it has required a great deal of effort, investment and faith in Aberdeen. If Dundee is compared with Aberdeen, for example, it is clear that the absence of these factors has been the major reason why Dundee has 'missed out' on the oil industry to any major extent.

Turning specifically to Aberdeen's role, it is largely concerned with administration and servicing and the level of manufacturing and development work is relatively low. There is certainly none of the heavy manufacturing such as production platform and module construction, although virtually all of the inspection, maintenance and repair work is done from or through Aberdeen.

In most respects Aberdeen has succeeded in absorbing the North Sea developments without severe dislocation, either economic or physical. Serious conflicts of interest have been few, even in the harbour area where originally there were fears for the needs of the fishing industry. The worst problem has been presented by housing. The build-up of employment began at a time when housing building was at a low ebb and of all the local sectors subjected to new demands it was one of the slowest to respond. The result was a serious shortage, with steeply rising prices in the private sector. In the course of an earlier study (Mackay *et al.* 1978) a sample of 600 houses in Aberdeen showed an average price rise of 170 per cent over the period 1970-74, compared with 110 per cent in Great Britain and 90 per cent in Scotland, and it is believed that this differential growth rate continued at least until 1978.

In Scotland, including Aberdeen, a large proportion of the housing stock is provided by the public sector. The demands created by the North Sea oil developments for a rapid expansion of council housebuilding coincided to some extent with increasing constraints on public expenditure throughout the UK, which made the financing of such housebuilding more difficult. Also, it would be misleading to believe that no housing problems existed in the area pre-oil. The price rises and associated shortages are not as great as those in other oil-affected areas, such as Edmonton, Calgary and St. John's in Canada. In Aberdeen the worst current problems are at the bottom end of the market and it is still very difficult for new families, for example, to obtain council housing or private-rented accommodation.

The housing problem—and similar difficulties with schools and community facilities—has had social and economic effects. Regarding economic effects, the main fear has been that the housing shortage would place limits on the immigration of labour and hence intensify the pressure on the local labour supply. The fact that during the decade the growth of population in the city region was markedly lower than that in employment is an indication that this situation has arisen, although it is important to remember that the Aberdeen employment figures include people working offshore who do not necessarily live in the Aberdeen area.

There has in fact been intense competition in particular sectors of the labour market, for example in the construction, metal-working and engineering trades. In other cases, some public sector services for example, normal processes of recruitment from elsewhere in the country have been inhibited because of the unwillingness of potential applicants to face the problems of moving into the area. However, it has to be said that the worst fears on this score have not been realised. The difficulties of some sectors and some firms notwithstanding, the local economy has adjusted itself remarkably well: some local firms have met the challenge by substantial improvements in productivity and involvement in the oil industry, and the city economy as a whole is certainly more efficient, particularly in its use of labour, than it was when the offshore industry descended upon it.

Nevertheless, the level of non-oil manufacturing activity has fallen in recent years, for reasons such as declining overseas markets, the EEC common fisheries policy, etc. Most local industries are feeling the effect of the industrial recession in the UK and the fishing industry is in a particularly bad state. It is unfortunate therefore that the government has removed development area status from Aberdeen, in the light of the low unemployment rate (7.4 per cent) in February, 1981 (compared with a Scottish average of 12.7 per cent) because this will further add to the problems of non-oil industries at a time when they need all the help they can (Begg and McDowall, 1981).

Although the region has an active and successful development body, the North East of Scotland Development Authority (NESDA), there is little a local area can do to counteract regional policy at the national level. If the industrial complex arguments outlined above are accepted, oil-related activity will continue to concentrate on Aberdeen, which means that the effects of the regional policy changes will be borne by the non-oil sector and over time that will mean a marked change in local industrial structure.

## St. Fergus

St. Fergus, about 50 kilometres north of Aberdeen is the location of the landfall terminal for the Frigg gas field. Since its completion it has been expanded to take Brent gas and is currently being expanded further to handle supplies from a number of smaller gas fields. The total site is about 250 hectares in a predominantly agricultural area, and distant from any large population centres. Permanent operational employment is about 300.

Three significant planning issues have arisen. The first concerned the actual location of the terminal. Total Oil originally submitted an application for a site to the north, close to the Loch of Strathbeg which is an important breeding ground for birds. A small but vociferous and well-organised group objected to the site. The outcome was that the developers, in cooperation with both the objectors and the local planning authorities, looked for an alternative and St. Fergus was the eventual choice. This happened before the planning authorities took a decision on the original application and is an excellent example of how cooperation at an early stage of the planning process led to an outcome which seems to have worked well in practice and to have been acceptable to most local people.

The second issue of pipeline routes has been more problematic. The main function of the St. Fergus terminal is to treat gas for onward transmission into British Gas' national pipeline grid. The latter involves a pipeline system taking the dry gas (methane) south to the main markets in central Scotland and England. The current level of gas production is such that four trunk pipelines exist and it may be that a fifth will be needed. In addition there will be a Natural Gas Liquids (NGL) pipeline to Shell-Esso's plant at Moss Morran, plus a number of smaller local lines. Safety considerations require the lines to be well away from houses and other 'at risk' buildings and also the lines have to be well apart from each other. It has proved difficult to find an acceptable route for the NGL pipeline and the Grampian Regional Council are becoming concerned about the network of pipes crossing the region and in particular the safety implications. There is also the issue of security, given the crucial role played by St. Fergus in the UK gas industry.

Thirdly, there is the issue of petrochemical developments. Some of the gas landed at St. Fergus is wet, i.e. it contains liquids which have to be removed before the dry gas is handed over to British Gas. These liquids—principally ethane, butane and propane—are important feedstocks for the petrochemical industry and have raised the opportunity of building up such an industry in Scotland. The original expectation was that any such plants would be located in the St. Fergus area in order to minimise the distances between the gas terminal and the processing plants.

A great deal of land speculation took place in the St. Fergus and Peterhead areas. Large amounts of land were zoned for industrial development and the local authorities even went to the stage of building new houses, schools and other infrastructure for the proposed developments. Nothing has happened. There has been considerable planning blight, primarily of agricultural land, and a surplus of council housing and school places, with the local authority facing substantial debt and interest payments (Moore, 1982). The surpluses are now being used for general development needs.

Again, the major problems have been the authorities' well-intended desire to attract industrial development and their lack of understanding of the industry, in particular the elements of uncertainty. The developments have not happened for a complex mixture of reasons. Three economic ones are the UK's membership of the EEC (which affected a Norwegian proposal), the high value of sterling (which has made petrochemical exports relatively unattractive) and the international recession (which has reduced the demand for petrochemical products and created overcapacity on the supply side). The main local problem is the lack of a suitable harbour for the export of natural gas liquids and other petrochemical products.

This last fact, or judgement, was the outcome of special studies which relied heavily on the hazard advice of the Health and Safety Executive and expert consultants. It has been difficult for local councillors, and the local population in general, to understand these reports and assessments because of their highly-technical nature. Also, it is difficult to comprehend the relevances of a judgement that an explosion, for example, is likely to occur once in 180 years and is therefore an acceptable/unacceptable risk.

The gap between the expert and the layman in relation to hazard analysis has been highlighted in the case of the one major new petrochemical development which is under construction in Scotland—the Moss Morran NGL plant in Fife. Some local residents were worried about the potential risks. A public inquiry, and subsequent investigations, led to the Secretary of State accepting that the risks were small enough for planning permission to be granted but it is clear that the local opponents have had great difficulty in understanding and accepting the technical advice presented (Rodgers, 1979).

*Easter Ross*

This is the area surrounding the Cromarty Firth in the Highlands, which is one of the best natural harbours in Scotland. The availability of flat land adjacent to the water and a reasonably large labour pool have long made it one of the obvious sites in the north for large scale industrial development. The authorities concerned—the old Ross and Cromarty County Council, its successors Ross and Cromarty District Council and the Highland Regional Council, the Highlands and Islands Development Board and the Cromarty Firth Port Authority— have been very active in promoting the areas, with a large measure of success.

Recent industrial history dates back to the establishment in the late 1960s of British Aluminium's smelter (reduction plant) at Invergordon on the north shore of the Cromarty Firth (which unfortunately closed at the end of 1981). In the present context the main oil-related developments which have located there are a steel platform yard at Nigg Bay, a pipecoating plant at Invergordon, the landfall storage terminal for the Beatrice oil field, also at Nigg, and the supply base for Beatrice. Other proposals have included an oil refinery and, more recently, the petrochemical plants mentioned above.

A series of public inquiries in the 1960s established the eagerness of the public bodies and the majority of the population for large scale industrial development. Large areas of land were then zoned for industry and housing, and the local authorities set about providing the necessary supporting infrastructure. At this time it is difficult to make a fair judgement of the effectiveness of the planning system. The existence of actual oil-related developments demonstrates success in that regard. However, it is not certain that the efforts to secure petrochemical developments will succeed. Unfortunately, the public plans for Easter Ross and the wider Moray Firth area in general attracted a few speculators and 'shady' developments. The authorities found it difficult to distinguish between serious and speculative projects, and in some cases between those which were likely to bring long-term benefits to the area and those which would not. Thus the attractiveness of the development concept has been reduced in the public eye by a few unsatisfactory developments and land speculation, particularly regarding the oil refinery and petrochemical proposals.

On the positive side, the actual achievements have demonstrated a praiseworthy degree of cooperation on the part of the public bodies. The Highlands are blighted by a proliferation of public agencies and Easter Ross is no exception, but in this area they have built on each other's special expertise and responsibilities rather than duplicating and competing. Their experience deserves examination by other areas faced with the speed, scale and uncertainty of offshore oil developments.

An outstanding example of this cooperation is the Moray Firth Working Party, set up in the late 1960s to provide a coordinating role for the planning and provision of housing and related infrastructure. It included representatives of the local authorities, the Scottish Office, the HIDB, the industrial developers and local construction firms. A good forecasting system was introduced and the relatively informal atmosphere encouraged the exchange of views and the emergence of a coordinated approach to infrastructure planning. More recently, the original group's successor, the Cromarty Firth Joint Working Party, was involved in considerable research and planning regarding possible petrochemical developments in the area.

Mention was made earlier of the problems of forecasting the onshore implications of the North Sea developments. A notable feature of the two working parties has been their willingness to consider the views of different bodies and individuals, including the author's pessimistic forecasts, and to try to devise a planning system which could take account of the inherent uncertainties. This has been in marked contrast, for example, with the central government attitude to the platform sites. The cooperation that occurred in Easter Ross is a good model for similar developments elsewhere.

*Shetland*

The factor of scale has been most important in the case of Shetland. In addition to the Sullum Voe terminal, Shetland has a number of supply bases and has experienced a substantial expansion of its main airport. In an island group with a permanent population of under 25,000 at the peak level there were around 7000 temporary construction workers and when the Sullum Voe terminal is fully operational permanent oil-related employment will be between 1500 and 2000 on present indications.

It has been very difficult for such a small and remote area to plan these developments satisfactorily. To their credit, Shetlanders, and their island neighbours in Orkney to the south, did not adopt an all-welcoming approach to the oil industry and many people raised serious questions about the benefits the industry would bring and what effects it would have on traditional industries such as fishing and fish processing, knitwear and crofting, and the social life on the islands. In the event many of their fears have proved justified.

In the face of great pressure both from the oil companies and central government, Shetland accepted that an oil terminal and related facilities would have to be located there but tried to ensur that the developments would come on Shetland terms rather than those of the industry. The main instrument of that approach has been the the Zetland County Council Act of 1974, mentioned earlier. The County Council commissioned consultants to identify a site for a multi-user terminal rather than a series of separate terminals for the different fields in the East Shetland basin and insisted that the companies built their facilities at the remote Sullum Voe location (see Livesey and Henderson, 1973). The 1974 Act gave the Council jurisdiction as a harbour authority, compulsory purchase powers for about 5000 hectares of land around Sullum Voe and other powers to take equity in any incoming company. Developers require a licence from the Council before any works can be constructed in the area. The powers have really only been used in relation to the siting and operation of the terminal and equity stakes in three companies.

Another key aspect was the formal agreement made in July, 1974 between the Council and the oil industry. This is known as the disturbance agreement by which the oil companies made a commitment to pay substantial sums of money to Shetland as compensation for the disturbance which oil-related development had brought and would bring. These sums are separate from and in addition to the profits the Council will earn from Sullum Voe. The disturbance payments are based on a complicated formula which takes into account the number of pipelines, the quantity of oil passing through the terminal, the rate of inflation and guaranteed minimum payments. The formula is weighted towards higher payments in the early years. At the time of the signing of the agreement it was stated that the minimum payments with two pipelines would total £25.25 million by 1999. Given that this was based on 1974 prices the current minimum presumably exceeds £50 million, or at least £2 million per year on average. The disturbance payments are now paid into a charitable trust which has created some problems regarding how the money can be spent within Shetland.

A ports and harbour agreement was signed in July, 1978, which sets out the obligations of both the Council and the oil industry. Those of the Council include the financing and construction of the four tanker loading jetties, the maintenance of the harbour and its facilities and the provision of a boat mooring service. The oil industry is obliged to reimburse the Council for the provision and appropriation of the jetties. The reimbursement consists of the Council receiving each year the costs of providing the jetties plus (a) 2 per cent profit on the actual capital cost and (b) one pence per long ton of crude oil and liquid petroleum gases exported over the jetties. The payments are protected against inflation by indexation provisions and are also likely to exceed £50 million by the year 2000. In Orkney there are similar but less complicated arrangements for the Flotta terminal there.

It is important to realise that these policies are unique in the UK. They have given Shetland (and Orkney) much greater powers to control oil-related developments than those available to any other area. Nevertheless it is important to distinguish between having such powers and how they are exercised in practice. Over the last few years Shetland has found it extremely difficult to protect its indigenous industries, discovering that the availability of capital is not a prerequisite of economic health (Mackay and Moir, 1982). With the rundown of construction activity at Sullum Voe, the increasing threat of unemployment among locals as well as temporary immigrants is forcing the Council to shift its attitude radically, even to the point of investigating downstream oil opportunities in order to create new employment.

Nevertheless Shetland, and Orkney to a lesser extent, have shown a novel approach to the planning of oil developments. Although their success has to be qualified, the fact that Newfoundland and Norway have copied some of their policies in their own legislation indicates the attractiveness of such an approach to areas where the advent of oil may not bring obvious and immediate benefits. Initially there was considerable conflict between the local authority and the oil companies, as is currently the case in Newfoundland with the provincial government. In Shetland now there is a healthier cooperation, borne from mutual respect, and a willingness to try to plan the developments in ways which are beneficial to all parties.

## Conclusions

The planning of the oil developments has occurred at three key levels—the UK, Scotland and local. The interests of the bodies concerned are not identical and inevitably there have been conflicts of interest. In the main the UK interest has been for rapid exploration and development and a high level of oil and gas production, primarily to reduce the burden of oil imports on the balance of payments. The Scottish interest has been for a rapid build-up of oil-related employment. Although a slower rate of development would have given Scottish industry a greater opportunity to become involved in North Sea work, and reduce the volume of imports of oil equipment and services, on the whole the Scottish and UK interests have been compatible.

In the 'national interest' the local areas have been left to cope with the detrimental effects of these policies. At the UK and Scottish levels the balance of benefits and costs have been heavily in favour of the former—for example, the savings in the balance of payments, increased government revenue through royalties and oil taxes, higher oil company profits and 70,000 or so new jobs in Scotland. At the local level, however, it is possible to argue that the costs have exceeded the benefits—or, at the very least, that there have been substantial costs. These include labour losses by local industries, increased competition for resources, shortages of housing, shortages of public services and facilities, and strains on local authority finances. On the other hand, there have been important local benefits such as greater employment, higher incomes and the reversal of population decline.

Largely by an accident of geography the onshore facilities needed for North Sea oil have been located in the North of Scotland and in the Northern Isles (Orkney and Shetland), which are the more rural and sparsely populated parts of the country. Any large scale industrial development would generate particular problems in the areas because of the limited experience of manufacturing industry, relatively poor infrastructures and small populations. In addition the oil industry has brought peculiar problems relating to speed, scale and uncertainty, all of which have made it more difficult for the planning authorities to cope.

The chapter has reviewed briefly the experience in the four main areas affected—Aberdeen, Peterhead/St. Fergus, Easter Ross and the Shetland Isles—which, although not comprehensive, offer a wide and typical range of the issues raised and the responses to them. Generally the planning of the North Sea oil developments has taken place within the established framework applying to the whole of Scotland.

Most of the major oil-related developments in the North of Scotland have involved public inquiries. This has meant lengthy delays, which have been criticised by the companies involved and their supporters (including many public bodies), but has resulted in an extensive public debate. In all major instances, except one, the outcome has been that the Secretary of State for Scotland has granted planning permission for the developments to proceed. The exception was the application for a production platform yard at Drúmbuie, on Loch Carron on the West Coast, when the inquiry reporter strongly recommended refusal because of fears about the detrimental social impact. The Secretary of State agreed but shortly after gave permission for a similar yard on the north shore of the same loch.

On the whole the system appears to have worked reasonably well and the present outcome, in terms of the scale, type and location of oil developments, appears acceptable to most parties. Thus those occasions when the system has been circumvented merit special attention and this chapter has discussed the two main legislative innovations—the Offshore Petroleum Development (Scotland) Act of 1975 and the Zetland County Council Act of 1974 (the latter paralleled by similar legislation in Orkney).

In the case of the 1975 Act the conclusion is that it was unnecessary and wasted a great deal of public money. Its history demonstrates a crucial factor, namely the civil servants' lack of experience and understanding of the oil industry. This problem also occurred at the local level, not least in the rural areas unused to large scale manufacturing industry. Most of the planning mistakes which have occurred are attributable to this lack of understanding. This does not imply that the planners should be blamed because there is no overriding reason why they should be expected to have this expertise, particularly at short notice. There has been a continuing obligation on the companies in oil industry to provide the planners (and the local populations generally) with the necessary information to enable them to make sensible decisions. In quite a few cases that information has not been provided, with the results that the authorities have been struggling to produce reasonable forecasts of land and housing requirements, labour demand and so on. The use of outside consultants has helped considerably but the lack of information is a recurring problem which requires a solution.

Finally the chapter has pointed to a few examples where successful planning has resulted from a flexible and cooperative attitude on the part of the bodies involved. In Easter Ross the daunting task of infrastructural planning was eased by the formation of the Moray Firth Working Party. In the Peterhead area a suitable site was found for the St. Fergus gas terminal after the companies' first choice proved unacceptable to some people. In Shetland a multi-user oil terminal replaced the original possibility of a number of separate ones. These are just a few examples but they demonstrate how planning can be acceptable at the local level, given a flexible system and cooperation.

It is essential to recognise that the needs and objectives of the various bodies involved (central government, local government and private industry) almost inevitably differ. Thus a crucial role for the planners has been to find solutions which minimise the differences. The Scottish experience has been quite successful but obviously not entirely so. Given the limitations at the local level, the main deficiency has probably been the lack of a policy framework in Scotland within which the local planners could operate. The Scottish Development Department's contributions, such as the national planning guidelines, have been helpful but in some cases were too late to influence decisions.

Other countries should be able to benefit from the UK experience. Not least is the simple provision of information on what has happened, since many of the offshore developments in the North Sea have been at the forefront of technology. In future many other offshore provinces will use equipment and methods developed in the UK, particularly for deep water and harsh environments. Obvious examples are the East Coast of the United States and Canada, as well as Australia, China and South America.

Lessons can be learnt from the mistakes which have been made. Key decisions and policies, which might not be apparent at first sight, can be identified in advance of the production and development phases. Examples are the importance of taxation policies, skilled labour requirements and the control of production platform construction. Finally, the policies of Orkney and Shetland show what local communities can do, even when faced with the largest multinational companies.

# References

Grampian Regional Council (1981) *Oil Related Prospects,* July, 1981, Grampian Regional Council, Aberdeen.

Lind, T. and Mackay, G. A. (1980) *Norwegian Oil Policies,* Christopher Hurst.

Livesey and Henderson (1973) *Sullum Voe and Swarbacks Minn Area Master Development Plan and Report,* Zetland County Council.

Mackay, G. A. (1974) *Revised Estimates of the Demand for Production Platforms, 1974–1980,* University of Aberdeen.

Mackay, G. A. and Moir, A. C. (1980a) *North Sea Oil and the Orkney and Shetland Economies,* Report to the Social Science Research Council.

Mackay, G. A. (1980b) *North Sea Oil and the Aberdeen Economy,* Report to the Social Science Research Council.

Mackay, G. A. *et al.* (1978) *The Economic Impact of North Sea Oil on Scotland,* HMSO.

McDowall, S. and Begg, H. M. (1981) *Industrial Performance and Prospects in Areas affected by Oil Development,* Scottish Economic Development Department, Edinburgh.

Moore, R. (1982) *The Social Impact of Oil,* Routledge and Kegan Paul.

Rodgers, J. J. (1979) Inauthentic politics and the public inquiry system, *Scottish Journal of Sociology,* **3,** 103–127.

Scottish Development Department (1981) *Revised National Planning Guidelines,* Scottish Development Department, Edinburgh.

Scottish Development Department (1977) *National Planning Guidelines,* Scottish Development Department, Edinburgh.

Scottish Development Department (1974a) *Coastal Planning Guidelines,* Scottish Development Department, Edinburgh.

Scottish Development Department (1974b) *Pipeline Landfalls,* Scottish Development Department, Edinburgh.

Scottish Development Department (1974c) *Production Platform Towers: Construction Sites,* Scottish Development Department, Edinburgh.

Scottish Office (1979) *Oil Related Employment—Further Aspects,* Scottish Economic Bulletin, No. 18, Edinburgh.

# CHAPTER 4

# Planning for Gas in the United Kingdom

PETER ROBERTS and TIM SHAW

## Introduction

Gas is a major source of energy in the UK, used for the satisfaction of both domestic and industrial demand. It also provides a range of feedstocks for the petrochemicals industry. In many senses gas is a unique form of energy; it does not necessitate the use of a large number of vast sites for either production or distribution, it is relatively easy to transport, it produces few harmful waste products, and it is highly adaptable for a large number of purposes. These advantages, together with the existence of large indigenous natural gas reserves, have made gas a premium fuel, and a major feature of national energy policy. Despite the transition from localised town gas to national natural gas system which has occurred in recent decades, they have also meant that the development of the gas industry has created fewer major physical planning problems than other sources of energy.

## Gas in the UK

### Organisation

The UK gas industry was developed in the nineteenth century, and nationalised in 1949. The 1972 Gas Act established the British Gas Corporation (BGC), with monopoly powers of gas transmission and piped supply on the UK mainland and required to 'maintain an efficient, coordinated and economical supply of gas for Great Britain, and to satisfy so far as it is economical to do so all reasonable demands for gas in Great Britain'. A two-tier organisation for the supply of gas was created, with consumer supply the responsibility of twelve regional organisations, and strategic policy, the supply of gas to regions, exploration, research and development the concern of central headquarters. Major developments related to the extraction, production and distribution of natural gas are therefore the responsibility of a number of headquarter divisions. This includes an

101

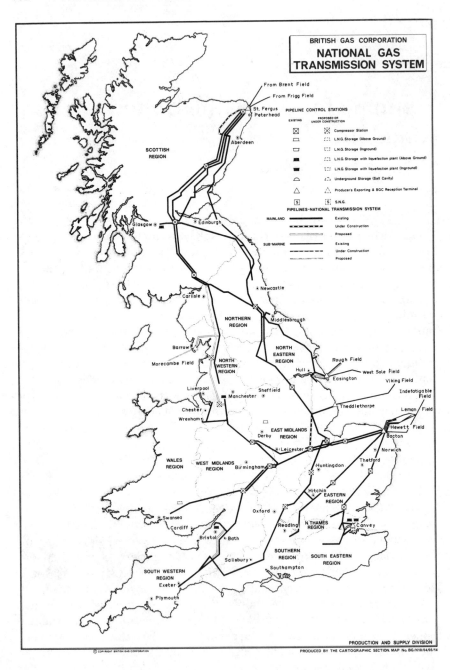

FIG 4.1 *The National Gas Transmission System in the United Kingdom*

Environmental Planning Department, established in 1967 by a BGC predecessor. In 1981 this had a staff of thirty, who were responsible for site selection and assessment and the obtaining of planning and other consents. All divisions have, since the early 1960s, worked closely with planning authorities in the development of natural gas reserves.

During 1981 the Conservative government began to dismantle the BGC monopoly position with legislation to end its sole purchasing rights to UK onshore and offshore gas production. The Secretary of State has also acquired powers to direct BGC to increase the capacity of its pipelines and to act as a 'common carrier' by conveying gas between private producers and consumers. Although the question is politically controversial and further changes may be made, the result will be a more diversified supply system. This will involve greater contact between the planning system and private sector gas producers.

The Department of Energy is the central 'sponsor' for the activities of BGC. This department plays a major role in the formulation of government policy and practice for the licensing of gas exploration, in relation to BGC purchase of gas from producing companies, and for the overall rate of depletion of gas reserves. BGC is also involved with the Department of the Environment (in Scotland, the Scottish Development Department) over onshore developments. Central government exercises a more general control over the activities of the BGC through the imposition of financial targets and the specification of external financing limits. Inevitably, given the high level of expenditure upon prime materials (i.e. the gas bought from producers operating gas fields)—£1,916 million in 1982/83—and upon materials, services and contractors' charges—£572 million in 1982/83—the activities of BGC are of great interest to a range of other central government departments, especially the Department of Industry.

During the 1980s BGC has also been a major source of funds to the Exchequer. A levy, imposed under the Gas Levy Act of March, 1981, was set at a penny a therm for 1980/81, at threepence a therm for 1981/82 and fivepence a therm for 1982/83. This applied to gas purchased from fields which are not subject to petroleum revenue tax. The levy for 1980/81 raised £129 million, and this had increased to £524 million by 1982/83. The payment of this levy to the Exchequer is intended to reduce any windfall profits accruing to BGC. As well as having a direct impact on consumer costs the levy will also reduce the funds available to BGC for future investment.

### Resources

The nineteenth century gas industry was based on 'town gas', produced by the carbonisation of coal. During the twentieth century coal was largely replaced by oil, which since the 1960s has itself been replaced (except in

TABLE 4.1 *Estimated Gas Reserves on the UK Continental Shelf as at 31 December, 1980*

|  | Proven | Probable | Possible | Possible Total |
|---|---|---|---|---|
| Southern Basin | 368 | 110 | 79 | 557 |
| Frigg and Brent | 164 | — | 3 | 167 |
| Morecambe Bay | 133 | 204 | 334 | 671 |
| Other Associated Gas | 74 | 48 | 42 | 164 |
| Total in billion cubic metres | 739 | 362 | 458 | 1559 |

Proven—those reserves which on the available evidence are virtually certain to be technically and economically producible.

Probable—those reserves which are estimated to have better than a 50% chance of being technically and economically producible.

Possible—those reserves which at present are estimated to have a significant but less than 50% chance of being technically and economically producible.

Source: Department of Energy, *Development of the Oil and Gas Resources of the United Kingdom,* London: HMSO, 1981.

Northern Ireland) by natural gas from UK and Norwegian fields, supplemented by a small amount of liquefied imports to the BGC Canvey Island terminal. These fields themselves have limited life, and BGC is retaining a number of sites in anticipation of a return to coal gasification as a major source of supply. To make the transition from synthetic to natural gas, a national grid system for gas transmission has also been built.

Most UK gas reserves are located in offshore areas (see Table 4.1). The initial period of offshore development was concentrated in the Southern Basin of the North Sea, south of 56° north. The 1959 discovery and subsequent exploitation of natural gas at Slochteren in the Netherlands, stimulated other West European governments to consider whether gas existed in areas within their territorial jurisdiction. A formal legal framework for offshore licensing, exploration and production was established, based on the international guidelines agreed in the 1958 United Nations Convention on the Continental Shelf. In the United Kingdom this was reflected in the 1964 Continental Shelf Act, which established a broad policy for the development of offshore gas resources. A drilling programme resulted in a number of major discoveries which were rapidly developed. The West Sole, Leman Bank and Hewett fields were in production by 1969, followed in 1971 by the Indefatigable field and in 1972 by the Viking field (Chapman, 1976). Three reception terminals were constructed on the east coast at Bacton, Easington and Theddlethorpe, to handle the gas which was landed by pipeline. Although a number of oil companies were involved in the production of gas, they were legally obliged to sell their production to the nationalised gas industry.

In the late 1960s the attentions of operating companies and the gas industry shifted to the Northern North Sea. In 1972 the massive Frigg gas field was discovered and developed with associated terminal facilities at St. Fergus. Gas from the Frigg field was first landed in 1977, followed by supplies from the nearby Piper field in 1978. Developments in the northern basin to the east of the Shetlands have concentrated mainly on oil production and large quantities of associated gas have been flared off on production platforms. The construction of a gas pipeline from St. Fergus to the Brent and Cormorant fields has provided some capacity for gas transportation and a large gas gathering pipeline system to serve most fields in the central and northern sectors of the North Sea has been proposed. Feasibility studies in the 1970s favoured the 'maximum use of existing pipelines' (Department of Energy, 1978) but a 1980 study by BGC and Mobil North Sea indicated that 'a new pipeline would be highly economic' especially given the condensate-rich nature of the gas which would be landed (Department of Energy, 1980). In June, 1980 the Government approved in principle construction of a 644 km gathering system running from the Magnus field in the north to the Fulmar field in the south, to be in operation in 1985, but financing difficulties caused the scheme's collapse in September, 1981. Several smaller pipelines to serve clusters of oilfields are likely to be built, although much of the gas which would have been tapped by the original plan will be wasted. The British National Oil Corporation is constructing a pipeline to gather gas from the Magnus, Murchinson and Thistle fields. This would join the existing pipeline running from the Brent field to the St. Fergus terminal.

During the 1970s exploration on the UK mainland and in the Irish Sea also occurred. In 1974 a commercially significant gas reserve was found in the Morecambe Bay area, with probable reserves in excess of 140 billion cubic metres of gas (200 Mtce). Production should begin by the mid-1980s, using an onshore terminal at Westfield Point, near Barrow-in-Furness. Further Irish Sea discoveries were made off Lancashire in 1982, and may further boost the importance of this gas-producing region. UK onshore gas production has been limited—mainly from the Lockton field in Yorkshire, opened in 1971 but now exhausted, and the Wytch Farm oilfield in Dorset. An increase in onshore oil and gas exploration during the early 1980s may lead to further discoveries, which can be exploited at lower cost than offshore equivalents.

*Gas and UK Energy Policy*

The energy policy of central government creates the framework for the operations of the gas industry. In recent years the aims of energy policy have been to increase natural gas production and use to exploit its economic advantages, but to limit its rate of growth to avoid a fall in the market share of other energy supplies and to extend the life of UK gas resources.

One aspect of national energy policy which has major planning implications is the rate of production from gas fields. Since the late 1960s successive governments have advocated and operated a policy of rapid depletion. The 1967 White Paper on Fuel Policy (HMSO, 1967) outlined the justification for a rapid depletion policy during the early years of exploration and extraction. It was argued (p.42) that:

> This policy (of a rapid build-up in supplies) will mean a shorter life for the gas fields than a policy of slow depletion and will involve using some of the gas in markets where the resource savings are relatively low. The Government believes that these disadvantages are outweighed by the value of giving an incentive to the further exploration needed to improve our knowledge of the ultimate resources available and by the benefits to the economy and the balance of payments which a fast build-up of supplies will bring.

The desire of government to deplete reserves rapidly was reinforced by the price escalation and difficulties of securing future supplies which followed the 1973 Arab–Israeli war. Rapid depletion, as a main policy of central government, was given further support in the 1974 White Paper on Offshore Oil and Gas Policy. This recognised a need for government to take powers to control the level of production but commented that, 'the question of reducing the rate of depletion is unlikely to arise for some years'. The 1978 Energy Policy Consultative Document (HMSO, 1978) continued this policy and the Department of Energy assumes a continuing rapid depletion of gas reserves with a reduction in output occurring in the 1990s, despite some opposition.

The importance for planning of an understanding of depletion rates is clear. Rapid depletion implies a hasty cycle of development whereby exploitation follows closely upon exploration. A plateau of production is quickly reached, followed by a rapid decline to the point where a reserve is exhausted. The rate at which a resource is to be depleted determines in part the speed at which gas and gas-associated developments occur. This can cause planning authorities to make hasty decisions which may conflict with other long-term objectives. In addition, expensive new infrastructure often has to be provided which may not have been amortised by the time a reserve is depleted. Another issue that has to be examined in relation to rapid depletion rates is the ability of local firms to engage in gas-associated activities. This in turn will condition the level of any multiplier effects which are generated by gas developments.

An alternative approach to the future development of the gas industry might be based on a lower rate of depletion with a reduction in the short-term in the level of current expenditure on development and an increased emphasis on the conservation of energy. By pushing back the date of exhaustion a better use of indigenous reserves might be established. Strategic policies can be generated which integrate gas developments with other attempts at regional and local economic regeneration. This approach may well question the immediate need for projects such as the Morecambe Bay development. Although BGC can point to the need to balance gas supplies and central government's desire for rapid depletion, a lower level of development has certain advantages. From the planning viewpoint it would allow the fuller integration of offshore developments and associated activities with strategic planning policy. Those developments which are seen as necessary can be subjected to a fuller examination within the context of agreed policy. This approach could resolve the dilemma of planning authorities when confronted by the needs of the offshore operator; of having to make rapid decisions, influenced by arguments of national interest, which affect the local well-being, but which can also generate short-term economic gains for a community.

Another important energy policy issue related to depletion rates is that of substitute natural gas (SNG) production by coal gasification, which may have an important role to play in the future, as well as increased imports of liquefied natural gas (LNG). Such a change in the source of raw materials would result in a new shift in the geography of the gas industry towards the coalfields and ports, and—as the Canvey Island LNG terminal demonstrates—is likely to be controversial on environmental grounds. In anticipation of this trend BGC has retained a number of urban sites from the town gas era, which can sterilise a valuable resource of scarce industrial land and this has aroused some concern (HMSO, 1981). As there are indications that offshore and onshore natural gas resources are greater than previously believed greater attention is likely to be directed to the effects of BGC land retention on local planning authorities.

## Planning for Gas: Issues

### General Features

The gas industry's move from a localised town gas operation to a national system, based on grid transmission of offshore resources, has had many planning consequences. New sites have been developed to accommodate reception and processing terminals, primary distribution facilities, compressor stations, and regional and local storage and distribution centres. In addition, a number of sites are used by BGC for the onshore production of hydrocarbons, and for the importation and storage of liquified natural gas. Many of these are in hitherto rural areas. Such sites are characteristically extensive in nature but with a low level of site coverage. All installations for the reception, processing, transmission and distribution of natural gas are subject to normal planning procedures and, given the national significance of gas supplies, many applications submitted by BGC have been 'called in' by the Secretary of State for his own determination and have resulted in a local public inquiry.

These trends have highlighted a number of planning issues. Both in the early period of development during the 1960s and at present, concern has been expressed by planning authorities over the safety of gas installations. This is reflected in the attention paid by BGC to the assessment of hazard. The wider environmental impacts of gas terminals, pipeline routes, compressor stations and other plant has also merited attention. At the exploration, proving and development stages of offshore gas resources many onshore economic activities can benefit. In some areas, given the contract preference obligation placed upon public companies, a potential exists for economic regeneration or expansion. The gas industry has a number of additional infrastructure requirements, according to the type of development and the area within which it is located. There are also social consequences, though generally of a lesser magnitude than the major disruption generated by the introduction of oil-related activities in north-east Scotland.

The availability of gas as an energy source can itself influence planning policy. In one recent structure plan the lack of a readily available supply of gas was seen to be a constraint upon industrial development (West Midlands County Council, 1980). The reservation of sites (at present under BGC ownership) for the location of possible future coal gasification plant has also caused planning problems in areas suffering from a shortage of available industrial land. Furthermore, there are questions concerning the long-term future of some reception terminals, which may be used (in reverse) for the transmission of synthetic gas to exhausted offshore reservoirs for storage. A related matter is the present and future development of terminals for the reception, storage and transmission of imported liquified natural gas.

### Onshore Impact of Offshore Development

Due to the rapid nature of gas exploration and extraction, there is often little or no time to develop a strategic planning framework for the provision of onshore facilities. Although highly desirable everywhere, such a framework is essential in heavily urbanised areas which are subject to development pressures. The discovery and current exploitation of the Morecambe Bay field provides a clear example of the difficulties that face planners. It is the offshore operators who have the expertise and experience relating to the technical and financial aspects of their activities, yet local planning authorities are faced with the need to respond. In such circumstances authorities need to be aware of the requirements of offshore operators at the earliest possible stage in the development programme and should, through a cooperative approach, attempt to accommodate these needs.

A broad categorisation of the issues facing planning authorities includes:
  (i) Environmental, land use and hazard issues relating to the construction and operational phases of development;
 (ii) Infrastructure problems, especially the strain put upon existing facilities and the financing of new provision;
(iii) Economic issues related to the development, both direct and indirect;

(iv) Social disruption and local concern;

(v) Integration of onshore development with matters of local, county and regional strategic planning.

The environmental concern expressed by local authorities and residents has been expressed by Dean and Graham (1974) as the 'anywhere but here' syndrome and was an early reaction to the activities of BGC. Through collaboration with local authorities BGC has quelled much of the initial opposition to the construction of terminal sites. Such sites are extensive in the amount of land required, the Bacton terminal covering some 80 hectares, while at St. Fergus over 200 hectares was initially used. The level of site coverage is far less, in some cases as low as 20 per cent of the total site. Gas reception terminals have to be located near to the coastal pipeline landfall, so that during the construction phase there will inevitably be some disruption of natural habitat. In the case of Theddlethorpe the site was adjacent to a National Nature Reserve. Through careful and sensitive planning it is possible to avoid major disruption and to ensure a competent restoration of any areas which are affected. Pipelines, both onshore and offshore also create environmental difficulties. Given the high cost of undersea pipeline, operators always attempt to minimise the total length of pipeline run, while at the same time ensuring that essential safety criteria are met. In the offshore zone, areas subject to strong currents, tidal flows, shifting seabed and scour are avoided. It is also important to avoid areas of intense marine activity, due to the dangers of fouling from anchors and moorings. At the coast, pipeline routes should attempt to avoid any coastal defence works. One of the alternatives to the Bacton site, at Northgap, was dismissed because the pipeline would have breached the coastal defences. In addition, at the point of landfall, it is desirable from the operator's view to bring the pipeline ashore across a sandy beach backed by an area of gentle slope. Although cliffs of up to 30 metres can be crossed, if composed of soft materials, larger hard rock obstacles present major engineering problems but conditions attached to permissions which are granted by local planning authorities attempt to ensure full restoration (Project Appraisal for Development Control, 1977).

The safety of terminals and other plant and the hazard involved in the movement of liquified gas or condensates is a central concern in the appraisal of onshore gas installations and a number of hazard assessments have expressed disquiet at proposals made by BGC. These include the findings of the Health and Safety Executive on the operation of the liquified natural gas terminal at Canvey Island (Health and Safety Executive, 1978), and the concern expressed by the Secretary of State for Scotland regarding the Moss Morran complex in Fife (Scottish Office, 1979). A more general concern for the monitoring and control of hazard has been expressed (Macgill, 1981). From analysis it is apparent that many planning authorities are not aware of the hazard created by the very existence of liquified gas installations.

Furthermore, there are organisational, legal and institutional difficulties in either measuring hazard or controlling the activities of the liquified gas industry.

At the BGC St. Fergus terminal, the previous experience of Banff and Buchan District and Grampian Regional Councils is reflected in their Contingency Plan (1980) for future gas and gas-based developments. This argues that in any gas-based developments, normal planning controls and advice/regulations of the Health and Safety Executive would need to be adhered to. At Morecambe Bay, an assessment of the application for a reception terminal stated that although the proposed terminal was hazardous and although this could be a question of balancing economic arguments against public safety, the risk is of an order that has been considered acceptable elsewhere (Barrow-in-Furness, 1980).

One final matter related to the operation of gas installations is the extent to which granting of permission for such installations pre-empts further development due to the need to maintain a separation or buffer zone. Even if the operation of installations can be accepted as presenting no significant hazard beyond normal criteria, the movement of liquified gas and condensates has proved to be a cause for concern. High capacity reception terminals, especially those handling wet gas (i.e. gas rich in condensates) can generate large quantities of condensates which have to be transported by pipeline, road, rail or sea. Concern has been expressed at the dangers involved, especially if the road transport option is selected.

Accepting that the environmental standards specified by local planning authorities and other agencies can be met during the operation of gas installations, the question of the disruption caused by construction activities remains. It has already been noted that pipelaying can cause disturbance to coastal and inland habitats. The construction of terminals and storage facilities is even more disruptive. In order to minimise the problem, planning authorities have attempted to impose duration limits. Barrow-in-Furness Borough Council recommended that, if permission was granted to BGC to construct a reception terminal at Westfield Point, its development should be phased and limits set on the construction period. Other detailed conditions relating to the character and extent of construction activities were also suggested. At the other end of the construction phase, local authorities have attempted to impose conditions upon gas installations related to the constant monitoring of pollution and safety standards. Many of these conditions cannot be directly enforced by local planning authorities, the competent organisations being the Health and Safety Executive or other public bodies, including the Fire Service. In order to ensure that environmental damage is minimised, it would be desirable to have an environmental monitoring system prior to and during both the construction and operation of gas installations.

The infrastructure requirements of gas operations differ according to the site and type of installation which is proposed. Onshore pipelines can be laid without major demands, although traffic congestion may be a temporary nuisance. Other onshore facilities (reception terminals, compressor stations, storage facilities and associated developments) have a variety of requirements. Major new sites located in rural areas have created a need for improved and new infrastructure. The construction of the St. Fergus terminal necessitated major road improvements, while the majority of other terminals have required the extension of public utilities (especially mains electricity and water). Associated activities also create a demand for additional serviced industrial land.

It is during the offshore development phase that gas operations create large new infrastructure requirements. In all offshore operations a service base is an essential facility. The intensity of use varies according to the stage of offshore activity, of which there are five—exploration, appraisal, development, production and depletion. The demand for facilities is at its peak during development. The production pattern for gas follows a similar cycle, normally typified as build-up, plateau and decline (Hepple, 1973). The demand made upon a service base include supply vessel berths, (preferably available at all stages of the tide) an extensive back-up and storage area (of between 3,000 and 4,000 square metres), the availability of deep water berths (for pipelay barges and other vessels) and a range of utility and related services, such as helicopter facilities. Other inshore requirements include the provision of land for rig, platform and module construction, pipecoating and other activities, all requiring a high level of infrastructure (Roberts et al. 1979; British Gas Corporation, 1974; Barrow-in-Furness, 1980).

Natural gas and associated developments have a significant economic effect upon their host areas. As well as requiring an increased level of public expenditure on infrastructure and other facilities, the gas industry can increase the level of economic activity in an area. Direct employment in gas and gas-related activities will vary according to the stage of development. During the construction of the Barrow-in-Furness reception terminal it is estimated that employment will rise to 920, while when the terminal is in operation a maximum of 90 jobs will be available. A comparable exercise for the additional terminal at St. Fergus estimates that the peak construction employment of 1200 is expected to fall to 76 at the terminal and 200 at the substitute natural gas plant.

Offshore developments present considerable opportunities to regional, national and international suppliers. The British Government established the Offshore Supplies Office in 1973, to ensure that British industry obtains a full and fair opportunity to meet the demands of the offshore market. Local authorities both directly and through sponsorship have also become involved with directing and attracting gas and gas-related expenditure. Through the activities of planning and industrial development departments the production capacity and potential of local areas can be matched to the requirements of BGC and their suppliers. Certain local authorities have also sponsored the formation of industrial consortia as with the Contractors and Offshore Traders Association of Merseyside. Local initiatives to promote industrial growth have emphasised the need for firms to achieve approved supplier status, in order that they are eligible to tender for BGC contracts. A further emphasis has been placed on the obligation of nationalised firms to give contract preference to suppliers who are located in assisted areas such as Merseyside or Cumbria.

The total of gas-related indirect and induced employment is not easy to estimate. Lewis and McNicoll (1978) calculated that on the basis of the direct effect of oil and gas activities in Scotland 26,650 jobs were created, an additional 11,350 indirect jobs (i.e. employment in firms only partly involved in the offshore industry) were stimulated and between 9,300 and 18,500 induced jobs (i.. employment generated through an increase in consumption) were subsequently generated. This scale and concentration of indirect and induced employment is unlikely to be repeated elsewhere in Britain.

The extent to which gas-related development will result in self-sustaining growth is also difficult to estimate. To date, gas and gas-related activities have not led to the establishment of major new production facilities (for example, the construction of platform building yards), so that a downturn in gas-related activities will not have catastrophic economic side effects. A limited number of long-term jobs can be identified. However, the majority of industrial activities that have been stimulated by the needs of British gas developments will have a future role only if they can trade in the international market. The downstream effects of gas development (in petrochemical and associated operations) have a longer-term existence.

Experience from Scotland during the past decade has demonstrated that there are many social issues associated with both offshore and onshore associated activities. These have mainly related to the construction phase of development and have been most severe in areas selected for the construction of platform yards. The social consequences of an influx of migrant workers are less severe in gas-related developments. Evidence from Banff and Barrow-in-Furness indicates that the major social disruption associated with, for example, the Nigg Bay platform yard, has not occurred and is not anticipated. There is, however, a significant level of local concern over pollution, hazard and loss of visual amenity that planning authorities must take account of. Set against this is the prospect of an improved rate income base for the local authority, from the presence of gas installations and other associated activities.

It is frequently difficult for local planning authorities fully to integrate the activities of BGC and associated industrial and commercial concerns with existing planning policies. Procedures exist within BGC for the management and planning of development proposals. These follow a standard commercial pattern from project appraisal to approval and onwards through site selection to an application for planning permission. Detailed consultations, both within BGC and with a wide range of statutory and non-statutory consultees, interact with this process. In all cases BGC follow their own and other guidelines, which provide details on site selection, safety criteria and operational constraints. Although local authorities are normally consulted prior to a planning application, it is only at the point of submission that authorities become formally involved. It is normal BGC practice to submit an environmental impact analysis in support of their formal application. In the case of small or non-controversial projects this evidence has been accepted by local authorities, as in the case of the application for permission to construct a compressor station at Kirriemuir. However, this is not always the case. The terminal at St. Fergus was subject to a detailed independent hazard assessment which, taken together with other assessments, has been used by Banff and Buchan District Council in their monitoring and contingency planning exercises. The BGC analysis for the Westfield Point terminal was considered by the district planning authority to be limited in value and furthermore the document was said to be 'inadequate and . . . not an Environmental Impact Analysis in the accepted sense' (Barrow-in-Furness, 1980). The council therefore prepared their own assessment, a remarkable achievement for a small district. The importance of this confrontation is that it highlights the frequently argued need for a more comprehensive form of assessment (PADC, 1976; Roberts *et al.*, 1979; Roberts *et al.*, 1980). With the move onshore of BGC, as seen in the development of the Dorset oil and gas field, this need becomes even more pressing.

In conclusion, planning authorities in the UK have been hampered by the practice of considering offshore-related applications on their own merits. Yet as Begg and Newton (1980) comment 'local authorities have only a limited ability to influence the timing, site, scale, nature and extent of (petrochemical) developments, . . . development decisions largely rest with the production companies, and, to a lesser extent, with central government'. In such a situation local authorities are limited in their scope for action. Moreover, gas developments can pre-empt future planning and land use in areas adjacent to their sites.

Examples of alternative approaches have been provided by Scotland, where the National Planning Guidelines for Petrochemical Developments (Scottish Development Department, 1977) provide local planning authorities with the ability to respond to individual operators within the context of agreed regional policies. The value of a coherent and comprehensive approach is also demonstrated by Shetland County Council (in their 1974 Zetland County Council Act) who attempted to minimise the undesirable effects of onshore provision, and to maximise the financial returns to the local community with some success.

**Planning for Gas: Morecambe Bay**

The Morecambe Bay gas field is the most recent of the major UK reservoirs to be developed and the first significant discovery on the west coast of Great Britain. It is also the only field over which BGC has complete control for it acts as sole offshore operator in addition to its normal onshore functions—and therefore provides a useful case-study of the relationship between an energy organisation and the planning system.

Irish Sea exploration for oil and gas began in 1965 and the Morecambe reservoir was first discovered in 1974. Further drilling revealed its extent and in July, 1978 BGC announced that the field was commercially viable and would be developed as rapidly as possible. A number of sites for the onshore terminal for gas from the reservoir were considered by BGC, which chose six for serious consideration. Westfield Point, at Barrow-in-Furness, emerged as the most favourable location and in December, 1979 BGC applied to Cumbria County Council (the responsible authority) for permission to build a pipeline landfall and a gas and gas liquid reception and treatment terminal at this site. After considerable discussions beteen BGC and the planning authorities, consent in principle was given by Barrow-in-Furness Borough Council in June, 1980 and Cumbria County Council in July, 1980. Work on construction of the terminal began in April, 1981. In the same month, the planning authorities and BGC reached agreement on a monitoring and notification system for the site, while further agreements have been made to cover the construction of offshore pipelines and associated activities.

Given that this major energy resource is within the control of a state-owned industry, it might be expected to provide a model for the efficient and harmonious development of a national asset. Many of the difficulties that have been experienced elsewhere (in, for example, the development of gas in the North Sea) should have been of minor importance, while the attention of the BGC, planners and politicians could have been focused on an integrated development programme to ensure that the maximum economic benefits accrued from the exploitation of the Morecambe Field. Matters of strategic importance (such as the selection of a terminal site, the full assessment of development proposals and the contribution that gas-associated activities can make to regional economic regeneration) would have been, in an integrated programme, the subject of co-operation, consultation and joint planning agreement between BGC, central government and local authorities in North Wales, the North West and Cumbria.

However, since 1978 BGC has concerned itself with the rapid provision of facilities to bring the gas ashore. This is not surprising given the constraints placed upon it and the expressed desire for rapid development. The central planning issue in the exploitation of Morecambe Bay gas has been the selection and approval of a terminal site. Many potential sites were considered by BGC in an area extending from Anglesey to St. Bees Head in

Cumbria, using a number of criteria. These were that a level of 120 hectare site should be located near to the coast, without the intervention of major roads or railways, with good access and service provision. In addition, the site should be one kilometre from residential or industrial development, as free as possible from environmental or ecological restraints and should avoid the use of high grade agricultural land. At six sites a score was calculated which expressed the length and practicability of the offshore pipeline, the existing land use of the site, environmental considerations, safety considerations and overall costs. A final summary evaluation showed Westfield Point to be an optimum location for the terminal.

This analysis, while demonstrating a rigorous approach to the selection of a site for a specific facility, does not incorporate the broader regional economic development objectives that might have been specified for a project of this magnitude. To an extent this is the result of a certain reluctance by one of the planning authorities in north-west England to welcome the location of a gas reception terminal within its area. It is also the case that, despite the existence of the North West regional Chemical Industry Working Party (a group comprising representatives of the county authorities in north-west England, the chemical industry and the regional offices of the Departments of the Environment and of Industry) little attention was given during the process of site selection to matters of overall regional economic growth which might be induced by the utilisation of port facilities, by the use of condensate products, or by the multiplier effects of all of these activities. In addition, the broader strategic site-search study undertaken by the Working Party seems to have had little influence upon BGC. It has been argued elsewhere that local planning authorities have only a limited ability to influence oil and gas related development (Begg and Newton, 1980). This limited ability was clearly demonstrated in the selection, by BGC, of the Westfield Point site. Indeed, the only real local authority influence upon BGC was the representation made by Barrow-in-Furness Borough Council.

The present authors have argued elsewhere (Roberts and Shaw, 1980) that in a heavily urbanised and industrialised area like north-west England, it is vital that a coherent strategy is prepared and agreed before any major hydrocarbons development occurs. This strategy should provide a basis for site selection and the preparation of a development schedule. It should also include details of plant construction and operation, including the need for port facilities and other infrastructure. The rapid selection of the Westfield Point site by BGC effectively pre-empted any real discussion of the regional significance or the long-term consequences of Morecambe Bay gas.

A policy of rapid development is also likely to preclude many local companies from being able to tender for construction or plant contracts. This is because such firms have insufficient time to gain approved supplier status. To date major contracts have been awarded to a French firm, operating at Clydebank, for the provision of a jack-up drilling rig and to a number of British companies. The objective of BCG in letting contracts was stated by James McHugh (the Corporation member responsible for gas production and supply) as developing the Morecambe Bay Field 'in a way which is technically right, on schedule and within budget'. This emphasis on rapid development is aimed at getting gas ashore by 1984. It can therefore be seen that at a strategic level the selection of a terminal site can work against the best overall interests of a region, especially if a rapid development option is proposed.

At the local level, planning was initially influenced by the high reputation of BGC which 'meant to a great extent that their views were held in high regard and with complete trust by both members and officers of the Local Authority' (Klosinski, 1981). Through the process of assessing the application this high reputation was somewhat diminished. The reasons for this change in attitude related both to the process of planning assessment and to the way in which major issues were presented by BGC.

After the BGC applied for planning permission in 1979, there were many important matters which Barrow Council wished to resolve before indicating approval to the County Council. The value of the BGC supporting documents, an Environmental Impact Analysis and Visual Impact Analysis was, in the opinion of the Borough Planning Officer, limited because little detailed information was given on the nature of the plant or the process to be used. Doubts were also expressed about the content of the Environmental Impact Analysis.

Barrow therefore requested additional information from BGC in the form of a detailed questionnaire. Until mid-October 1979 (i.e. prior to the formal application) the partnership between the local authority and BGC was proceeding well. Then, for reasons which were never entirely made clear, BGC decided to suspend further discussions and to submit a formal application giving the basic necessary information and asking for a decision within 8 weeks (Klosinski, 1981). In the view of the borough council it would have been unwise to expedite the granting of planning permission until a full assessment of the proposal had been carried out. In January, 1980 a statutory request for additional information was sent to BGC. The reply was received in late February. Meanwhile, Barrow-in-Furness had commissioned consultants to examine the safety and hazard aspects of the proposed terminal.

By May, 1980 the Borough Planning Officer had prepared a detailed 'Environmental Impact Appraisal and Report' (Barrow-in-Furness, 1980). This indicated that many details of the terminal could be dealt with by conditions of consent and agreements with BGC and asked whether 'national interest (can) be achieved without unacceptable local effects on aspects such as amenity or safety'? Earlier in May the Borough's consultants believed there was a risk of some significance, a view challenged by BGC and the Health and Safety Executive, who regarded the risk as negligible

(Klosinski, 1981). At the meeting of the Barrow-in-Furness Planning Committee on May 19th two options were considered. It could refuse permission (in which case it was anticipated that BGC would gain permission following an appeal or at Inquiry) or it could grant permission subject to a list of 61 conditions. In the event, following a period of public consultation, the borough council decided on June 4th, 1980 to recommend to Cumbria County Council that it grant planning permission. The County Council approved the application on July 4th, 1980 after a series of meetings with Barrow-in-Furness Borough Council to consider the details of conditions. It is the original 61 conditions that demonstrate the depth of analysis and thought which characterised the Barrow 'Environmental Impact Appraisal'. Outline and duration limits were suggested within a phased construction programme, a daily maximum nominal intake of gas was specified, transport modes for condensate were restricted to either rail or pipeline and height limits were imposed on plant and other equipment. Other suggested conditions were related to matters of visual impact and landscaping to be applied during and after construction, throughout the operational life of the terminal and following the cessation of operations. Questions of access and car parking and the diversion of footpaths were also dealt with.

However, the majority of the suggested conditions relate to issues of hazard, safety and the monitoring and control of pollution. Until April 28th, 1981 the question of monitoring remained unresolved, when BGC agreed to a monitoring and notification system for difficulties or incidents, and to take any remedial action necessary.

On April 13th, 1981 work began on the construction of the terminal. Subsequent agreements have been reached between BGC and Barrow-in-Furness regarding the construction of the offshore pipeline and any associated activities. To date the monitoring system has worked well (Klosinki, 1981) and the exploitation programme for Morecambe Bay gas is on schedule. A more detailed system has now been established jointly between Barrow-in-Furness and a team from Aberdeen University. This will monitor the development of the terminal during both the construction and operational phases, giving emphasis to the effects of activities upon the natural environment. In addition, the effectiveness of the conditions that were attached to the granting of planning permission will be evaluated. A longer term Environmental Impact Assessment of the terminal's operation will also be prepared.

This case study demonstrates three major issues. First, it is clear that the decision to locate a gas reception terminal at Westfield Point was considered mainly on criteria specified by BGC with little regard for the more general strategic planning objectives that might have been identified. Secondly, the way in which BGC presented their application and conducted the subsequent discussions indicates their unwillingness to enter into a partnership with the local authority in order that the best possible analysis and evaluation might be undertaken. Thirdly, it is to the credit of Barrow-in-Furness Borough Council that they produced a detailed and comprehensive assessment of the direct and indirect consequences of the gas terminal. Even given a small professional staff and limited financial resources the example provided by this district authority demonstrates what can be achieved by way of an environmental impact assessment.

The speed at which the detailed assessment was prepared by Barrow-in-Furness Borough Council illustrates the potential offered by environmental impact analysis for clarifying difficult issues, while at the same time accelerating the process of planning assessment. This assessment might have been prepared even more rapidly had BGC worked fully in harmony with the District Council and not suspended discussions in October, 1979. Given that the BGC has claimed that the preparation of environmental impact analyses has saved the Corporation at least £30 million (House of Lords, 1981), it might have been expected that they would have welcomed the opportunity to have worked in partnership with the District Council and thereby further expedited the assessment of the Westfield Point application.

The lesson to be learned from the Morecambe Bay experience can best be summarised in the words of one of the officers involved in the assessment of the Westfield Point terminal; 'at least in Furness the British Gas Corporation's intentions are viewed more cautiously, even now' (Klosinki, 1981).

### Conclusions

The value of gas to the UK economy makes it important that planning policy does not hinder development. However, it is also important to ensure that planning is not simply responsive to the demands of the gas industry but considers the exploitation of gas resources within a strategic framework for land use, economic development, social adjustment and the maintenance of environmental quality.

Demand responsive provision, associated with the early period of hydrocarbons development (particularly the oil industry), tends by its very nature to be incremental. It is typified by the provision of sites and social and economic infrastructure with little regard for its pre-emptive nature or the longer term consequences of such action. To an extent it therefore abrogates the responsibility of local authorities for the long-term well-being of their population. In extreme cases proposed developments are regarded as *fait accompli*; they are in the national interest and should proceed with haste. An illustration of the effect of hydrocarbons-related development and the pressures exerted on planning authorities, can be seen in Uden's study of the Drúmbuie public inquiry (Uden, 1976). Gas and gas-related developments in the period since the mid-1960s have not completely lapsed into this situation for BGC has been aware of the environmental consequences of hydrocarbons production and processing and has adopted a responsible approach, although further improvements could be made (Roberts *et al.*, 1979). In recent years attempts have been made to introduce demand-anticipatory strategic planning. It has been argued elsewhere (Roberts and Shaw, 1980; Begg and Newton, 1980) that there is a need to consider hydrocarbons development within a broader land use, environmental, social and economic framework at local, regional and national levels.

Oil and gas operators may rightly argue the need for rapid decision-making, due to the high cost and long lead-times involved in offshore developments. However, the quick decision may not be the optimum one for the areas involved. Great Britain already has enough resource-based regions, developed with haste in previous eras, that suffer from almost intractable problems of decline. The adoption of a new resource frontier mentality, succinctly described by Spooner (1981), should not be allowed to add to the list of such regions. Arguably, it is in the long-term national interest to develop gas resources (which meet consumer demand), while at the same time minimising social costs and maximising economic benefits. Thus, for example, offshore gas resources located in reservoirs adjacent to assisted areas should be developed within the context of other policy measures applied to such areas.

The merits and failings of these approaches can be equated with the critiques advanced more generally regarding incremental as against longer term strategic planning (Alden and Morgan, 1974). Whatever approach is adopted by planning authorities, it is clear that decisions which relate to the development of hydrocarbons cannot be divorced from national issues and the policies which are pursued by central government (Begg and Newton, 1980). During the consideration of major industrial applications local authorities are required by central government to take account of national economic interests, which may well result in an authority having to balance the optimum planning solution against other factors. In order to allow the county and district planning system to extend and reinforce the range of its activities, central government would have to move towards the establishment of explicit national energy objectives which could form the basis for regional strategic planning.

A significant aspect of this would be specification of natural gas depletion rates. One of the failings in the development of the gas industry in the 1960s and 1970s has been the emphasis placed upon rapid extraction and depletion, often to the exclusion of rigorous planning at both site and regional levels. Demand responsive provision has been the order of the day, with all the potential loss of benefits that such an approach suggests. Although there is still a long way to go in achieving demand-anticipatory planning, with the integration of BGC development proposals into the strategic planning activities of central government and local authorities, some advances have been made. The Scottish National Planning Guidelines have illustrated the way in which strategic guidance can be offered to developers and local authorities (Scottish Development Department, 1977). The North West Regional Chemical Industry Working Party attempted to develop a future strategy for chemical developments (including offshore gas), giving valuable information to local authorities for the preparation of their structure and local plans. In the absence of a regional strategy, local authorities have demonstrated that they can produce a rigorous analysis of the consequences of a proposed development. The assessment of the Westfield Point application by Barrow-in-Furness District Council has already been quoted and other district and county authorities have indicated a similar capability.

The important issues that arise from these varied experiences are that there is great benefit to be gained from co-operation between the developer (in the case of gas this is normally BGC) and the planning authority; that there is a need to examine an individual application within the context of national and regional strategic policy; and that a full project assessment can be undertaken with no threat to its viability. It has been stated by BGC that environmental impact assessment can result in significant cost savings without generating major delays (House of Lords, 1981). In an era of low economic growth, where the opportunities for economic development are limited, the assessment of a project's likely contribution to the industrial growth of an area can be justified, even if this results in more lengthy consideration.

In the interim there are a number of lessons that can be put into practice. Firstly, on the matter of institutional arrangements, it is clearly in the interest of the developer to enter into an early dialogue with the relevant planning authorities, the Health and Safety Executive and the various central government departments likely to be involved. Through a better understanding of the scale and ramifications of a proposed project it is possible to clarify the major issues that will need to be resolved. Secondly, the potential costs and benefits of a project need to be identified at an early stage. There will always be problems in reconciling local and national interests, which are not unique to the development of gas resources (Roberts and Shaw, 1982). They are real issues and have often remained obscure and in certain cases have resulted in costly and lengthy public inquiries. Thirdly, having established a working relationship and identified the major issues, a detailed environmental, social and economic assessment of the consequences of a project can be undertaken. This should involve the examination of alternative sites, the potential contribution of the proposed project to the local economy and the financial, social and environmental costs that may be incurred. Finally, this assessment should be prospective—it should be set within the context of expected future trends in the energy industry, it should deal with matters of plant operation and safety and the likely problems of after-use, decommissioning and site restoration.

Although the above may appear to suggest a new, more bureaucratic approach to the assessment of gas and gas-related developments, in reality it reflects best existing practice. Much of the information required is already supplied by BGC, while local authorities have available most of the other necessary data. Mutual benefits would accrue from partnership in assessment, while both the national and local economy would be better served through an examination of the multiplier effects of a development. On questions of monitoring, partnership in assessment might reduce the number of conditions which are attached to a planning approval and would enable the operation of a plant to occur efficiently while allaying the fears of local residents.

The major changes that have been brought about in the gas industry during the past 20 years have created an extensive production and supply operation. In most cases these changes have occurred with the minimum of local disruption and with a high degree of responsibility. Future developments should be capable of making an even greater contribution to national and local economic growth through the adoption of more rigorous assessments, while at the same time minimising social and environmental costs. The challenge that confronts central government, planning authorities and the gas industry is to take any future opportunities that are offered in a manner which continues to be responsible, but which also maximises the benefit that can be obtained.

## References

Alden, J. and Morgan, R. (1974) *Regional Planning: A Comprehensive View*, Leonard Hill, Leighton Buzzard, Bedfordshire.

Banff and Buchan District Council and Grampian Regional Council (1980) *Contingency Plan for Petrochemical Industries*, Banff and Buchan District Council and Grampian Regional Council, Banff and Aberdeen.

Barrow-in-Furness Borough Council (1980) *Environmental Impact Appraisal and Report on the Outline Planning Application for a Gas Terminal at Westfield Point*, Barrow-in-Furness Borough Council, Barrow-in-Furness, Cumbria.

Begg, H. M., and Newton, K. (1980) Strategic planning for oil and gas-related development, *Town Planning Review*, **51** (No. 1).

British Gas Corporation (1974) *Onshore Requirements for Gas and Oil Reception*, British Gas Corporation, London.

Chapman, K. (1976) *North Sea Oil and Gas*, David and Charles, Newton Abbot.

Dean, F. E. and Graham, G. (1974) *To See or Not To See—Some Environmental Aspects of the Onshore Natural Gas Programme*, Institution of Gas Engineers, London.

Department of Energy (1978) *Gas Gathering Pipeline Systems in the North Sea*, Department of Energy, London.

Department of Energy (1980) *Development of the Oil and Gas Resources of the United Kingdom*, HMSO, London.

Health and Safety Executive (1978) *Canvey: An Investigation of Potential Hazards from Operations in the Canvey Island–Thurrock Area*, HMSO, London.

Hepple, P. (ed.) (1973) *Outlook for Natural Gas: A Quality Fuel*, Applied Science Publishers, Barking, Essex.

HMSO (1981) *Coal and the Environment*, Report of the Commission on Energy and the Environment, HMSO, London.

HMSO (1978) *Energy Policy: A Consultative Document*, Cmnd 7101, HMSO, London.

HMSO (1967) *Fuel Policy*, Cmnd 3438, HMSO, London.

House of Lords (1981) *Environmental Assessment of Projects*, Select Committee on the European Communities, 11th Report, Session 1980–81, HMSO, London.

Klosinki, S. (1981) *Major Industrial Application Appraisal at Barrow-in-Furness*, Paper presented to a seminar on Environmental Impact Assessment, Liverpool Polytechnic, May 27th, 1981.

Lewis, T. M. and McNicoll, I. K. (1978) *North Sea Oil and Scotland's Economic Prospects*, Croon Helm, London.

Macgill, S. M. (1981) Liquified energy gases in the UK: what price public safety?, *Environment and Planning A*, **13** (No. 3).

Project Appraisal for Development Control (PADC) Team (1976) *Assessment of Major Industrial Applications: A Manual*, Department of the Environment, London.

Project Appraisal for Development Control (PADC) Team (1977) *The Environmental Impact of Selected Linear Developments*, Department of Geography, PADC, University of Aberdeen.

Roberts, P. W. and Shaw, T. (1982) *Mineral Resources in Regional and Strategic Planning*, Gower Publishing Co., Aldershot, Hampshire.

Roberts, P. W. and Shaw, T. (1980) Onshore planning implications of the offshore development of mineral resources, *Marine Policy*, **4** (No. 2).

Roberts, P. W. *et al.* (1980) *Environmental Impact Assessment—A Practice Guide*, Coventry (Lanchester) Polytechnic, Coventry.

Roberts, P. W. *et al.* (1979) *The Effects of the Development of Irish Sea Gas on Liverpool*, Liverpool Polytechnic, Liverpool.

Scottish Development Department (1977) *National Planning Guidelines*, Scottish Development Department, Edinburgh.

Scottish Office (1979) *Go Ahead for Fife Petrochemical Complex*, Scottish Office, Edinburgh.

Spooner, D. (1981) *Mining and Regional Development*, Oxford University Press, Oxford.

Uden, J. (1976) *Public Inquiries and the Planning Decision-Making Process*, University of Glasgow, Glasgow.

West Midlands County Council (1980) *County Structure Plan*, West Midlands County Council, Birmingham.

CHAPTER 5

# Local Impacts of Power Station Developments

JOHN GLASSON*

In an urban and industrialised country such as Britain there is always a shortage of sites that are technically suitable for new projects, let alone acceptable on environmental grounds. Modern power stations are one of the most technically demanding but also one of the most ubiquitous forms of industrial development. The Central Electricity Generating Board (CEGB) is responsible for planning almost all the new generation capacity in England and Wales. Over 40 new power stations have been built in the last 20 years; the stations have become much larger and more varied in fuel source and further developments are planned.

The CEGB has the statutory duty to develop and maintain an economic and reliable system of bulk electricity supply. In addition, since its establishment in 1958, the CEGB has had a statutory duty to take into account the effects of its activities on natural amenity (Hawkins, 1974). Potential loss of amenity has been a prime cause of objections to power station proposals and the most frequent occasion for a public inquiry (see Gregory, 1971; Matthews and Usher, 1977). it is therefore understandable that the CEGB should be prepared to consult fully on amenity grounds. However power stations are also major employers, often in rural areas, and may have significant local social and economic effects. Little work has yet been done on the local economic and social issues associated with power station development. However, increasing concern about the effects of large scale development, controversy over nuclear power and the rapid exhaustion of uncontentious sites is focusing attention on a wider range of local effects.

* Some material in this chapter is drawn from a CEGB sponsored research project on power station impacts carried out at Oxford Polytechnic. The contributions of other members of the research team—Martin Elson, Ralph Leavey, Paul Nichols and Susan Squires—are gratefully acknowledged.

123

## The Electricity Supply System in England and Wales

### *Nature of the System*

The large-scale supply of electricity involves the *generation* of electricity in power stations, the *transmission* of the electricity from the stations to points of bulk supply, and the *distribution* of electricity from the bulk supply points to individual consumers. In England and Wales the CEGB is responsible for the generation and transmission system, a system which is the largest integrated power system operating under unified control in the western world (Figure 5.1). There are over 100 major power stations which are linked in the national grid system of 7700 route kilometres of high voltage

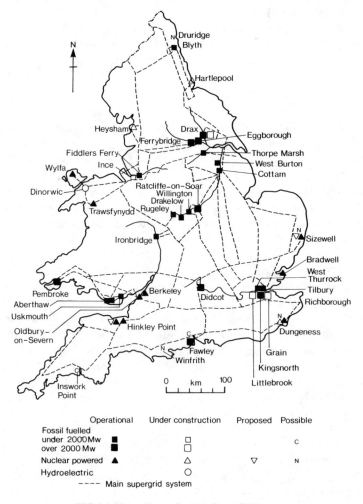

FIG 5.1 *Major Power Stations Since 1961*

transmission lines. Transmission is to 800 substations, including 202 super-grid substations, which are the primary points for distribution.

The CEGB's five regions are responsible for the generation and transmission, operation and maintenance in their particular geographical areas of England and Wales. Control of the entire CEGB power system is supervised by the National Control Centre in London. Electricity distribution is the responsibility of 12 area electricity boards which purchase supplies in bulk from the CEGB to meet the needs of their 20 million customers. The CEGB, the area boards, and the Electricity Council—the central consultative body—together form the nationalised electricity supply industry of England and Wales. The CEGB employs about 60,000 (1980), the area boards employ another 100,000 and employment in many other industries (e.g. coal mining, nuclear fuel, and generating equipment manufacture) is heavily dependent upon the electricity supply industry. Northern Ireland and northern and southern Scotland are served by their own electricity boards which also organise their own generating systems.

### Power Station Characteristics

Power stations vary greatly in size and type. In March, 1973, CEGB plant for England and Wales included 174 stations; by March, 1980, only 7 years later, there were 132 stations. This reduction in stations has been achieved, without any loss in output, through the replacement of smaller stations by larger stations. The biggest leaps in size have taken place over the last 20 years, mainly through the introduction of larger generating sets. During the 1950s most of the plant built was based on multiples of generating sets of an output of 60 MW(e); the next step was to 100 or 120 MW(e) sets. During the 1960s, 200 and 300 MW(e) sets were introduced, and there was a further increase to the 660 MW(e) units commissioned at Drax in 1974 (the gross declared capability of Drax is 1980 MW(e), which will be doubled to almost 4000 MW(e) when Drax (phase 2) is finished in the mid-1980s). The main reasons given for the constant increase in size are the enhanced operating and thermal efficiencies available and, it appears, a relative diminution in the size of variable costs, such as operating staffs.

Power stations also differ according to fuel type. Table 5.1 indicates the subdivision in 1980. Most generating plant built post-war has been coal-fired, followed by oil-fired and nuclear-fuelled. At the present time, plant of all types is still under construction. The largest oil-fired plant to be ordered was Littlebrook 'D' in 1974 and it seems unlikely for economic and policy reasons that more large oil-fired plant will be ordered. There have been few recent orders for coalfired plant, the last one being for Drax (phase 2), where site work began in 1978. There had been no orders for nuclear plant since those for Hartlepool and Heysham I (1968 and 1970 respectively) until the order for Heysham II in 1980. Two main types of nuclear plant have been built by

TABLE 5.1 *Power Station Types—England and Wales (1980)*

| Type | Number of Stations | Declared Gross Capability | |
|---|---|---|---|
| | | Megawatts (MW) | % of Total |
| Steam: Coal-fired | 76 | 38315 | 63 |
| Oil-fired | 18 | 9247 | 15 |
| Coal and oil[1] | 3 | 945 | |
| Coal/oil[2] | 1 | 2000 | 8 |
| Coal/gas[3] | 2 | 1690 | |
| Total steam | 100 | 52197 | 86 |
| Nuclear: Magnox | 8 | 3986 | 8 |
| AGR | 1 | 1090 | 8 |
| Diesel | 1 | 8 | 5 |
| Gas turbine | 14 | 2969 | |
| Hydro | 7 | 113 | 1 |
| Pumped storage | 1 | 360 | |
| Total | 132 | 60724 | 100 |

[1] Stations where some boilers burn coal, others burn oil.
[2] Dual fired boilers capable of burning coal or oil.
[3] Boilers capable of burning coal or gas, or coal and gas.

Source: CEGB Statistical Yearbook (1979–80), 1980.

the CEGB. The earlier nuclear programmes were based on the gas-cooled 'Magnox' reactor design, and the later one on the Advanced Gas-cooled Reactor (AGR). In January 1983 a public inquiry began into a proposed Pressurised Water Reactor (PWR) at the existing Magnox site of Sizewell, Suffolk.

The expected 'lives' of power stations vary from about 25 years (nuclear) to 30 years (fossil-fuelled), but this can be lengthened through the development of additional capacity or, often, by technical improvements. To the operational life must also be added lengthy construction and decommissioning periods. The stage of development of a station, particularly the construction-operational distinction, is significant in terms of local impacts and is discussed below.

### Transmission and Distribution

The scale of transmission has also increasd greatly over the years. In 1900 there were 400 small electricity undertakings in Britain, providing supplies at a variety of voltages and frequencies. Each supplied its own locality and carried spare capacity to cover changes in local demand, breakdowns and maintenance. The spare capacity in the system was of the order of 70 per cent. Few of the undertakings were interconnected with neighbouring undertakings; thus there was generation and distribution, but no transmission or sharing of share plant capacity.

Today the electricity generated at modern power stations is fed to the national grid system, where it is transmitted at high operating voltages (from 132 to 400 kV). The development of a transmission network allows the bulk transfer of electricity to load centres which leads to greater flexibility in the siting of power stations and industry. It also allows selective generation to be adopted, whereby supply can be rapidly adjusted to changes in the availability and price of fuel, and has allowed a reduction in the planning margin of the system to a current figure of 28 per cent.

Transmission lines (with 50 m towers from 400 kV lines) can have a major effect on the visual amenity of the country. To minimise the impact, the CEGB seeks to follow a number of basic rules drawn up by the late Lord Holford, Professor of Town Planning, University College, London, in 1959 (Howard, 1980). For example:

> 'Avoid altogether, if possible, the major areas of highest amenity value, by so planning the general route of the line in the first place, even if the total mileage is somewhat increased in consequence', and 'Approach urban areas through industrial zones, where they exist, and where pleasant residential and recreational land intervenes between the approach line and the substation, go carefully into the comparative cost of undergrounding, for lines other than those of the highest voltage.'

The CEGB's 202 Supergrid substations provide bulk supplies of electricity at 132 kV and lower voltages for primary distribution to towns and industrial areas. The 400 kV and 275 kV substations are large in area. Outdoor air-insulated substations need large clearances around electrical conductors to avoid flashovers and to provide safe working clearances between sections for maintenance, and much of the equipment is large. Advantage is taken of natural contours in the ground and existing woodlands in siting substations, but their siting can generate considerable concern. This was true of a recent development at Sellindge, Kent, of a converter station as part of a scheme to augment the CEGB's cross-Channel DC cable link with Electricité de France.

The lines from the major substations are fed into intermediate substations, where transformers reduce the voltage to 11 kV. Secondary distribution lines radiating from these substations carry the power into the locality to be supplied and terminate as distribution substations, where the voltage is reduced to its final level of 240 V for use in shops, schools, homes and so on. Many of the local lines are underground.

*Electricity Supply and Demand*

In developing its system, the CEGB faces two major planning problems. The first is the overall size of the system, the second the mix of generating fuels used.

The forecasting of electricity demand is a difficult and complex exercise. It has become particularly difficult in the uncertain economic climate of the last decade (England, 1980). Forecasts must consider many factors, including trends in domestic and commercial demand and the impact of government policies on the price of other fuels and energy conservation. On the basis of demand forecasts, the CEGB estimates its necessary supply capability. Allowance must be made for the decommissioning of old plant, the nature of transfers with other systems (for example, Scotland), the need to meet the maximum demand experienced during the winter and the margin for breakdowns and other contingencies (currently 28 per cent). Because of the long lead time in developing new stations, forecasts must be made many years in advance. CEGB demand estimates have been too high in recent years; this may be explained by several factors including the impact of cheap natural gas, the economic recession and possibly too much optimism on the part of the forecasters. Indeed some commentators have suggested that, with appropriate government policies (e.g. giving more financial support to home insulation schemes), the need for new electricity supply capability could be reduced considerably (Energy Research Group, 1976).

The present fuel mix of CEGB power stations is given in Table 5.1. Coal-burning stations are likely to remain dominant into the foreseeable future, but, to be prepared for eventualities, such as greater constraints on chimney emissions, the CEGB is collaborating with the NCB to explore the possibility of developing a coal gasification combined cycle plant. The 'oil shocks' of the 1970s make the development of further oil-fuelled plant unlikely.

The current central plank of CEGB and the UK Government policy for future electricity supply capacity is the further development of nuclear power. The medium term, future nuclear plant programme is likely to be a combination of AGR and PWR designs. Nuclear stations are the most demanding with regard to site requirements and any future developments are likely to be a major topic of planning debate in the 1980s.

Other potential energy sources include pumped storage and hydro-electricity. Pumped-storage schemes use off-peak surplus generating capacity from base-load nuclear and fossil-fuelled stations to raise water from a lower to an upper lake, where it is stored in the form of potential energy for later conventional hydro-electric generation. The system uses roughly one-third more power than it produces, but it does facilitate the efficient non-stop running of base-load stations and provides a ready 'on-tap' supply of power for topping up at peak demands. Installations are operational at Foyers, Loch Ness and Cruachan, Loch Awe in Scotland and at Ffestiniog, Snowdonia, in Wales. The major Dinorwic plant, also in Snowdonia (1320 MW(e) ), will be operational in the mid-1980s. Further schemes are being considered. Conventional hydro-electric schemes, on the other hand, make only a limited contribution to electricity supply in Britain and there would appear to be little additional potential.

There has been a growing interest in the exploitation of other renewable energy sources for electricity generation. Those of most interest are wind, wave, tidal and geothermal energy. The CEGB has chosen several sites for a large aerogenerator and there may be input into the grid by 1985. On a different scale a tidal barrage across the Severn Estuary could generate 6 to 10 per cent of the electricity currently consumed in England and Wales, according to the first report of the Severn Barrage Committee (Department of Energy, 1981). However, the Committee concluded that economic viability depends on the size of the nuclear component in the generating system. The barrage could only save expenditure on fossil-fuels if nuclear stations, with their cheaper fuel, did not fill the gap.

### Power Stations and Planning

A power station goes through four distinct stages of development: planning (5–6 years), construction (6–10 years), operation (^0–25 years, depending on fuel type) and decommissioning (varied). These stages have different requirements regarding labour, resources and material inputs and are the responsibility of different branches of the CEGB. Planning is the responsibility of the Board's Headquarters' Corporate Strategy Department (System Strategy Branch), whilst the Generation Development and Construction Division organises the design and construction of new plant and is responsible until the station is commissioned (i.e. begins to supply the national grid), at which point the station becomes the responsibility of one of the CEGB's five regions.

### Planning and Site Selection

Detailed planning procedures have been developed by the CEGB over the years. The Board must make an application for statutory consent for a particular power station development from the Department of Energy (S.2, Electricity Lighting Act, 1909); the consent may also carry deemed planning permission (S.40, Town and Country Planning Act, 1971). The System Strategy Branch of CEGB Headquarters is continually searching for sites in rough anticipation of demands, so that once a demand estimate is agreed, the Board has a choice of sites which may be developed as part of the programme to meet that demand. The relationship between demand estimates and individual power station developments is therefore not direct. The pool of sites held at any one time allows for flexibility in response to increased demand, allowing for a choice to be made between different locations and different station types. The choice needs to be sufficient to allow the Board to take account of certain external limitations on choice, for example altered priorities regarding fuel type.

The CEGB search for sites to put into the pool involves a number of phases and criteria.

1. *Area of search*—This involves the study of a region extending over several thousand square kilometres to identify potential sites and constraints. An important criterion here is the nature of regional demands relative to the national system. Factors such as the extent of regional self-sufficiency are taken into account. Trends which are likely to affect demand in future, such as prospects for future industrial growth are also considered. Because of the scarcity of suitable sites for power station development, it is likely that once a broad area has been selected, the Board will select a number of possible sites within that area and explore their suitability concurrently.

2. *Detailed and exacting technical investigations of alternative sites*— Direct cooled stations may require up to 400 m litres per hour of water, which can only be met in coastal locations. The alternative is the use of tower cooling, but such cooling still needs access to a major river. Fossil-fuelled stations also need good access to fuel. A 2000 MW(e) coal-fired station will burn up to 5 million tonnes per year, (equivalent to twenty 1000 tonnes trains per day). Nuclear sites are less constrained by fuel availability and delivery, but they must be sufficiently remote from large population centres to comply with nuclear licensing requirements. Coal-fired stations have the additional problem of the disposal of pulverised fuel ash (up to 1 million tonnes per year for a large station). All stations need a sizeable area of reasonably level land with subsoil conditions suitable for foundation construction. In England and Wales many of the sites which best meet the locational requirements have already been used for one purpose or another. In addition, over 40 per cent of the land area and 60 per cent of the coastline are protected in some way. New stations must also be planned in relation to the existing pattern of electricity supply and demand. A supply and demand balance within a region minimises the economic, technical and environmental problems of additional and long transmissions routes.

3. *Site selection/conflict resolutions*—This involves the selection of specific sites for which consent may be applied. Special local factors may be taken into account—for example the local economy, the amenity value of the area, and the political implications of developing a power station in that location—which may be local or national. It is likely that the CEGB will be required to justify its proposal to make it acceptable locally. This is not to imply that CEGB planners deliberately go for easy options. If, in a region, only one site meets the strict technical criteria then it is probable that CEGB would press ahead with its application for consent despite local opposition.

The lead time required for a power station development, and the policy of the Board to hold a number of sites in a pool in advance of demand, means that site surveys will be taking place many years ahead of development.

The locations of major new power stations vary in their degrees of rurality and remoteness. The topographical requirements for pumped storage schemes are usually found in rural locations such as Ffestiniog and Dinorwic in North Wales. The bulk of the recent coal-fired stations are less remote and rural and many have been located in the main mining regions of Nottinghamshire and Yorkshire. Oil-fired stations are located on estuaries and adjacent to oil refining centres. The most rural sites are largely nuclear stations. Early nuclear stations were located in North Wales and the south and east of England where fossil fuel supplies were in limited supply and expensive to transport. They were also sited away from population centres to meet the stringent government siting policy. With the exception of Trawsfyndd, they were also on open coasts or estuaries to satisfy water requirements. A relaxation of siting policy in 1968 led to the development of more urban nuclear developments at Heysham and Hartlepools. However, the Health and Safety Executive, who license nuclear installations, require stations with reactor types new to this country to be on remote sites, at least for the first few stations.

Future locations vary according to fuel type adopted. Additional coal-fired capacity is under construction at Drax. Several other sites have been investigated and proved suitable for fossil-fuelled stations and are owned by the Board. The development of new coalfields, for example at Selby, Vale of Belvoir, Warwickshire or Oxfordshire, is an important locational determinant. The Board also owns a number of sites which should meet nuclear siting criteria, but suitable isolated sites are few in number. The problems of nuclear site selection in rural areas with high amenity value are illustrated by the CEGB search for a site in South West England. As noted earlier, investigations for a nuclear site at Druridge Bay in Northumberland have also led to much local debate. Several recent nuclear stations have been developed as 'B' stations on existing sites; the proposed PWR development at Sizewell would be the second station on the site. This is not always possible however, for transmission reasons. At Sizewell, another station would require little transmission work because the existing lines out of the station can be uprated to 400 kV operation to take a further 2600 MW(e). At Dungeness, transmission capacity has been fully used and further generation plant would necessitate 120 kilometres of 400 kV line across areas of high amenity value to supply London.

If there is considered a need for peak-load as well as base-load capacity, there could be more pumped storage capacity. A possible CEGB development adjacent to the Longendale Valley reservoir complex, at Tintwistle in the Peak District National Park, has raised major environmental objections. In Scotland, the North of Scotland Hydro-Electricity Board's proposal for a station at Craignroyston on Loch Lomond has raised similar objections.

During the 1970s encouraging signs emerged of local authority influence of strategic planning by the CEGB. Thus in 1979 the Standing Conference on London and the South East Regional Planning (SCLSERP) and the

CEGB produced a report on the prospects of demand for electricity in the South East of England and on the power stations that might be needed over the next 10 years (SCLSERP, 1979). The aim was to provide a regional context for the local consideration of specific power station and transmission line proposals which are likely to be forthcoming from the Board in the 1980s. The Standing Conference is an inter-authority body of local authorities, its roles are consultative and advisory. Its reports are not binding on its constituent local authorities but they may be influential. The report on South East power stations contains much very useful information for local planning authorities. The South East is a major centre of electricity demand and more supply capacity may be needed in the region. Five broad areas of search are identified which meet technical and environmental criteria, and nine suitable sites are noted: Bradwell, Essex; Fawley, Hampshire; Didcot, Oxfordshire; Cliffe Marsh, Dungeness and Kingsnorth, Kent; Elstow, Bedfordshire; and Beddington and Barking in London. However, a programme of primarily nuclear stations could cause some re-examination of these potential locations by the South East local planning authorities.

### Consultation procedures

As one study noted, 'any proposed major development has an underlying configuration of interests, strategies and perspectives' (Gregory, 1971). But whatever the development, be it a power station or aluminium shelter, it is possible to divide the 'actors' in the planning and development process into two broad groups; the developers and those directly or indirectly affected by or having an interest in the development. The status and character of the two groups will vary in each situation. For example, where the developer is a statutory undertaker (as is the CEGB), the powers of national and local government agencies normally concerned with the control of development may be reduced.

The CEGB is not required to apply for planning permission to local authorities. However, there are agreed procedures for consultation with government departments and agencies (especially the Departments of Energy and Environment, and the Nuclear Installations and Industrial Air Pollution Inspectorates), local planning authorities and other agencies, such as the regional water authorities, affected by the project (Department of the Environment, 1976). In addition consultations occur with local political interests, including MPs and the amenity groups (Figure 5.2). These consultations cover a number of development criteria related to technical and environmental issues and to the public acceptability of the project (Gammon, 1978). It has been argued that such consultations, prior to application for consent, are critical in terms of ability to influence the Board (Drapkin, 1974). The interaction between the CEGB as the developer and the local planning authority is of particular concern.

TECHNICAL                                              ENVIRONMENTAL

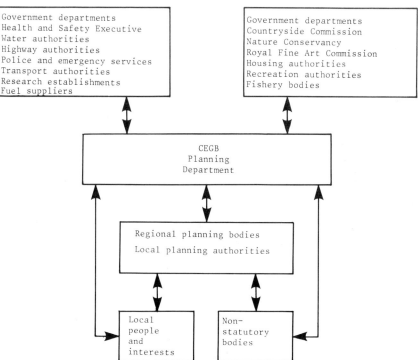

FIG 5.2 *Power Station Planning Consultations*

The Board does appear to give weight to advice received from local authorities in all phases of the planning process. In the initial identification phase, discussions take place with local authorities on the broad policies and constraints on development in the broad area of search. In the detailed site investigation phase, consultations take place on the comparative merits of alternative sites and their impact on other developments, water supplies, sewerage, transport, employment, etc. Where the Board decides to nominate a site as a reserve against long term needs, the local authorities are asked to include it as a potential site in structure and local plans. When the Board decides to make an application to the Secretary of State for Energy for consent to develop a site, the formal views of the local planning authority are requested. If the local authorities have objected to the development and their objections are not withdrawn, and/or if the Secretary of State so decides, a public inquiry into the application will then be held. If consent is given for a development, the local authority is likely to be further involved in such aspects as sites for construction camps, routes for the transport of labour and materials and contributions to improvements to local structure.

In most cases, the proposal for a new station will be handled by the planning committee of the relevant county, although occasionally special *ad-hoc* committees are set up. In the two major case studies of Drax (phase 1) and Sizewell 'A' carried out by the Power Station Impacts (PSI) team, no local public inquiry was held, nor was there any outright opposition to the station developments. Informal discussions between the CEGB and local authorities were however important in resolving certain objections (for example, at Drax the then West Riding County Council was concerned about any development which would increase the County's dependence on heavy industry). Conflict is sometimes greater betweeen local authorities than between authorities and the developer. For example, at Hinkley Point, there was dispute between the County and Rural District on whether new population associated with the development should be dispersed or concentrated. At Sizewell, the local Leiston UDC, foreseeing local economic benefit, took the initiative; Suffolk County Council was less enthusiastic. For some developments, there may be special conditions. At Dinorwic, the County Council took the opportunity to ensure that, in its eyes, most of the potential employment benefit of the proposed construction would be channelled locally. The Caernarvonshire County Council and the CEGB made the North Wales Hydro-Electric Power Bill Agreement in 1973. This required the CEGB to 'use their best endeavours to secure that at all stages of construction of the works not less than 70 per cent of the labour force employed are workmen normally resident in the district'. Of course, the nature of consultations noted here may not be typical of the future: local authorities are now likely to be more critical and require answers to a wider range of questions. Thus initial CEGB investigations at Druridge Bay in Northumberland generated considerable local concern, leading to the publication of a CEGB report outlining the characteristics and potential impacts of a station development in the locality. New site applications are also likely to lead to public inquiries.

CEGB consultation with local authorities does not end with the beginning of construction. Indeed the construction stage can be a source of a number of issues, such as employment, contractors' traffic, accommodation and noise but, as in the planning stage, the nature of such consultations can vary greatly. The most expensive liaison procedure has been operated at Dinorwic. The main interest of the local authorities here was to ensure that the local employment agreement was implemented—as it has been. In the operational stage, local authority interests tend to focus more on the provision of services such as accommodation and education. All the operating stations in the PSI research study claimed to maintain a close liaison with their respective local authorities. In the case of nuclear stations this is formalised as a Local Liaison Committee.

## Local Effects of Power Stations

### Anticipated effects

Arguments about the anticipated effects of power station developments change through time, influenced partly by the growth of political pressures, such as the environmental movement and partly by changing requirements on developers. Arguments also straddle the national-local continuum. Until recently, existing procedures have tended to limit the debate to the local level and have excluded the discussion of programmes, rather than individual developments. However, in the 1979/80 inquiry into the proposal by the National Coal Board to mine in the Vale of Belvoir the opponents were able to discuss the need for the development. In the public inquiry into the Sizewell 'B' PWR development, national issues relating to need and safety have taken a central role, although local issues are also extremely important. The discussion below concentrates on these local issues.

The arguments for a power station development tend to be framed in terms of increased quality of life and opportunities for local residents both immediately and in the long-term. The advantages of an increased pool of secure, permanent, power station jobs are often put forward as a major benefit of development, especially in areas of otherwise declining job opportunities. In certain cases the station may be seen as providing direct job replacement (as at Sizewell 'A' where workers were expected to be shed by a major employer). In other cases more general arguments of economic regeneration, diversification of the economy, reversal of decline and reduced out-migration may be made. These arguments are likely to be strongest in peripheral areas which may be subject to pressures to accept 'jobs at any price'. The types of jobs provided, in an industry with a certain future, with generally good wage levels and working conditions, may be seen as an advantage, particularly in rural areas which have provided limited job opportunities and little competition for labour. Power station development may also provide training in skills which are useful in the future in contrast to the skills obtained in the traditional industries of rural areas.

It is frequently argued of major developments that the increases in local expenditure as a result of employee and CEGB expenditure on goods and services will increase turnover in certain sectors of the local economy. The increased rate income provided by the station may also be argued as a benefit. Advantages for infrastructure improvement, wholly or partially financed by the Board, may also be anticipated. Improvements to the road network may be brought forward and new structures such as bridges may be built. Such infrastructure may assist other types of economic activity in the area. The housing added to the public sector stock as a result of guarantees by the Board may also be seen as a long-term benefit accruing to the locality. More generally, the development of a power station may be seen as having symbolic significance, is that it may be seen as a modernising, or status element, generally expressed by the view that it would be 'putting the place on the map'. This appears to have been important in the case of the Hartlepool nuclear power station.

Those opposed to power station developments often argue that few of the jobs may actually benefit the local population, as a result of mismatch between the skills of the workforce in the area and employment generated. Associated with this are fears that the construction stage may build structural unemployment into the economy (the skills being redundant after construction), the only alternative being for the area to develop a construction-dependent economy. In addition, there are arguments about the effects of increased labour and craft competition which may create problems for small firms and for certain sectors of the local economy. The agricultural lobby often argues strongly against industrial developments in rural areas, for reasons of labour shortage and upward pressure on wages (Newby, 1978). Resources used for construction of the power station and associated infrastructure may be seen as being diverted from the needs of the local population, such as local roads and housing.

Both the construction and operation of major developments may be considered damaging to local amenity. Amenity issues are only briefly noted in this chapter. However, certain environmental changes may have economic or social effects, such as the effect of visual intrusion on tourism, or the disincentive to development that may be caused by the existence of a nuclear station. Fears of social disruption may also be expressed. These are expected particularly in the construction stage, when the influx of a large labour force with no permanent attachment to the area, is seen as a threat.

### Demonstrated effects

In all fields of policy making, there may be quite a gap between the anticipated and actual outcome of a policy or development initiative.

The Power Station Impacts (PSI) study analysed in detail the social and economic impacts of several power stations on their localities, of which two were studied intensively (PSI, 1980). These are at Drax and Sizewell and they differ markedly in type, stage of development and site and locational characteristics. Drax is a large (2000 MW(e)) coal-fired station which was commissioned in 1974; Sizewell is a smaller nuclear station (580 MW(e)) of the first generation Magnox type, commissioned in 1966. Drax is located in the Selby District of North Yorkshire on the edge of a large conurbation, in an area with a recent history of growth and prospects of further expansion. Sizewell, in contrast, is located in a peripheral rural area, with an agricultural base and limited growth prospects.

Drax and Sizewell are both operational stations. To increase the relevance of the findings and their explanatory and predictive value for other locations, further studies were undertaken (PSI, 1982 (a); 1982 (b)). The commence-

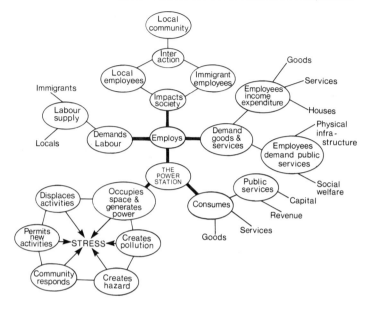

FIG 5.3 *Socio-economic Impact Model for Power Station Construction and Operation*

ment of the Drax Completion Project, where construction began in 1978 to expand the existing Drax station from 2000 MW(e) tp 4000 MW(e) capacity, provided an opportunity to study power station construction. Further comparative studies were conducted at a number of sites of different station types, in different locality types and at different stages of development.

The precise nature and range of effects are a function of the interaction between the power station development and the locality. Figure 5.3 outlines the range of effects investigated and their inter-relationships and provides a simplified view of the impact process. Working out from the power station into the local community, it illustrates some of the more important interactions, with the direct effects of the development (e.g. employment demand) filtering into the community and generating a range of inter-related indirect effects (e.g. power station employees' expenditure). A number of effects models were identified as the most significant from within the general framework. These relate to labour market, expenditure, social structure, service requirements and physical development effects.

*Construction*—Employment associated with power station development is particularly high in the construction stage. Peak employment on recent British construction sites has been of the order of 2000 to 2500. The level of employment varies during construction according to the mix and overlap of civil works and plant (mechanical and electrical) works. The geographical and industrial sources of construction labour are influenced by a number of factors including the recruitment policies of the contractors, CEGB policies, the nature of local and regional labour markets and trends in recruitment practices in the construction industry. For example, the large plant contractors tend to import sizeable numbers of 'travelling men' from their main works. Managerial and technical staff are recruited from a national labour market and are highly mobile geographically. Site service jobs (e.g. canteen and hostel facilities) on the other hand are almost wholly locally provided. Estimates of local recruitment are complicated by varying definitions of 'local'. At Dinorwic there were special arrangements to maximise local recruitment and local labour (from an approximate 50 km radius of the site) constituted 82 per cent of the workforce at its 1979 peak. At most other sites studied the proportion of locally recruited labour has been considerably lower. The significance of large scale construction employment at a single site is perhaps most strongly felt locally during the period of construction rundown. At the sites studied which had experienced this period, the associated growth in unemployment was of a much smaller order of magnitude than the actual numbers laid off from the respective construction sites. This supports the picture of construction workers as being generally 'travelling men' and that the local component on a construction site at this phase is often quite limited.

Large amounts of expenditure are associated with the construction of power stations (approximately £1000 million for a nuclear station in 1981). Up to two-thirds of this expenditure may be for manufacture off-site. Of the on-site expenditure, the main injection into the local economy is via wages and salaries of site employees. However, although the initial injection may be large, a very high proportion of expenditure is on goods and services not produced locally; hence there is a high leakage out of the local economy. The local benefits of local spending are thus reduced. Work by Archer for the county of Gwynedd (Gwynedd County Council, 1976) estimates that for the year of peak construction employment at Wylfa power station, wages and salaries of £7.8 million paid to construction workers generated an increase in income in the Gwynedd economy of £1.7 million (this must be adjusted by the loss in unemployment benefits received locally). Similarly, the patterns of contract letting for power station construction in a largely national market have resulted, at all the sites studied, in only a small percentage of the sums spent on site goods and services being spent locally. However, the total amount of local spending may still be sizeable by virtue of the total size of power station construction expenditure.

The large numbers of non-local construction employees has considerable social effects. They may commute, relocate near the development temporarily or relocate on a permanent basis. Major influences on their decisions are the likely length of contract, the availability, cost and acceptability of local accommodation and the levels of lodgings and travel allowances. Typically, the contract length for managerial and technical staff on site is greater than for hourly paid workers and relocation is a more feasible alternative for the senior staff. Accommodation is usually provided at or near construction sites in the form of site hostels and caravan sites. At their peaks in 1963 and 1964, Dungeness 'A' and Sizewell 'A' site hostels accommodated 800 and 600 employees respectively. At more recent developments reduced figures were found—possibly reflecting a tendency amongst contractors to recruit on a more regional basis, a reduction in the working week, the payment of travel allowances and greater personal mobility.

A detailed study of public perceptions of the construction stage was carried out on the civil works stage of the Drax Completion Project. The perceived environmental effects of construction activity were concerned largely with traffic, noise, dusty and visual impacts. Traffic disruption was the most frequently mentioned physical effect. Overall, 14 per cent of respondents in a survey of over 400 local households mentioned traffic effects and in selected locations on main transport routes to the site the frequency of mentions was considerably higher.

*Operations*—Employment levels at large operational stations currently vary between about 400 and 750, according to the age and size of the plant, plant design, whether the station is base-load or not and whether maintenance work is carried out by a permanent team within the plant, a regional team, contractors or by some combined approach. Such levels represent significant contributions to employment in rural locations and over a period of 30 to 40 years. However, the direct employment benefits to a community can be greatly diluted by high levels of in-migration to take up the power station jobs. At Drax and Sizewell some 60 per cent of the power workers had their previous work-place outside a 17 km radius of the stations. High grades were more likely to be geographically mobile and less likely to be industrially mobile than were lower grades (many higher grade jobs were recruited from within the electricity supply industry). The local/non-local ratio of power station employees is a central factor in the nature of socio-economic effects.

Direct employment can of course generate a range of indirect effects in the labour market. Evidence from the sites studied suggests that these effects are limited. Little independent impact on local unemployment rates has been observed. The situation for employers of female labour was potentially improved; for local employers of male labour, there was undoubtedly some loss the the power station although it appears to have been limited. Power stations may have contributed also to local wage inflation and perhaps, to a lesser extent, to local labour shortages in particular skills. Estimates of the net long-term local employment effects of power station development depend on a number of not easily quantifiable factors: the extent to which local industries may benefit from power station contracts, the degree of local utilisation of power station waste products (e.g. pulverised fuel ash, waste heat for horticulture), and the extent of replacement by local firms of jobs lost to the power station development.

Operational power stations and their employees are sources of major expenditure. However, as with construction, the local benefits of this expenditure are limited. Of the power station purchases of goods and services (exluding fuel) in 1977/78, less than 2 per cent of £8.9 million (Drax) and less than one per cent of £1.5 million (Sizewell) were made within a 17 km radius of the power station. In general terms, the national and regional purchasing policies operated by the CEGB have not greatly benefited small local suppliers. The expenditure of the power workers also suffers from the high import leakages associated with small areas. A third element of expenditure is the rate contribution made to the host local authority on behalf of power station activity. This represents a sizeable contribution to the rate base of a local authority: £2 million (Drax, Selby District) and £0.75 million (Sizewell, Suffolk Coastal District) in 1977/78. However, such apparent gains did not in fact constitute 'profit' to the local authority because of the offsetting pound for pound reduction in the resources element of the Rate Support Grant received from central government. The modified rate support grant system introduced from 1981 has replaced the former needs and resources elements by a block grant. However, as with the old system, a higher rateable value still reduces the amount of block grant payable. Thus an expectation of substantial financial gains locally from operational power stations may be optimistic, although this is not to deny that some traders in particular localities may benefit considerably from power station-associated expenditure.

Attention has been drawn by many sources to the potential social tensions resulting from the influx of a large new workforce into a locality, especially a rural locality. At the major case study sites at Drax and Sizewell there were sizeable increases in population as a result of the power station development. Relative impacts, however, must be seen in the context of population trends in the locality. In the growth area of Drax, the additional population associated with the operational power station was only a small percentage of the change taking place anyway. Even in areas such as Sizewell where recent population change had been more limited, the additional population was so distributed as to be of only minor impact. 'Us and them' attitudes between the indigenous local population and in-migrants to the power stations do of course persist in the minds of some people, but the hypothesised social tensions were not thought significant enough to be mentioned by most people. This may be because, in both study areas, a large number of power station recruits already had social attachments and involvements. More people saw benefits (of a vague nature) accruing from 'new blood' than expressed hostility towards outsiders.

The additional population associated with the development of a power station places demand on certain services in the area, such as housing and education. The power workers display a high level of owner occupation: 81 per cent at Drax, 62 per cent at Sizewell, in 1978, compared with the national rate of 54 per cent. However, in both cases, at the Board's request, there was some provision of local authority housing. Such council accommodation tends to be a temporary resource, before workers enter the private housing market. Thus after a while the Board can hand back housing to the local authority to be used to meet general local need. (Studies at a number of sites do tend to suggest a downward trend in CEGB requests for local authority housing). Housing availability as between tenure types is an important factor in determining where the greatest population impact from incoming power workers would be felt.

Education impacts appear to vary with the age of the station. A new power station appears to recruit a young workforce, in or entering the age of peak family creation. Thus demand for school places will be substantial initially and there will be additions each year until the station is roughly half way through its planned life. Impacts also vary with distribution. At Drax the local impact was spread over many primary and secondary schools. At Sizewell there was more concentration but in both cases local authority response was largely pragmatic, such as temporary provision of extra classrooms.

The measurement of physical effects such as chimney emissions, noise or the quality of water discharges was not undertaken in the impact study. It was considered important, however, to assess local opinions and attitudes and the decisions and actions taken in consequence of attributing certain physical effects to the presence of a power station. Concern over the effects of the initial development was in both cases quite limited, although at Sizewell there was some concern over access to the beach adjacent to the development. At Drax, more local feeling was aroused by an ancillary development—the proposals for ash disposal sites in the area. Communications in both areas have received limited benefits from power station development, via improved/new road links in the vicinity of the power station and the keeping open of a railway link in East Suffolk previously earmarked for closure by British Rail.

Overall, the actual local economic and social effects of power stations may be less dramatic than the anticipated effects but may nevertheless be significant. Much depends on the perspective of the assessor. From the perspective of the research team, the effects considered under the headings of labour market, service requirements and physical development would appear to be more noticeably important in their local implications, for both construction and operation, than the other effects considered. In several instances, such as expenditure effects and social disruption, there would seem to be some mismatch between anticipated and demonstrated effects.

### Perceived effects

Individual perceptions of effects may be as important as the actual effects and local opinions about effects constitute an important source of information. They not only allow a comparison with findings from data from other sources but also allow a comparison of the views of the general public with those put forward by pressure groups. Individuals' views are arguably the strongest influence on their future decisions, so that perceptions of effects are as important in conditioning behaviour as more scientific measurements carried out by monitoring agencies. Opinions were obtained from a household survey (n = 565, Drax; 504, Sizewell) and a power station employees' survey (n = 210, Drax; 128, Sizewell) undertaken in 1978. The opinion questions sought to distinguish between categories of effects, and for convenience distinguished 'favourable' and 'unfavourable' effects. Open-ended questions were used, unprompted responses were recorded verbatim and at the editing stage grouped into appropriate categories. However, no claim can be made about the relative weights which respondents attached to the various effects mentioned. In 1980, a similar household survey (n = 402) was carried out in relation to the Drax Completion Project. In this survey, respondents were asked to weight their own views on a common scale. In both 1978 and 1980, more respondents noted favourable than unfavourable effects.

Some 20 per cent of those interviewed in the 1980 Drax survey did not know that a major construction programme to double the size of Drax Power Station was under way (at the time of the survey, site employment was approximately 850). Over 50 per cent of the sample mentioned at least one favourable effect of construction (predominantly employment); 19 per cent of the sample mentioned one unfavourable effect (predominantly traffic).

In the 1978 household surveys of the perceived effects of the operational stations at Drax and Sizewell, comments about the favourable effects of power stations also outnumbered unfavourable comments. The creation of employment was again perceived as the main favourable effect and was mentioned by 60 per cent of the respondents at Drax and 75 per cent at Sizewell. Environmental effects (pollution, noise, visual effects) accounted for the majority of mentions at both sites. At Sizewell, there was the additional concern that the station was nuclear. There was also concern about the possible impact of the control of development around a nuclear station on the potential housing and industrial development of nearby settlements. Evidence to support or offset such concern is sparse although it is possible that the negative impact on development is more apparent than real.

An attempt was also made to assess broad shifts in the opinions held by local people about the power station over the period since the development began. At Drax, it was found that there was a large shift of opinion in favour of the power station, with no shift in the opposite direction. At Sizewell, the favourable movement outweighed the unfavourable movement, but was smaller than at Drax.

**Conclusions: Improving the Planning Process**

Even in the climate of economic recession and public expenditure restraint of the early 1980s, future expenditure on power stations In Britain is planned to increase substantially. Many of the issues relating to such developments, such as national need, type of plant, and the balance of supply and demand in different parts of the country involve considerations which cannot be resolved by the planning system. Yet planning authorities can perform a useful role at the broad strategic level by anticipating the scope and nature of potential developments and their implications for regional planning, as with the Standing Conference on London and the South East Regional Planning.

At the local level, there is a growing awareness by both local authorities and the CEGB of the social and economic effects as well as the physical effects of developments on localities. During the proposals stage, questions are raised about many aspects of power station development and frequently questions about economic and social effects are inadequately answered because of the paucity of information available. Estimates may be made which are often, at best, wide of the mark and sometimes completely misleading. Yet, in parallel with national trends, it seems likely that local debate about the effects of such massive developments will intensify. The growing interest in environmental impact assessment suggests that in future local authorities and other interested parties are likely to be seeking more precise and detailed answers to their points from the developer. An improvement in the quality of information on the local effects of power stations requires a better understanding of the processes at work when such a development is introduced into a locality, plus a more systematic approach to the prediction and monitoring of effects.

The various local social and economic effects of power stations are the outcome of many factors but it is possible to identify a number of key determinants. The actions and decisions of the CEGB are of central importance. Decisions on the recruitment policy pursued—that is the balance between locals and in-migrants—have effects which filter into the community in a variety of ways. However, the availability of relevant local skills, plus union pressure on the electricity supply industry to recruit internally as more stations are de-commissioned may limit flexibility of policy. CEGB purchasing policy, with its emphasis on contracts tendered nationally, also has significant effects. At the local level, the local authority can influence the nature of effects by, for example, objecting to the development proposals and bringing them much more into the public arena. Local planning and development decisions can partly condition factors such as 'journey to work' length and housing availability. Private sector decisions such as local labour agreements and housing investment also help to determine the nature and extent of the impact of power station development. The nature of the locality—its population size and economic organisation, its rate of growth and diversity—can influence the nature of effects. The stage of power station development is also important. Limited evidence on the construction stage suggests that its effects may be more marked locally than operational effects, although even here there are different phases of efforts. Thus the initial 'civil' phase, with site employment of around 1000, is followed by a 'plant' phase, when site employment can be well in excess of 2000.

The identification of key determinants of effects is an essential element in the development of a more systematic approach to the prediction and monitoring of the economic and social effects of power station developments. Hopefully a more systematic approach will produce estimates of effects which are less wide of the mark. Better prediction involves the clarification of complex sets of interconnected events and the isolation of the key variables influencing those events—for example, developer labour recruitment decisions appear to be a key factor in predicting labour market effects. A monitoring system involves identifying both indicators of the variables and sources of information. Thus actual recruitment policy is the indicator, relevant information is from management interviews. The development of a more systematic approach could be useful not only in proposal assessment but also in forward planning. For example, monitoring of relevant indicators might give early warning that housing estimates associated with a development had been inaccurate—thus allowing outcomes to be changed.

A more systematic and wide ranging approach to the planning and development of large projects, such as power stations, is likely to be required in the future and is already operating overseas. In Canada, Ontario Hydro (the public utility supplying electricity to Ontario province) has a well-developed system for estimating likely effects of power plant development. Project assessment is used as a basis for negotiation between developer and local authority for the payment of costs for provision of the required infrastructure and services resultant upon the development. Both groups then monitor the actual requirements over time.

Pressure from the European Community (EEC) for wider use of Environmental Impact Assessment is also likely to intensify. The draft EC directive identifies two categories of projects for assessment. In the first category, which includes nuclear power stations, assessment will be mandatory. In the second category, which includes fossil-fuelled stations, a more limited form of assessment may be agreed (Commission of the European Communities, 1980). However, impact assessment is an ongoing process; a power station, from planning to decommissioning, may impact a locality for over half a century and the interactions between the development and the locality need to be regularly monitored. There must be an important role for local planners in both these prediction and monitoring exercises.

## References

Commission of the European Economic Community (1980) *Proposal for a Council Directive Concerning the Assessment of the Environmental Effects of Certain Public and Private Projects*, COM(80) 313 final, CEEC, Brussels.

Department of Energy (1981) *Tidal power from the Severn Estuary: Volume 1*, Energy Paper Number 46, HMSO.

Department of the Environment (1976) Circular 34/76, *Procedure for Consultation and Consent for New Electricity Generating Stations and Overhead Lines*.

Drapkin, D. B. (1974) Development, Electricity and Power Stations: Problems in Electricity Planning Decisions, *Public Law*, Autumn.

Energy Research Group (1976) *A critique of the electricity industry*, Energy Research Group, Open University.

England, G. (1980) *Planning for Uncertainty*, CEGB.

Gammon, K. M. (1978) Power Station Planning, *CEGB Newsletter*, No. 107, September.

Gammon, K. M. (1979) CEGB Experience in Selecting and Developing Nuclear Power Station Sites, *CEGB Newsletter*, No. 111, December.

Gregory, R. (1971) *The Price of Amenity*, Macmillan.

Gwynedd County Council (1976) *The Impact of a Power Station on Gwynedd*.

Hawkins, A. (1974) *Electricity Supply and the Environment*, CEGB.

Howard, R. (1980) *Transmission of Power*, CEGB.

Matthews, R. R. and Usher, E. F. F. W. (1977) *CEGB Experience of Public Communication*, CEGB.

Newby, H. (1978) *Property, Paternalism and Power*, Hutchinson.

Power Station Impacts Research Team (1980) *Power Station Impacts: the Socio-Economic Effects of Power Stations on their Localities*, Department of Town Planning, Oxford Polytechnic.

Power Station Impacts Research Team (1982(a)) *Drax Power Station Completion: A Study of the Social and Economic Effects of Construction—Part 1 Civil Works*, Department of Town Planning, Oxford Polytechnic.

Power Station Impacts Research Team (1982(b)) *A Comparison of the Social and Economic Effects of Power Stations on Localities*, Department of Town Planning, Oxford Polytechnic.

Standing Conference on London and South East Regional Planning (SCLSERP) (1979) *Electricity supply in South East England:* a review, SC1242R.

# CHAPTER 6

# Energy Projects and the Planning Process: A Canadian Perspective

JON O'RIORDAN

## Introduction

The decision-making process associated with the development of both energy policies and projects in Canada has to tackle many of the same issues that have been described earlier in this book in the British context. These issues revolve mainly around the questions of project justification, the management of demand (rather than expansion of supplies) and the impacts of large-scale energy developments on the natural and social environments. Over the past decade decision-makers have faced mounting public pressure to consider these broader aspects of policy and this has resulted in a gradual change in the institutional arrangements for making such decisions.

This chapter provides a broader perspective on the British approach to energy project analysis by reviewing some of these developments in Canada and in particular in the Province of British Columbia (BC). Examples of specific issues associated with energy developments and land use planning in Canada and British Columbia are described first to provide background for the policy making system that is evolving to tackle these issues. In the second part of the chapter a number of examples of project and non-project energy decision-making processes are described to illustrate how legislation and institutions are adapting to new challenges. The final section concentrates on analysing the present policy-making system in British Columbia and some of the new directions it might take over the next few years. It also reflects on the potential success of these developments in terms of improved decision-making within the context of the province's political economy.

## Energy Developments in British Columbia

British Columbia, with a land base covering 95 million hectares and a population of 2.6 million would at first glance appear to be a province with almost unlimited resources. However, the rapid development of its forests, mineral wealth and agricultural base, combined with the fact that over one-third of the area is alpine or sub-alpine have changed this perception to one of a finite land base that is almost fully committed for various resource uses. For example, the province's vast timber resources are already fully utilised by existing industry. There is a great concern that in the future there will have to be a reduction in the annual permitted timber harvest since the reforested lands are generally not as productive as the virgin timbered lands. Agricultural development has taken place on the province's most fertile lands, which represent less than 2 per cent of the total land base. Any further expansion will be at the expense of already committed forest base.

The province's underground natural resource base does have considerable development potential however. Both metal and coal mine developments are on the increase. In 1979 there were 62 operating mines in the province, of which four were producing 12 million tonnes of metallurgical coal and 23 were major metal mines. Present mineral and coal licences for exploration cover approximately 6 million hectares. As a result, 10 coal mines and 17 metal mines are currently being planned for development under the province's environmental assessment guidelines (O'Riordan, 1981).

The province has some supplies of natural gas, which will soon be the subject of a public inquiry to be held by the BC Utilities Commission to determine how much can be safely exported without jeopardising the future domestic market. These large gas and thermal coal deposits have attracted a number of proposals for energy conservation projects such as coal liquefaction and liquified natural gas and petrochemical plants. At the time of writing there is approximately $12 \times 10^9$ worth of potential investment in energy-related industrial projects on the drawing boards.

These industrial projects have in turn fuelled a demand for electric energy, arguably the most controversial energy developments affecting land use and environmental resources in the province. Almost all of the province's installed capacity of 7 GW(e) is produced by hydro-electric power (HEP) (Figure 6.1), the 41 existing reservoirs flooding 329,000 hectares of some of the most productive valley bottom lands in the province. These HEP projects have provided cheap electric power in financial terms because of their economics of scale (the largest exceed 2000 MW(e)) and low operating costs but have been increasingly expensive in terms of forestry, fisheries, wildlife, agriculture and amenity values foregone. With the possibility that a number of large-scale energy-intensive industrial projects could be built in the province, the forecast growth rate for electrical energy demand is high relative to other Canadian provinces, ranging between four and six per cent per year (BC Ministry of Energy, Mines and Petroleum Resources, 1981). This high potential demand has encouraged BC Hydro and Power Authority, the Crown corporation responsible for electric energy developments in the province, to study four major additional projects with a combined capacity of 9400 MW(e) and a major thermal (coal) project at Hat Creek in the interior of the province with an initial capacity of 2600 MW(e).

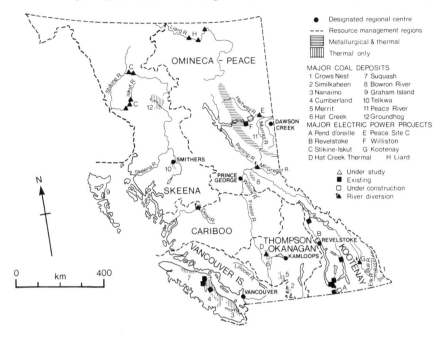

FIG 6.1 *Major Coal Deposits and Electric Power Projects in the Province of British Columbia*

Because these electric energy projects are all located in environmentally sensitive areas of the province, the construction of any one of them will cause a major public controversy. The HEP projects proposed in the Stikine-Iskut river basin will raise the important issue of flooding a wilderness river, the Stikine Canyon being considered one of the most important scenic attractions in the province. The Kootenay Diversion will threaten some of the most productive wetlands for migrating waterfowl in Canada. The Liard project would regulate downstream flows in the Mackenzie River Basin in Alberta and the North West Territories, resulting in a possible delay in ice break-up which could have a major impact on migrating waterfowl populations. In addition, the project would create a direct confrontation with native indians who are claiming the return of their aboriginal rights in the area. Additional diversion of water in the Kemano HEP project in northwestern British Columbia to provide power for expansion of the aluminium smelting industry threatens valuable stocks of Pacific salmon and steelhead trout. The thermal projects also give rise to environmental concerns. The proposed Hat Creek project would use highly sulphurous coals that will require very expensive pollution control equipment to reduce $SO_2$ emissions. The province is very sensitive to the prospect of 'acid rain' caused by high concentrations of $SO_2$ in the atmosphere, especially when such environmental problems are already a reality in the eastern provinces and the north-east industrial zone in the United States.

Electrical energy projects are not the only ones that are giving rise to environmental concerns in the province. There has been a recent renewal of interest in drilling for oil and gas in the offshore waters between the mainland and Vancouver Island and south of the Queen Charlotte Islands. Exploration activity was initiated in the early 1960s, but a 10-year moratorium was imposed on all activities in 1971 as the result of a legal dispute between the federal and provincial governments regarding ownership of these offshore resources. Although this legal dispute has still not been settled, the moratorium has come to an end. With the rising price of oil in Canada and a national policy to strive for oil self-sufficiency by 1990, both governments are now interested in resuming exploration activities. However, the prospect of drilling and piping oil on to the scenic west coast of the province with its highly-valued salmon fishery has aroused the concern of the province's most influential public interest groups.

Significant deposits of metallurgical coal are located under the western slopes of the Rocky Mountains which straddle the British Columbia-Alberta border (Figure 6.1). As noted earlier, there are presently four operating mines located in the southern part of this region producing an output of 12 million tonnes annually. As a result of recent studies conducted by the federal and provincial governments, a major regional coal development is now under way in the northern section, south of the Peace River, which when fully developed will double the province's current coal production (O'Riordan, 1981). The new mines with the associated infrastructure of roads, railways, new towns and industrial support facilities will create major impacts on a relatively untouched natural environment. Because the mines are located close to or in the alpine zone, the main environmental concerns are centred on the protection of small but ecologically important populations of mountain caribou, mountain sheep and mountain goats and the difficulty in revegetating and reclaiming disturbed areas.

In many ways, the above description of the conflicts between energy developments, land use and environmental quality represent a microcosm of the situation across Canada. All provinces face major decisions on energy developments which have important impacts on the environment. These include the very large scale HEP projects in Quebec, Newfoundland and Labrador, nuclear power stations in New Brunswick and Ontario, uranium mining in Saskatchewan and Ontario and large petrochemical complexes in Alberta. Although each province and the federal government have developed their own specific institutional arrangements to deal with these issues, the policy appraisal and project decision-making systems tend to follow an overall pattern. This is described in the following section.

## Evolution of the Policy-Making Process in Canada

### Federal and Provincial Policy-Making Contexts

Before analysing this policy-making system and the changes that have taken place across Canada and particularly in British Columbia, it is necessary to outline the Canadian federal system.

Under the current constitution, the federal government, through its National Energy Board (NEB) has powers over energy export out of the country and inter-provincial energy transfers. The NEB also sets the domestic and export prices of petroleum and natural gas and thus has a major influence on the rate of energy development and provincial price structures for alternative sources of energy such as electricity. In addition, the federal government has direct control over land and resource use in the Canadian north, specifically the Yukon and the North West Territories where many of the future energy projects in oil and gas are expected to be developed. Last and by no means least, the federal government has directed responsibilities for fisheries management, with a strongly-worded Fisheries Act which contains enforceable powers to halt developments that have deleterious impacts on Pacific and Atlantic salmon. For example, recently the British Columbia Supreme Court ordered Alcan, a major aluminium smelting company in the province to release up to 28.3 $m^3$ of water per second from its privately-owned HEP project into the Nechako River to maintain salmon populations. These flows are worth literally millions of dollars annually, if converted into electric power and sold to the NW United States.

The provinces have direct control over land use and natural resources. Consequently, they exert regulatory controls over energy developments to protect environmental quality and in general, make the final decisions on all projects that produce, transmit or process energy resources within their own provincial boundaries. As noted earlier, the one exception to this is the development of offshore oil and gas: the jurisdictional complexities of resource ownership have yet to be resolved in the Supreme Court of Canada.

Because over 90 per cent of the land in British Columbia is owned by the Crown, the provincial government has a direct control over land use allocation and resource management. It has not developed a comprehensive approach to land use planning, however, so all major energy projects are in a sense 'called-in' for review by the provincial government (or the federal government in Northern Canada, where its jurisdiction over the land base is paramount). Generally across Canada, municipal and regional levels of government have a much smaller influence over energy projects than is the case in Britain.

The general policy-making framework for energy project decisions used in the ensuing analysis is shown on Figure 6.2. The broad issues are subject to value judgements developed by a number of interest groups to form the

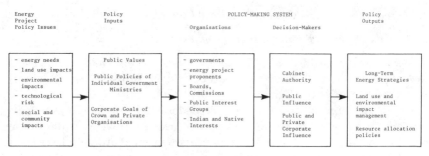

FIG 6.2 *Energy Project Policy-making Framework*

main policy inputs to the decision-making system. This is composed of cabinet and corporate groups which are in turn influenced by a wide range of public interests, appointed boards and commissions. The decisions become policy outputs both in the form of project implementation and longer-term energy and land use planning strategies.

During the 1950s and 60s, energy developments were relatively few in number, small in scale, generally involved well-tested technologies and were usually perceived by the public to be both necessary and good for economic and social growth. Major projects were developed under a relatively simple regulatory system. There were no formal environmental assessments, public hearings under NEB and provincial regulatory bodies dwelt mainly on technical or financial aspects and the necessary licences and permits were generally routinely granted by the various regulatory agencies in government.

The 1970s witnessed the rapid change in size, costs and technology of energy projects across Canada. This, plus an aroused public consciousness over environmental quality and resource allocation, brought demands for comprehensive environmental and risk assessments prior to project decisions. The slow-down in economic growth following the dramatic oil and gas price increases in the mid-1970s encouraged the public to question the need for continued expansion of energy supplies and to demand greater accountability from developers on project justification, with more emphasis on energy conservation.

Perhaps the most significant social and economic consequence of the energy development proposals of the mid-1970s in Canada was the awakening of the native peoples across the nation to the implications of such developments in their lifestyles. The major pipeline proposals to bring natural gas from the Canadian Arctic down the Mackenzie Valley to serve southern Canada and the United States stimulated the native peoples to stake their aboriginal claims for land and resources both in the north and the provinces. Indian land claims now affect many energy project decisions, an issue made all the more difficult to resolve as native peoples and their lands are not ordinarily subject to provincial legislation. As a result, Native Indian Associations are now a major political force in the group bargaining process that pervades the decision-making process on major energy projects. Recently, large financial settlements have been made to Indian groups in Northern Quebec and northern British Columbia as compensation for the use of energy resources in lands claimed by these groups.

The policy-making systems in Canada have responded to these broader issues and changing public values in three major ways. First, a number of special inquiries have been commissioned by both federal and provincial governments to consider the questions of energy need and land use planning in more depth before final decisions are made. Second, there has been an extension of the regulatory process within existing legislation to consider these broader issues for specific energy projects. Third, some jurisdictions across Canada have brought in new legislation to come to grips with the growing public unease over large scale energy developments.

### Inquiry Commissions

One of the first moves to expand the decision-making system came in 1974, when the federal government appointed Mr. Justice T. R. Berger of the British Columbia Supreme Court as Chairman of the Mackenzie Valley Pipeline Inquiry. The inquiry was responsible for examining the land use, environmental and social implications associated with two alternative proposals by Arctic Gas and Foothills Pipelines Ltd. respectively to build a multi-billion ($10^9$) dollar pipeline that would bring natural gas from the Alaskan and Canadian Arctic to markets in Canada and the USA. It is interesting to note that the federal government had already made a commitment to the American government to build a pipeline; the inquiry's terms of reference were limited to establishing the routing and conditions for its constructions that would limit impacts on the environment and maintain native Indian lifestyle.

The process developed by Berger revolutionised the public inquiry system in Canada. The inquiry lasted 3 years, cost over $5 million, with public hearings being held in every small community throughout the North West Territories and northern Yukon as well as major cities in the south. Berger, a man of infinite patience and obvious respect for the feelings of the people of the north, developed an informal approach to these hearings to encourage the many native groups, environmental coalitions and other non-technical interest groups an opportunity to express their concerns outside the rigour of a formal, legalistic inquiry process (Berger, 1976).

In addition, Berger's inquiry set a precedent in Canada by funding a number of interest groups which would not otherwise have the resources to participate at the hearings. To ensure that there was a fair distribution of these funds, Berger developed the following criteria (Sewell, 1981):

(i) each group must represent a discernible public interest.
(ii) separate and adequate representation of each group must be relevant to the inquiry.
(iii) each group must have an established record for representing that interest,
(iv) each group must demonstrate that they lacked adequate funds to represent that interest, and
(v) each group must present a clear proposal for the use of funds.

The inquiry also ensured that there was extensive coverage of all hearings by the news media. The Canadian Broadcasting Corporation Northern Service employed a team of native reporters to broadcast a summary of each day's proceedings in all six native languages and in English, thus permitting all of the northern population access to the issues being discussed.

Following nearly two years of formal and informal hearings, the inquiry recommended a 10-year moratorium on pipeline development to provide time for the federal government to settle the native land claim issues and to increase the development of renewable resources in the north to offset the negative economic impacts that generally follow a construction boom. The report also advocated the establishment of a wilderness park in the environmentally sensitive north slope of the Yukon, thus ruling out any pipeline development in that area and the creation of a whale sanctuary in the Beaufort Sea.

Because of the overwhelming concerns expressed by the peoples of the north and the great uncertainties of all the impacts of the pipeline in the fragile northern environment, the federal cabinet quickly considered and approved a less environmentally and socially damaging route for the pipeline which generally parallels the Alaska Highway. This alternative was also subjected to hastily convened environmental and social impact analysis and a major public inquiry (Lysyk et al., 1978). Nevertheless, the Berger inquiry is one clear example where the broadened decision-making structure had a major influence on the policy outcome.

As noted earlier, the Mackenzie Valley Pipeline Inquiry became the prototype for several other public inquiries into energy resource development proposals such as the Thompson Commission on the West Coal Oil Ports, the Bates Commission on Uranium Mining in British Columbia, the Hartt Commission on the Northern Environment and the Porter Commission on Electric Power Planning in Ontario. The latter inquiry deserves some comment because it specifically dealt with the issues of electric energy demand and the interrelationships of power stations and transmission lines on environmental quality and land use. The Porter Inquiry was initiated in 1975 as a result of public controversy over the siting of thermal (coal and nuclear) power stations and 500 kV transmission lines on high quality agricultural lands. There was also mounting public concern over the environmental risks associated with uranium mining to supply Ontario's nuclear stations and the potential for acid rain resulting from the high $SO_2$ discharges from thermal power stations. Between 1958 and 1973, the annual consumption of electric energy rose at a rate of 4.5 per cent, but after the 1973–75 economic recession in Canada, growth rates dropped dramatically. By 1975, Ontario Hydro had a large surplus capacity as a result of project commitments made in the late 1960s and early 1970s. Hence the public outcry over more loss of farmland due to high voltage transmission lines, at a time when it appeared these projects were no longer needed.

The commission held a large number of public meetings on energy demand; conventional and alternative generation technologies; nuclear power; transmission and land use; financial and economic issues and public participation in decision-making (Porter, 1980). Although it provided almost $360,000 over the 3 years of hearings to support the major intervenors, in general public involvement at these hearings was low. At many critical debates on the key issues listed above, attendance at public meetings (apart from official representatives from government, BC Hydro and the commission) was rarely more than ten people. Only when there was a significant local issue involving Ontario Hydro was there a large attendance at the commission's hearings. Apart from the difficulty of arousing the interest of the general public in the long-term issues affecting power planning and land use in Ontario, there was a clear indication that the hard-core proponents and opponents on these issues were not influenced by the commission's findings. In the words of Lord Ashby, cited to the Porter Commission, 'their prejudice is impenetrable' (Porter, 1981).

The commission reported to the provincial government in February, 1980, with an extensive list of recommendations which emphasised conservation, development of alternative technologies to coal and nuclear power generation and much tighter controls on transmission line construction. The whole philosophy of Ontario Hydro should be changed from one promoting electric energy supply to one concentrating on demand management and the selected use of electric power for end uses that specifically require this form of energy. Considerable attention was also paid to reducing the possibility of environmental risk at nuclear power plants, uranium mining operations and waste disposal sites with a call for a new division in Ontario Hydro exclusively concerned with nuclear power safety. Although almost 2 years have elapsed since the commission filed its report, there has not yet been any formal response from the provincial cabinet to these recommendations. However, it does appear that as a result of the inquiry process, Ontario Hydro has become much more sensitive to public concerns over these broad policy issues and will tread more carefully in the future.

### Extension of Existing Institutional Processes

In addition to these specific inquiries, many provincial governments and the federal government found they had to extend their decision-making processes associated with energy developments within existing legislation.

The Province of British Columbia's response in this regard perhaps illustrates this type of reaction as well as any province. In the early 1970s, decisions on major projects were based largely on a financial review by the Cabinet and a technical (engineering) analysis conducted under the province's *Water Act* (1960) (O'Riordan, 1981). All diversions and storages of water required a water licence under the Act. This was granted by a civil servant—the Comptroller of Water Rights, who made his decision largely on questions of dam safety and the protection of the rights of existing water users. He had discretionary powers to call public hearings under the act to discuss these issues.

Because these hearings were the only forum at which the public could question the need for these projects and their environmental impacts, their scope was greatly expanded at hearings into the Pend d'Oreille and Revelstoke projects in 1974 and 1976 respectively (O'Riordan & O'Riordan, 1980). BC Hydro produced fairly comprehensive environmental and social impact assessments based on a set of guidelines produced by the Environment and Land Use Committee of the Cabinet. Subsequent to these project hearings, the government developed Guidelines for Benefit Cost Analysis and for Compensation and Mitigation (1980) which required BC Hydro and other major developers to evaluate generation alternatives and pay financial compensation for the impacts of their project on public resources.

Compensation for loss of private property rights is required under law, as is the case in Britain, but unavoidable losses to recreation, fisheries, wildlife, timber and mineral resources are now also subject to compensation. Generally, the developer is required to pay up to the estimated value of these public resource losses to the provincial government, which in turn allocates the funds towards improving resource management programmes in the region affected by the project. These programmes, plus mitigatory measures such as pollution control devices and the regulation of reservoirs to avoid particularly sensitive environmental areas, do lead to a better allocation of resources than has been the case in the past. Recently, British Columbia Hydro and Power Authority has paid out over $10 million in compensation for loss of fish and wildlife habitat and for the development of recreational facilities associated with the Pend d'Oreille and Revelstoke projects. These funds are currently being used to construct and operate spawning channels and hatcheries and to increase the productivity of key wildlife areas in regions affected by the major power projects.

In addition, there are now strengthened procedures for monitoring project construction and operation to ensure that the environmental guidelines and regulatory provisions are adhered to by the developer. Generally, the proponent pays for these project monitors, though they report directly to the provincial environmental agencies. Similar arrangements have been made to monitor changes in the social environment, from inflation in local markets caused by the influx of construction workers to the provision of a range of social and community services required by the affected municipalities.

Although the Water Comptroller expanded the scope of the hearings under the *Water Act* to deal with these environmental, social and economic issues, when it came to granting a Conditional Water Licence, he was required by the narrow provisions of the act to restrict the terms and conditions associated with the licence to matters of public safety and compensation/mitigation for water-related resource impacts. He could not judge directly on social concerns, nor on the question of project need. As the granting of a water licence is appealable to the provincial cabinet, major public interest groups in fact appealed of his decisions on both the Pend d'Oreille and Revelstoke projects on these broader issues. In both cases, the cabinet upheld the decision to construct these projects.

Although these two project decisions made the cabinet aware of the deficiencies in the legislation, it was the result of a controversy over a major transmission line that tipped the scales and forced the cabinet to change policy. In 1978, BC Hydro proposed a 500 kV transmission line to bring additional power from the mainland to Vancouver Island. The proposed route crossed a major cottage recreational area located on the mainland coast about 100 km north of Vancouver. Unlike HEP developments, there is no equivalent requirement under the provincial *Land Act* to call a public hearing on such a project. Consequently, the transmission line was approved without a hearing* though it was subject to a detailed environmental assessment. The lack of any formal public hearing to discuss project need and alternatives raised public frustrations to the point of localised civil disobedience akin to the problems with motorway inquiries in Britain in the mid-1970s. Clearly some new legislation was required that provided a consistent review for all major energy projects in the province. Other provinces also expanded their regulatory procedures without changing legislation. Alberta, for example, has an established Energy Resources Conservation Board that is mainly responsible for considering questions of project need and energy depletion policies. However, environmental issues were recently tacked onto the hearing process for the Cold Lake Oil Sands project proposed by Imperial Oil Ltd. through the appointment of senior officials from the provincial Ministry of Environment on to the panel that conducts the hearings. But generally, land use and environmental issues are not given the same emphasis as the energy resources issues in the board's report to the cabinet.

In many ways, these extensions to the public hearing process parallel a similar process in Britain, where the local public inquiry has also become the only public forum at which policy as well as regulatory issues can be debated prior to formal energy project decisions.

The success of these adjustments varies across the country and depends upon the personality of the public official conducting the hearings and the

* BC Hydro conducted an informal public consultation programme, but there was no formal hearing under an impartial commission or inspector.

avenues for appeal. In British Columbia, the willingness of the Water Comptroller to listen to all issues diffused some public anxieties. The fact that there was a political avenue for appeals also helped to limit frustrations over the process for a while until it became apparent that the policy issues on the public mind were not really tackled head-on by the cabinet at appeal hearings. In other provinces a similar pattern emerged. No matter how broad-minded the public servant conducting regulatory hearings, the constraints inherent in such a regulatory process simply did not provide an avenue for informed public discussion of the more general policy issues. Accordingly, pressure continued to mount for major changes in legislation.

### Legislative Charges

A number of provinces have recognised that the public concerns over energy developments on land use and resource planning are so extensive that new legislation is required to tackle the problem. Tinkering with existing institutions or even the occasional inquiry commission is simply not adequate to satisy a general discontent with existing policy-making processes. To resolve this concern, the British Columbia government recently enacted *the Utilities Commission Act* (1980) which establishes a Utilities Commission with both policy advisory and regulatory powers. Under the act, all major energy projects in the province must obtain an Energy Project Certificate before a project can be built. This certificate can be granted only by the cabinet based on the advice of the Utilities Commission after it has held public hearings. The terms of reference for these hearings are set by both the Ministers of Energy and Environment. Any exemptions from public hearings must be agreed to by both ministers. Thus, these two ministers have statutory responsibilities under the act to ensure that both their mandates are protected. The terms of reference that are passed to the Utilities Commission for its public hearings into major energy developments and can include the major issues of project need in the context of provincial energy policy and that management of land use and environmental impacts. A general diagram of the project planning and approval process is outlined in Figure 6.3.

In the case of major projects the application for an Energy Project Certificate is supported by an environmental assessment, a social-community impact statement and a comprehensive benefit-cost analysis prepared in accordance with provincial guidelines (1977). These documents are reviewed by a wide range of government ministries for compliance with regulations and various policies and a deficiency statement may be prepared where the proponent has not submitted adequate documentation. If the application is sent to the Utilities Commission for a public hearing, then any government ministry or public intervenor may prepare a brief for the commission. In the case of government resource ministries, the main

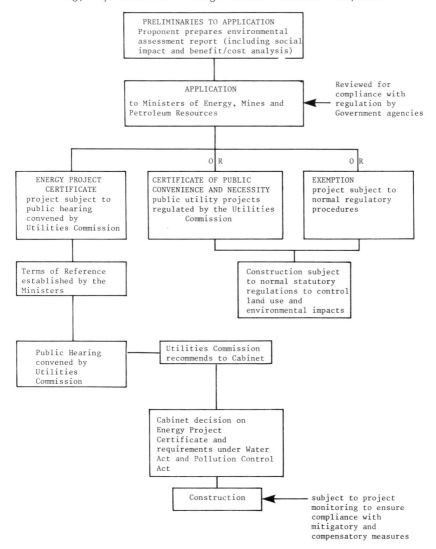

FIG 6.3 *Energy Project Review Process in British Columbia*

emphasis is placed on ways to mitigate and compensate for project impacts, rather than to state direct opposition to the project. Any major differences of opinion between ministries would have been resolved during the review of the application before the Ministries of Energy and Environment collectively decide which path the application should follow.

The provisions of the act are now in the process of being tested, and there are already indications of problems in its application. The first major project hearing involved a proposed 900 MW(e) hydropower project located at 'Site C' on the Peace River in northern British Columbia (see Figure 6.1), which began in November, 1981. The terms of reference provided to the hearing panel (which is established by cabinet order) were comprehensive and included questions of both project need and management of environmental impacts.

The main issue centres around the need and timing of the project, since the lower range of demand forecasts would suggest that the project is not required until after 1990, whereas BC Hydro has applied for completion by 1988. The corporation argues that surplus power could be exported to the United States. The principal environmental concern involves the flooding of approximately 2000 hectares of highly productive agricultural lands, which, because of a local micro-climate in the valley-bottom, are capable of producing quality grains and vegetables. In a province where the protection of agricultural land is a sensitive political issue, this impact will provide a major focus to the environmental phase of the hearings.

As a beginning, the hearing panel completed two months of testimony on electrical energy demand forecasts. A further four phases of hearings then followed, dealing with alternative sources of supply; project cost and design; social, environment and land use factors and benefit/cost and financial analysis. The panel conducted an independent and rigorous examination of all participants, including representatives of various provincial government ministries. To provide technical information on the project to the hearing panel and the public at large, a number of government ministries released background papers covering impacts on agriculture, environment, outdoor recreation, labour and energy forecasts and other items. Representatives from each ministry were required to appear at the hearings and were subject to cross-examination from registered intervenors. From the very early stages of the process, it appeared that all participants were on their mettle to achieve their own individual goals and thus set precedents for future headings. This does not always make for an efficient process, fostering some prolonged legal debates at times. The hearings on Site C lasted from November, 1981 to November 1982.

The costs of the hearings were not covered by the commission or the provincial government, but were being directly passed onto BC Hydro. These expenses included the legal and consulting fees for the hearing panel itself, plus costs borne by public interest groups and other individual intervenors judged by the panel chairman to be justified. In this way, there was no financial incentive for the panel or the intervenors to make the hearing process more efficient, another factor contributing to the protracted length of these hearings.

The cabinet also has the power to require the Utilities Commission to hold public hearings into the more general issues of energy that are not related to any specific project. For example, the commission has been asked to determine whether there is a surplus of natural gas in the province over and above anticipated domestic requirements in the forseeable future. Under the Utilities Commission Act, no energy resources in any form can be exported out of the province without an Energy Removal Certificate, which is granted by the cabinet on the advice of the commission. The commission might thus recommend on the scope of the terms and conditions that would be placed on Energy Removal Certificates involving natural gas. In addition, the government is currently considering terms of reference for a public inquiry into whether offshore oil and petroleum exploration should be resumed, the environmental and social consequences of this programme and the terms and conditions that should be applied. Subsequent hearings would also have to be held by the Utilities Commission on any specific discovery before production and trans-shipment to shore could begin.

Ontario has also made a major legislative change with the introduction of the *Ontario Environmental Assessment Act* in 1975. An Environment Assessment Board has been established to hold public hearings into the environmental consequences of all projects that are regulated under the act. The act itself contains provisions that proponents will consider alternative projects and their consequences as part of their environmental assessment. In recent years, the board has become involved in hearing energy project proposals from Ontario Hydro and, as it is, an open public forum, the public has demanded that it consider issues pertaining to project need. However, as the Porter Royal Commission largely exhausted public input into this topic in the late 1970s, the main emphasis is placed on environmental and land use issues. The assessment board makes its reports and decisions public. Though there are provisions under the act to permit the cabinet to overturn the decision within 28 days, the board's decision is otherwise binding.

Other provinces have recently brought in or have strengthened their statutory powers requiring that major developments be subject to a complete environmental assessment prior to decisions. Newfoundland, Quebec and Saskatchewan have all introduced this type of legislation. The pattern of these acts is roughly the same; the energy developers must prepare comprehensive assessments of project impacts on the natural and social environments and general land use in the area. These reports are subject to public scrutiny and debate by an assessment board or commission, which in turn reports to the cabinet.

**Reflections on the Policy-Making Framework**

The broadened energy project planning process upstream of a cabinet decision in British Columbia and generally across Canada has resulted in more sensitive environmental designs for energy projects. With the advent of compensatory and mitigatory programmes, there is certainly a more equitable regional balance between energy production and environmental management. But these relatively small gains are being achieved at the considerable cost of extended planning horizons, complex administrative arrangements to review project applications and expensive public hearings. Given the experience from other countries, including Britain, that such costs are difficult to control, it seems appropriate to question whether the benefits of a more comprehensive and public energy policy appraisal and project review process are warranted.

It is postulated here that policy outcomes relating to long-term energy development and land use strategies cannot be made 'rationally' i.e. according to some explicit or even implicit set of values that balance economic, social and environmental issues. This is because energy project developments such as the Mackenzie Valley Pipeline or the Stikine HEP project in British Columbia now involve a complex set of policy issues for which no defined frame of reference has yet been developed. Lowi (1970) categorised public policy-making into three broad areas—distributive or allocative (e.g. allocation of resource and land use, tariffs), redistributive (e.g. taxation, social programmes) and regulatory (e.g. project design). Until the mid-1970s energy project decisions largely belonged to the regulatory category, with emphasis placed on controls to project design to reduce impacts on the local environment and land base. Perhaps the main reason why energy project decisions are now so difficult is that they cut across all three policy sets.

Distributive issues are well illustrated by the two-tier pricing system that now exists in Canada for oil and gas—the world price for exports and a lower domestic price. Redistribution policies are used to maintain a unified domestic price for oil across Canada, even though the eastern provinces must import oil at world prices. Major issues of regulation are now raised by the need to control emissions of $SO_2$ from smoke-stacks of large-scale thermal plants. But even the regulatory issues are of such a scale that they effect the allocation of resources such as the flooding of large areas of productive lands for HEP projects, or the opening up of Canada's northlands with pipelines and access roads. All three types of issues and many more are inextricably intertwined in today's energy project decisions, resulting in a smorgasbord in which decision-makers must attempt to balance distributive and regulatory policies through procedures that must constantly be modified to match the dynamics of the situation.

Recently, a number of analysts of the energy policy-making system in Britain have argued in favour of a two-tier hearing process that would separate the distributive issues from the regulatory ones (O'Riordan and Sewell, 1981; Outer Circle Policy Unit, 1979; Pearce *et al.* 1979). Under such a system, the first stage would consider the broader issues associated with project need, levels of public safety and alternatives (both on the demand and supply sides). These are generally issues that are generic to a class of energy projects and about which general policies could be formulated, or so the theory says. The second stage would be directed at the regulation of specific projects to meet site-specific environmental and land use concerns, which should be resolved in the context of the broader first-tier policy decisions. The conventional inquiry process can safely be applied at the second-stage, since the substantive policy questions had already been resolved at the first stage.

There are a number of reasons why this process cannot work at present. First, in British Columbia at least no overall resource management framework exists in which to make 'distributive' or allocation decisions such as the amount of energy development required or the amount of resources (fisheries, forestry, agriculture) that can be sacrificed to permit large-scale HEP developments to be built. Such a framework would be extremely difficult to develop because it would require sound information on resource potentials and an ability to forecast development with some reasonable degree of confidence.

Second, the public at this time are not organised to exert political leverage at the generic level of energy development issues. This has been demonstrated by the lack of informed public input to structure planning programmes in Britain and at the Porter Commission hearings described earlier in this chapter. The main public response is associated with 'backyard' issues which are generally project-specific. A major educational programme is required to encourage significant numbers of the public or even organised public interest groups to become actively involved in these broader issues outside the context of a specific project. Unfortunately in British Columbia and probably elsewhere in Canada, governments are not yet prepared to develop such a programme.

Third, the realities of the political system in Canada are such that few politicians are willing to make such broad policy decisions on controversial energy projects any earlier than they absolutely have to. As a result, they prefer to wait until a project is well advanced in its planning before any decisions are made. Thus, energy projects that are subject to public hearings and inquiries at assessment boards or utility commissions in Canada tend to be the only options immediately available for development; their advanced engineering and environmental designs require substantial costs in time and money, all of which build up the proponent's commitment to these projects. This level of commitment in turn places considerable political pressure on the decision-makers to the frustration of the public interest groups, who often feel that project decisions are made prior to the hearings themselves. As a result, single energy project decisions are made without sufficient thought being given to the allocative aspects of resource and land use.

There are doubtless many other reasons why there cannot be a smooth transition from policy appraisal to project analysis at this time. However, the policy-making process has come a long way in the past decade in response to public pressure and there are already signs in British Columbia at least that such a two-tier system may yet develop in some rudimentary form over the next decade.

Consideration of a two-phase hearing for off-shore petroleum exploration and its subsequent development (if proved justifiable) is one example of a move in this direction. The second move is the development of a regional resource management framework for the province. As noted in the introduction to this chapter, it is becoming increasingly clear that the province cannot meet all the demands for timber extraction, mining developments, energy production, agricultural expansion, fisheries and wildlife protection. Conflicts in resource use inevitably occur, though to a small extent these can be reduced through more intensive resource management. But this costs money. To develop a framework for making the necessary allocative decisions, the government introduced its *Land Use Act* as a bill before the provincial legislature in December, 1981. Under Part II of this Act, the resource ministries in the government together with the Crown corporations such as BC Hydro are required to develop quantified resource management objectives for each of seven major regions in the province. These objectives will set out the resource production (cubic metres of timber, numbers of big game species, sport fisheries, cattle, settlement etc.) required to meet current and future demands. They will also assess the land base required to support these levels of production at specific levels of management. Clearly there will have to be trade-offs where conflicts occur, or where the costs of intensive management cannot be justified in social and economic terms. Nevertheless, through a more systematic approach to resource planning, the critical land base required to achieve approved resource production objectives can be identified and the implications of not meeting specified resource management targets can also be made more explicit.

A third opportunity to come to grips with the broader issues of energy policy would be for the cabinet to direct the BC Utilities Commission to call a series of public meetings on a whole systems plan for electrical power planning for the next 20 years. A number of generation and conservation alternatives should be proposed and their impacts on the province's resources analysed in the context of these regional resource management strategies. It remains unlikely that the cabinet would commit itself to any specific project until after project-specific hearings. However, the larger issues of energy planning and resource management strategies would be publically aired and would thus provide more focus to the debate at the project hearings themselves.

It is difficult to believe that an energy and regional resource policy framework will ever be established to satisfy public concerns over project design, land use and resource compensation. The loss of wilderness rivers or unique stocks of Pacific salmon and steelhead trout are not easily evaluated in 'rational' terms. It is also difficult to develop explicit policies relating industrial development, economic growth and energy generation especially in a province such as British Columbia where the public tends to be sharply divided over environmental and economic issues. As a result, any energy policy statement released by the provincial government tends to be too vaguely defined to provide any specific direction on energy project development. Even a small step towards developing such a systematic framework could pay big dividends however. If regional resource management objectives were quantified, each resource ministry would have a clear set of targets against which it would claim compensation, should these targets not be met because of project development. In cases where strategically important resources would be irreparably lost, each ministry would have a stronger case for vetoing project proposals. Hopefully, with an embryonic system in place, energy developments could be steered towards the less sensitive environments before there is a large commitment of time and money into project design.

**Conclusions**

The decade of the 1970s witnessed great strides in improving the energy project decision-making process in Canada, with the advent of environmental assessments, compensation and mitigation, and more attention to controlling environmental risk. This process needs to be further consolidated in the 1980s by tying it with regional land use strategies and energy development programmes that are closely inter-linked.

Such a process will not be achieved without some political costs. In British Columbia, the time and costs of project planning have increased exponentially in the past 5 years. There is no doubt that the expanded democratic process now evolving under the *Utilities Commission Act* will have to be traded-off against increased administrative costs. BC Hydro applied for an Energy Project Certificate in September, 1980, the public hearings commenced in November, 1981, and a decision was not made until two years later. Such delays are also evident in Britain with the Belvoir coal inquiry and the petro-chemical complex at Moss Morran in Scotland.

In the final analysis, it appears most likely that the political systems in Canada will 'muddle through' based on a slowly evolving policy-making process such as described above. Given the inherent complexities in the policy issues, there can be no turning back to a site-specific project assessment based on regulatory issues. The larger questions of energy need, economic growth and resource allocation at a regional scale will dominate future energy project assessments in British Columbia. However, the province, like its counterparts across the country, has not yet developed a well-conceived regional resource management policy linked to an industrial and energy development strategy to provide the framework for site-specific project decisions. It seems unlikely that such a policy will be formulated for the next several years, because it represents a major analytical challenge to any society with its mix of values and powerfully entrenched interest groups. If the decade of the 1970s witnessed a major thrust into environmental assessment procedures, it appears that the decade of the 1980s will see an expansion of both the time and geographic horizons to forge major improvements to regional resource and energy policy-making. History has shown that progress in developing energy project appraisal policies in Canada has generally been positive; perhaps that provides the best source of optimism for the future.

## References

Berger, Mr. Justice T. R. (1977) *Northern Frontier, Northern Homeland. The Report of the Mackenzie Valley Pipeline Inquiry; Volumes 1 and 2.* Ministry of Supply and Services, Ottawa.

BC Ministry of Energy, Mines and Petroleum Resources (1981) *British Columbia Energy Supply and Requirements Forecasts, 1980/1985,* Victoria, B. C.

Environment and Land Use Committee Secretariat (1980) *Environmental and Social Impact Mitigation and Compensation Guidelines,* Province of British Columbia, Victoria, B. C.

Environment and Land Use Committee Secretariat (1977) *Guidelines for Benefit-Cost Analysis,* Province of British Columbia, Victoria, B. C.

Lowi, T. (1970) Decision-making vs. policy-making: Towards an antidote for technocracy, *Public Administration Review,* Volume 30, May/June, pp.314–325.

Lysyk, K. M., Bohmer, E. E. and Phelps, W. (1978) *Alaska Highway Pipeline Inquiry,* Ministry of Supply and Services, Ottawa.

O'Riordan, J. (1981) The British Columbia Experience, in *Project Appraisal and Policy Review* (Eds. o'Riordan, T. and Sewell, W. R. D.), 95–123, J. Wiley & Sons, Chichester.

O'Riordan, J. and O'Riordan, T. (1980) How Can Citizen Input Best be Utilised by Decision-Makers? Proceedings of a National Workshop *Public Participation in Environmental Decision-Making: Strategies for Change,* Ed. Saddler, B. The Environmental Council off Alberta, Edmonton, Alberta.

Outer Circle Policy Unit (1979) *The Big Public Inquiry,* Council for Science and Society, London.

Pearce, D., Edwards, L. and Bueret, G., (1979) *Decision-Making for Energy Futures,* MacMillan Press, London, England.

Porter, A. (1980) *The Report of the Royal Commission on Electric Power Planning,* Queen's Printer of Ontario, Toronto, Ontario.

Sewell, W. R. D. (1981) How Canada Responded: The Berger Inquiry, in *Project Appraisal and Policy Review* (Eds. O'Riordan, T. and Sewell, W. R. D.), 77–94, J. Wiley & Sons, Chichester.

CHAPTER 7

# Nuclear Power and Land-Use Planning in the Netherlands

ANTOINE H. M. JANSSEN

## Introduction

In many respects the problems which arise from conflicting land-use requirements in modern industrial societies are found in their most intense form in the Netherlands. The very high population densities, averaging 415 persons per square kilometre and rising to over 900 persons per square kilometre in the densest parts of the western Netherlands, combine with the unique geographical circumstances of the country to create a situation where the ordering of activities in space is of singular significance. As the Dutch Ministry of Housing and Physical Planning notes (1981): '(a) sound land-use policy in the Netherlands is a matter of extraordinary importance: it is even an absolute condition for the proper continued existence of Netherlands society'. The response of the society to this planning imperative has included the development of sophisticated interrelated planning processes operating at the national, provincial and local levels but retaining a very important role for the lower levels of administration.

Part of this planning response includes the provision for integrated thematic planning of major structural features required in a complex industrial country. In recent years, attention has been given to planning for open-air recreation, airports location, military training facilities, traffic and transport, housing, water supply and so on. However, energy supply facilities have inevitably been the subject of considerable attention as well. Energy matters have a particular significance for the Netherlands. Not only was the country especially badly affected by the oil supply difficulties of 1973-74 but its economy is notably dependent on the modern petro-chemical industries and the petroleum and coal entrepôt functions clustered in the country's sea ports. The discovery of the massive Slochteren gas reserves in Groningen in the north east has had both beneficial and adverse impacts on the Netherlands' economy and made the issue of energy management a very transparent one in the economic and political debate occurring there. This chapter considers the way in which the sophisticated Dutch planning system

167

has interacted with the issues arising from the attempt to develop nuclear power as a major contributor to electricity generation capacity. It discusses how the resulting problems have demanded particular responses and how the considerations which have come to light, at least in part, from the operation of a systematic, rational, anticipatory siting procedure have required the introduction of protracted and wide-ranging political advice-seeking and decision-making procedures.

**The Current Energy Situation in the Netherlands**

Despite extensive natural gas reserves the national energy situation in the Netherlands is not without its problems. At present more than half of the national primary energy consumption is met by indigenous natural gas. Domestic gas consumption amounts to about $45 \times 10^9$ m$^3$ annually and a somewhat greater quantity is exported. Even if an extensive energy conservation policy is adopted, as intended by the government, Dutch gas reserves will be exhausted in about 40 years. Oil and related products meet about 40 per cent of the country's primary energy needs, a lower proportion than other western countries (IEA, 1981). At present therefore, more than 90 per cent of total national primary energy demand is met by oil and natural gas.

Because of uncertainties about future energy availability, especially of oil, the promotion of other energy sources is being actively pursued. This includes coal and nuclear energy as well as relevant renewable energy sources. This programme can yield results only in the long run because of the difficulty of re-orienting the energy supply and use system based on oil and gas. The Netherlands will need to import all the quantities of coal it will require. Indigenous coal production ended in the early 1970s when the price of energy made it uneconomic to keep the existing coal mines in operation. The re-introduction of coal, especially in the industrial sector, will be a laborious affair because of difficulties related to environmental impact and infrastructure requirements. At present there are two nuclear power stations operating at Borssele and Dodewaard with a total capacity of around 500 MW(e) and it is not likely that any new capacity will come into operation for the next 10 to 15 years. If there were to be no expansion of nuclear electricity generating capacity at all then for both the replacement of the existing generating capacity and for any eventual growth of consumption, coal is the only practical alternative to natural gas and oil. Whatever their eventual possibilities, renewable energy sources are at present too limited in their ability to change this picture drastically.

Total present public sector electricity production capacity is around 16 GW(e). Present demand levels for electricity mean that about 4 GW(e) is now superfluous over and above a back-up capacity of around 3 GW(e). Given an annual growth in demand of 1 per cent this superfluous capacity would not become fully utilised until the mid-1990s. In 1980 almost 80 per cent of the fuel consumed in public electricity generation was oil or gas, both fuels tied to high prices in the world energy market. In other EC countries the oil and gas share in electricity is around 35 per cent. In the main countries in economic competition with the Netherlands—France and the Federal Republic of Germany—the oil/gas share is below 25 per cent. This heavy concentration on oil in the Netherlands is not only unattractive from an energy policy point of view (especially as oil makes up around 40 per cent of the consumption) but it is also extremely unfavourable from a price policy viewpoint. There is considerable concern about the effect of high energy prices on industrial competitiveness and the problem is made more important by the energy-intensive structure of the Netherlands' economy. It is now an aim to meet at least 40 per cent of electricity demand in the year 2000 by coal-fired generation. (Editor's note: a general review of the Netherlands' energy situation in English is given in van Stein Callenfels and Bunge, 1982).

**Energy Policy and the Nuclear Debate**

*The Emergence of Energy as a Political Issue*

In September, 1974, the Dutch government, which at the time included members of the socialist party, published an Energy Memorandum in which the emphasis of energy policy was on slowing down consumption and increasing the security of energy supply provision (Tweede Kamer, 1974–75a). It was argued that it would be inappropriate to employ hazardous methods of electricity production whose development had been justified on the need to meet high rates of growth of energy consumption. Nevertheless it was decided in 1974 to allow a moderate extension of nuclear power capacity by around 3,000 MW(e) (three plants each of 1,000 MW(e)). These plants were intended to come on stream around 1985. Further expansion was held to be unwise for the reasons just mentioned and also unnecessary because of the availability of Dutch natural gas which was expected to be able to cover an important part of the national requirements for energy. This latter interpretation displayed a certain superficiality and complacency which would certainly not be adopted at present, given current policies over the preservation of national gas supplies. The 3,000 MW(e) expansion was tied to 4 conditions:

1. Central government was to have a decisive voice over a number of essential points in the organisation of electricity production.
2. A complete risk analysis would have to be drawn up by those concerned, with due observance of government directive.
3. The Gezondheidsraad (the national medical advisory board) was to provide advice about the influence of nuclear energy on public health and the environment.

4. The Commissie Reactorveiligheid (Commission on Reactor Safety) was to deliver a report on the safety aspects of the nuclear energy cycle in the Netherlands.

Of these 4 conditions, the risk, public health and reactor safety studies were delivered in 1975, within a short time of their being required (Tweede Kamer, 1975–1976). There has been little change in the organisation of the Netherlands' electricity supply system, which is in the hands of several semi-public companies which act more or less independently of central government. It is generally recognised that such a structure would be inappropriate for any extension of nuclear energy, so that although the existing nuclear capacity is controlled by such companies, it is intended that future licences would be issued only to a fully state-owned organisation. The Ministry of Economic Affairs, responsible for the country's energy policy, would *not* participate in the licensing, to ensure the separation of policy-making and policy overview and regulation.

In the years after 1975 the question of the trend and composition of future national energy policy came to be a very dominant issue in national political discussion. A vociferous anti-nuclear movement emerged in the Netherlands and this has had a strong influence on the focus and intensity of the debate.

The form of this debate and the responses of successive governments to it is of considerable interest because various features, three in particular, reflect some of the policy responses which have been suggested in other countries, including the UK, to deal with the problems of achieving a national consensus on energy policy and reconciling land-use constraints with the supply of energy. The three particular features are:

(a) the emergence of the debate on energy policy has, at least to an extent, been the result of attempts to lay down a rational planning basis for the location of energy facilities;

(b) the preparation of a detailed national energy policy statement, including a discussion of the location of energy facilities, within the constraints of national spatial planning guidelines;

(c) the decision to have a national debate on the future form of the Netherlands' energy supply policy, the so-called 'Brede Maatschappelijke Discussie over Energie' (Broad Public Debate on Energy) (BMD).

As noted in the section below on the selection of sites for nuclear power stations, a special Aanvullend Structuurschema Electriciteitsvoorziening (Complementary Electricity Power Supply Structure Plan) (Tweede Kamer, 1976–77) was published in 1977 which identified twelve potential sites for nuclear stations which were to be whittled down by a process of public consultation. However, the general awareness of location issues raised by the publication of the plan, coupled with subsequent political changes, led to considerable uncertainty about the future form of energy supply. At the end of 1977, a new cabinet decided that as far as possible, nuclear power should be a policy of the last resort in a country as populous as the Netherlands and that the plans contained in the Principle Decision of 1974 for 3000 MW(e) should not be implemented until the problem of nuclear waste disposal had been finally resolved as well as uncertainties over the safety of nuclear plants.

Such fundamental rethinking of the future pattern of energy supply policy provided the spur for the developing conviction that the advantages and disadvantages of nuclear energy should be examined in the course of a wide-ranging examination of the entire Netherlands' energy situation in which there should be the widest possible participation. The government accepted the desirability of such a Public Discussion in 1978 and published its basic ideas in 1979 (Tweede Kamer, 1978–79).

## The Government Statement on Energy Policy

It was accepted that before the Public Discussion could take place, there should be published a comprehensive statement on the government's interpretation of the options for energy supply and management open to the country, which could be critically evaluated as part of the Public Discussion. The first section of this important statement—*Part 1, General*—was published in September, 1979 and raised the question, based on insights acquired since the first Energy Memorandum of 1974, of how energy consumption may develop and ways in which energy conservation might be promoted (Tweede Kamer, 1979–80a). The Memorandum concentrated on general policies for ensuring adequate energy supplies within the limits fixed by the goals of social and economic policy. It discussed the future role of oil and natural gas in energy supply and the role which renewable and other novel sources of energy might play, together with the timing of such possibilities. Finally, it dealt in detail with the possible use of coal for the country's energy supply. It aimed to promote an understanding of the size of the energy consumption requirements to be covered by various sources of energy.

*Part 2, 'Coal Memorandum'*, was published in February, 1980 and dealt with the possibilities and problems of an increased use of coal as a substitute for oil and natural gas, notably for fuelling power stations and for industrial heat and steam raising (Tweede Kamer, 1979–80b). The Memorandum identified what were considered as minimum coal requirements but decisions on whether to use coal on a larger scale were found to be related to other possibilities, including further use of nuclear energy. The Coal Memorandum also introduced an extensive research and development programme in coal energy. Finally, it discussed the infrastructural aspects of increased coal consumption.

*Part 3, The Memorandum on Power Generation Fuels* was published in July, 1980 and in it the cabinet set forth its views of fuels in electricity power stations, explaining in detail the considerations supporting these views

(Tweede Kamer, 1979–80c). The publication of this Memorandum served as the culmination of the other two Memoranda. It sought to sketch out a complete picture of all aspects of the expansion of the country's nuclear energy capacity. It derived its general energy policy framework from the Memorandum, Part I and augmented this by paying extra attention to more specific economic and industrial energy aspects. It focused on the problems caused by nuclear power stations in the fields of public health, environmental control and urban and regional planning. Of course, it also considered the particular aspects of nuclear energy such as proliferation, safety, storage of nuclear waste, terrorism and sabotage and the safety measures and procedures to be adopted against such hazards.

Part III of the Memorandum therefore also raised the physical aspects of nuclear power station siting. Based on these aspects a selection was made of prospective locations for nuclear power stations. This physical consideration was made in a separate chapter (13) of the Memorandum which has been seen as having independent character because the questions raised in it were not necessarily considered to be part of the Public Discussion on energy policy. In fact this chapter is concerned with the translation of a Principle Decision of the government into actual concrete development. However, as this Principle Decision was one of the main objects of attention of the energy debate, it was decided to include planning aspects of nuclear power within the Public Discussion, but channelled through the normal planning institutions, rather than the special organisation set up for the more strategic questions by the Plan Memorandum of August, 1979 (Tweede Kamer, 1978–79) (the Stuurgroep of the BMD discussed next).

### The Broad Public Discussion on Energy (BMD)

The object of the Public Discussion was 'to involve the population in the shaping of an opinion on energy problems in general and the nuclear energy issue in particular on the basis of the fullest possible information, duly tested for reliability, for the purpose of a justified subsequent decision-making by the government and parliament'. The chief elements of this goal were defined as follows:

(a) Information

Public opinion-shaping should be based on the fullest possible comprehensive information, duly tested for reliability;

1. Relevant facts and arguments should be available to anyone desirous of knowing them.
2. To this end a Stuurgroep (steering group) should be established initially to draw up an inventory of opinions, facts and views contributed from all sides and subsequently to derive the best possible objectivification by verifying the data contributed and testing assumptions and views for their probability and reliability.

3. Next, information on these matters should be distributed on a large scale in a form which everybody would be able to understand.

(b) Opinion-shaping

On the basis of the information so made available, a thorough opinion-shaping, covering the widest possible circles, should be stimulated.

1. To this end, a discussion should be organised under an independent leadership, ensuring large-scale participation by the population and the hearing of all views. Following this discussion there must be no ground whatever for claims that there had been insufficient opportunity for opinion-shaping.

2. The public discussion should result in a systematic collection and evaluation of the opinions, facts and views proffered for the purpose of decision-making by the government and parliament.

(c) Decision-making

The Public Discussion will have to help the government and Parliament make the final decision subsequent to the provisional decision mentioned above, on the basis of the fullest possible understanding of the matter and after an intensive and structured process of public opinion-shaping. The Public Discussion cannot affect the responsibility borne by the government and Parliament for the 'ultimate decision' (Tweede Kamer, 1978–79).

It should be noticed that the Public Discussion in no way substituted for the decision-making by Parliament. It was seen as a new preliminary phase of parliamentary decision-making which, if it showed a consensus in one direction or the other, would certainly have a great influence on the political decision subsequently taken. The government proposed that the Public Discussion should be led by a Stuurgroep composed of government-appointed persons who could command confidence in the widest circles and who would be capable of arriving at a balanced judgement on the complicated problems of nuclear power and energy policy. However, special expertise on nuclear energy was not seen as a prerequisite for membership of the Stuurgroep. In carrying out its duties the Stuurgroep was required to take great care that all the relevant problems were to be considered, that participation in the discussion was to be as wide and varied as possible, that the information to be furnished to the public at large should be both easily intelligible and of high quality, that the Public Discussion should be completed in the allotted time and that the results of the discussion should be reported fully and scrupulously.

It was intended that the Public Discussion should not take more than 2 years and should consist of two phases. The first, the so-called 'information phase' should be concerned mainly with the collection and testing of the information to serve as the basis of the second phase which was the actual Public Discussion.

In detail the plan for the Public Discussion was as follows:

*Phase I:* Information Phase

1. The Cabinet will publish an Energy Memorandum, and summaries of this would be widely distributed.
2. The Stuurgroep will collect reactions to the Memorandum. In the first place these would be comments and contributions by groups and organisations which are already actively concerned with energy policy and nuclear power issues or which might be expected to have an interest in these matters. In principle, however, the Stuurgroep was to welcome any contributions whatsoever.
3. The Stuurgroep will subject the collected reactions to systematic investigation, analysing the arguments on energy problems in terms of the assumptions and facts on which they are based. The Stuurgroep will then attempt to 'objectify' these arguments as far as possible by verifying the alleged facts and testing the assumptions for their proba- bility. To this end the Stuurgroep may hear both sides to any argument, consult experts at home or abroad or employ any such means as it considers suitable. The Stuurgroep will prepare an interim report containing its findings as verified facts and tested assumptions. It will also state in this interim report what it considers to be the main issues for discussion during Phase II and to do this the Stuurgroep will identify those questions to which it considers that answers are given, stating the facts, arguments and hazards involved.

*Phase II:* Discussion Phase

1. The Stuurgroep will ensure a wide circulation of information about results of Phase I, including distribution of the interim report on a large scale.
2. The Stuurgroep will stimulate public awareness of energy problems in general and opinion on nuclear energy in particular by promoting an intensive and structured discussion of the results of Phase I amongst the widest sections of society.
3. The Stuurgroep will collect, analyse and assess the arguments, opinions and standpoints advanced during this discussion, prepare a final report containing its conclusions and publish this report which will then mark the end of the Public Discussion.

However, the appointment of the Stuurgroep members took a long time. In the first place it was difficult to find a chairman for the group. Many potential chairmen were unwilling to take on such a potentially controversial task. In the end, in January, 1981, a former cabinet minister, Dr. D. R. de Brauw took on the task. Subsequently there was again a delay before other members of the group could be appointed. The group consists of nine members with very different backgrounds. They hold, or have held, high positions in academia, trade, industry and the judiciary. The composition of the Stuurgroep seeks to reflect as closely as possible a balance of the main social positions over nuclear energy. For example, a former member of parliament who has always maintained the need to shut down existing Dutch nuclear capacity is a member of the group. However, it still remains to be seen whether this broadly-based group will be able to gain the confidence of the anti-nuclear movement in the Netherlands.


## Land-Use Planning in the Netherlands

### Planning Goals and National Characteristics

In a densely populated, highly educated, prosperous and small country such as the Netherlands, development of town and country is extraordinarily strongly interwoven. Many urban elements are to be found in rural areas. People from the towns move to the country and large parts of the rural areas serve as the towns' 'back gardens'. However, Dutch environmental policy aims to preserve the particular identity of the rural areas as much as possible. In the Orienterings nota Ruimtelijke Ordening (guidelines for physical planning) the government mentioned as a basic goal of planning policy the promotion of physical and ecological conditions such that:

1. The essential efforts of individuals and groups in society are demonstrated to a full advantage;
2. The diversity, coherence and survival of the physical environment are guaranteed as much as possible.

In the policy for the development of rural areas a strong emphasis used to be placed on the useful economic value of the areas for functions such as agriculture, forestry, recreation and so on. However, in recent years different grounds of valuation have emerged based on the experience of the landscape in its totality. As a result resistance arose against the construction of roads which affected natural beauty, against harbour works, high rise building, electricity stations, power transmission lines and so on.

There has also been an increasing awareness of the ecological interdependence of rural areas. Policy is therefore now aimed at doing justice to weighing environmental data, the experience of the landscape, economic aspects, the preservation of the rural population's living circumstances and the wishes and needs of the urban population. (Editor's note: a comprehensive review of the Netherlands' physical planning situation, in English, can be found in van Embden, Thoenes and Witsen (forthcoming)).

In the Netherlands land-use planning is not regarded as a discrete, autonomous policy sector but is integrated as one particular part of the many policy sectors which together form total government activity. The aim is to evaluate the land-use planning aspects of the entire range of policy sectors including traffic and transport, waterways, public housing, preservation of the natural and aesthetic environments, airport location, military training grounds, port facilities and the electricity supply system. The intention of land-use planning is to identify, evaluate and integrate the physical planning effects of decisions taken in all these different policy sectors. In the

Netherlands, with its high population density, this is of some importance if one accepts the principle that space should be subservient to man and society.

However, in 1973, in the third government 'Report on Physical Planning' (Rijksplanologische Dienst, 1973) the government ventured to raise the question of whether existing society and social and economic structures would gradually have to be adjusted to the constraints of space and environment if current social arrangements were to survive in the future. At present land-use planning in the Netherlands bears marks of both these interpretative approaches.

### Planning Processes

(Editor's note: English language accounts of physical and regional planning in the Netherlands are given in van Houten (1977), Brussaard (1980), Hazelhoff (1981) and Ministry of Housing and Physical Planning (1981)).

The Netherlands has many specific planning instruments and responsibility for their operation rests variously with each of the administrative levels of the country (state, province and municipality). The nature and strength of relations between these three levels of administration are determined by the decentralised structure of the Netherlands. Each level of the administration is essentially at liberty to conduct its own policy and to make its own regulations so long as conflict with the policy or regulations of a higher authority is avoided. Generally, the lower the level of administration the less abstract are the plans made and it is particularly at the municipality level that various policy directives are given shape in the form of specific obligatory regulations.

Quite often the plans worked out by a lower administrative level will not concur with the plans or policy of a higher level and may even go against these in a completely unacceptable manner. In such situations the higher authority has some means at its disposal to interfere in the planning process. In this respect at the state level, structural designs, structural schemes and the procedure for Planologische Kernbeslissing (crucial planning decision), play a part (Tweede Kamer, 1972, 1980–81). Structural designs give an indication of the overall spatial development of specified areas on a longer term basis, especially developments which the national government wishes to encourage in specific directions. In the case of electricity generation the 'structural scheme' and, above all, the procedure for a Planologische Kernbeslissing are of greater importance. To construct any major industrial development, especially electrical generating stations (irrespective of their fuel usage) a comprehensive planning process is regarded as indispensable in the Netherlands. Electricity supply is considered a matter of national importance and the associated costs of the provision of infrastructure and the environmental effects go well beyond mere local impacts and therefore require more than a local response.

The policy intentions of the central government over developments which have such a national importance have been contained in 'structural schemes' for several years. These schemes are subsequently subjected to a broadly-designed procedure for public participation, the procedure for a Planologische Kernbeslissing.

Although this procedure has as yet to be incorporated in any formal legal framework it has already been used for handling a considerable number of developments. It is designed to guarantee that a policy intention of the government is associated with the opportunity for the public to give their opinion on the policy. Experience has shown that many people freely use this opportunity. While the participation is taking place the government consults with the councils of the provinces and municipalities where realisation of the proposed policy could cause effects. Also, advisory bodies whose subject matters relate to the development proposed are expected to provide relevant advice to the government.

On the basis of the outcome of the participation exercise, the results of administrative consultation and the advice received, the government reviews its policy and then publishes a decision. In so doing the government mentions the reasons for rejection or acceptance of any modifications of its original policy intention. After this the government decision is brought before the Second Chamber of Parliament. The Second Chamber does not move to consider the decision immediately. For a six month period after the government notification the Chamber has the opportunity to exchange views with the government and to attempt to modify the proposed policy decision.

Since 1977 a Bill has been pending in parliament which would give a legal framework to the procedure mentioned and would give to the Second Chamber the power to make its approval a condition for the execution of any government decision. This would imply a considerable enlargement of the power of Chamber in this respect (Tweede Kamer, 1977–78).

Once the government decision has been finalised the actual execution of the proposed project will require the co-operation of the lower administrative levels. Reservation of the land required will, for example, have to be worked out in the affected provincial and municipal plans. In the case of controversial developments, the co-operation of the lower administrative levels will not necessarily be excessively cordial and therefore, as mentioned earlier, the higher levels have the possibility of interfering if necessary. As the most significant example, it may be mentioned that the Wet op de Ruimtelijke Ordening (Wet van 27 oktober 1972, Stb. 578) (Spatial Planning Act) provides the Minister concerned with the authority to grant dispensation from the observance of municipal regulations. However, experience shows that such interference is only rarely necessary as points of dispute are usually resolved harmoniously.

When these procedures have resulted in a final government decision which enables the policy intention to be carried out on a particular site there is still a long way to go before the construction can actually start. This is

particularly the case with nuclear power stations and it means that government consent after the planning procedure has been carried is by no means
a charter for the plant's construction at the selected site. The procedure
simply results in the electricity company concerned being in a position to
apply for a building licence without their proposal possibly being in danger
from national political considerations.

## Planning for Nuclear Power

### Nuclear Site Licensing Procedures

Under the Nuclear Power Act of 1963 (Wet van 21 februari 1963, Stb 82,
amended most recently by Wet van 13 juni 1979, Stb. 443), it is forbidden to
erect, put into, or keep in operation a nuclear power plant without a licence
granted jointly by the ministers of Economic Affairs, Social Affairs and
Public Health. An electricity utility will therefore begin by applying for a
licence to erect the nuclear generating station. This application needs to
include many data of which those related to the concern of this chapter are a
statement and description of the site on which the station would be constructed, stating all the relevant circumstances of geographical, geological,
climatological and other natural environmental considerations. From this
description it can be seen that once again a type of planning survey is being
constructed. However, interest in this can not be expected to be particularly
great because it has been preceded by the procedure for a Planologische
Kernbeslissing (crucial planning decision), as described earlier. In that
procedure the site for which the licence is being applied for has been selected
specifically on the grounds of its suitability from a planning viewpoint and to
do this a considerable amount of data has to be presented including a
description of the structure, the contained installations and their working; a
description of the way in which the applicant intends to dispose of fissionable
material after use and a description of the measures to be taken by or on
behalf of the applicant for the protection of people, animals, vegetation and
property. This review covers both measures for the prevention of danger and
nuisance during normal operation and also the dangers which would arise as
a consequence of accidents.

These must be those which can be reasonably deemed possible to occur
and which may have effects, especially contamination, on the surrounding
area. Such a 'safety report' provides parties with an insight into the possible
dangers and the measures which might be taken against these.

After receiving the application for the licence the government will consult,
among others, two independent advisory bodies for assessment of the
potential building and operation of the installation. These are the Gezondheidsraad (Medical Council) which has the general task of advising ministers about scientific and technical knowledge over problems in the field of

public health and the Commissie Reactorveiligheid (Commission for Reactor Safety) which has the task of providing advice on nuclear technology safety aspects of nuclear generating stations. Any data required for these bodies to carry out their studies must be submitted by the applicant. If they decide that the proposed plant does not present extraordinary risks they return favourable advice. This will also contain proposals on the regulations which would attach to any licence issued for the construction of the nuclear generating station.

After having sought further advice, such as that of the Interdepartmental Commission for Nuclear Power (a standing consultative committee on nuclear affairs with representation of a large number of government ministries) and after the conclusion of a procedure for objections, the ministers concerned may or may not proceed to grant a licence.

This objection procedure will now be described in some detail as it will make clear the precise nature of the efforts that are made to take the ordinary citizens' interests into account in planning policy for nuclear power station siting.

For some time now the Nuclear Power Act has declared relevant for its purposes the Wet Algemene Bepalingen Milieuhygiene (General Provision Environmental Hygiene Act) which came into force in 1979. This means that procedures originally laid down in an act specifically designed for nuclear energy, are now dominated by an act which is concerned with a number of subjects in the field of environmental hygiene. It is intended to extend this General Provision Environmental Hygiene Act to give an outline Environment Act. This would, in the first place, include general regulations for public participation opportunities and for appeals over the granting of decrees (such as licences for operating nuclear power stations) and a regulation designed to co-ordinate the preparation and discussion of the application for such decrees.

The application for a construction licence is announced through various channels (press, posting of notices, notices to users of buildings in the immediate vicinity) and apart from the citizens who are informed in this way, the provincial and municipal councils in whose territory the plant will be located are informed along with the councils and municipalities with territory within 10 kilometre distance from the proposed site and also the authorities in charge of quality control of surface water also within 10 kilometre distance.

After the application has been announced it is deposited for public inspection together with accompanying papers and the reports and recommendations to the authorities which are relevant to judgement on the application. For a period of a month after the deposition for inspection anyone who wishes to do so, including all the bodies previously mentioned, may submit objections in writing. After this a public session is held at which verbal objections may be submitted in addition to the written ones. An account of the public session is added to the papers deposited for inspection and also sent to the applicant, the government's advisers and to those present at the session. After the period of objection the government, as soon as possible, draws up a draft decree which is sent to the applicant and the government agencies involved. The issuing of this decree is publicly announced in the same manner as for the receipt of the application discussed earlier. The draft decree also has to be sent to all those who entered written or verbal objections to the application.

For a period of a fortnight from the day on which the draft decree is deposited for inspection, the applicant, those who had entered objections against the application and those who can prove that they had reasonably been unable to do so previously, may enter written objections to the draft decree.

The overall time period within which the definitive decree is intended to be granted is 7 months from the receipt of the application. However, this time may be extended should the complexity of the subject give cause to do so and it can reasonably be expected that this will always be the case with an application for a nuclear power plant licence.

If the decree is finally granted it is, among others, sent to the applicant and to those who entered objections to the application for the draft licence as discussed earlier. Along with the granting of the decree will be a statement on interpretation of the objections lodged against the application or the draft decree.

There is however, another possibility for appeal against the final decree. For a period of 4 weeks after the issue of the definitive decree an appeal may be lodged with the Crown (the Queen and the ministers, with the ministers assuming responsibility). This possibility for appeal has to be clearly mentioned in the definitive decree. As well as this, the Raad van State (Council of State)—the government advisory board which also has jurisdictional functions in administrative matters such as these—may be called upon to suspend the decree forthwith until the Council has passed the judgement on an appeal against it. The act of requesting suspension automatically brings about this suspension until judgement has been passed on the request. The possibility of appeal is open to, among others, the applicant, those who raised objections against the application or against the draft decree and also to anybody who had been 'reasonably unable' to appeal at the earlier stage. This may mean that even at this very advanced stage of the decision-making process, individuals who had not hitherto been involved in the procedure may try to thwart the licence with new counter-arguments.

From all this, it can be seen that the procedure has been designed to give objectors every possible opportunity of making their position known and it may be possibly wondered whether the limits of what is reasonable are not occasionally exceeded or that the procedure may be somewhat unbalanced. For example, on the one hand it is laid down that an appeal has to be lodged within 1 month after the deposition of the draft decree for inspection while also provision is made for an objector who proves that an appeal 'could not be reasonably demanded within that period'. Because a decree becomes operative after 1 month has passed, except for adjustments resulting from appeals lodged within that month, the tolerance shown towards tardy opponents causes a high degree of legal insecurity for the applicant.

As noted, the Raad van State plays an important part in any appeal to the Crown. All disputes which are submitted for judgement of the Crown have to be brought before a special department of the Raad van State where a formal legal procedure takes place with investigation, the hearing of parties, witnesses and experts, position statements and so on. After the 'trial' the department of the Raad van State proposes a judgement which is passed as a draft decision to the Crown. It is very rare for this advice not to be followed by the Crown but the ultimate decision is vested with it.

In December, 1980, the Netherlands' Cabinet Council agreed to the insertion of a section on environmental impact statements in the previously-mentioned General Provision Environmental Hygiene Act (Staatsuitgeverij, 1979; Tijdschrift voor Milieu en Recht, 1979; Tweede Kamer, 1978–79b). The bill to do this ordains that no decision may be taken on activities which may have significant negative consequences for the environment until an environmental impact statement has been made. The applicant for the licence is responsible for the drafting of the environmental impact statement. The report has to be open for general participation and the quality of its contents are to be examined by a special commission of independent experts. Subsequently the government is required to state explicitly the ways in which consequences for the environment have been taken into account. The environmental impact statement is regarded as an aid, but only an aid, to the decision-making process. This means that a statement which identifies highly-negative consequences need not be prohibitive to the granting of a licence. Social or economic interests may be at stake whose significance exceeds the environmental objections identified. However, in respect of nuclear energy where public attention is directed more to the identification of a wide range of potential dangers than to their extremely unlikely occurrence, environmental impact statements mean an additional heavy burden for the developer, both psychologically and operationally.

Once the licence has been issued for the erecting of a nuclear power plant, construction activities may start. However, the plant can be put into operation only after the granting of a separate operational licence. This licence does not require such a broad formal granting procedure as that for the construction licence but one again objections in writing may be submitted and, the licence having been given despite these, appeals may be lodged with the Crown. It can be seen that here again there are opportunities for opponents to a plant to express their criticisms.

FIG 7.1 *Site Selection Process for the Location of Nuclear Power Stations in the Netherlands*

●    site chosen in 1975 Electricity Power Supply Structure Plan as suitable for power station location but not considered suitable for nuclear power station in the 1977 Complementary Structure Plan (20)

○    site chosen as potential location for nuclear power station in 1977 Complementary Structure Plan but rejected on the basis of the absolute site selection criteria (see text) (6)

⊙    site chosen as potential location for nuclear power station in 1977 Complementary Structure Plan but rejected on the basis of mutual comparison (see text) (4)

-⊙-    preferred sites for location of additional nuclear power station(s) (2)

Locations

| | | |
|---|---|---|
| 1 Eems | 12 Veluwemeer/Eemmeer | 23 Tiengemeten |
| 2 Groningen | 13 Flevo | 24 St. Philipsland/Tholen |
| 3 Bergum | 14 Markerwaard | 25 Borssele (existing reactor) |
| 4 Urk | 15 Wieringermeer | 26 Ossenisse |
| 5 Ketelmeer | 16 IJmuiden | 27 Bath/Hoedekenskerke |
| 6 Harculo | 17 Velsen | 28 Amer |
| 7 IJssel-Zuid | 18 Hemweg | 29 Maas-Waal |
| 8 Nijmegen | 19 Diemen | 30 Boxmeer |
| 9 Dodewaard (existing reactor) | 20 Maasvlakte | 31 Buggenum |
| 10 Lek | 21 Rotterdam | 32 Maasbracht |
| 11 Lage Weide | 22 Regio Dordrecht | |

An operational licence will be granted only if it has been proved that during the construction the requirements of government inspections have been met. The reactor system designs, of which only the principles were available at the time of the application for the erection licence, are elaborated during the construction activity. Before the actual building activity starts, detailed surveys and system calculations are given by the constructor and owner to two government inspection services, the Kern Fysische Dienst (Nuclear Physics Service) and the Dienst voor het Stoomwezen (Steam Engineering Service). The Commissie Reactorveiligheid is also involved to ascertain whether the actual construction meets the safety principles incorporated in the reactor plan. There is always the possibility that the reactor owner will be required to make modifications to the reactor system after the actual construction. All the construction and equipment assembly supervision results are reported to the committee, including at the later stages of the construction the results of functional tests of the different reactor systems. If necessary the committee will advise on modifications of the design or other measures to guarantee maximum safety. In the last phase of construction the committee lays down the test procedures for putting the plant into active operation. A step-by-step indication is given of which functional tests are to be carried out. Only when the committee has been convinced that safe operation of the reactor is possible will a favourable notification be given.

*Selecting Nuclear Sites*

In July, 1975 the government published a 'Structuurschema Elektriciteitsvoorziening' (Electricity Power Supply Structure Plan) (Tweede Kamer, 1974–75b). This aimed to make clear in a general way the possible consequences for the physical structure of the Netherlands of the planning of electricity supply facilities on a longer term basis and to ensure that the actual siting decisions to be made later on would be well-grounded. This 'Structuurschema' was submitted to general discussion by means of the procedure prescribed for this—the 'Procedure voor een Planologische Kernbeslissing' (Procedure for a crucial physical planning decision).

Thirty-two sites were identified as possible locations for the establishment of electricity power plants. Because of the particular characteristics of nuclear power plants, it was decided to exclude them from the Structuurschema and consequently from the procedure for public participation associated with it. A special plan was published in 1977 under the title of Aanvullend Structuurschema Elektriciteitsvoorziening (Complementary Electricity Power Supply Structure Plan) (Tweede Kamer, 1976–77).

This complementary structure plan was also required to pass through the procedure for a 'Planologische Kernbeslissing'. Using specified criteria, twelve sites out of the thirty-two mentioned above were identified as possible sites for nuclear power stations. This selection was based on:

*(a) Absolute Criteria*

The main selection of sites was made with the help of absolute criteria derived from requirements for, among other matters, cooling water availability and data regarding population density. This latter criterion is the most interesting one and it will be discussed in some detail.

In formulating a criterion for population density a model was used developed by the Gezondheidsraad (medical board) which was representative of the average Netherlands situation. This model permits only one thousand persons to reside within a radius of 1.5 km of a nuclear plant, 200 persons per square kilometre up to 5 km and 400 persons per square kilometre beyond that distance. The last mentioned figure corresponds to the average population density of the Netherlands. To take into account the unequal distribution of the population around a location, a population density two and a half times as large as those specified above is allowed to occur in the 45 degree sector.

In the actual application of this model a demand was made that up to a distance of 20 km the population density should not exceed the Netherlands average, except in a 45 degree sector as mentioned. The distance of 20 km was chosen because within that there is, in the case of an extremely serious accident at the plant, an immediate death risk. Furthermore, in such a case, consequences might also occur at an even greater distance and therefore attention was also paid to the circumstances of the area up to 100 km from the plant's location. Any consideration of greater distances is, because of the existing population distribution in the Netherlands and the adjoining foreign territories, not likely to lead to the identification of any significant differences between potential locations. A further refinement of the model was to attach greater weight to the significance of population near the nuclear plant than to the remoter population because of their greater risk. The factors used for this weighting were deduced from meteorological dispersion models. In this way a population criterion was formulated which allowed, as a yardstick for the average risk around a potential location, for a weighted total number of inhabitants of 14,400 in the area up to 20 km distance and 42,400 up to 100 km distance. The weighted number of inhabitants in the previously mentioned 45 degree sector, representing the yardstick for the *maximum* risk, should be not greater than 4500 and 13,100 within the 20 and 100 km limits.

After the population around the potential location was counted and weighted, three sites were identified which did not meet the requirements and these were consequently rejected. After the application of all the absolute criteria, of which the population criterion was one, six places were left which were considered to be generally suited to the establishment of a nuclear power station.

As well as these population-related selection criteria, three other types of consideration enter into the site identification and facility design procedures.

These are the consequences of highly unlikely catastrophic events, 'system linkage' factors and the special circumstances created by the need for transfrontier planning.

Highly unlikely catastrophic events:

—earthquakes

The major part of the Netherlands is aseismic. There are no tremors of any importance. The construction requirements for nuclear power plants guarantee the function of the safety components in the event of an earthquake with a force which could occur more than once in one million years. Consequently earthquakes are not an element in mutual comparison of sites.

—tornadoes

Tornadoes are very rare in the Netherlands. The construction specifications of nuclear power plants take into account a tornado which could occur once in one million years, which means a wind-force of 125 m/sec and a maximum pressure fall of 13 kN/m$^2$ within 2 seconds. This covers all potential sites and consequently is of no importance to the mutual comparison.

—gas cloud explosions

Construction requirements guarantee a nuclear power plant can stand up to an effective pressure of 30 kN/m$^2$, which is similar to the pressure in the event of an explosion of an explosive gas cloud with a diameter of 50 m at the same spot as the reactor building or to the explosion of 20,000 tonnes of TNT within a distance of 3 km. Installations with a risk of explosion are only allowed within a distance of 3 km from the reactor when their explosion-potential does not exceed the figures mentioned.

Already existing activities within that territory have to be studied during the licensing procedure. If it appears that certain activities could cause greater risks, supplementary safety measures could be required. Thus the risk of gas cloud explosions does not affect the mutual comparison of sites.

—toxic gas leakages

Construction of an installation with a toxic gas leakage risk is not allowed within a distance of 1 km from the reactor building, unless that risk is met by additional safety measures. Similar safety margins are adopted when such installations already exist in the neighbourhood of a site which could be chosen for a nuclear station. Consequently also toxic gas leakages do not affect the mutual comparison.

'System linkage' factors:

—linkage to the national grid

The six sites have been mutually compared with regard to the possibility of as simple as possible a connection to the national 380 kV high tension grid. For example, the site at Wieringermeer would oblige the construction of a connection line of about 60 km, which makes the site less desirable.

—carrying capacity of the grid

With regard to the carrying capacity of the grid, it can be pre-determined whether a certain power concentration is desirable or not and this consideration does not affect the mutual comparison. The only relevant conclusion which can be drawn is that a certain spread of nuclear capacity is desirable over the north east and the south west of the Netherlands. Certainly, a total concentration of 3000 MW(e) of nuclear power (the capacity aimed at in the Memorandum) would severely diminish the flexibility of the high tension grid.

The criteria used in the site selection process are not limited to the territory of the Netherlands. If a site is situated in the borderlands, data related to the situation in Belgium or the Federal Republic of Germany on the other side of the border are taken into account and could, if they so indicate, prohibit the construction of a nuclear power station at a borderland site. The Netherlands government expects that the country's interests will be similarly taken into account by the Belgium and German Federal Republic governments in the planning of nuclear plants in their marchlands. To guarantee this international dimension, as well as the general obligations under article 37 of the Euratom treaty which obliges mutual consultation of public health experts, some specific and general international liaison organisations have been established. These are:

   (i) the Nederlands-Duitse Commissie voor Kerninstallaties in het Grensgebied (Netherlands-German Commission on Nuclear Installations in the Border Area) which has a general overview on nuclear matters.

  (ii) the Nederlands-Duitse Commissie voor de Ruimtelijke Ordening (Netherlands-German Commission on Spatial Planning) concerned with general land-use planning of all types, and

 (iii) the Bijzondere Commissie voor de Ruimtelijke Ordening (Bilateral Commission on Spatial Planning) with a similar remit for liaison with Belgium.

*(b) Mutual Comparison*

The 6 places identified as a result of the absolute criteria were then mutually compared with the intention of picking those which were the most appropriate for nuclear power station locations. The factors taken into account comprised, among others,

1. The quantities of available cooling water. All 6 places met the absolute requirement in this respect but some had a greater cooling water potential than others.
2. Cooling water quality. Sites near the open sea are better as regards treatment of effluent water than sites located on estuaries or rivers or, to an even greater extent, on standing fresh water.

3. Location with respect to standing water. Especially with regard to the supply of drinking water, location near large fresh-water basins was considered undesirable. In this respect whether the water was to be used for cooling purposes was immaterial as it could possibly be indirectly contaminated in a particularly serious accident.

4. Population density. As well as being used as an absolute selection criterion, population density was also important for the mutual comparison of potential locations. To this end, the population density was expressed as a Site Population Factor (SPF). The SPF is considered to be unity at an average population density of 1000 persons per square mile (corresponding to 386 persons per square kilometre, close to the average population density for the Netherlands). The population density was considered up to a distance of 20 km from the potential location and again was weighted according to the distance of the populations from the location under consideration.

5. Flooding. The Netherlands' sea walls and dykes are designed to resist water levels occurring only once in 4000 or 5000 years. The directive of the Commissie Reactorveiligheid (Commission on Reactor Safety) required nuclear power plants to be designed so that they can withstand even higher water levels. The plant design must guarantee the operation of safety factors even when the extremely improbable water levels have occurred and the normal retaining walls have been inundated. The possibility of flooding is therefore not a significant factor in distinguishing between potential sites for nuclear power plant location.

6. National physical structure. National physical planning policy is designed to maintain as far as possible, the diversity of urbanised and lightly urbanised areas. The largest part of the electricity consumption occurs in urban areas and therefore location of the generating facilities outside these areas is not desirable from the physical planning viewpoint.

7. Population fluctuation. It is obviously important to identify whether there are any temporary increases in the population densities at potential plant locations. These might arise from the influx of the working population at industrial establishments in the area or the recreational use of adjacent land.

8. Agriculture. The loss of high quality agricultural land resulting from the land requirements of a nuclear power plant is obviously unsatisfactory and should be avoided if possible.

9. Use of surplus heat and agglomeration effects. The extent to which at present or in the future there might be a potential availability of users of surplus heat and the degree to which agglomeration effects from the concentration of industry near a nuclear power plant could be accommodated at a potential location was also taken into consideration.

10. Land use. The economic activity on land adjacent to the potential locations was considered in respect of the possibility of contamination by radioactivity. Stoppage of industrial production and harbours would cause the greatest amount of economic damage and therefore locations with these activities adjacent were not considered desirable.

11. Accumulations in the biosphere. In the normal operation of a nuclear power plant a degree of accumulation of radioactive matter may occur in the biosphere. Although, according to present opinions, this does not comprise any hazard, it is nevertheless considered desirable to keep such radiation doses as low as possible. Site selection can contribute to this to a certain degree, especially by locating plants in aquatic surroundings, in particular close to the open sea.

12. Organisational and safety aspects. The arguments for and against concentrating or dispersing nuclear potential between various locations have been considered. Apart from such advantages as the lesser degree of disturbance of the landscape and the smaller space requirements, it is also an advantage of the concentration of nuclear power plants that the possibility of combining certain provisions for their operation arises, such as the operation of safety measures, storage of fuel elements, temporary storage of waste, transport of radioactive material and so on. These other aspects mentioned are also desirable from a safety viewpoint and the advantages which arise are considered to outweigh the objection that the individual risk for residents in the surrounding area will be increased by the concentration of nuclear power plants at a particular site. Of course, the average risk to the nation as a whole is not increased.

On the basis of the comparison of the 6 places considered as potentially suitable for the location of nuclear power plants the government arrived at a preference for two locations—Borssele, where there is already a nuclear power plant in existence, and in the vicinity of the Westelijke Noordoostpolderdijk on the IJsselmeer near the town of Urk.

### Nuclear Energy Policy and Nuclear Waste

In the emergence of nuclear energy policy in the Netherlands several factors, some of which are still in need of close attention, have assumed a special importance. This applies above all to policy over nuclear waste management. The problem of nuclear waste has been increasingly in the limelight in the Netherlands in the last few years. Little by little, this problem at the tail-end of the nuclear cycle seems to have become the crowbar of opponents of nuclear power. In the mid-1970s the Netherlands government came to the view that an extension of nuclear power would be unwise without there being a solution for the problem of nuclear waste in sight.

In 1975, 1977 and 1979 official reports were produced examining the solutions for nuclear waste disposal which were open to the Netherlands.

The most important of these is the 1979 report (Ministry of Economic Affairs, 1979). One conclusion was that the Netherlands does have the possibility of geological disposal of waste in salt domes situated in the northern part of the country which, if certain requirements are met, can guarantee very good isolation of the waste from the biosphere. Further field investigation, including test drilling will be required to show whether one or more of these salt domes meets the demands which were broadly described in the 1979 report. To this end, the government asked the local and provincial authorities concerned to consider jointly how these field investigations could be carried out and in so doing the government made public for the first time specific plans for nuclear waste disposal. There was an instant reaction. The lower authorities involved refused to co-operate in any way and a grim mood arose among the population in the northern provinces. A campaign was launched, named the 'van Aardenneoffensief' derived from the name of the Minister of Economic Affairs who was also responsible for nuclear energy and alluding to the Ardennes offensive at the end of World War II. The climate became so explosive that the government dropped attempts to deliberate with the lower authorities in the north of the country and decided to maintain the integrity of the salt domes there for the time being.

The peak of the issue was reached in the spring of 1980 when the Tweede Kamer (second, lower, house) carried a motion that the Public Discussion 'was not to be burdened by starting the test drilling' (Tweede Kamer, 1979–80d). The drillings were to be postponed until the end of the Public Discussion and in the interim, other possible solutions had to be studied. As a result, a rather curious situation arose where the Public Discussion, which was aimed at providing clarity for everyone, was not allowed to be 'burdened' with scientific clarity over a possible solution to one of the most crucial problems related to the subject of the Public Discussion.

Subsequently the government turned its attention to salt domes in the North Sea. These may be seismologically investigated and this clearly causes fewer political problems. At present test drilling in such structures are equally out of the question in view of the parliamentary motion mentioned. Recently a national programme of investigation has begun which embraces all aspects of nuclear waste policy as well as geological disposal this programme also considers deep sea bed disposal possibilities and interim storage. Despite this it must be concluded that even if the programme identifies one or more possible options, actual solutions to the problem will exist only when the political seal of approval has been given to them. Optimism that this will occur is not justified if the case of the investigation into the salt domes underneath the mainland are any illustration.

**Conclusion**

This chapter has shown that even with a highly-developed planning system, responsive to both national and local level issues, and with a general public consensus on the desirability of fairly rigid land-use planning controls, the development of future energy infrastructure has presented this system with dilemmas. These have not been primarily of a technical nature. As the chapter illustrates, a comprehensive site selection procedure has been able to identify potential sites for nuclear power expansion even given the very tight physical constraints which have to be overcome in the Netherlands.

However, to an extent the very exercise of carrying out such a selection has created some problems in terms of the acceptability of the wider premises on which the selection procedure was based. Some have argued that it has been the very sophistication and rigidity of the Netherlands' spatial planning which is at fault and that a greater flexibility would have accommodated the concern which was accumulating over the trend of official energy policy at a much earlier stage. Others believe that the political uncertainties created by or exacerbated by uncertainty over energy policy, especially nuclear power, have undermined what were perfectly adequate planning methods and procedures which could identify sites for future generation capacity expansion.

The Netherlands has decided to address these problems, at least in part, by an extensive 'Public Discussion' on energy and, although there was some initial uncertainty, and a continuing administrative singularity, over the inclusion of site-specific considerations in this Discussion, it has proved impossible to exclude them completely. The Dutch experience has also shown that a formally organised 'national energy debate' may create, as well as hopefully resolve some problems. The initial creation of the BMD, the composition of its steering group and its funding and grant dispersing activities have all been problematic, especially with the difficult economic circumstances in which the country finds itself.

These dilemmas have added to the convictions of some observers that the process of consultation, debate and evaluation has gone too far and has not helped to develop a widespread confidence that the outcome of the BMD will be the national consensus on the future pattern of energy security which the government hoped for when it initiated the procedure. To an extent, the pressure is off the energy front at the moment, as demand slackens and supply eases. Other national concerns have risen to overtake energy in the forefront of consciousness. However, to accept this view uncritically would be to prejudge the final outcome of the BMD and whatever this may be, the Netherlands' experience over the reconciliation of national energy and planning goals is worth close examination by other countries with similar existing or emerging dilemmas.

### References

Brussaard, W. (1980) *The rules of physical planning, 1979,* Ministry of Housing and Physical Planning, Central Department of Information and External Affairs, The Hague.

van Embden, F., Thoenes, P. and Witsen, J. (eds) (forthcoming) *Physical Planning in the Netherlands*, Elsevier.

Hazelhoff, D. (1981) *Government reports on physical planning*, Ministry of Housing and Physical Planning, Central Department of Information and External Affairs, The Hague.

van Houten, D. (1977) I. Planning in the Netherlands. II. Urban and regional planning in the Netherlands. Notes on planning organisations and on physical planning at the level of central government, April, 1977. University of Kent. Canterbury.

IEA (International Energy Agency) (1981) *Energy Policies and Programmes of IEA Countries, 1980 Review*, OECD, Paris.

Ministry of Economic Affairs (Ministerie van Economische Zaken) (1979) Interdepartmental Nuclear Energy Commission: Report on the feasibility of radioactive waste disposal in salt formations in the Netherlands, April, 1979, (English translation).

Ministry of Housing and Physical Planning (1981) *Main characteristics of the land-use policy in the Netherlands*, Central Department of Information and External Affairs, January, 1981, The Hague.

Rijksplanologische Dienst (1973) Derde Nota over de Ruimtelijke Ordening, 's-Gravenhage Staatsuitgeverij.

Staatsuitgeverij (1979) Raad van advies voor de Ruimtelijke Ordening. Advies over milieu-effectrapportering in de ruimtelijke ordening, 22 juli, 's-Gravenhage.

van Stein Callenfels, G. W. and Bunge, E. F. (1982) The energy situation in the Netherlands, in *The European Energy Scene*, papers presented at the Tenth Consultative Council of the Watt Committee on Energy, 21 May, 1981, Watt Committee on Energy, London.

Tijdschrift voor Milieu en Recht (1979) Themanummer Milieu-effectrapportage, 4–5, Zwolle, Tjeenk Willink.

Tweede Kamer (1972) zitting 1972, 12006 Nota over de openbaarheid bij de voorbereiding van het ruimtelijk beleid.

Tweede Kamer (1974–75a) zitting 1974–75, 13122.

Tweede Kamer (1974–75b) zitting 1974–75, 13488.

Tweede Kamer (1975–76) zitting 1975–76, 13122 nr. 11

— Risico-analyse van de splijtstofcyclus in Nederland (RASIN), uitgevoerd door de NV Samenwerkende Elektriciteits-Productiebedrijven te Arnhem, Ultracentrifuge Nederland NV te Almelo en Interfuel BV te Petten.

— Het advies van de Gezondheidsraad 'Kerncentrales en Volksgezondheid; invloed van kernenergie op volksgezondheid en milieu in Nederland bij een totale capaciteit van 3500 MW' (a supplementary report was issued in September, 1978).

— Het advies van de Commissie Reactorveiligheid over de veiligheidsaspecten van de splijtstofcyclus in Nederland.

Tweede Kamer (1976–77) zitting 1976–77, 14363.

Tweede Kamer (1977–78) zitting 1977–78, 14889 Ontwerp van Wet tot wijziging van de Wet op de Ruimtelijke Ordening.

Tweede Kamer (1978–79a) zitting 1978–79, 15100 nr. 18. An English translation has been published under the title 'Public Discussion on the use of Nuclear Energy for Power Generation, 1978–79 Session. The Stuurgroep has also published a monthly 'Nieuws brief' since January, 1982.

Tweede Kamer (1978–79b) zitting 1978–79, 15715, nrs. 1–2. Nota hordende het regeringstandpunt inzake de milieu-effectrapportage.

Tweede Kamer (1979–80a) zitting 1979–80, 15802, nrs. 1–2. An English translation of the summary has been published 'Memorandum on Energy Policy, Part I, Summary', 's-Gravenhage, Directie Externe Betrekkingen.

Tweede Kamer (1979–80b) zitting 1979–80, 15802. An English translation has been published as 'Summary of the Memorandum on Energy Policy, Part II: The Coal Memorandum', Ministry of Economic Affairs, The Hague.

Tweede Kamer (1979–80c) zitting 1979–80, 15802, nrs. 11–12. *Nota Energiebeleid Deel 3: Brandstofinzet centrales.*

Tweede Kamer (1979–80d) zitting 1979–80, 1500, nr. 24.

Tweede Kamer (1980–81) zitting 1980–81, 16799, Nota van de Minister van Volkshuisvesting en Ruimtelijke Ordening.

# CHAPTER 8

# Renewable Energy Resources and Planning in Ireland

MICHAEL GOUGH and J. OWEN LEWIS

## Introduction

While there may be other contenders for the claim, there can be no doubt that Ireland has been one of the countries most adversely affected by the energy traumas of the 1970s. The late 1960s and early 1970s saw a concerted effort to develop what had been a somewhat peripheral and stagnant economy into a more integrated and expanding position, especially in the context of the European Community (EC). The early 1970s economic growth was an indication that this effort was beginning to bring benefits. Unfortunately, the experience of the later 1970s suggests that the difficulties of energy pricing and supply may have seriously disrupted this early promise and has accentuated the urgency of breaking the energy constraints.

In all countries facing such constraints, the response has universally been to try to secure *reliable* sources of external energy supplies but, above all, to evaluate, and if possible develop, opportunities for a high level of energy supply *self-sufficiency*. Ireland has been no exception and, again like most countries, the emphasis to date has been on development of conventional energy systems. Progress with the Kinsale gas field has been rapid while the search for other hydrocarbon resources in the waters around the country has been extensive, although to date comparatively unrewarding.

The exploitation of Ireland's extensive peat (turf) resources is probably the most singular and widely-known feature of the Irish energy situation and is a good example of the way in which the determination to maximise self-sufficiency can lead to the exploitation of 'unconventional' resources. However, as this chapter notes, the peat resource is limited in both scale (around one-fifth of all electricity generated is turf-fired) and the length of time that the resource will be available.

Because of the apparent poverty of Ireland's conventional energy resource endowment, the potential of various renewable energy supply options demands at least a careful examination of their possible contribution to

193

energy self-sufficiency. Similar examinations in countries with predominantly dense, urban-based populations have been pessimistic about the contribution which can be expected, especially from dispersed 'soft' sources. However, for predominantly rural economies and societies, this conclusion is by no means so clear-cut.

Rural areas have a particular relevance for land-use planners. Issues of employment generation and protection intermix with amenity and agricultural resource considerations and energy matters can be expected to interlink closely with these and other factors. Furthermore, as this chapter shows, because of their extensive nature many renewable energy options may have regional scale consequences to a much greater extent than point-based, concentrated fossil-fuelled systems.

Inevitably, compared with fossil energy sources, experience with renewables (other than hydro power) has everywhere been limited and most countries, Ireland included, are in the early stages of project development. Consequently the findings of this chapter are inevitably more speculative than those of some others. However, in as much as planning attempts to be integrative and anticipatory, and because it is becoming increasingly clear that practicable renewable energy systems may pose many problems in their integration with the land-use planning system, the planning issues raised by renewable energy demand considerable attention *now*.

**Energy in Ireland**

Total Irish primary energy demand in 1980 was 14.4 Mtce, of which 68 per cent was supplied by oil, 14 per cent by peat, 9 per cent from coal, 6 per cent from natural gas and 3 per cent from hydro-electricity (the sole renewable source in use). All oil and most coal is imported, and subject to disruption in times of major price changes or supply interruptions. It has been the main priority of successive Ministers for Energy to reduce this dependence, for example by rapid exploitation of the Kinsale gas field (a significant native source discovered in the early 1970s) and oil exploration at various offshore locations.

Over the period from 1960 to 1980 total primary energy consumption rose by 95 per cent, although since 1973 the growth in primary energy consumption has been an average of 2 per cent a year. This slackening in demand has been due to a slow down in economic growth, increased energy conservation and other factors. In 1980 the domestic sector consumed an estimated 32.5 per cent of primary energy, the commercial sector 13 per cent, the industrial sector 32.5 per cent and the transport sector 22 per cent.

The primary energy supply mix has changed dramatically over this period. During the early 1960s coal, oil and peat each accounted for about 30 per cent of the total with hydro-electricity making up the balance, giving a flexible energy system with a reasonable diversity of supply and without

TABLE 8.1 *Irish Primary Energy Inputs 1973–80*

| | 1973 | 1974 | Million tonnes of Coal Equivalent 1975 | 1976 | 1977 | 1978 | 1979 | 1980 |
|---|---|---|---|---|---|---|---|---|
| Peat | 1.902 | 1.959 | 2.027 | 2.064 | 2.149 | 2.057 | 2.018 | 1.985 |
| Coal | 0.990 | 0.931 | 0.748 | 0.854 | 0.901 | 0.959 | 1.371 | 1.274 |
| Oil | 9.126 | 9.281 | 8.787 | 9.048 | 9.629 | 10.052 | 10.852 | 9.925 |
| Hydro | 0.306 | 0.372 | 0.247 | 0.282 | 0.355 | 0.322 | 0.374 | 0.372 |
| Natural Gas | — | — | — | — | — | — | 0.449 | 0.856 |
| Total | 12.324 | 12.554 | 11.809 | 12.248 | 13.034 | 13.389 | 15.065 | 14.412 |

critical dependence on any single fuel. The increased availability of cheap, convenient, efficient and clean oil stimulated a rise in the market share of this fuel while the supply of the indigenous fuels, hydro-electricity and peat, remained static. This was due to the limited availability of new hydro sites suitable for large scale electricity generation, and a combination of unfavourable economics and a limited quantity of readily-exploitable peat bogs. Considerations of cost, pollution and inconvenience all played a part in the decline of coal use.

Power generation in Ireland is mainly carried out by the Electricity Supply Board (ESB), a small utility by international standards—at mid-1981 its generating capacity was 3117 MW(e). At 31 March, 1981, 54 per cent of installed capacity was oil fired, 15 per cent was natural gas fired and only 0.5 per cent was coal fired (the remainder was peat and hydro). There are proposals under way to diversify from high oil usage for electricity generation. By 1987/88 oil-fired capacity is expected to drop to 44 per cent and coal-fired capacity will be 21 per cent (increased by a new power station at Moneypoint, on the Shannon estuary). Natural gas will be 11 per cent and renewables and peat together will be 24 per cent. Further diversification away from oil is aimed at and although a proposal for a nuclear power station has been put back to the 1990s, the ESB is investigating the possibility of using renewable and indigenous sources.

A number of forecasts of future levels of energy consumption have been published. A 1978 Government discussion document gave an 'expected growth case' total primary energy requirement in 1990 of 28.7 Mtce (Dept. of Industry, Commerce and Energy, 1978). It was proposed to meet this demand by construction of a 1200 MW(e) coal-fired plant and a 650 MW(e) nuclear-generating station in the electricity sector, and a continuing dependence on imported oil—83 per cent of non-electricity supply in 1990, despite increased use of coal. A maximum achievable saving through conservation measures of 2.6 Mtce was assumed.

The economic and energy growth projections were challenged by many, and the Solar Energy Society of Ireland projected a total primary energy

FIG 8.1 *Renewable Energy in Ireland*

demand of 20.9 Mtce in 1990 (SESI, 1978). Arguing that Ireland makes relatively ineffective use of energy consumed the Society sought to change this by vigorous conservation measures, reshaping of industrial structures and development of renewable energy resources. In another response to the Government paper An Taisce, the National Trust for Ireland, projected a 1990 demand in the range 16.7 to 25.2 Mtce (An Taisce, 1979).

In 1980, the National Board for Science and Technology published a study entitled *Energy Supply and Demand—the next Thirty Years,* (Kavanagh and Brady, 1980). This sought a balance between economic, political, social and technical considerations while taking account of energy system requirements such as flexibility in planning, diversity of resources and security of supply.

Projecting a primary energy demand of 22.7 Mtce in 1990, the study considered the composition of primary energy demand and supply over the period to 2010 and identified a strategy which would be cost-effective and flexible and avoid an over-commitment to any single fuel. Among the elements of such a strategy those with particular planning implications are the following:

— the planning and development of an infrastructure to cater for the widespread use of coal, including importing, handling and storage facilities;
— the investigation, identification and resolution of environmental considerations resulting from increased coal usage;
— the planning and development of facilities for importing and distributing natural gas and liquified natural gas;
— the use of biomass;
— demonstration and development programmes on wind and wave energy;
— the introduction of coal-burning co-generation facilities for industrial usage;
— the planning and development of district heating schemes;
— the integration of combined heat and power systems in the electrical system;
— preparation for the large scale direct consumption of natural gas and solid fuels;
— the planning and implementation of conservation strategies.

**Renewable Energy Resources**

Ireland is well-endowed with renewable energy resources. It has been argued that solar energy could be of greater significance in Ireland than any other country of the European Communities because of the country's low population density and low absolute level of energy demand:

> The ratio of solar energy availability to primary energy demand is higher in Ireland than in any other EEC country. It is two to three times as high as that for France or Italy, about ten times that of Germany and the UK and sixteen to seventeen times that of Belgium and the Netherlands. It follows that certain solar energy applications should have a greater impact in Ireland that in any other EEC country (Lalor, 1975).

Hydro power already makes a large contribution to electricity supply which could be increased. Wind, wave and tidal power resources are also considerable.

*Hydro*

Hydro is a well-established renewable energy resource, which makes a valuable contribution to electricity generation in many countries.

In Ireland, prior to 1927 there were 182 small hydro-electric power (HEP) installations supplying 8 million kWh and the first project undertaken by the newly founded ESB was the development of the Shannon HEP scheme in 1929. There are now 9 ESB HEP stations totalling 220 MW and a single-pumped storage scheme of 292 MW. The major Irish rivers have been harnessed and attention is now switching to smaller schemes. In 1980, a small 600 kW HEP scheme was commissioned at Parteen on the River Shannon, the first HEP scheme since the 1950s. HEP has some clear advantages over other sources of energy. There is very good security of supply (except in exceptional cases of severe drought) and there are long term economic attractions *vis-a-vis* fossil fuel stations (in 1980/81 in Ireland, electricity generation costs for HEP plants varied from 0.26p to 0.54p per kWh as compared to costs of 1.31p to 16.43p per kWh for fossil-fuel plants). For a country such as Ireland, there are some additional benefits. Long experience in the design, construction and operation of HEP plants makes them attractive while the possibility of exporting package plants must be considerable in view of the large volume of untapped HEP potential in developing nations.

The Department of Industry and Energy introduced in 1981 a scheme of financial support for small HEP demonstration projects as part of that Department's overall programme to encourage the development of alternative energy using native resources. HEP systems from 10 to 250 kW will be considered for support and the amount awarded in each case will not exceed £30,000. The Industrial Development Authority (IDA) also offers a 25 per cent grant on schemes costing up to £400,000 for HEP production. The Industrial Credit Corporation (ICC) offers low interest loans to industry with money made available through the European Energy Fund (EEF). The IDA and ICC schemes can also be used in other energy projects.

While there is still some untapped HEP potential in Ireland there is conflicting opinion on the amount. The government discussion paper on energy (Department of Industry, Commerce and Energy, 1978) stated that development of some six additional rivers as far as is practicable might provide an extra 20–30 MW. The Fine Gael Party's policy document on energy policy, however, states that an additional capacity of about 150 MW was considered but was not proceeded with for reasons of cost, land use or amenity constrictions (Fine Gael, 1980). Duggan (1978), who has examined some existing weirs and civil engineering structures previously used by the many former privately-owned electricity supply companies, contends that these could be used to provide a further 25 MW. It is possible, therefore, that a potential total of 175 MW exists at the present time (80 per cent of existing HEP capacity) of which 75 MW could be developed by the year 2000 according to SESI (1978). The ESB has decided on a programme of investigation to identify sites suitable for HEP potential as small as 250 KW. It is known that the River Erne has potential for a further 30 MW and that the development of the Ballisodare River is now economically feasible.

Recent technological advances in small-scale HEP such as electronic load governors reduce the capital costs considerably and make it more possible for private individuals to generate electricity for their own needs. New micro-HEP schemes will be run-of-the-river and will not require dams and reservoirs as the river flow provides the power. Not only will this mean more small HEP schemes, but it will eliminate many of the environmental impacts associated with larger HEP.

In pumped storage schemes, off-peak electricity from the national grid is used to raise water from a lower lake (or reservoir) to an upper lake (or reservoir) where it is retained in the form of potential energy for later use in conventional hydro-electric generation during times of heavy day-time demand. Ireland's only pumped storage scheme has a capacity of 292 MW and has been in operation since 1974. A number of technically attractive sites for pumped storage schemes have been identified by the ESB and geological investigations are in hand. One of the most attractive of the sites is Coumshingaun, in County Waterford, an upland cirque lake in the Comeragh Mountains. Brady and Kavanagh (1980) state that by 1990 pumped storage capacity will be 590 MW or a doubling of the present capacity. If a high level of development of wind and wave generating facilities takes place, then it is conceivable that additional pumped storage schemes will be required to create a firm source of supply from the daily and seasonal fluctuations of wind and wave facilities.

*Biomass and Peat*

Biomass includes agricultural and forestry crops, animal wastes, marine plants and other energy crops grown specifically for fuel through the use of solar radiation. The subsequent routes by which this biomass may be transformed into fuel and many and varied and include fermentation, anaerobic digestion, biophotolysis, combustion, hydrogenation, partial oxidation and pyrolysis. The development of biomass as an energy source has several inherent advantages. The resource is renewable (in the case of coppice short rotation forestry (SRF) replanting would be required every 25-30 years); energy can be stored for later use; conversion techniques are available; it has low environmental impact and it is relatively non-polluting. The main disadvantage is the large land area required. However, Ireland has the lowest population density in Western Europe (48 persons per square kilometre), with five times more land per person than in the United Kingdom and eight times more than the Netherlands. More importantly, if population density is calculated per unit of utilised agricultural area, Ireland's potential for biomass production becomes even clearer.

In addition to a mild climate and adequate rainfall, Ireland has further advantages for the exploitation of SRF. These include the availability of agriculture/forestry research and development expertise; the existence of a developing forestry programme, and the land use possibilities of marginal sites. In addition, the experience of Bord na Mona (Irish Peat Development Authority) in peat harvesting is a valuable asset because of the similarities between the technology of harvesting biomass for energy and that of the peat development programme. The Irish national biomass R & D programme involves growth and production experiments, harvesting and transport systems, conversion, forestry energy demonstration projects, assessment studies and systems analysis, new project definition and consideration of national and international programmes.

The present preferred strategy for biomass production is SRF on non-agricultural land. This involves coppice harvesting every 3 to 5 years for 25 years of plantation life. Thereafter, the area would be replanted and a second 25-year plantation commenced. Species selection results from An Foras Taluntais (The Agricultural Institute) suggest that hybrid poplar, willow and alder are likely to be suitable, with annual yields up to 12 tonnes/hectare dry matter. More conventional non-coppicing Sitka Spruce looks promising on blanket bog. A £IR5 millions project to develop SRF and burn the fuel, with forest residues, in an existing peat-fired power station has begun, with EC support (Kearney, 1979). One forecast suggests that use of biomass for electricity generation alone could be 140 MW(e) in 1995, rising to 700 MW(e) in 2010, or 2.6 and 9.5 of total installed capacity respectively at these dates (Brady and Kavanagh, 1980).

Although peat is a non-renewable resource, nevertheless, it is relevant to Irish biomass production because of possible re-use of cut-away bogs for SRF plantations and the use of peat-fired electricity stations for biomass combustion. At present 52,600 hectares of peat bog is in production and an additional 25,300 hectares is being developed under the Third Bog Development Programme. There is a further 1.1 million hectares with varying potential for peat fuel production. In 1980, 2.0 Mtce of peat was produced which was 14 per cent of national primary energy. Output is planned to increase to a peak of 3.06 Mtce by 1985 with a progressive decline to 2.46 Mtce by 1990.

As the peat is cut from the bogs, an average depth of 1.5 m is left after the sod peat process and 0.5 m after the milled peat process.* This cutaway bog will accrue at an annual average rate of over 400 hectares during the 1980s, and more quickly afterwards. By the year 2030 some 80,000 hectares of cutaway bog will be available for new uses, including the growing of biomass.

Experiments are currently in progress on the planting of cutaway bogs with trees for SRF. These are funded by the EC in co-operation with the ESB and the Department of Forestry and Fisheries, with Bord na Mona as project managers. SRF grown in counties Mayo and Offaly is expected to be harvested in 1983/4 for burning in an existing 5 MW(e) peat station at Screeb, Connemara. A small biomass project of 5 MW(e) is already under

---

* Sod peat is cut in brick-sized lumps, milled peat by scraping the bog surface with a blade.

way in County Kerry utilising forest thinnings. Recent tests by the ESB indicate that a blend of wood chips and domestic coal slack can be successfully burnt at sod peat stations.

Healy (1979) suggests that the Bord na Mona cutaway bog is the most suitable area of land in Ireland for biomass production and that Bord na Mona itself is a suitable organisation to lead this work, because:

1. The eventual 80,000 hectares of flat land is in state ownership and does not involve the difficult task of private land acquisition or persuading private landowners to commence biomass production.
2. The land already has a complete network of small gauge railways used for transporting peat, which may also be suitable for biomass.
3. The existing peat-fired stations are in immediate proximity to these cutaway areas and are readily convertible to biomass combustion.
4. There is an experienced labour force, 90 per cent of it in rural areas where it is socially desirable to maintain employment levels. Biomass seems to offer the best prospect of this. The *Development Strategy for the Midland Region* recognised that the energy sector is a labour intensive industry employing one person per 10 hectares. This compares with agriculture which employs perhaps one per 40 hectares.
5. There is a high degree of mechanical expertise within Bord na Mona, including experience in machine design and manufacture. The Irish Sugar Co. are currently developing under contract to Bord na Mona a prototype biomass harvester which will be capable of cutting two rows of young trees with stems up to 60 mm, harvesting on a 30° slope and chipping 160 tonnes/hectare.

Even if all the 80,000 hectares of cutaway bog is used to grow biomass it would only reach one-third of the 700 MW(e) generation capacity of peat when full production is reached. McNulty (1979) stresses that if biomass is to make a major contribution to the total energy requirements of the nation, it will necessitate a major intrusion into agricultural lands.

Ireland is noted for grass production and during the 1974–77 period approximately 31.4 Mt (22.3 Mtce) dry biomass was produced. Eliminating cattle production except for liquid milk would release at least 3 million hectares of grassland for fuel energy cropping, either with grass or other energy crops grown on grassland. This could yield 8.4 Mtce or 58 per cent of the 1980 total energy requirement. However, the elimination of 68 per cent of the country's grassland from cattle production to energy crop reduction would be a major radical event and is cited here only as an example of the potential of grassland for energy production.

One possible biomass energy route is conversion to ethanol, especially if new technologies increase present conversion efficiencies. It is estimated that diversion of 10 per cent of currently tilled land would provide sufficient ethanol to substitute 'gasohol' (90 per cent petrol, 10 per cent ethanol) for present uses of petrol. Suitable crops for such conversion include sugar and fodder beet, wheat, grass, potatoes and Jerusalem artichokes. Whey, a by-product of cheese production, could also be diverted from cattle food to ethanol conversion. Another possibility is to use oils from rape seed or other brassicas as diesel extenders or replacements. Finally biogas production from farm wastes could be another source of useful energy, as well as reducing pollution problems.

*Wind Energy*

Ireland has good wind resources, the potential of which is greatest in northern and western coastal areas, although local topography can create promising sites elsewhere. Wind power can be used on a variety of scales for electricity generation or pumping and a variety of designs are now emerging. An important characteristic of wind power is its seasonal and diurnal variations. June to September are generally the months of lowest mean wind speed while strong winds are most frequent in the period November to March. Lowest mean speeds occur during the night hours and the highest average is generally in the early afternoon, thus broadly coinciding with periods of peak demand. A £IR1 million national wind energy programme was initiated by the Department of Energy in 1980, with construction and operation of a variety of machines in various applications. A 50 kW Danish wind generator has been installed on Inisheer, the smallest of the Aran Islands, to provide electricity for the island community. An American machine at Fermoy will be used to heat water by mechanical means for a dairy. At Ballinamore in Leitrim an Irish-made generator will provide electricity for water heating in another dairy. A Dutch-made machine is being used at Creagh in Mayo for water pumping in a land reclamation project. It is also reported that 200–300 water pumping windmills were installed in Ireland during the 1970s (Brady, 1981).

The Electricity Supply Board also decided in 1980 to undertake a wind power test and demonstration programme. Four medium-sized machines have been erected at different locations around the country, with 10 kW, 50 kW, 55 kW and 120 kW generators. Electricity generation specifically related to the grid is likely to take the form of 'wind farms' and the ESB has studied the feasibility of combining a large number of wind energy turbines, each rated at 3 MW, with a pumped storage reservoir. The programme is intended to assess the reliability, efficiency and economics of commercially available wind turbine generators and sites. As well as operational data, the ESB is also monitoring 'environmental and social acceptance' (Hally, 1981). In parallel with this research, the Meteorological Service has been asked to map the detailed wind climate of the country and the Department of Energy is preparing a design manual.

*Solar Energy*

Solar energy can be used directly for water or space heating (solar thermal) or converted to electricity via photovoltaic cells. As some 60 per cent of the solar radiation reaching Ireland is diffused by clouds and other factors, there are some constraints on its use.

Although there has been little government support for solar thermal applications other than through EC research and development programmes, private installations have been made in the domestic sector. For space heating these have been mainly passive in which solar energy captured by building components rather than 'active' (which capture solar energy by special collectors and working fluids) designs, and this situation is likely to continue in the future. Traditional forms of buildings often have 'passive solar' features and the carefully sited, sheltered traditional thatched cottage presents a sharp contrast in the Irish countryside to contemporary exhibitionist overglazed bungalows. There are some encouraging signs of renewed interest in climate-responsive buildings. Opportunities for greater use of solar water heating are related to construction rates of new houses, where it is much cheaper to install collectors than to 'retrofit' existing buildings. The current Irish construction rate is about 26,000 houses per annum. If a target of 60 per cent of new houses, together with 20 per cent of existing houses, were to be achieved there would be about 40 per cent market penetration by 2000. This would save some 0.05–0.14 Mtce per annum by 2000 (SESI, 1978). There is also potential for the use of solar water heating in other sectors such as industry and agriculture but it is too early to make an assessment of the possible impact.

The main Irish photovoltaic application is a demonstration project, partially financed by the EEF at a dairy farm on Fota Island, County Cork. As photovoltaic cells are made from silicon, the basis of modern electronics, they may provide opportunities for the many Irish companies already using this raw material.

*Wave Energy*

Ireland participates, through the ESB, in the wave research programme of the International Energy Agency. The area to the west and north west of Ireland is possibly the most attractive part of the world in which to exploit wave power (Murphy, 1978), and may have great potential in the medium to long term.

*Tidal Energy*

Preliminary studies of Irish tidal energy resources made some years ago indicated that their potential was limited due to the relatively small tidal ranges. However, these studies are being reviewed to take account of present circumstances and the resources of the estuary of the River Shannon and Carlingford Lough in the north east are being re-examined. Another analysis has shown that Strangford Lough, with a 3.6 m tidal range, could provide 350 MW and an annual production similar to the La Rance tidal barrage in France (McMullen *et al.*, 1977).

### Geothermal Energy

Six major granite intrusions exist in Ireland, and three—in Galway, Leinster and Donegal—are being examined for geothermal potential (Brock, 1979).

## The Planning and Development System

### Structure

The Local Government (Planning and Development) Act 1963 is the basis of Irish planning. This Act established a flexible planning system to be operated by 87 planning authorities who were required to prepare development plans and to operate a development control system. The Act did not contain the term 'energy' and the first two generations of development plans did not contain any planning policies for energy use. Even the most recent development plans (each plan must be reviewed at least once every 5 years) did not have energy policies, with occasional exceptions, such as the 1980, Waterford Draft Added Area Plan. However, the 1963 Act does allow planning authorities to indicate objectives for energy-using such as housing, transport and industry, and to control the density, layout and orientation of structures.

The 1963 Act was further improved by the Local Government (Planning and Development) Act 1976 which was based on the experiences and insights gained from operating the planning system in the intervening period. New concepts were included, for example, environmental impact assessment but once more the word 'energy' was not contained in the new Act. A 1976 Act instituted An Bord Pleanala (The Planning Appeals Board) to adjudicate on the appeals emanating from the decisions of the 87 planning authorities. Formerly, this function had been carried out by the Minister for Local Government, (now the Minister for the Environment).

Under the planning acts, authorities have 2 months in which to decide on development applications (the time period can be extended by mutual agreement or by seeking further information). When reaching a decision on any application, the planning authority must consider 'the proper planning and development of the area of the authority (including the preservation and improvement of the amenities thereof), regard being paid to the provisions of the development plan, the provisions of any special amenity area order relating to the said area' and a variety of other matters, none of which include energy considerations. Third parties may object to the proposed development and, if overruled by the planning authority, may appeal to An Bord Pleanala. The applicant may also appeal and An Bord Pleanala can hold an oral hearing which is conducted without undue formality. The decisions of An Bord Pleanala, an independent body chaired by a Judge of High Court status, can only be reversed by the Courts on matters of law and procedure and not on planning grounds.

At the regional level are nine Regional Development Organisations (RDOs), which could become an important influence at the interface of energy policy and land use planning policy. The nine regions were defined for physical planning by the Irish government in 1964 and their RDOs established in 1969 to provide a national framework for the co-ordination of regional planning policies. They are non-statutory bodies, representative of local authorities and other development agencies. Their principal function is to help co-ordinate development in the regions by facilitating information exchange, undertaking relevant studies and advising central government on problems which may arise in the implementation of regional policy at sub-national and local levels. All the RDOs prepared regional strategy reports in the early 1970s and the second generation of more detailed and more specific regional plans are currently being published.

These new regional reports are now more likely to contain a discussion of energy objectives than the statutory development plans. For example the South East RDO 1980 report contains a chapter on energy which includes specific conservation, biomass, coal mining and the impact of energy on the settlement and transportation patterns (South East Regional Development Organisation, 1980). Similarly the Midlands RDO recently considered policies for the exploitation of peat resources (20 per cent of the region is peat land) including the use of cutaway bogs for SRF as an aid to regional development.

While local planning authorities can control energy developments within their own areas, they rarely initiate any energy projects (except for town gas supply). Hydro-electricity is mainly generated by the semi-state body—the Electricity Supply Board (ESB). Peat is mainly produced by Bord na Mona and it is likely that SRF would be grown on the large scale by either a state or semi-state organisation. There are very few cases where local authorities have opposed government-initiated energy developments although local groups have done so in a number of cases. The relative balance of power lies with the central authority even though national gain could mean local loss of amenity, land or other advantages. As the renewable energy development anticipated to take place in Ireland tends towards decentralisation and low environmental impact, it is likely that such national-local conflict will be minor, unlike, for example, the siting of a nuclear power station (Gough, 1979).

Local authorities are also responsible for the control of water pollution under the Local Government (Water Pollution) Act, 1977. The Regional Health Boards control air pollution and general health matters while the Department of Labour is responsible for occupational health and safety. Only the local authority and the Health Boards can influence a decision as to whether or not a particular development goes ahead. The Department of Labour enforces legislation in regard to safety for workers employed in a particular project.

After a planning authority grants permission subject to conditions, it may monitor the development to ensure that these are being fulfilled. In some cases, such as monitoring of effluents, periodic checking on a regular basis may be required, either by the developer or by the planning authority. Other agencies such as Health Boards or the Department of Labour Industrial Inspectorate, may also monitor certain aspects. The planning authorities work closely with the Health Boards but the working relationship between the planning departments and Industrial Inspectorate is not very close and may sometimes be non-existent. There is less danger of overlap of monitoring functions than of some monitoring procedures not being done at all.

### Planning Controls and Renewable Energy Developments

Under current Irish planning legislation some renewable energy projects require planning permission but others are 'exempted developments'—defined by Section Four of the 1963 Act as 'development consisting of the use of any land for the purposes of agriculture or forestry (including afforestation), and development consisting of the use for any of these purposes of any building occupied together with land so used'. Therefore SRF or biomass production is likely to be exempted development. Section 84 further implies that buildings which are to be constructed or extended in connection with afforestation by the State do not require planning permission. Peat production is also an exempted development and Bord na Mona only applies for planning permission for briquette factories and similar plant. Similarly the exploitation by private individuals of blanket bogs on mountain sides does not require planning permission.

The Local Government (Planning and Development) Regulations 1977 has set restrictions on exempted developments which could be important in deciding whether or not individual renewable energy developments require planning permission. Such restrictions relate to the creation of traffic hazards; the contravention of building regulations; the restriction of views or prospects whose preservation is an objective of a development plan; the enclosure or fencing of public land and other matters. As a result wind machines for agricultural purposes require planning permission if they exceed 7 m in height within 100 m of a public road.

Exempted developments are set by ministerial regulation and it would be relatively easy for a Minister for the Environment to add to the list of exempted developments or to require existing exempted developments to be the subject of planning permission in the future. For example, to expedite the development of the Kinsale gas field, new regulations were introduced which made the construction of the underground pipelines by the newly-founded Irish Gas Board exempted development (but not the construction or erection of any apparatus, equipment or other things ancillary to such a pipeline save cathodic protection equipment and market posts). A variety of matters arising from the construction process as well as wider development issues are thus placed outside the normal planning process. Presently exempted renewable energy developments could in the future require planning permission particularly if the environmental impacts of such developments become serious or noticeable.

All aspects of electricity undertakings require planning permission except certain minor developments, such as undergroundings of cables, pipes and mains; the provision of overhead transmission or distribution lines of less than 10 kV and construction of small sub-stations. All HEP schemes require planning permission and are therefore subject to public scrutiny and possible appeal procedures.

Solar panels erected on a building would not normally require planning permission except in a situation where the alteration would render the character of the building inconsistent with that of any neighbouring structures. Both 'active' and 'passive' solar houses require permission in the normal way. On the other hand, wave power machines do not require planning permission as these would be outside the jurisdiction of the planning authorities (which stops at the high-water mark).

Article 28 of the Local Government (Planning and Development) Regulations 1977 makes mandatory the submission of two copies of an environmental study with certain types of planning application. These are for trade or industrial (including mining) developments comprising any works, apparatus or plant used for any process which would result in the emission of noise, vibration, smell, fumes, smoke, soot, ash, dust or grit, or the discharge of any liquid or other effluent, and which are likely to cost £IR 5 million or more. Such an environmental impact assessment (EIA) would therefore be required for a large wind generator costing £IR 5 million or more and causing noise and vibration, although these are likely to be rare. Major HEP schemes and biomass combustion plants would inevitably be subject to the requirement of EIA. Under a 1980 EC draft directive, energy developments which produce and distribute electricity, gas, steam and hot water would be subject to EIA. This provides much more detailed guidelines on EIA than the existing Irish legislation, which Lee and Wood (1978) have described as 'project appraisal'. For example, the planning authority would have to make publicly available its assessment of the environmental effects of the proposed energy developments, a synthesis of the main comments and opinion sought in the consultation and participation process, and the reasons for granting or refusing the planning permission. There would also be greater scope for public participation. The directive stresses the relationship between the proposed project and land-use plants for the affected area, and permits the consideration of socio-economic effects such as contribution to employment and effects on the built-up environment, including the architectural heritage and the landscape.

## Planning for Renewables

The development of renewable resources in Ireland will be influenced by national goals and the pattern of Irish economic geography.

Energy production and supply in Ireland has been determined by population geography, with the primate city of Dublin, a small number of medium-sized towns and a low density rural population. This is a result of a large agricultural sector, and an industrial policy of bringing jobs to the people rather than people to jobs. This has resulted in a dispersed pattern of industrial development in each of the nine regions.

The dispersed rural population makes it expensive to distribute electricity, oil and gas (peat distribution was never a comparable problem). Few towns have had town gas supplies as most were too small to support viable services. Oil is transported by truck and not by pipeline. Low population densities and car numbers means that many rural petrol filling stations are too small and uneconomic to be supplied by the oil companies. The ESB has had to build expensive and intrusive electricity transmission lines to remote areas where industry was set up to utilise large quantities of fresh water, deep water port sites or other natural advantages.

Despite these problems successive governments have encouraged rural electrification to provide amenities and economic opportunities in remote areas, with the result that nearly every rural dwelling in Ireland has electricity. In the year ending 31 March, 1981, some 1160 houses were connected and work was going ahead on providing a supply to a further 240 premises under the rural electrification scheme (ESB, 1981). Renewable energy sources are clearly suited to such schemes, and may have economic advantages over the expensive provision of electricity from the centralised system. In Denmark, the government envisages small windmills providing half of the energy for space heating and most of the electricity for houses in rural areas. In the Highlands and Islands region of Scotland (similar in many ways to the west of Ireland), the Highland and Islands Development Board has explored the effects of decentralised use of renewable resources on employment opportunities (Hughes, 1981). Some commentators have stated that increased local employment and manufacture in remote rural areas is more likely to happen by harnessing the dispersed renewable forms of energy and using these at low intensity in the vicinity, rather than bringing in supplies from centralised sources or concentrating the renewable supplies for export to urban complexes (Twidell, 1981).

Another national goal of relevance to the introduction of renewable energy is the desire to develop the Gaeltacht (Gaelic-speaking areas) and other parts of Western Ireland. As a large proportion of Irish renewable resources are concentrated in this region, their development could do much to overcome their present energy and economic disadvantages, and provide job opportunities and new investment. For example where peat supplies are being depleted, the growing of biomass crops on the cutover (worked) bogs could provide alternative jobs for workers. This will become increasingly important from the mid-1980s onwards. The provision of renewable energy supplies, such as electricity from windmills, may be necessary for the survival of island communities and other especially remote. Inisturbot inhabitants have left their island and settled on the mainland because the peat supply on the island was depleted and the only energy alternative was expensive bottled gas. Recently the Government approved the construction of a windmill on Inisheer, the smallest of the Aran Islands, to avoid this outcome.

However, without care, renewable energy installations could conflict with other environmental or planning goals. Some 1.2 million hectares of Irish countryside (one-seventh of the total land area) is classified as being outstanding landscape (An Foras Forbartha, 1977). These landscapes feature not only in tourist literature but are designated in many county and regional plans as areas of strict development control. They include areas of high relief, both mountain and coastal, and areas of low relief as lakes, river valleys, estuaries, and low-lying coastal areas. A number of renewable developments, such as the growth, harvesting and combustion of SRF, the development of peat bogs, the construction of windmills and hydro-electric schemes (including pumped storage schemes) could be detrimental in some of these outstanding landscapes. Although there is probably sufficient rural land not in the category of outstanding landscape to provide for the acceptable location of renewable energy developments it can be expected that conflicts will arise in the future between the provision of renewable energy developments and the protection of Ireland's scenic heritage. Such conflicts have already occurred in the past as with the Turlough Hill pumped storage situation in the Wicklow Mountains.

Each of the main renewable sources will have their distinctive impacts. The environmental effects of large HEP schemes can be considerable, especially at a local level. The major impact is often the raising of the water level to create new lakes and reservoirs behind dams. Water supplies can be altered, habitats destroyed and new marshland created. The disturbance of valuable fishing stocks, for example, of River Lee salmon, has caused much concern, although coarse fishing has been encouraged by hydro reservoirs. Large areas of land become permanently submerged and other land uses can be reduced in value although amenity value is often raised by water-based recreation opportunities. The regulation of water levels may erode lakeside edges, cause damage to river banks downstream of dams and alter silting patterns. At a time of industrial unrest in other power stations in Ireland in 1979, many of the HEP lakes were run down very quickly, resulting in serious disturbance to the tourist pleasure boat industry on the River Shannon and its lakes in the summer of 1979, as water levels dropped rapidly and rivers and lakes became unnavigable.

Controversy over HEP has not been as great as that over pumped storage schemes, especially the Turlough Hill scheme. Selman (1979) states that their sheer scale increases environmental impact and rightly insists that a number of planning constraints should be added to the geological and engineering criteria which presently guide the location of such developments. In particular the impact of pumped storage is likely to be the most prominent:

— where proposals affect a 'wilderness' area;
— where the upper reservoir is starkly visible from popular vantage points;
— where the site to be inundated is of botanical or recreational value;
— where the lower water body is of major biological interest;
— where extensive workcamps have to be constructed or large numbers of workers have to transported to the site; and
— where marginal local industries and communities are liable to be disrupted.

Anfield (1979) has argued that the environmental effects of pumped storage makes construction of increased capacity a better alternative.

Large scale biomass production will have some environmental, planning, and ecological impacts, principally because of the large areas needed for growing and storing the biomass crops. It has been calculated that to provide enough biomass to keep a small 50 MW(e) generating station supplied the land take would be 11,700 hectares cropped on a 4-year cycle (Lyons, 1979). There will be some landscape effects, not least the 'greening' of cutaway peat bogs, which could be considered by some to be a visual gain. Biomass production on blanket bog and marginal land on hillsides will have a different visual effect, but such lands are, in any case, more suited to conventional forestry than SRF. There are unlikely to be any new biomass-fuelled power stations for a considerable time until most of the existing peat-fired stations have been converted. Thus the landscape effects of new power stations in rural areas will be kept to a minimum. Noise pollution will also be minimal as harvesting noise is unlikely to be a problem in the remote rural areas where most biomass will be grown. Air pollution at the biomass-fired power stations will not be a problem because of its low sulphur and nitrogen content; the emission of particulates would be equivalent to that from a peat-fired station and less than from similar coal-fired stations. The biomass fermentation process can produce characteristic odours but as this is likely to be done close to the plantations in rural areas, they should not become too significant. Ash production from biomass combustion is almost negligible and can be stored in lagoons with acceptable environmental impact.

The main ecological hazards are likely to arise through water pollution resulting from the large-scale application of fertilisers, herbicides and pesticides which could affect fish life and drinking water and produce localised eutrophication effects. Aerial spraying of large areas of biomass could affect neighbouring lands. Proper control over fertiliser application, times and rates (leaf fall will also cut down on fertiliser applications) and the proper selection of herbicides and pesticides will limit the water pollution effects. Water pollution from biomass fermentation can occur but recycling the waste water reduces this problem. Large land areas of biomass could affect hydrological patterns locally and may lower water tables. However, until large scale biomass production for energy purposes takes place on a large and organised scale, it is difficult to be certain about the ecological, environmental and planning impacts.

Studies of the physical planning implications of an extensive exploitation of solar energy for space or water heating or for photovoltaic electricity generation in decentralised installations are still at an early stage. It has been suggested that the use of this source would be prejudiced by densities of more than 40 houses to the hectare in low-rise residential developments. The mid-winter sun angle can be a major dimensioning factor in the planning and layout of neighbourhoods and architects and planners will need to manipulate shading diagrams when designing groups of buildings.

Planning and building control requirements must also be met. It would seem that the fixing of solar panels to the roof of a house where it is hidden from the public street may be exempt from any requirement to seek planning permission. The attitude of planning authorities towards installations visible from the street has not yet become clear. Similarly, building controls will impose certain constraints on the solar system and its fixing and connection to the water service but detailed requirements have not yet been clarified. From experience elsewhere, one may anticipate that the principal concerns will be security of the panel fixing to the roof; the satisfactory weathering of any interruption to the roof finish; adequate arrangements to ensure that the public water supply is not contaminated and care that anti-freeze additive will not lead to health hazards if part of a heat exchanger, for example, fails.

Where an individual has installed collectors he will naturally be concerned if a neighbour undertakes development which causes the shading of his collectors. Ireland has no 'right to sun' analogous to the rights of light as found in English common law, and this may be needed to encourage solar use. The visual impact of solar collectors 3 m$^2$ to 6 m$^2$ in area on the southern side of pitched roofs in northern Europe or North America is not great and has not usually produced serious opposition, possibly reflecting the generally favourable public attitude towards what is seen as a benign energy technology. The visual problem can be more problematic when collectors are mounted on low rise flat-roofed buildings or fixed to frameworks mounted off the external walls. When installed on low flat-roofed buildings, solar collectors may create an ugly skyline. Such planning considerations must constrain the implementation of solar water heating in a proportion of existing housing, especially in historic and conservation areas where large areas of glazing are not likely to be appropriate. In certain circumstances glare may be caused by the reflection of sunlight off collector covers. This particularly arises at high sun angles and when collectors are mounted on low buildings. Proper planning of a district may require that where collectors are mounted in a low area, for instance facing a road north, some screening of the collectors may be necessary to prevent glare hazardous to approaching drivers.

A number of environmental impacts of wind power have been noted. At high wind speeds, above Beaufort force four, some noise may be heard but it is not unlike the whistling of wires and is usually masked by sounds such as trees rustling. Infrasound can be a more serious problem in certain sites if topographical effects are not adequately considered. This very low frequency (2–3 Hz) noise may cause perceptible vibration if focused by ground contours. Some television microwave interference may be experienced in a cone extending up to one mile from large machines, though plastic blades reduce this effect compared with metal ones and cable television can resolve it fully. Safety questions may arise in gusting or gale force winds and brakes are usually incorporated to control the machine in such circumstances. Vibration detectors are fitted to large machines to warn off any defects and to shut down the machine before any catastrophic failure might occur. Finally, in a similar way to 'rights to sunlight' for solar collectors, it may be necessary some time in the future to regulate new developments to prevent the sheltering of windmills (a 17th century Dutch Law required that windmills should be 200 m apart, or 8 to 10 diameters). Preferred sites for wind energy are likely to consist of wide, flat, open areas with road access and ideally located close to the existing grid, rather than the most obvious but probably problematic coastal sites.

The environmental effects of tidal schemes are likely to be considerable both during the 10 to 15 years of construction and the post-construction period. These effects include interference with port traffic and shipping, ecological change in estuary habitat, changes in fishing patterns, and hydrographic alterations. But there are also beneficial impacts, such as flood protection, provision of road/rail links on the barrage and enhanced recreational facilities due to reduced tidal currents and less tidal range.

Most proposed devices will be located several kilometres out to sea and will not be visible from shore and thus will have minimal visual impact. On the other hand the vicinity of wave energy installations would be restricted areas for shipping and fishing activities. Site specific geomorphological and ecological impacts could result because of changes in the wave regime and the creation of calmer water areas between the installation and the shore. Shore facilities will have to be carefully sited and designed to minimise visual impact, and problems with transmission lines coming ashore in scenic locations must be anticipated.

## Conclusion: Planning and Renewable Energy Systems

It is now clear that in the medium and long term, renewable energy sources will make an important contribution within the Irish energy economy. The existing planning system already provides a basic framework within which these developments can be assessed but improvements will be needed at the regional and local levels. The planning system must be able to do more than simply respond to the emergence of new technologies, many of which will pose considerable environmental challenges.

It is in the wide field of renewable energy that some of the most significant technological developments in the whole area of energy supply are likely to emerge and the planning process must be able to anticipate, guide and nurture this emergence. As Hall (1979) has urged, 'it is beholden upon the planning authorities to be tolerant towards experimentation' with alternative energy sources. Any inertial tendencies towards suspicion of and disfavour towards the unconventional, as aspects of renewable energy are likely to be, can be minimised by planners having a considerable technical familiarity with the different renewable supply systems. They must also develop procedures, regulations and statutes so that these can cope with the rapid change which introduction of renewable systems could precipitate and also so that the systems themselves, if an accelerated need emerges, can rapidly be propagated. In particular, as well as appreciating that future renewable energy policies will inevitably influence regional and county plans (and even smaller-scale urban plans) planners dealing with the issues of economies such as Ireland's need to be especially aware that many of the renewable energy systems are very labour intensive.

The advantages, disadvantages and impacts of each potential energy option, including renewables, must be evaluated on an equivalent basis. Here planners have a particular role in constructively questioning the energy policies of central government and the energy supply utilities when these affect the areas for which they are responsible. Planners must ensure that national gains do not cause unacceptable local losses of amenity, environmental degradation and health hazards and have a central role in minimising the conflicts which such losses can precipitate. Looked at in general, the broad characteristics of every major energy supply option, except renewables, have emerged in the period before planning was accorded the significance it enjoys today. Sites and impacts have to a degree been a legacy. With renewables, however, there is a *tabula rasa* and the successful reconciliation of their introduction with the problems that might arise will be a powerful vindication of the necessity and efficacy of land-use planning.

## References

Anfield, J. (1979) Peak Park pumped storage electricity, in *Energy Policy and Local Planning*, Council for the Protection of Rural England, London.

Brady, J. (1981) Opportunities for the Irish engineering industry, in Institute for Industrial Research and Standards conference on *Wind Power Technology*, April, Dublin.

Brock, A. (1979) Geothermal Energy in Ireland, National Board for Science and Technology, December, Dublin.

Department of Industry, Commerce and Energy (1978) *Energy—Ireland: Discussion Document on some Current Energy Problems and Options*, Stationery Office, July, Dublin.

Duggan, J. C. (1978) Small scale water power, in proceedings of Solar Energy Society of Ireland conference, *Wind, Wave, Water Conference*, Solar Energy Society of Ireland, April, Dublin.

ESB (Electricity Supply Board) (1981) *Annual Report for the year ending 31 March, 1981*, Dublin.

Fine Gael (1980) *Aspects of Energy Policy*, Fine Gael, Dublin.

An Foras Forbatha (1977) *Inventory of Outstanding Landscapes in Ireland*, Dublin.

Gough, M. (1979) The integration of national energy policy within the framework at regional and local level, paper presented at the Irish Planning Institute conference on *Town Planning Implications of Energy Demand and Supply*, November, Dublin.

Hall, D. (1979) The way ahead—practical proposals for action by planners, in *Energy Policy and Local Planning*, Council for the Protection of Rural England, London.

Hally, M. (1981) Wind energy—a utility programme, in Institute for Industrial Research and Standards conference on *Wind Power Technology*, April, Dublin.

Healy, J. (1979) Planning implications of biomass as a future energy source, paper presented at the Irish Planning Institute conference on *Town Planning Implications of Energy Demand and Supply*, November, Dublin.

Hughes, J. T. (1981) Alternative energy and rural development, in *Energy for Rural and Island Communities*, Pergamon Press, Oxford.

Kavanagh, R. and Brady, J. (1980) *Energy Supply and Demand—the Next 30 Years*, National Board for Science and Technology, June, Dublin.

Kearney, D. (1979) Overview of national and international programmes in biomass energy development, in *The Key role of Biomass in Ireland's Energy Future*, Solar Energy Society of Ireland, Dublin.

Lalor, E. (1975) *Solar Energy for Ireland*, National Science Council, February, Dublin.

Lee, N. and Wood, C. (1978) EIA—a European perspective, *Built Environment*, **4**, 2.

Lyons, G. T. (1979) Storage and combustion of wood fuel chips, in *The Key Role of Biomass in Ireland's Energy Future*, proceedings of a conference, An Foras Taluntais, May, Dublin.

McMullen, J. T. and Morgan, R. and Murray, R. B. (1977) *Energy Resources*, Edward Arnold, p.39, London.

McNulty, P. B. (1979) Energy from biomass, in *Energy and Power in Ireland*, Dublin.

Murphy, E. S. (1978) Natural energy resources, in proceedings of Solar Energy Society of Ireland conference, *Wind, Wave, Water Conference*, Solar Energy Society of Ireland, April, Dublin.

Selman, P. (1979) Pumped storage electricity: the latest threat to the uplands, *The Planner*, May.

SESI (Solar Energy Society of Ireland) (1978) *Toward Energy Independence*, SESI, December, Dublin.

South East Regional Development Organisation (1980) *Regional Report and Development Strategy*, Waterford.

An Taisce (1979) *Energy in Question*, An Taisce, Dublin.

Twidell, J. (ed.) (1981) *Energy for Rural and Island Communities*, Pergamon, Oxford.

CHAPTER 9

# Spatial Structure and Energy Demand

SUSAN OWENS

## Introduction

During the 1970s, society was made acutely aware of its dependence on secure supplies of low price energy. Following a series of interruptions to the flow of oil and in the face of steeply rising prices, most organisations began to assess the relevance of the changed energy situation for their activities. The planning profession was no exception and recognised that there are relationships between energy, land use and planning which have hitherto received little attention but which could now emerge as an important planning issue.

The focus of debate on energy and planning—as demonstrated by all other contributions to this book—has been on the planning implications of energy supply systems. This emphasis is a particular case of a more general bias towards concern with energy supply rather than energy demand. This is frequently explained (and often justified) by comparing the inherent difficulties of influencing energy demand, controlled by myriads of individual consumers in the market place, with the alleged relative simplicity of a 'technical fix' on the supply side. Furthermore, there are highly organised and influential institutions to promote energy supply, but no equivalent organisation to 'lobby' for conservation (although the need for such a body is increasingly recognised. See, for example, Williams, 1981). Additional factors account for the emphasis on energy supply in the planning field, particularly the significant impacts of many energy-related developments and the increasing use of planning inquiries as a forum for debate on national energy needs and policies.

The opportunities for local authorities, and more particularly local authority planners, to have any immediate and direct influence on the energy consumption of individuals and organisations within their area is limited, although they can try to set an example in sectors, such as public housing, under local authority control. There may, in fact, be little incentive for them to try, since to do so will incur local costs but not necessarily any immediate local benefits (any resulting reduction in the impact of new supply facilities, for example, is unlikely to be enjoyed in the same area). Nevertheless, it is argued in this chapter that there may be significant opportunities for planners, in their role of monitoring and guiding the evolution of society's spatial structure, to contribute to the more 'rational' use of energy resources in the medium to long term. The term 'rational' is used throughout this chapter to imply that energy conservation be given due consideration, but not to the exclusion of other important goals.

Little attention has been given to the fundamental relationship between the spatial organisation of society and the way it uses energy. The relative neglect of this subject and its policy implications may be attributed to a number of factors in addition to the more general emphasis on supply facilities already outlined. These include the intrinsic difficulties of identifying energy-efficient settlement patterns, the long-term nature of the policies involved and the existence of innumerable physical, social and institutional constraints which some believe would prevent any significant modifications to urban form within a realistic planning period.

Land-use patterns which developed during a long period of relatively cheap and abundant fuel are clearly 'energy intensive' and may provide considerable scope for improvement of their energy efficiency. Although some have argued that energy considerations should form an integral part of any long term policies which influence the structure of the built environment (e.g. Ashworth, 1974; Brown, 1977; Odell, 1975, 1977), very little progress has been made towards the implementation of these ideas in planning practice. In the UK, for example, the energy issue was virtually ignored in the recent round of structure plans. Although in 1975 the House of Commons Select Committee on Science and Technology urged that regional, structural and transport plans should consider the energy implications of their proposals, the Department of Energy, while accepting the importance of the issue, rejected the idea that energy considerations should be separately identified in such plans (Select Committee on Science and Technology, 1975; Department of Energy, 1976).

This chapter addresses the potential for planners to guide the evolution of settlement structures and the built environment into forms which are more compatible with an energy-constrained future. A prerequisite for an assessment of this potential is some knowledge of the spatial distribution of energy demand although very little research has been done in this field. Secondly, an attempt must be made to describe how energy requirements for different end uses are influenced by spatial structure—in other words, to model the relationship between spatial structure and energy demand. It should then be possible to explore the way in which settlements might adjust to the changing energy situation and to identify development patterns which would contribute to the more rational use of energy sources. Where these patterns seem unlikely to evolve without planning intervention, it may be possible to develop and implement appropriate policies. All of these issues, which remain largely unexplored, are considered in turn in this chapter.

## Energy Use in Spatial Systems

We are still a very long way from understanding energy flows in complex urban and regional systems. There is both a paucity of studies on the energy budgets of urban communities and a lack of acceptable and well-defined methods for energy use inventories (Kalma and Newcombe, 1976). In particular, there is a lack of data on the spatial distribution of energy demand which are sufficiently disaggregated to permit exploration of its relationship with urban structural variables.

There is, however, an increasing quantity of information about the distribution of energy demand between different sectors of the economy and, though less frequently, between different end uses. Although often not spatially disaggregated, such data are useful for identifying, in broad general terms, those areas where planning policies might conceivably influence energy requirements.

One of the most detailed studies to date of energy use in the United Kingdom has been provided by Leach *et al.* (1979). The main aim of this work was to produce a 'low energy scenario' for the future but the methodology involved a very detailed breakdown of UK energy demand into nearly 400 separate categories. The considerable detail for each sector cannot be reproduced here, but the aggregated breakdown of delivered energy requirements for different end uses is of some significance to the subject of this chapter. This breakdown is shown in Table 9.1.

TABLE 9.1 *Delivered Energy Requirements by End Use (Leach, 1979).*

| End Use | % delivered energy |
|---|---|
| Low temperature heat (<80°C) | 34.8 |
| High temperature heat (>80°C) | 25.0 |
| Essential electricity[1] | 8.1 |
| Transport | 21.2 |
| Non-energy uses[2] | 11.0 |
| TOTAL | 100.1 |

[1] lighting, machinery, electro-chemical processes, etc.
[2] chemical feedstocks, international bunkers, bitumen, lubricating oil, industrial spirits, etc.

The relevance of Table 9.1 for planners lies in its demonstration that no less than 56 per cent of delivered energy is for low temperature heat (the bulk of which is for the space heating of buildings) and for transport (almost three-quarters of which is for land-based transport in the UK). Since buildings and transport networks constitute the built environment and since it is the development and use of the built environment with which planners are primarily concerned, it would seem, even from this rather crude breakdown of energy demand, that planners could have a significant influence on future energy consumption. Nor should other sectors be ignored, since there may be circumstances in which planning policies could influence energy requirements for such purposes as lighting ('essential electricity') and high temperature industrial processes. Furthermore, most policies which influence the built environment will involve the provision of, and therefore an energy 'investment' in, infrastructure. Thus, while transport and space heating are the two sectors within which the most obvious energy/land use interactions take place, the possibility that planning policies could influence energy requirements for other end uses should not be ignored.

Ideally, planners should have for their own areas (counties, districts, etc.) the detailed breakdown of energy consumption by end use that Leach and his colleagues have provided at the national scale, together with some idea of the spatial distribution of this energy demand. This issue is touched upon in a study of the implications of more decentralised energy planning in the United States conducted at Oak Ridge National Laboratory. Wilbanks (1981) notes that 'the potential for energy conservation and the use of renewable resources is nearly always underestimated when evaluations are based on national averages and aggregates; it shows up more clearly when a "fine-grained localised analysis" is done'.

Clearly, energy budgets will differ quite markedly between geographical areas; that of a rural agricultural area with dispersed settlements, for example, will be quite different from that of a heavily industrialised urban region. In theory, the more disaggregated the data, the more appropriate the planners' policies could be in relation to energy conservation. In practice of course there will be considerable costs attached to obtaining detailed information whereas the potential benefits of such knowledge may not be fully realised because of the many constraints which planners face in policy-making and implementation.

A certain amount of research has been carried out on the energy budgets of specific geographical areas (e.g. Borg, 1978; Kalma and Newcombe, 1976; Newcombe, 1975 a and b, 1976) but such work has usually involved no spatial dimension in the sense that energy flows are usually disaggregated by fuel and end use sector but not at any finer level of spatial resolution *within* the geographical area concerned. In most cases, fundamental research will be required to determine the spatial distribution of energy demand for different purposes in a given geographical area. The results of such work would provide a sound basis for the incorporation of energy considerations into the planning process. However, until it is carried out, the concept of spatially disaggregated energy budgets provides a useful theoretical framework for the discussion of energy, land-use and planning interactions.

## The Relationship between Energy Use and Spatial Structure

While it is often accepted that 'the spatial organisation of society is fundamental to the way in which it uses energy' (Steadman, 1980, p.27) the mechanisms of the relationship are difficult to define and cause and effect cannot easily be distinguished. Empirical investigation is hampered by the large number of variables involved, while theoretical work has tended to be so abstract and simplified that its applicability to any 'real world' situation is severely limited.

As a first step in attempting to define the relationship between energy demand and spatial structure, three groups of variables may be distinguished. For simplicity, these may be termed 'energy system variables', 'structural variables' and 'interaction variables'. The first group, as its name suggests, describes aspects of the energy system, these would include, for example, the spatial distribution of energy demand for different end purposes, the fuels used, the source of these fuels etc. It might also include such variables as incident solar radiation, wind speeds etc. which would enable the potential for renewable energy sources in the area to be explored.

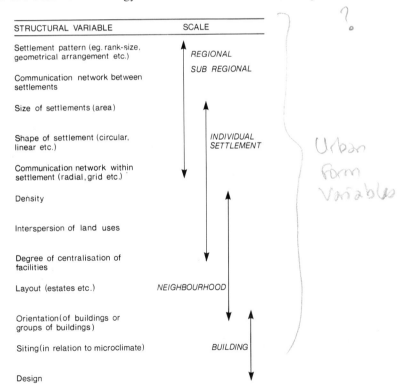

TABLE 9.2 *Significant Structural Variables at Different Scales*

Structural variables describe 'urban form' and other aspects of the built environment. Much depends on the *scale* at which the analysis is being conducted, since different structural variables will be relevant at different scales. This is illustrated in Table 9.2.

The third group of variables is less easy to define; these variables are involved in the mechanisms of interaction between the energy system and spatial structure. They might include, for example, the deterrent effect of distance on trip making, modal split (proportion of travellers using different modes of transport), the efficiencies of heating equipment or the level of thermal insulation. Trip making and modal split would influence the relationship between the interspersion of land uses and energy requirements for transport, while the extent to which densities influence space heating requirements will depend partly on equipment efficiencies and levels of insulation in houses. The prices of various fuels and the elasticities of energy demand for different end uses are also important interaction variables.

A simple model of the relationship between the energy system and the spatial structure of society may now be postulated. In this model, (Fig. 9.1), the nature and availability of energy sources exert an influence on land use patterns. The location of early industrial development, for example, was largely determined by energy sources—first water power, then coal. Later, with the development of national energy distribution grids, industrial location became less tied to energy sources. During times of cheap and readily available energy the built environment was planned and developed in a form which reflected the *absence of energy constraints*. Thus, the urban sprawl and increasing separation of activities experienced by most of the western world throughout the 1950s and 1960s reflected the relative lack of energy constraints in the transport system and the absence of much concern for space heating efficiency in the predominantly low density, dispersed residential development which took place during this period.

Once constructed, the built environment constrains the level and pattern of energy demand. This is incorporated in the model as the influence of spatial structure on energy requirements for various activities. For example, in low density suburbs, segregated from employment and service opportunities and lacking efficient public transport systems, the inhabitants are necessarily dependent on a high level of personal mobility, while the potential for reducing energy requirements for space heating is limited to measures which can be applied to individual buildings.

An important aspect of the model is the ability for parts of the energy system to change much more rapidly than it is possible for spatial structure to respond. In the period of steadily increasing energy availability and economic growth of the 1950s and 1960s, the built environment was able to respond to the diminution of energy constraints. When the price of oil virtually quadrupled overnight in 1973, it was quite impossible for a settle-

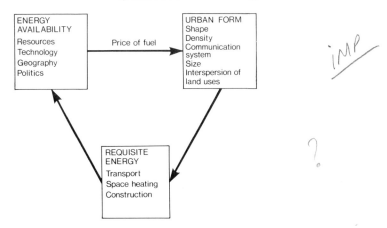

FIG 9.1 *Relationship between Energy and Urban Form (after Owens, 1981)*

ment structure, much of which had developed on the assumption of uninterrupted, low-cost supplies of this fuel, to adjust. The problem has of course been compounded by a much lower rate of growth and development in the ensuing decade, itself related to energy supply traumas.

The model must allow for some 'feedback' in that the difficulties experienced because of the inelasticities of energy demand in spatial systems would themselves stimulate new developments and adjustments in the energy system. For example, ways of meeting space heating requirements from renewable energy sources may be explored.

Of course, the energy/spatial structure relationship is vastly more complicated than the simple model outlined above and no attempt has ever been made to analyse, or even to describe, it in its entirety. The aspect of the relationship which has received most attention has been the influence of various structural variables on energy requirements in different sectors. Within this, the most commonly explored interactions have been those between various attributes of 'urban form' (size, shape, density, etc.) and energy requirements for transport. Some attention has also been given to the influence of densities and built form on space heating requirements.

The influence of spatial structure on other energy uses—perhaps because it is conceptually more difficult to contemplate—has been virtually ignored, although there must be ways in which the spatial arrangement of activities influences energy requirements for infrastructure, industrial processes etc. The influence of the energy system on spatial structure (as opposed to the other way round) has likewise received little attention, although there have been some tentative efforts (described below) to assess how cities might evolve in response to energy constraints and also to determine the spatial implications of technologies which might be introduced in the interests of energy efficiency (such as combined heat and power (CHP) systems * or solar heating). However, while progress has been made in certain areas, most research to date has been unco-ordinated and has not been conducted within the context of a sound theoretical framework.

Given the existence of a relationship between a society's energy system and its spatial structure, whether considered in all its complexity or at the level of more mundane and easily identified interactions, a strong case can be made for the inclusion of energy considerations into the planning process. Urban and regional planners, whose policies are intended to influence the spatial structure of society, should at least be *aware* of the energy implications of the plans which they seek to implement, even if these plans are developed with a main emphasis on issues other than energy factors. However, before considering how such integration might be achieved, some attention should be given to the question of how the built environment might in any case tend to evolve in response to a more constrained energy situation.

### The Evolution of Settlement Patterns Under Energy Constraints

Because the spatial structure of society became increasingly energy intensive in an era of plentiful and cheap fuel, it may gradually respond to a more constrained energy situation by becoming more energy efficient. It has been suggested that such changes could be brought about by the operation of market forces in the urban economy without any need for planning intervention. Keys (1976, p.235), for example, considers the possibility that 'smoothly functioning private land markets composed of numerous informed and willing participants will adequately reflect the scarcity value of energy and create more efficient urban structures'.

Others have attempted to predict the form which such structures might take. A utility analysis carried out by Romanos (1978) suggested that the effect of higher energy prices on housing and transportation costs would be to produce residential areas located closer to employment centres with an increase in the density of development. This confirms a conclusion which might well have been arrived at intuitively. If energy prices rise, and this is reflected in the cost of travel, people will seek to live nearer to their work, and to accommodate enough residences close to employment centres, densities will have to rise. (It would be the reverse process of the residential dispersal and decreasing densities which took place during the 1950s and 60s). The analysis also suggests, however, that these more compact future residential areas are likely to develop around semi-independent suburban

---

* Systems producing both electricity and heat (usually steam or hot water, for either industrial use or district heating).

centres of economic activity and employment, the steady trends of employment relocation from the central city to the suburbs having been reinforced
by the need to reduce the travel requirements of the suburban labour pool.
The resulting spatial structure, Romanos suggests, could be one of compact
urban clusters each consisting of a suburban employment centre and a
relatively dense residential centre around it.

There has also been some debate as to whether the 'electronic revolution'
will permit continued interaction between widely spaced activities even if
energy costs rise to constrain physical mobility. Others have argued that an
increase rather than a reduction in trip-making could result from the
contacts made possible. (For further discussion see, for example, Clark,
1981; Young, 1981).

Dendrinos (1979) has examined the impact of changes in transport energy
costs on urban form, using a very simple model of a city with employment
concentrated at the centre. His analysis found that in certain situations, for
example, if travellers trade off travel time for work time, higher energy
prices would not necessarily result in the city becoming more compact.

Dendrinos' analysis suggests that other factors such as the value of time
may moderate or counteract the influence of energy prices on 'urban form'.
In contrast, van Til (1979) argues that the elasticity of energy for transportation will be of critical importance in determining future settlement patterns:

> 'The shape of the future metropolis may take a form determined almost entirely by energy
> availability: values and preferences may become submerged to necessity as our resource
> options disappear'. (p.321).

Van Til's argument is that under energy constraints, a determined attempt
to protect overall economic health may be made at the direct cost of a radical
decline in energy available for transportation. His analysis, based on five
alternative energy scenarios, applied to four models of spatial form and
structure, suggests that spatial options will decrease dramatically as energy
prospects diminish and that in an energy-short future the only viable form of
urban spatial structure would be 'diversified-integrated' cities. He suggests
that (in the United States at least), future settlement might take the
following form:

> Most transportation will be confined within 2–3000 regional nodes, with the most desirable
> housing located within 2 km of the node. The nodes will occupy, in large part, 'existing
> shells'. They will be characterised by high densities and energy efficient transportation
> modes, with limited transport of persons. Large cities and more spread out smaller cities
> would see the development of multiple nodes within their present limits, each of which
> would take on an increasing autonomy. Many suburbs and small towns would become
> largely depopulated. (Adapted from original).

Incidentally, van Til has little faith that any effort to re-shape settlement
patterns to accommodate energy shortfall will be undertaken, considering it
much more likely that we will be left to 'muddle through'.

Not everyone would agree that the changing energy situation will inevitably affect spatial structure. A recent US Presidential Commission suggested that:

> ' . . . there are multiple options for accommodating higher energy costs that make the prospect of a large-scale return to compact, centralised, high density urban development extremely unlikely . . . Firms and households will likely be able to avoid profligate energy consumption in a variety of ways without resorting to relocation'. (President's Commission for a National Agenda for the Eighties, 1980, p.32).

Wood and Lee (1981, p.220) argue that 'in the short term, large scale structural adjustments in urban areas are highly unlikely. It seems more likely that urban change produced by the fuel factor will occur gradually and reflect the compensatory adjustments of individuals and households'.

Thus, there is a variety of views on the extent to which the market mechanism will cause spatial structure to be modified in response to energy constraints. Clearly, a critical factor will be the relative elasticities of energy demand in those sectors which can be related to spatial structure and in those which cannot. The *nature* of the energy constraint will also be important. A series of sudden supply shortfalls, for example, might induce a quite different response from a gradual upward trend in energy prices. This question deserves further investigation.

Among those who consider that energy constraints *will* influence spatial structure, there is a marked degree of consensus about the form which future settlement patterns will take. This suggests a trend towards higher densities and more compact centres, but also a degree of decentralisation resulting in concentration around small, semi-autonomous centres based on existing employment areas in cities, suburbs and small towns.

The question remains whether any anticipated changes should be guided by planning intervention into socially desirable forms. Van Til, for example, argues that in the absence of a strong planned commitment to guide the process of concentration (which he sees as the inevitable outcome of energy constraints), land and house values will increasingly reflect accessibility to central locations and inequalities between citizens will be exacerbated. Where, as in the United Kingdom, changes in spatial structure are already under some form of land-use planning control, the choice is not so much one between market mechanisms or planned development but rather between planning with regard for future energy availability and planning which fails to recognise energy as a constraint. The problem then becomes one of identifying spatial structures which are both efficient in their consumption of energy resources and realistic, in the sense that planning policies designed to achieve them can be implemented in a democratic society. In developing such policies, it will be important to recognise that planning for longer-term energy efficiency may well impose additional *present* costs, for example, in terms of capital or inconvenience while changes are made. An example of the latter would be the disruption caused by the need to lay street mains in any programme of retro-fitting of district heating or combined heat and power/district heating. Such short-term costs clearly affect both the economic feasibility and public acceptability of policies.

## Energy Efficient Environments

If planners are to incorporate energy considerations successfully into their policies, it is necessary to identify the characteristics of land-use patterns which are compatible with the efficient use of energy resources. Two broad approaches to this problem may be identified. The first is a deductive approach, in which the energy implications of alternative spatial structures are investigated and an attempt is made to identify the characteristics of a form with low energy requirements. Both empirical and theoretical studies have employed this technique. The second is a more normative approach and involves designing spatial structures around energy-saving principles—for example, ensuring that spatial structure is compatible with the use of energy-conserving heat and power systems and/or district heating. This section shows how both approaches may be used to identify 'energy efficient' spatial characteristics. They are not entirely independent and it seems likely that both would need to be employed in an 'energy-integrated' planning process.

An enormous number of variables influences the level of energy use for different purposes within society and not surprisingly it has been found to be very difficult to isolate the effects of urban form on energy demand. The results of empirical work in which attempts have been made to relate energy consumption in different communities to aspects of their spatial structure have for the most part been unsatisfactory and ambiguous. Firstly, there are problems of defining and quantifying the various dimensions of urban form in existing areas which, as Stone (1973) has pointed out, are only the current stage of a long process of evolution and adaptation to changing needs. Next, considerable variation in energy demand patterns due to climatic, socio-economic and many other factors tends to obscure any variation which might be attributed to spatial structure. Finally, great caution must be exercised in claiming causality, even when a high correlation between structural variables and energy consumption is observed.

Empirical work has mainly been concerned with transport energy requirements, although a few studies have also included residential energy consumption. Results have tended to be inconclusive with significant relationships not always emerging clearly and contradictions between different studies. However, there is a certain degree of consensus that higher densities and clustering of land uses result in lower energy consumption, for both transport (due to shorter and fewer trips) and for space heating (because of more efficient built forms). (See for example, Hamer, 1976; Markovitz, 1971; RPA and RFF, 1974; Weiss, Burby and Zehner, 1974).

Most research on energy and spatial structure has adopted a more theoretical approach, usually involving urban modelling, although sometimes 'real world' values for some of the variables have been incorporated. Again, the emphasis has been on the transport sector, with investigation most typically using gravity type models to predict the travel and energy requirements associated with alternative arrangements of land uses. Studies have ranged from the highly abstract (e.g. Hemmens, 1967; Schneider and Beck, 1973) to those which consider alternative development patterns for existing geographical areas (e.g. Clark, 1974; Roberts, 1975), although even the latter have been highly simplified and essentially theoretical. As the literature has been reviewed elsewhere (see Gilbert and Dajani, 1974; Owens, 1981), the main emphasis here is on the results rather than the methodologies of the various studies.

Size, shape, density of development and interspersion of activities have all been found to influence transport energy requirements and to some extent those for space heating. For example, there is a general agreement that large single settlements are relatively inefficient in their use of energy for transport (Stone, 1973; Edwards and Schofer, 1975). Thus, a cluster of smaller settlements would be more energy efficient than one large one, and there is some indication that an upper threshold population size would be between 150,000 and 250,000 (Ashworth, 1974; Stone, 1973). Even when incremental developments to existing urban areas have been considered, some of the results indicate that development in secondary centres, to produce a multi-centred form, would be more energy efficient than continued growth based on a large single centre (Clark, 1974).

Investigations of the most energy efficient shape for a settlement have tended to be unsatisfactory, largely because this variable may be interpreted in many different ways. It has frequently been defined in terms of the transport network, in which case energy efficiency also depends on many other assumptions about the network. Jamieson, Mackay and Latchford (1967), for example, investigated different transport network configurations, but considered only private transport, which must limit the general applicability of their results. Nevertheless, there is a certain degree of consensus that linear forms may result in low transport energy requirements (Jamieson, Mackay and Latchford, 1967; Edwards and Schofer, 1975). Roberts and Barrell (1975) have urged planners to explore the 'inherent energy and accessibility advantages of the linear city'.

Most authors agree that low densities will inhibit energy efficiency. Higher densities result in lower physical separation of activities, thus reducing travel requirements, and also tend to be associated with built forms which have relatively small space heating requirements (Clark, 1974; Roberts, 1975; Edwards and Schofer, 1975). Very high densities, however, are *not* required. Dickins (1975) has shown how a density of only twenty-five dwellings per hectare would allow facilities with a catchment area of 8000 to be within 600 m of all homes, and Thomas and Potter (1977) suggest that a 'pedestrian scale cluster' of 20–30,000 people would provide a sufficient threshold for many facilities without resort to high densities. Energy efficiency could certainly be achieved without needing high-rise development. In fact, such forms may be quite inefficient in energy terms, requiring the use of highly energy-intensive construction materials, greatly increasing the 'energy investment' in infrastructure. Also they may have high heating requirements (due to weather exposure) and will almost certainly be inimical to the use of dispersed renewable energy (as discussed further later).

A reduction in the physical separation of activities has been urged in nearly all studies of energy and spatial structure. This could be achieved by more compact development, more interspersion of different land uses, or both (Hemmens, 1967; Schneider and Beck, 1973; Stone, 1973). Thus, Thomas and Potter (1977) have criticised 'land-use apartheid', Boothroyd (1976) has suggested that neighbourhood land use should become more heterogeneous and Odell (1975) has called for 'more effective integration at a smaller geographic scale'. This implies that some degree of decentralisation of employment and commerical opportunities might be desirable although care must be exercised that any savings in transport energy requirements are not outweighed by losses in economies of scale—including energy economies of scale, for example, in space heating or industrial processes. As in some empirical studies, it was commonly found in theoretical work that some degree of clustering of activities would result in lower transport energy requirements, by making multi-purpose trips possible.

To summarise, comparative analysis of different structures suggests that an energy efficient settlement pattern would consist of small to medium-sized settlements or settlement 'clusters'. Within settlements, over-centralisation of employment and services would be avoided. Instead, residential areas would be planned around more dispersed clusters of employment and services in relatively compact 'urban sub-units'. High densities would not necessarily be a feature of this settlement pattern.

The spatial structure described above might be thought of as 'inherently' energy efficient, in that it reduces the need for *useful* * energy because, for example, travel and space heating requirements are smaller. Even if useful energy requirements remain unchanged, however, it might still be possible to make savings by reducing *delivered* * energy requirements. For example, if the same number of people still have to travel to work from A to B, or the same building stock still has to be maintained at a comfortable temperature (implying the same, basic, *useful* energy requirements), this could be achieved by using more efficient transport or space heating methods, thus

---

* The distinction between useful and delivered energy is important. *Useful* energy is the energy actually required to perform a specific function. *Delivered* energy requirements for the same function are greater because the equipment used is not 100 per cent efficient, the departure between the two varying with the equipment and fuel used.

reducing delivered, and in most cases primary, energy requirements. Some advantages in terms of conserving depletable resources may also be gained by employing renewable energy sources such as sun and wind. The relevance to planners is that the implementation of some energy-conserving technologies may be facilitated or prejudiced by the structure of the built environment and this clearly has implications for all new development. Furthermore, in the *existing* built environment, planners will inevitably be closely involved in the implementation of policies which might result in energy savings and should clearly be aware of the opportunities and potential problems with which they will be presented.

It is well-known, for example, that certain land-use patterns are much better suited to the efficient and economic operation of public transport systems than others. Relative concentration of residences and facilities maximises accessibility to the transport route and induces a high load factor (Roberts, 1975; Jamieson, Mackay and Latchford, 1967), whereas public transport is particularly bad at serving spread out, low-density areas typical of residential suburbs. This implies relatively high residential densities and concentration rather than dispersal of facilities. However, Steadman (1980) points out that while it is undeniable that increased densities in general favour public transport, there are also significant *shape* factors involved; he argues that a linear grid form may combine high densities along the route served with moderate overall densities, compatible with a high quality environment. If it is agreed, therefore, that a shift towards public transport from energy-greedy private vehicles is a legitimate way of saving energy (as well as conferring certain social and environmental benefits which are already widely recognised), then planners should try to ensure that the form of the built environment is compatible with this aim. Policies might include discouragement of dispersed, low density suburbs, some degree of concentration (though not necessarily *centralisation*) of facilities, relation of new development to transport routes and the maintenance of moderately high densities *along* these routes. Such policies could be applied to green field developments and also to re-development, growth and 'infilling' in existing settlements.

It should be noted here that there may be potential for local authorities to influence energy demand in the transport sector more directly, rather than through its relationship with land-use configurations. This subject is not considered in detail here since it is worthy of extensive coverage in its own right. Banister (1981) has provided an excellent summary of the scope for energy conservation in the transport sector and has identified certain specific policy areas where local authorities would be involved (sometimes in conjunction with Central Government). These include promotion of public transport (which may involve politically controversial subsidies), provision of pedestrian and cycling facilities, consolidation of freight loads, urban traffic control, parking control and area licencing. He also considers the potential for car sharing, but suggests that at the local level, most benefits come indirectly from traffic management schemes. The point to be emphasised is that 'non-spatial' policies may be effective in reducing transport energy requirements as well as measures aimed at modifying the form of the built environment, which are the main focus of this chapter. Both sets of policies involve many conflicts of interest (witness the recent controversy over London Transport fares) and it goes without saying that *all* the costs and benefits, and not only the energy implications, must be carefully considered.

The from of the built environment may also be a significant factor in determining the feasibility of various technologies of energy supply and distribution. Knowledge of the constraints involved will be important in assessing the feasibility of their introduction in existing areas, and also in avoiding unnecessary constraints on such technologies in areas of new development.

The potential for the introduction of combined heat and power and district heating systems, for example, depends (among other considerations) on the density of development and on the degree of mixing of different land uses. This is not to say that such systems would not be *technically* feasible in, for example, low density residential suburbs, but that they may not be economic in comparison with other means of energy supply. Combined heat and power/district heating (CHP/DH) systems will almost certainly be economically feasible, however, even in areas of moderate and moderately low densities. The Combined Heat and Power Group (1977) found that in existing cities the costs of CHP/DH schemes, discounted at 10 per cent over 60 years, could break even with those of the current fuel mix at densities of thirty to thirty-seven dwellings per hectare (typical of many modern developments), when they assumed that fuel prices would double every 18 years in real terms. On a 'green field' site the 'break-even' density would be lower; it could also be reduced by lowering the discount rate, or by assuming a more rapid increase in real fuel prices (Combined Heat and Power Group, 1977). Odell (1977) has suggested that densities of no more than thirty dwellings/hectare would be necessary. Thus, it seems probable that, while the costs of CHP/DH schemes will generally be inversely proportional to the density of development, high densities will not be essential in order to make such schemes economically competitive, especially where they are planned as an integral part of new development.

The economics of CHP/DH are also enhanced by some degree of mixing of land-uses, so that the demand for heat and power is spread over different types of consumer. This implies that in an area served by any one scheme, land-uses should be heterogeneous rather than homogenous. This is not inconsistent with the requirements for closer integration of different land uses (e.g. industrial, residential, commercial) which was advocated above as a means of reducing the physical separation of activities.

The decision to introduce CHP/DH systems would clearly involve many technical, socio-economic and environmental considerations. However, spatial factors will be important and planners must be involved in identifying existing areas where such schemes would be beneficial and in deciding where they could be incorporated into new developments. In Denmark, where energy policy has favoured considerable development of CHP/DH and DH systems, planners are already closely involved in the division of the country into areas where CHP/DH can be introduced (mainly in towns of more than 10,000 population), areas which would be better served by natural gas and areas where space heating must be provided in some other way. Kommunes (districts) are obliged to map present and future energy needs at the local level and the county council draws up a heating plan for the county, including the location of specific heat-producing or consuming activities and details of the areas in which particular heat supply methods will receive priority in future. Physical planning and planning for heating in Denmark now seem likely to take place simultaneously (Christensen and Jensen-Butler, 1980). In the UK, following the recommendations set out in the 'Marshall Report' (Combined Heat and Power Group, 1979) the feasibility of a number of 'lead city' combined heat and power schemes is currently under investigation and it is to be hoped that these studies will add considerably to our knowledge of the spatial and other planning implications of such schemes.

The potential for the exploitation of renewable energy resources will also be influenced by the structure of the built environment. Perhaps the most obvious example is the use of solar technology on a small scale for space and water heating. Any extensive use of solar power on the scale of the individual dwelling would require densities low enough to avoid overshadowing and to permit access to sunlight for fairly large collecting surfaces. Boothroyd (1976) suggests that the need to preserve access to sunlight for solar heating systems might counter any move towards higher densities resulting from other energy considerations. However, it should be quite feasible to take advantage of solar energy at moderate densities, for example, of forty or forty-four dwellings/hectare (Roth, 1977; Green, 1980), which would not necessarily conflict with other energy-related objectives. Indeed, in this context, density is probably not as critical as layout and orientation, which should be carefully selected to take maximum advantage of potential solar gain.

The characteristics of an 'inherently' energy efficient environment and those which allow maximum opportunity for energy-conserving technologies are similar in many respects. For example, a land-use pattern with moderate overall densities (and possibly high *linear* densities), with mixing of land-uses but local concentration of facilities could be both inherently energy efficient and well-suited to public transport, CHP/DH or small scale solar power. Some aspects of a theoretically efficient land-use pattern are illustrated in Figure 9.2. Interestingly, the emerging 'ideal' pattern also has much in

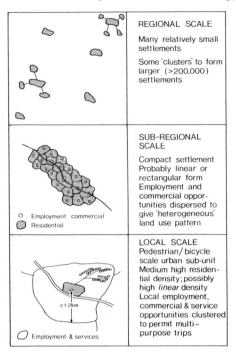

FIG 9.2 *Illustration of Consensus of opinion on 'Ideal' Energy-efficient Form (after Owens, 1981).*

common with the kind of spatial structure which the results presented above suggest might emerge from the spontaneous evolution of urban areas in response to energy constraints. The greater compactness, the decentralisation of employment and services and the semi-autonomous nature of the emerging 'sub-units' are all common features. This suggests that in attempting to encourage the more rational use of energy resources in their land-use policies planners will not necessarily be involved in the conflict with market forces which has frequently been suggested (see, for example, Pauker, 1974). Their role may rather be one of encouraging such trends and ensuring a smooth and socially equitable transition to the new spatial structures with minimum economic and environmental costs.

It has been shown above how the characteristics of an 'energy efficient' spatial structure might be identified although clearly much work remains to be done in this field. However, the improvement of energy efficiency in the existing built environment will be constrained by many factors. Some of these, together with the policy implications and the potential for integrating energy considerations into the planning process are considered in the concluding section below.

## Policy Implications and Constraints

The potential for energy conservation by modification to the built environment will be limited by many factors. Not the least of these is the vast investment in existing infrastructure, since the real world in no way resembles the 'clean slate' assumed in so many of the theoretical studies. There is considerable inertia in the built environment, particularly in periods of slow economic growth and change. When marginal adjustments do take place, there is inevitably pressure for them to conform with and reinforce existing land-use/activity patterns. Other constraints on the achievement of energy efficiency will include the multiplicity of planning objectives, the limited *effectiveness* of planning policies in achieving the desired land-use patterns and the failure of individuals to behave in an energy efficient manner, even when the built environment gives them the opportunity to do so.

The existence of such obvious constraints has disheartened many planners and has led them to conclude that they have no significant role in relation to energy conservation. Wright (1979) probably sums up the view of many practicing planners when he concedes that they 'will have a minor interest in changes of appearance to buildings from conservation measures and in changes to the transportation system', but can see 'no key role for planners in energy conservation'.

The fact remains that the spatial structure of society and the energy system are closely inter-related. Since planners influence spatial structure it is difficult to accept, as we enter an era in which energy is widely expected to become increasingly scarce and expensive, that they should continue to ignore the energy implications of their plans and policies. Planners may well have been discouraged, however, because the *wrong questions* have generally been asked about their role in relation to energy demand. It may be argued that too much attention has been focused on energy *conservation* by large scale modification of settlement patterns. In developed societies, the achievement of an 'energy efficient' spatial structure may well be too ambitious an objective. The 'ideal' end state is as unattainable (and as alarming) as all the other 'utopias' which have obsessed the planning profession from time to time.

Planners need not, however, be deterred by the seemingly limited potential to develop energy efficient spatial structures, since energy *conservation* need not be their primary energy-related objective. Instead, they should aim for flexibility and for the *rational* use of energy resources. One of their main goals should be to reduce the inelasticity of energy demand in the built environment. They should try to ensure, for example, that land-use patterns will not lock people into lifestyles of high energy consumption but will provide an alternative, should energy become scarce and expensive. Where other objectives can be achieved by policies with low energy costs, these should be implemented in preference to less energy-efficient alternatives but energy efficiency need not—and should not—be given unwarranted priority over other goals.

The point which should be emphasised is that the inclusion of energy considerations, where they have previously been ignored, should in itself result in the more *rational* use of energy resources. Policies which conflict with energy-related objectives may well be adopted because there are sound reasons for preferring them on other grounds but they will not be implemented by default. All efforts to integrate energy considerations into the planning process should be based on the principle that energy conservation is not an end in itself but a means by which society can continue to function without the social, economic and environmental costs of the profligate use of a scarce resource. The implications have been expressed simply by Goode *et al.* (1980, p.9):

> 'Clearly, if the economic and social costs of allowing energy considerations to modify other areas of public policy exceed the economic and social benefits, then such modifications should not take place'.

Two questions remain in relation to the integration of energy considerations into the planning process. The first is whether the resources and expertise available to typical local authority planning departments would be sufficient for the successful development of 'energy-integrated' planning. Secondly, if the inclusion of energy considerations is judged to be valuable and feasible, there is the question of how best this could be achieved within the context of the overall planning process.

The complexity of energy/land-use interactions, and the difficulties which have been experienced in attempting to identify and quantify the energy implications of alternative spatial structures might suggest that it would be impractical in a busy local authority planning department to undertake any such assessment of the energy implications of alternative plans and policies. Indeed, the apparent hopelessness of this task is probably one of the main reasons for the continued neglect of energy as an issue in the majority of land-use planning exercises. However, to some extent the difficulties of taking at least some account of energy constraints in the planning process may have been exaggerated. Much of the necessary information in any particular planning area (for example, the rate of growth and change, physical constraints, travel patterns, housing densities) will already be available in the planning department or will be needed in any case in relation to other aspects of policy. Much more is now known about patterns of energy use for different human activities than at the beginning of the 1970s and data are rapidly increasing. In some cases, as in transport modelling, energy co-efficients could be incorporated into techniques with which planners are already familiar. Finally, some of the problems of fitting a new type of assessment into everyday planning practice and acquiring the relevant expertise could be overcome by taking the issue out of the normal planning

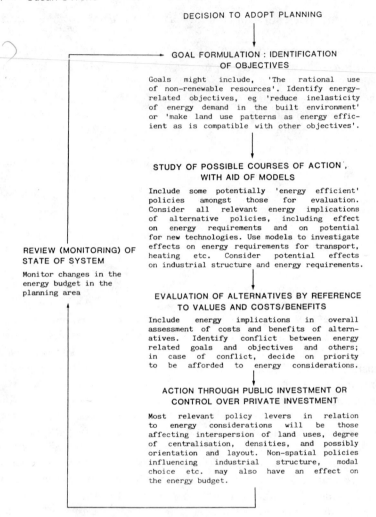

FIG 9.3 *Planning Process with Energy Considerations (after Owens, 1981).*

sphere in the initial stages. Such an approach has been adopted by Cheshire County Council which has established a 'long range futures' group to consider longer term issues which might be 'squeezed out' by everyday local authority activities. A study recently completed by the county planning department has recommended the establishment of an 'Energy Co-ordinating Group' along similar lines (Cheshire County Planning Department, 1981).

Perhaps the best way to illustrate how energy considerations might be included in more general terms in the planning process is by reference to a

TABLE 9.3 *Sample Checklist of Energy Considerations for Use in the Study of Alternative Planning Policies (Owens, 1981).*

1. How will the policy influence travel requirements—for journeys to work, to shops, to schools, to recreation etc.? Will people be trapped in expensive travel patterns if fuel prices rise? Does the policy encourage or discourage the use of the private car, public transport, walking/cycling?
2. Does the location of development take sufficient account of micro-climate?
3. Would the development densities implied by this policy (a) encourage or discourage the use of energy-efficeint built forms; (b) prejudice the use of solar energy for space and water heating; (c) permit the economic introduction of district heating schemes or combined heat and power/district heating?
4. Is there any potential, apart from control over densities, to influence built form, orientation and layout of buildings to maximise energy efficiency at this 'micro' level?
5. Does the policy encourage decentralisation of employment and services? Does this involve the loss of 'energy economies of scale'; how do these compare with potential savings in transport energy requirements?
6. Is new industry likely to be energy intensive? Could less energy intensive industries be encouraged by industrial location, or any other policies?
7. How do the energy implications of this policy vary in the short/medium/long term?
8. Could the policy be modified in any way to improve energy efficiency whilst still meeting all the other objectives?
9. In comparison with alternative policies under consideration, is this policy energy efficient/energy intensive/robust?

well-known model of this process. Such a model (adapted from McLoughlin, 1969, as illustrated by Hall, 1974), is shown in Figure 9.3. The suggested energy-related activities are not exhaustive, of course, but are a sample to illustrate the considerations which might be relevant at each stage in the planning process.

At the outset of any planning process, the current situation in the planning area must be investigated and documented; during implementation of planning policies, it is reviewed in the monitoring process. In relation to energy considerations, it would be very useful to document the energy budget in the planning area. This would enable the most significant energy flows which might be influenced by planning policies in the area to be identified and in the subsequent monitoring exercise would show whether the relevant planning policies were being effective in modifying energy flows. It will be important to identify *all* the effects of planning policies on energy requirements to make sure that unsuspected influences (which might outweigh the more obvious savings) are not overlooked.

During the *study of alternative courses of action,* a checklist of relevant considerations might be useful. Such a checklist is shown in Table 9.3; again, this is illustrative but clearly not exhaustive. Similarly, use might be made of simple 'interaction matrices', such as that shown in Table 9.4 to aid identification of significant relationships. The matrix shown here shows only the most obvious interactions but clearly the rows and columns could be further subdivided to permit more disaggregated analysis. With these and similar tools, and with use of appropriate models to explore effects on energy

| | location and degree of dispersal of residential development | location and degree of dispersal of industrial development | location and degree of dispersal of services | density of development | built form layout and orientation | industrial structure | siting in relation to micro-climate |
|---|---|---|---|---|---|---|---|
| energy investment in infrastructure | X | X | X | X | | | |
| energy requirements for transport ✓ | X | X | X | X | | | |
| energy requirements for space heating | X | X | X | X | X | | X |
| energy requirements for industry | | | | X | | X | |
| potential for efficient public transport system ✓ | X | X | X | X | | | |
| potential for walking/cycling ✓ | X | X | X | X | | | |
| potential for introduction of CHP/DH | X | X | | X | X | | |
| potential for use of renewable energy sources | | | | X | X | | X |

lighter crosses indicate interaction possible in certain circumstances

TABLE 9.4 *Simple Interaction Matrix to Show How Energy/Spatial Structure Relationships Might be Identified (after Owens, 1981)*

requirements for transport and space heating it should be possible to build up a picture of the system of energy flows which would result from any particular planning policy.

The most difficult stage of the process will be the evaluation stage, since it will then be necessary to come to some decision about the priority to be attached to energy-related objectives. It may be difficult to quantify energy implications in financial terms (for inclusion, for example, in a cost benefit analysis), but it should be possible at least to rank alternative policies according to their performance in relation to the specified energy objectives. In the case of conflict between energy related and other objectives, a subjective judgement would then have to be made about the relative importance of each. Planners are, of course, familiar with the problems of incorporating considerations which are difficult to quantify into the evaluation of alternative policies. In many situations, such a judgement may not be necessary, since the longer term energy implications may be the only way of choosing between otherwise equal policies. At the very least, the energy consequences of alternative policies will have been considered and if policies which are sub-optimal from an energy point of view are preferred, this will be on the rational grounds that conflicting objectives were considered to be more important, rather than by default because of ignorance of their energy implications.

The *implementation* of planning policies with energy-related objectives could largely be achieved by the normal means of selective public investment and control over private development (although it may not be easy to achieve consensus over such objectives in the first place). This permits some degree of control over the location, degree of dispersal and density of development, all of which may influence energy requirements. More influence on design, layout, orientation and specific siting might also be useful if any attempt to control space heating requirements is to be made. A case could also be made for imposing more stringent insulation standards on energy intensive built forms, but this falls within the realm of building regulations rather than that of planning policies. Planners would not require wide ranging new powers in order to implement energy-related policies, although some minor modifications to existing powers might be necessary.

Although our understanding of the relationship between the energy system and spatial structure remains imperfect, the potential for planners to contribute to the more rational use of energy resources has been repeatedly demonstrated by theoretical studies. The need now is for the theory to be tested by application in the 'real world'. Some attempts have been made in recent years to incorporate energy considerations into the planning process. Sewell and Foster (1980), for example, report on the experience of several American cities in trying to adopt energy efficient land-use policies but such experience is very limited. Virtually no serious attempts at energy-integrated planning have been made in the United Kingdom.

The most appropriate way to develop experience in the integration of energy management considerations into the planning process would be to engage in specific exercises in a few particular local authority areas. Several counties, metropolitan districts or districts could be selected, based on the active co-operation of their planning authorities, as case studies. The objective would be to document the energy budget of these areas, to identify the points at which planning intervention might influence energy requirements, to consider energy implications of alternative plans and policies and, where appropriate, to show how existing policies might be modified to take better account of potential energy constraints. Although such policies would need to be tailored to specific local conditions, the practical experience gained should permit development of a set of guidelines for more general application.

The value of this experience would be enhanced by co-ordination of the activities of individual authorities for the exchange of information and expertise but also because the viability of many initiatives will depend on activities which straddle area boundaries. This co-ordination might better arise from initiatives by local authorities themselves rather than relying on a stimulatory role being played by central government energy or environmental departments.

The closest that policy-making has come to such activity in the UK has been the developments which followed the report of the Combined Heat and Power Group (1979). Although the Department of Energy has initiated a programme to identify potential 'lead cities' where district heating schemes might be developed to exploit the waste heat potential from pre-existing generating stations, there is little doubt that the progress which has been made so far on the possible large-scale development of this important energy-conserving technology has been largely the result of the initiative and enthusiasm of a combination of a few local authorities such as the London Borough of Southwark, Newcastle MB, Tyne and Wear CC., local energy action groups, the District Heating Assocation and a number of committed individuals.

Although the Department of Energy has argued that the pace of examination of CHP/DH potential has been determined by the need to establish in detail the specific local circumstances which might condition the success of any trial schemes (Select Committee on Energy, 1982) outside opinion has argued that governmental restraint on spending, political dogma about the role of government in relation to market developments and a tendency for the Central Electricity Generating Board to be somewhat lukewarm towards CPH/DH proposals have combined to slow the pace of 'test-bed' developments.

Such difficulties are, however, but some of the problems which any 'test-bed' development would face if it came to implementation. The history of urban experiment in Britain is somewhat chequered. Energy management programmes would need a resilience to carry them through the exigencies of changes in local administrations and a financial basis to insulate them from premature curtailment arising from budgetary stringency. Similarly, it would be naive not to recognise that local initiatives in as central an area of economic and general public concern as energy would inevitably give rise to political conflict. Achievement of the desirable overall goal of reducing energy consumption would probably not come about by uniform distribution of the advantages and disadvantages through all sections of the population. Adverse side effects of disruption, disturbance and loss of markets would affect some interest groups more than others. It is perhaps only because there has to date been so little initiative at the local level that an almost ritualistic affirmation of the desirability of conservation pervades much discussion, and the general public image of energy policy.

While these dilemmas might be thought to be a challenge to far-sighted and enthusiastic planners, many planners and policy makers have regarded recent research on energy and spatial structure as vaguely interesting but with little practical importance. If successful, studies and programmes such as those proposed would do more to overcome such apathy than further theoretical work. Only within the many constraints of a 'real' planning situation can it be shown whether energy considerations have as crucial a role in planning practice as theory and intuition suggest.

### References

Ashworth, G. (1974) Natural resources and the future shape of Britain, *The Planner*, **60**(7), 773–778.

Banister, D. (1981) *Transport policy and energy: perspectives, options and scope for conservation in the passenger transport sector.* Town Planning Discussion Paper No. 36, University College London, Gower St., London WC1E 6BT.

Boothroyd, P. (1976) The energy crisis and future urban form in Alberta, *Plan Canada*, **16**(Sept./Dec.), 137–146.

Borg., N. (1978) Regional energy requirements: energy usage in transportation. Paper presented at PTRC Annual Meeting, University of Warwick.

Brown, B. G. H. (1977) The planning challenge of tidal power, *Town and Country Planning*, March, 159–163.

Cheshire County Planning Department (1981) *Energy and Cheshire. The way ahead.* Report on a project co-ordinated by Roger Lowe, Cheshire County Planning Dept., Commerce House, Hunter St., Chester CH1 1SN.

Christensen, B. and Jensen-Butler, C. (1980) Energy, planning of heating systems and urban structure. Paper presented at Regional Studies Association Conference, July, Edinburgh.

Clark, D. (1981) Telecommunications and rural accessibility: perspectives on the 1980s, in *Transport and Public Policy Planning*, eds. Bannister, D. J. and Hall, P. G., Mansell, London, 134–137.

Clark, James W. (1974) *Defining an urban growth strategy which will achieve maximum travel demand reduction and access opportunity enchancement.* Research Report 73, 7 UMTA WA 0003, 74. Washington University, Seattle, USA.

Combined Heat and Power Group (1977) *District heating combined with electricity generation in the United Kingdom.* Discussion document prepared by the District Heating Working Party. (Energy Paper No. 20). HMSO, London.

Combined Heat and Power Group (1979) *Combined heat and electrical power generation in the United Kingdom.* Report to the Secretary of State for Energy. (Energy Paper No. 35). HMSO, London.

Dendrinos, D. S. (1979) Energy costs, the transport network and urban form. *Environment and Planning A*, 11, 655–664.

Department of Energy (1976) *Energy Conservation.* The government's reply to the First Report from the Select Committee on Science and Technology, session 1974–75, HC 487, Cmnd. 6575, July, HMSO, London.

Dickins, I. (1975) Travel patterns and the built environment. *The Planner*, **61**(9), 338–340.

Edwards, J. L. and Schofer, J. L. (1975) *Relationships between transportation energy consumption and urban structure: results of simulation studies,* Dept. of Civil and Mineral Engineering, 112, Mines and Metallurgy Building, Minneapolis.

Gilbert, D. and Dajani, J. S. (1974) Energy, urban form and transportation policy. *Transportation Research*, **8**, 267–276.

Goode, J., Roy, D. and Sedgewick, A. (1980) *Energy policy: a reappraisal.* Fabian Research Series 343, Fabian Society, London.

Green, C. W. B. (1980) *Solar housing experimental design.* University of Sheffield. Ecotecture Group, Dept. of Architecture.

Hall, Peter (1974) *Urban and regional planning.* Penguin, Harmondsworth.

Hamer, M. (1976) *Getting nowhere fast.* Friends of the Earth, London.

Hemmens, G. (1967) Experiments in urban form and structure. *Highway Research Record*, **207**, 32–41.

Jamieson, G., Mackay, W. and Latchford, J. (1967) Transportation and land use structures. *Urban Studies*, **4**(3), 201–217.

Kalma, J. D. and Newcombe, K. J. (1976) Energy use in two large cities: a comparison of Hong Kong and Sydney, Australia. *International Journal of Environmental Studies*, **9**, 53–64.

Keyes, D. L. (1976) Energy and land use: an instrument of US conservation policy. *Energy Policy*, **4**(3), 108–116.

Leach, G., Lewis, C., Romig, F. Buren, A. van and Foley, G. (1979) *A low energy strategy for the United Kingdom.* Science Reviews Ltd., London.

Markovitz, J. (1971) *Transportation implications of economic cluster development.* Interim Technical Report 4245–4424, Tri-State Regional Transportation Commission, New York.

McLoughlin, J. Brian (1969) *Urban and regional planning; a systems approach.* Faber and Faber, London.

Newcombe, K. (1975a) Energy use in Hong Kong: Part I, an overview. *Urban Ecology*, **1**, 87–113.

Newcombe, K. (1975b) Energy use in Hong Kong: Part II. Sector end-use analysis. *Urban Ecology*, **1**, 285–309.

Newcombe, K. (1976) Energy use in Hong Kong: Part III. Spatial and temporal patterns. *Urban Ecology*, **2**, 139–172.

Odell, P. (1975) Settlements and energy. *Planning and Administration*, **1** (Habitat Issue), 43–50.

Odell, P. (1977) Energy and planning. *Town and Country Planning*, March, 154–158.

Owens, S. E. (1981) The energy implications of alternative rural development patterns. Ph.D Thesis, University of East Anglia, Norwich, Norfolk.

Pauker, G. J. (1974) Can land use management reduce energy consumption for transportation? Paper presented at Caltech Seminar Series *Energy Consumption in Private Transportation*, 29th April.

President's Commission for a National Agenda for the Eighties (1980) *Urban America in the Eighties: Perspective and Prospects*. Report of the Panel on Policies and Prospects for Metropolitan and Non-Metropolitan America, US Govt. Printing Office, Washington.

RPA and RFF (Regional Plan Association Inc. and Resources for the Future) (1974) Regional energy consumption. *RPA Bulletin*, January, **121**.

Roberts, James S. (1975) Energy and land use: analysis of alternative development patterns. *Environmental Comment*, September, 2–11.

Roberts, John and Barrell, David (1975) Tomorrow's transport. *Built Environment*, **4**(1), 38–40.

Romanos, M. C. (1978) Energy price effects on metropolitan spatial structure and form. *Environment and Planning A*, **10**, 93–104.

Roth, U. (1977) The impact of settlement patterns on low temperature heating supply systems, transportation and environment, in *Papers and proceedings of the International Congress of the International Federation for Housing and Planning, 'Towards a more humane urban technology'*, Den Haag International Federation for Housing and Planning (IFHP).

Schneider, J. and Beck, J. (1973) *Reducing the travel requirements of the American city. An investigation of alternative urban spatial structures*. Research Report 73–1, US Dept. of Transportation, Washington DC.

Select Committee on Energy (House of Commons) (1982) *Report on Energy Conservation in Buildings*, Session 1981–82, HC 401-I and 401-II, HMSO, London.

Select Committee on Science and Technology (House of Commons) (1975) *Energy Conservation*, First report for the session 1974–75, HC 487, July, 31, HMSO, London.

Sewell, W. R. D., and Foster, H. D. (1980) *Analysis of the United States experience in modifying land use to conserve energy*. Working Paper No. 2, Lands Directorate, Environment Canada, En 73–4/2E, Ottawa.

Steadman, Philip (1980) *Configurations of land-uses, transport networks and their relation to energy use*. Centre for Configurational Studies, Open University, Milton Keynes.

Stone, P. A. (1973) *The structure, size and costs of urban settlements*. Cambridge University Press.

Thomas, R. and Potter, S. (1977) Landscape with pedestrian figures. *Built Environment Quarterly*, **3**(4), 286–290.

Van Til, J. (1979) 'Spatial form and structure in a possible future: some implications of energy shortfall for urban planning'. *American Planning Association Journal*, July, 318–329.

Weiss, S. F., Burby, R. J. and Zehner, R. B. (1974) *Evaluation of new communities: selected primary findings*. Centre for Urban and Regional Studies, University of North Carolina, USA.

Wilbanks, Thomas, J. (1981) Local energy initiatives and consensus in energy policy. Energy Division, Oak Ridge National Laboratory, Oak Ridge, Tennessee, March.

Williams, R. (1981) 'Britain's energy institutions' in Royal Institute of Public Administration, *Facing the energy future: does Britain need energy institutions?*

Wood, L. J. and Lee, T. R. (1980) Time-space convergence: re-appraisal for an oil short future. *Area*, **12**(3), 217–222.

Wright, David (1979) Do planners hold the key to energy conservation? *Planning*, **343**, November.

Young, I. (1981) The impact of telecommunications in planning and transport in *Transport and public policy planning*. Eds. Banister, D. J. and Hall, P. G., Mansell, 119–133, London.

CHAPTER 10

# Radioactive Waste Management and Land-Use Planning

DAVID R. COPE

## Acknowledgement

Considerable help was provided in compiling the information in this chapter from the following individuals and organisations.

Dinah Nichols and David Lewis of the Radioactive Waste Management Advisory Committee secretariat, Stephen Brown of the Department of the Environment Radioactive Waste Management Division, John Mather and Neil Chapman of the Environmental Protection Unit, Institute of Geological Sciences, Sidney Chapman, M.P., Kathleen Miller of the Scottish Conservation Society, Kelvin Macdonald of the Town and Country Planning Association, Mr. K. Ritchie of the United Kingdom Atomic Energy Authority, Tom Cotton of the Office of Technology Assessment, US Congress, Tom Wilbanks of Oak Ridge National Laboratory, Alvin Weinberg of the Institute of Energy Analysis, Oak Ridge, Roger Kasperson of the Center for Technology, Environment and Development, Clark University, Worcester, Mass., and the staff of the planning departments of Highland and Strathclyde Regional Councils, Northumberland and Somerset County Councils, Kyle and Carrick, Wychavon and Vale of White Horse District Councils, Rushcliffe, Charnwood and Tewkesbury Borough Councils and also from the Engineers Department, Durham County Council, the Scottish Office and the Department of the Environment Northern Regional Office.

Needless to say, the author assumes full responsibility for any errors and for all interpretations of material supplied.

## Introduction

Concern about nuclear-generated electricity has been the main force which has powered the entire evaluation of supply and use of energy and the resulting effects on the environment. Reviews of other energy supply options have, in most countries, come only after detailed investigations of either individual nuclear facilities or of the 'nuclear option' as a whole. The

241

pressure for this wider evaluation has often come from the nuclear industry itself (Inhaber, 1978), or from neutral decision-makers (General Accounting Office, 1981) to counterbalance what they have considered an unacceptable pre-occupation with nuclear power alone, threatening to overlook comparable or more severe environmental impacts from other sources of energy.

A major part of the debate on nuclear power and land-use planning has concerned issues of *reactor* siting and *reactor* safety. The situation in Britain has been slightly anomalous. The 1982–83 public inquiry into the proposal for a pressurised water reactor (PWR) at Sizewell, Suffolk, will be the first such occasion since the inquiry into the proposal for a station at Torness, Scotland, held in 1974. This inquiry lasted for 8 days. That statistic, set alongside the elaborate procedures for the Sizewell inquiry, encapsulates more than any other, the changing circumstances of planning for nuclear power.

This situation has arisen because Britain was relatively advanced in the introduction of commercial nuclear power and had by 1970 already installed 13 nuclear generating stations, with a capacity of around 3.5 GW(e). Moreover, during the 1970s, forward planning was constrained by the commissioning difficulties experienced with the second generation advanced gas-cooled reactors and the entire debate on the relative merits of these reactors compared with water-cooled systems (Williams, 1980). Only in December, 1979 did a government announcement of a nuclear station ordering programme which envisaged the commissioning of 'one new power station a year in the decade from 1982' (Department of Energy, 1979) confirm the possibility of a nuclear reactor proposal being subject to consideration at a public inquiry since 1974.

Consequently, in Britain, the development of the relationship between land-use planning policy and nuclear power in the later 1970s has occurred through the examination of phases in the nuclear fuel cycle other than the reactor stage (Fig. 10.1) and especially the 'back-end' of the cycle, involving reprocessing and waste management. A small amount of attention has been given to certain planning aspects of uranium exploration (Rowan-Robinson, undated a; Edwards, 1980) but as, at present, there is no commercial mining of uranium ores in the United Kingdom, the bulk of the attention has been to the back-end phases. Paradoxically, there are some parallels between land-use planning problems arising at the ore exploration and waste disposal stages, as discussed later in this chapter.

The 'Windscale inquiry' held between June and November, 1977, covered British Nuclear Fuel Limited's (BNFL) application to develop a Thermal Oxide Reprocessing Plant (THORP) at the existing works at Windscale (Sellafield), Cumbria. The proposal, the public inquiry and the decision-making process which followed it have all been the subjects of more coverage of the British land-use planning system and energy policy than any other single development, including a detailed study which used the

THE NUCLEAR FUEL CYCLE

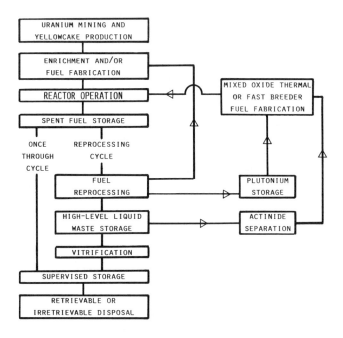

Notes:    All lines linking stages can involve transport of materials between
          facilities. Links between some stages invariably do so, e.g. from
          uranium mining to fuel enrichment. In other stages it is desirable
          to minimise transport, e.g. from fuel reprocessing through vitri-
          fication.

          Actinide separation and subsequent stages have been proposed but
          are not currently practised on a commercial scale.

          This diagram does not show routes for low or intermediate level
          waste production and disposal and is concerned with fuel alone.
          There are also wastes arising from contamination, e.g. of fuel
          cladding and from decommissioning.

FIG 10.1 *The Nuclear Fuel Cycle*

Windscale case to suggest revised procedures for the entire process of energy policy-making in Britain (Pearce, *et al.* 1979; Stott and Taylor, 1980; TCPA, 1978; Parker, 1978). Opinions on the preparation for and conduct of the inquiry and the following decision-making process have strongly influenced subsequent debate in Britain on ways to improve the handling of major energy-related and other large developments, as well as the exposition of national policy on energy and other important, nationally-provided systems such as airports and major roads.

However, even before the favourable decision on the BNFL proposal was taken, and certainly at a pace which was accelerated by it, events were leading to the exposure of the final stage in the nuclear fuel cycle to public debate and treatment by the land-use planning system. A series of planning applications were made, between 1978 and 1980, for proposals for test-drillings to evaluate the geological characteristics of rocks in several areas of Britain relating to their suitability for sub-surface containment of 'high-level' radioactive waste (radwaste) (HLW).

These events and their aftermath, although originating from policy decisions dating back to 1975 or before, have not received anything like the same degree of attention as the 'Windscale inquiry' and yet in many ways the entire field of radioactive waste management (RWM) policy, at least to the extent that it involves the possibility of on-land disposal or storage of radwaste, illustrates better than any other single stage, not merely of the nuclear fuel cycle, but even of all energy supply sources, the relationships between energy policy and land-use planning. Many of the issues raised at the Windscale inquiry, such as risks of weapons proliferation and sabotage, although undoubtedly important, were hardly the conventional concerns of land-use planning. However, most of the issues raised by RWM undoubtedly are. These include issues of procedure and decision-making, such as relations between central and local government, the role of impartial advisory committees, the place of national overview studies and ways of organising policy-making and waste management regulation. Also involved are important substantive dilemmas including locational problems and the characteristics which arise from the long-term nature of the possible developments.

National policy on RWM is still evolving and so the exact timing of some of the interactions with the land-use planning system is difficult to predict. However, it is clear that plans for development of facilities for intermediate level waste (ILW) management are likely to lead to significant planning-related dilemmas. The central theme of this chapter, after examination of the nature of RW, the current systems for its management in Britain and the experience so far with the applications for test-drilling, is that the progressive, logical development of RWM policy, which is the aim of the Department of the Environment (DoE) division responsible, must be matched by a similar progressive, systematic treatment of the planning and public discussion aspects of policy formation. This has not been the case to date in the development of RWM policy and this explains the impasse and political expediency which have characterised decision-making on the subject in the past few years.

Understanding the circumstances of radioactive waste management presents the land-use planner with an extreme example of the need for technical competence discussed in the introduction to this book. It also means that a chapter such as this must inevitably address technical considerations, such as the discussion of classification of types of radioactive waste which follows, if the subject is to be handled appropriately. This problem is exacerbated in the case of RWM because of the major uncertainties which exist in areas such as the nature of potential pathways whereby radioactivity might return from containment or dispersal to have impacts on human or other life forms. There is also uncertainty about responses, particularly at low dose levels. Other uncertainties arise from the imprecision about the amount of installed nuclear generating capacity in the future, and from aspects of reprocessing policy, such as whether foreign-originating waste should be returned to its country of origin.

It is not possible in this chapter to go into great detail on the operation of the nuclear fuel cycle, on reprocessing and many other features of nuclear electricity generation. Readers who wish to pursue this background material in greater detail can find an excellent account, even if slightly dated, in the sixth report of the Royal Commission on Environmental Pollution (1976), which concentrates especially on waste management. A brief discussion of waste management is given in the context of a general overview of nuclear power in Cottrell (1981), while Lindblom and Gnirk (1982) give an informal account of the specifics of geological disposal of waste.

## Radioactive Waste: Characteristics and Management Options

### Radioactive Waste in Perspective

The criticism is often advanced that in discussion of the problems of radioactive wastes, the level of the risk involved in their treatment is not often compared with other risks, especially the exposure risks which arise to populations from other sources of radioactivity. In particular, attention has been increasingly given in recent years to the exposure from natural sources of radiation. Figure 10.2, derived from the National Radiological Protection Board's report on *Living with Radiation* (1981), shows that the *average* dose per annum in Great Britain arising from all forms of waste discharge is indeed small, compared with the natural sources of radioactivity and with other man-made sources, especially medical exposure from the use of X-rays and to a lesser extent from radiochemicals used therapeutically. It is important to note that these figures refer to *average* exposures. One area of concern is that special groups of the population may be exposed to higher dose levels, either because of occupational risks, or because of routes whereby radionuclides dispersed into or disposed in the environment may find a way back into contact with humans. Of course, these figures do not take into account any abnormal exposure incidents which might occur as a result of accidental releases.

Most of the radioactivity in HLW arises from the fission products, especially strontium and caesium. These have half lives of around 30 years, so that by 300 years after production their level of radioactivity has declined to around only 20 times that of uranium ore, although the waste continues to contain long-lived transuranic radioactive isotopes, but these have radiation levels around $10^{-6}$ those of fresh HLW (Weinberg and Blomeke, 1982). Confusion frequently arises over the *amounts* of wastes for management.

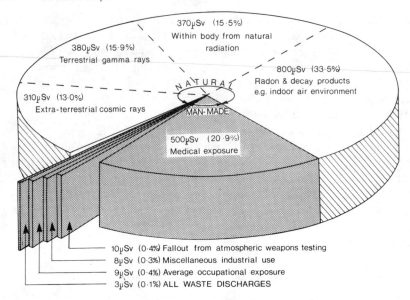

FIG 10.2 *The Varying Sources of Human Exposure to Radioactivity in Britain*
based on information and an illustration in National Radiological Protection Board (1981)

This is because accounts may give details of the weights, volumes or the specific activities of the wastes. While each of these measures is relevant to some aspects of RWM (large-volume, low-activity wastes may still be troublesome) it is the specific activity which is the most significant measure for comparing the nature of risks from radioactive wastes from different sources and against radiation from other origins. Figures on the total amount of wastes and the contained activity which will need managing at various dates in the future obviously depend on decisions about the scale and rate of future reactor commissioning, decommissioning and spent fuel reprocessing, but Duncan and Brown (1982) have given estimates being used by the Department of the Environment. These assume an installed UK nuclear power capacity of 20 GW(e) by the year 2000 which is probably an overestimate. However, the issues created by the presence of wastes arising from *existing* nuclear power stations are sufficient to give rise to major RWM problems.

### Classification of Radioactive Waste

Wastes arise at *all* stages of the nuclear fuel cycle, not only at the back end. Different classifications of waste exist and there is no consistent, internationally accepted definition of terms (Radioactive Waste Management Advisory

Committee, 1980, p.42). The Radioactive Waste Management Advisory Committee (RWMAC) uses a straightforward low (LLW), intermediate (ILW) and high (HLW) level division but notes that ILW embraces widely varying levels of radioactivity (RWMAC, 1980, p.42).

The committee has noted that a more logically consistent waste classification system would be based on matching of different types of waste to 'appropriate disposal' * outlets, as well as on the inherent radioactive characteristics of the waste. This is because criteria such as the phase (solid, liquid or gas) of the waste and its volume per unit of radioactivity also determine management policy. The DoE has initiated a classification study based on such an approach. The logic of the proposal is distinctly beneficial and should aid research and evaluation, systematic decision-taking and public appreciation of the issues involved in RWM. Table 10.1 identifies the various origins of radwaste arising from nuclear power generation. There are other sources as well, such as radio-chemical, radio-medical and defence wastes, not considered in this chapter, although their management is systematically included in the development of the DoE's RWM policy.

This chapter is primarily concerned with the intermediate and, above all, the high level wastes identified in Table 10.1 but, particularly in terms of public apprehension and public acceptability, low level waste disposal may also give rise to concern (Association of County Councils, 1982). In Britain, LLW is currently disposed of either by shallow land burial, especially at the Drigg site near Windscale, or by ocean dumping. In future, ocean dumping may be superceded by disposal in a near-surface concrete repository (Duncan, 1981, p.115; Duncan and Brown, 1982). ILWs include irradiated reactor components and plutonium-contaminated fuel cladding. Additional ILW problems will arise in future from the decommissioning of existing reactors as parts of the structures will emit neutron-induced beta and gamma radiation.

The Royal Commission on Environmental Pollution (RCEP) sixth report (1976) noted the lack of a clearly formulated policy on disposal of ILW and regarded the accumulation of more highly active solid ILW at nuclear sites for future ocean disposal as inadequate (recommendation 31). The second Annual Report of the RWMAC notes that work has been undertaken on identification and assessment of existing mines and cavities for possible LLW and ILW disposal as well as examination of some nuclear sites to assess their potential as ILW responsibilities, with test-drilling into clay beneath the Harwell site in Oxfordshire (RWMAC, 1981, p.30). Any site which might be chosen for storage or disposal of HLW could also be suitable for handling LLW and ILW (Hill, 1980, pp.6, 8). Of course problems of transport of waste to the repository, the capacity of the repository and the size of access shafts (some ILW may be quite bulky) may rule this out in

---

* Also, presumably, including in this term, in this context, the option of long-term storage.

TABLE 10.1 *Categories of Radioactive Wastes*

| Type of Waste | Phase and Principal Radioactive Source | Category | Current Handling Procedures |
|---|---|---|---|
| A. Fission product stream from fuel reprocessing | Currently liquid, to be solidified into borosilicate glass, contains fission products, some Pu and actinides | HLW | Stored at Windscale and Dounreay in liquid form |
| B. Reactor core components | Solid | HLW | Stored at power stations |
| C. Fuel cladding hulls | Solid | HLW | Stored at Windscale |
| D. Fuel element debris, e.g. fins from fuel cladding | Solid, with $^{60}$Co | HLW/ILW | Stored at power stations |
| E. Wet materials—spent filter material and ion exchange resins | Slurries with $^{137}$Cs and sometimes transuranics | ILW | Mostly stored at Windscale and power stations, some is solidified for ocean dumping |
| F. Pu-contaminated wastes from Pu-handling plants e.g. weapons plants | Solid, with Pu | ILW/LLW | Mostly stored at Drigg,* Windscale and Aldermaston, some is ocean dumped |
| G. Miscellaneous combustible wastes, e.g. contaminated swabs, filters, etc. | Solid | ILW/LLW | Incineration with ash incorporated in category H |
| H. Waste not able to be incinerated, e.g. metallic items | Solid | ILW/LLW | Stored on site or buried at Drigg |
| I. Liquid effluent, e.g. water from spent fuel storage ponds | Liquid, with $^{35}$S, $^{45}$Ca, $^{55}$Fe, $^{137}$Cs and tritium | LLW | Filtered or treated by ion exchange, then discharged to sea |
| J. Waste lubricating oil | Liquid | LLW | Injected into furnaces of oil-fired power stations—combustion gas discharged through stack to atmosphere |
| K. Gases, arising at various stages in the fuel cycle | $^{41}$Ar, $^{85}$Kr, $^{137}$Cs, $^{35}$S, $^{14}$C, $^{90}$Sr, $^{129,131}$I, tritium | LLW | Discharged to atmosphere |

\* Shallow-burial site near Windscale.
Pu = Plutonium, Co = Cobalt, Cs = Caesium, S = Sulphur, Ca = Calcium, Fe = Iron, Ar = Argon, Kr = Krypton, C = Carbon, Sr = Strontium, I = Iodine.
Source: modified from RWMAC (1980), pp. 43–44.

certain cases and a general management policy of on-site storage and disposal of LLW and ILW may be adopted.

### High Level Wastes

Although the management of ILW is rapidly emerging as the focus of the most urgent attention in RWM, to date in Britain the greatest amount of concern, and certainly the closest contact with the planning system, has occurred over management for high level wastes (HLW). These arise from the operation of power reactors and the periodic need to replace the fuel due to 'poisoning' by fission products. In Britain, the spent fuel is reprocessed to separate the unused uranium of the original fuel and the plutonium created in the fission reaction (originally for military purposes but now for use in thermal reactors as a partial substitute for $^{235}U$ and, in particular, as a potential fuel for fast breeder reactors). The reprocessing also produces liquid HLW which contains residual products as well as about 0.5 per cent of the uranium and plutonium which is not separated. Figure 10.3 shows the sequence by which HLW arises through reprocessing.

The two chief components of HLW are the 'transactinides', elements in the periodic table beyond actinium (less of course the separated uranium and plutonium) and fission products. The transactinides, of which

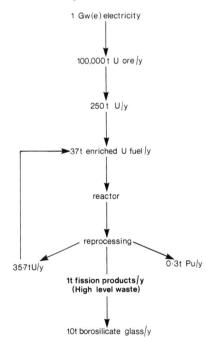

FIG 10.3 *The Origin of High-level Waste*
based on information contained in *Nuclear Power Technology*, ed. W. Marshall, Oxford University Press, to be published in 1983

[241]Americium and its decay product [237]Neptunium are the most significant in terms of potential doses to individuals arising from geological disposal, are mainly alpha radiation emitters and their relatively short half-lives mean that they are extremely radiotoxic if ingested and need very careful control (RCEP, 1976, p. 61; Hill *et al.*, 1980). The fission products, mainly beta emitters, include a large number of elements from arsenic to europium of which the most important in terms of potential doses to individuals from geological disposal are [99]Technetium and [129]Iodine (Hill *et al.*, 1980).

### High Level Waste Management and Conditioning *

In the early stages, HLW is intensely heat-emitting, mainly from radioactive decay of the fission products and in Britain is currently stored at Windscale and Dounreay in double-skinned stainless steel tanks with seven independent cooling systems. There is a consensus that the long-term storage, let alone disposal, of *liquid* HLW is not feasible although research is continuing into potential liquid disposal in geological formations (IAEA, 1977, p. 4). It is important to note that there are distinct handling and safety advantages to solidification of HLW independent of its eventual destination (storage or disposal).

Research has been carried out on the possibility of solidifying the waste by incorporation into glasses of various types, synthetic rock (synroc) or cermets (ceramic/metallic admixtures) (IAEA, 1977, 12–13; Lee, 1981). Although various advantages are claimed for the synroc option, British work has primarily been directed at borosilicate glass encapsulation since the late 1950s. The first commercial vitrification plant in Britain will use the French-developed continuous-process Atelier Vitrification Marcoule (AVM) method. This offers greater flexibility for different RWM options. The French plant at Marcoule stores the vitrified material in gas-cooled chambers pending a final decision on RWM policy.

### Storage and Disposal

The distinction between *storage* and *disposal* as two discrete options or as successive stages in waste management has come to be an important consideration in management policy. The government White Paper (Cmnd. 6820, 1977) issued in response to the RCEP sixth report, defined storage as emplacement in a facility, either engineered or natural, with the intention of, and such that it was feasible to, take further action on the waste at a later time. Disposal was defined as dispersal into an environmental medium or

---

* The term management implies the entire set of operations of satisfactorily accommodating radwaste. Conditioning is the treatment of waste to facilitate such management, e.g. by solidification of liquid waste.

emplacement in an engineered or mined facility without the intention of further action, except monitoring (p. 15). Since then, as management policy has moved towards greater preference for longer-term storage of waste, the distinction between the two options has tended to become blurred.

There is a continuum of RWM options ranging from explicitly-conceived temporary storage, through some form of storage which, by withdrawal of supervision becomes *de facto* disposal, through disposal where nevertheless the feasibility of retrieval exists and the waste is monitored to ensure that this is not required, to irretrievable, unmonitored, absolute disposal. Current UK policy on retrievability in the design studies which are being carried out on repositories is that no provision will be made for engineered retrieval as it is envisaged that large-scale disposal will not occur until there is 'sufficient confidence' in irretrievable disposal (Haytinck, 1980, p. 188).

Virtually all management pathways involve the interim storage of vitrified HLW for at least 50 years to reduce potential disposal problems from the high fission-product decay heat early in the life of the waste (RWMAC, 1981, p. 22). An important consideration for the subject of this chapter is that research work on geological *disposal* of HLW 'will also have a relevance to long-term *storage*' as such storage may well be in underground engineered facilities (RWMAC, 1981, p. 30).

The options are not mutually exclusive—long-term storage could be abandoned for disposal should this be proved feasible. Long-term storage is the most flexible of the options as well as having the lowest initial costs, although it does, of course, imply some continuing commitment of funds virtually indefinitely, even after the nuclear power programme which gave rise to the waste has long since ceased (RWMAC, 1981, p. 24–27). Facilities may be developed which combine different options for different waste levels and/or the possibility of moving from one option to another for the same waste without its removal. LLW might be *disposed* of in a facility which was also used for long-term *storage* of HLW, with the aim of reducing the total land commitment to all types of waste handling and/or the hazards of transporting HLW to a site which was suitable for HLW *disposal.*

The relationship between management based on storage or on disposal and on policy for the *siting* of facilities is a complex one. The move towards an emphasis on *storage,* whether 'temporary' (around 50 years) or longer-term, which characterises current thinking in Britain, obviously opens up greater opportunities for management of wastes on the sites where they arise. This may resolve some of the problems of identifying appropriate disposal sites and designing the transport systems by which the wastes would reach them. However, current British policy contemplates both disposal *and* storage facilities possibly being required at 'away-from-reactor' (and repro-cessing plant) (AFR) sites, so that the increasing emphasis on the storage option in the policy may not have a great significance for the land-use planning system, as siting issues are still likely to arise.

## Disposal Options

Research in Britain on radwaste, especially HLW, disposal is focused on three possible options—geological containment and emplacement below or on the seabed. Considerable dispute has arisen on whether there is a serious intention to pursue the two oceanographic options. The disparity of funding between geological and oceanographic research has been said to indicate central government perception of the feasibility of the different options. Possible international legal problems likely to arise from the oceanographic disposal options have been put forward as a strong reason for their potential unattractiveness. The government's response to such accusations has been that equal research *results* do not necessarily flow from equal research *expenditure* and that later in the research programme, spending on oceanographic work is likely to be stepped up (Scottish Office, 1980: UKAEA, 1980, 1, p. 51).

Another argument frequently advanced by opponents of geological disposal in attempting to demonstrate that behind the declared lack of commitment to any particular option lies a *de facto* intention to concentrate on terrestial geological disposal has been the balance of attention paid to the different options in British, foreign and international publications on RWM. There is no doubt that the great bulk of this is concerned with emplacement in geological formations on land. Responses to the assertion of a *de facto* concentration on land disposal have tended to suggest that there is a separate 'British' approach to RWM in which the avoidance of option foreclosure has been given a distinctively high priority, even to the extent of implying that there is a need to resist premature international pressure to concentrate exclusively on geological disposal (Hill, 1980, p. 17).

Land-use planners in areas which may be affected by radwaste developments will need to maintain a close watch on the progress of research and policy-making in the field of oceanic disposal. This is particularly the case as it is an option currently exploited for some forms of ILW disposal. If this option were to be restricted or foregone, then the pressure for development of on-land RWM options will inevitably increase.

## Disposal Sites

Three general rock types, crystalline, argillaceous (clay) and halitic/evaporitic (salt), have been identified as potential hosts for land-based geological containment of radwastes in the British Isles. The halitic rocks occur in bedded deposits rather than the intrusions used for experimental facility construction in the USA and West Germany and under consideration for radwaste disposal in countries such as the Netherlands. Each of the rock types has, to a greater or lesser extent, qualities which make them potentially appropriate for radwaste emplacement. They need to have low permeability—probably the most important criterion for minimising the potential return of radionuclides to the biosphere. For HLW, especially if it is deposited soon after vitrification, the rocks should be able to withstand heat emission. This requirement diminishes the longer the time interval between removal of spent fuel from the reactor and final emplacement of the waste and the problems which heat emission may create for guaranteeing containment integrity is a major reason for the emerging tendency to store HLWs to allow them to cool significantly. Resistance to heat is not important with ILW, which is not heat-emitting.

Ideally the rocks should have inherent properties which would minimise the corrosion of canisters emplaced within them and also the ability to absorb leakage of radionuclides by ion-exchange. Argillaceous rocks have particularly good absorbtion qualities but are liable to deformation from heat. For these reasons they are attractive for management of ILW and because ILW management is emerging as the main focus of attention in short-term RWM policy in the UK, areas of these rocks are likely to be of particular interest in the near future.

As well as the intrinsic properties discussed here it is important that the rocks should occur in formations of sufficient depth below ground level, of sufficient thickness and of sufficient areal extent. Figure 10.4 gives a general representation of a repository.

The expense of mining in the different rock types and the constructional engineering which would be required obviously has a bearing on choice of type. Costs tend to be higher for crystalline than sedimentary rocks. A US report quotes, for a standard 800 square hectare repository, figures of $1,200 million for salt, $1,300 million for argillaceous rock, $2,000 million for granite and $2,300 million for basalt (Lewis, 1981). Roadways and galleries in crystalline rock tend to maintain their integrity, while in argillaceous and halitic rocks there may be a need for active support measures. This natural closure of passages and drill-holes which tends to occur in the sedimentary rocks, especially at depth, may well be an advantage in guaranteeing isolation of deposited material in any total disposal procedure but it is obviously a burden in any storage facility where retrieval of deposited material may be required. As well as the characteristics of the rock types themselves, certain geophysical and geomorphological considerations also arise in choosing potential sites, including seismic stability, isostatic, glacial, periglacial and eustatic factors as well as resistance to catclysmic events such as meteorite impact (Gray, *et al.*, 1976; IAEA, 1977; Hill and Grimwood, 1978).

It is obviously undesirable to develop containment facilities in rocks which have a potential economic value or which under- or overlie other deposits which might be the subject of human attention for their mineral properties at some point in the future or have been explored and/or worked in the past. It was this last consideration which led to the 1972 abandonment of the

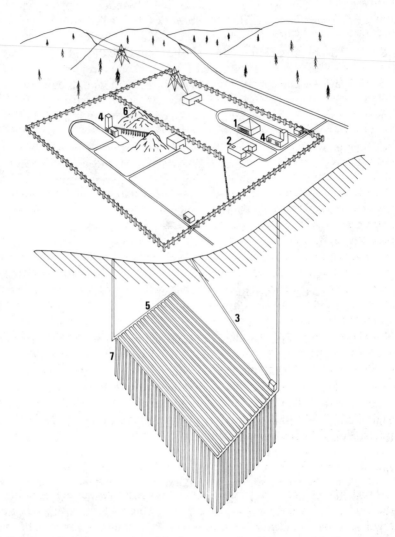

FIG 10.4 *Generalised Representation of the Appearance of an Underground Radioactive Waste Repository*

Key
1. Administration building
2. Waste reception building
3. Inclined access shaft
4. Winding tower buildings for vertical shafts
5. Roadways
6. Spoil from shaft and roadway construction
7. Waste emplacement boreholes

Source: modified from CEC (1978)

Lyons, Kansas salt facility in the USA (Weinberg, 1972, p. 33; Kasperson, 1980, p. 135). Both salt working and exploratory oil and gas drilling had occurred in the vicinity.

Of the rock types discussed, the most susceptible to future disturbance in this way would be the halitic rocks but it is generally accepted that supplies are such that it is highly unlikely that there would be any need to exploit the deposits proposed for waste containment investigation in Britain. However, the fact that the proposal involved operations on a *potentially* economic mineral did lead to a planning application for HLW test-drilling in Somerset being handled as a 'mineral' matter by the land-use planning system, requiring granting of permission by the county, rather than district authority.

As well as operations in or around the potential sites themselves it is also considered desirable to avoid areas where there are human activities or constructions which could possibly induce crystal instability or increase rock permeability within a certain distance of a potential repository. A 15 km radius *zone sanitaire* has been proposed (Gray *et al.,* 1976, p. 4). Such activities and constructions are deep mining, large dams, high pressure water tunnels and disposal wells. Obviously, as well as requiring the absence of existing activities and constructions, the location of a repository in an area would clearly tend to rule out possible future development of these types within the same radius. It is interesting to note that the prior existence of a waste repository may diminish the potential risk to inhabitants of the area from other risk-enhancing facilities, such as hydro-power dams, which might otherwise be constructed there (Weinberg, 1977, p. 57).

## The Development of Radioactive Waste Management Review, Policy and Regulation

### Introduction

Much of the discussion on the relation between national energy policy and the land-use planning system has considered the role of central government regulatory and overview responsibilities and their interaction with the needs and dilemmas of local government. The introduction to this book has touched on this issue and on the part which could be played in developing overall 'national guidelines' by commissions of inquiry of one form or another. Ongoing monitoring of complex technical activities may also have a part to play in disseminating information and possibly allaying public concern over the impact of these activities. All of these considerations are well illustrated by the case of radioactive waste and after reviewing the evolution of RWM, this section examines the impact which a 'one-off' Royal Commission study and the deliberations of a standing committee have had on the evolution of RWM.

*Early Experiences*

The problem of RW, at least of HLW in liquid form, was recognised early in the development of civil nuclear electricity generation. In 1951, Sir John Cockcroft observed that 'the dispersal of radioactive waste at one time seemed to be one of the major problems of a large scale atomic energy programme' but maintained that methods to concentrate and store the waste (the storage/disposal distinction was obviously not made by him) were being developed (Cockcroft, in Saunders, 1981). This appears to refer to the FINGAL vitrification of liquid HLW. Weinberg and Blomeke (1982) quote a 1952 US contention that 'the gigantic problems' of waste disposal meant that nuclear power was 'not worth the candle'.

An early example of intense local opposition to waste disposal occurred in the latter half of 1954 when plans for disposal of low-level liquid waste in four disused coalmines in the Forest of Dean provoked the local authority and other organisations to protest about lack of consultation and to oppose the plans on the grounds of the safety of miners in working pits and the effects on water supply and tourism. The proposal was abandoned in late 1954 because of the level of local opposition ('*The Times*', 17/8, 20/8, 21/8, 28/8, 20/10, 4/11, 1954).

The first systematic examination of British RW production came in 1956 when the Ministry of Housing and Local Government set up an expert panel. On its report, *The Control of Radioactive Wastes* (Cmnd. 884, 1959) the Radioactive Substances Act 1960 was founded. This came into effect in December, 1963, and has established the legislative basis of control for nearly 20 years. Cmnd. 884 noted that considerable work has been done on solidification of HLWs for economy in storage space or to 'dump them in inaccessible parts of the earth's surface'. It also noted that there were no present proposals to dump such waste at sea and that more research would be needed to establish this as a satisfactory method of disposal (p. 38). The report also emphasised the need for central and not local government waste control and provision of waste disposal facilities (pp. 39 and 40).

## The Royal Commission on Environmental Pollution and Subsequent Reviews and Responses

Early in 1974 the Royal Commission on Environmental Pollution (RCEP) decided to examine the interactions between nuclear power and the environment. Its report, published in September, 1976, has profoundly influenced subsequent debate on all aspects of nuclear power not only in Britain but in many European countries and in North America. RWM was subjected to particular scrutiny by the RCEP and it is clear that this led to intensification of activities to address the RW problem even before publication of the report, such as an expert group review of Cmnd. 884 begun in March, 1976

(DoE, 1979a). Several conclusions of the report have had particular ramifications for the entire subsequent unfolding of radioactive waste developments. The RCEP expressed concern at the absence of a clearly formulated
policy for RWM, which it attributed to the division of responsibilities
between a number of government departments. It felt in particular that the
long-term nature of the subject meant that existing governmental procedures were ill-equipped to deal with its particular problems.

The most important, possibly the most significant of all the Commission's
50 recommendations and conclusions was No. 27, that '(t)here should be no
commitment to a large programme of nuclear fission power until it has been
demonstrated beyond reasonable doubt that a method exists to ensure the
safe containment of long-lived, highly radioactive waste for the indefinite
future'. By explicitly establishing a link between the satisfactory resolution
of waste disposal problems and the entire future development of nuclear
fission power, this recommendation was seen as a powerful weapon by those
who sought to end or curtail the role of nuclear-generated electricity in
Britain.

The government's response to the RCEP report, published in May, 1977,
as *Nuclear Power and the Environment* (Cmnd. 6820) clearly tried to
diminish the force of this recommendation. It noted that the RCEP had itself
expressed confidence that a method would be found and emphasised the
*expectation* of achieving such a method from the implementation of current
research and development on waste conditioning and management. The
House of Commons Select Committee on Energy in February, 1981, noted
that 'we concur broadly with the conclusions of the Royal Commission on
Environmental Pollution that it would be unthinkable for any government
to commit this country to a substantial programme of nuclear power until
there is a firm prospect that the problems of the transport and long-term
disposal of nuclear waste can be managed safely' (HC 1141, 1980–1, p. 27).
Again, the emphasis was shifted from demonstration as the criterion to 'firm
prospect'.

The RCEP expressed doubt in its conclusions (No. 33) whether seabed
disposal of HLW would ever be internationally acceptable but the government response was that it was not yet an option to be ruled out. Two
recommendations were made that programmes of research into land-based
(No. 35) and sub-seabed (No. 36) disposal should be developed and it is from
these that the current activity essentially stems. The force of the
recommendations and their acceptance in Cmnd. 6820 have been important
factors in the cases put forward supporting test drilling by the UKAEA, the
SDD, the DoE and the IGS in the planning applications made for test
drilling and at the subsequent public inquiries.

Two other important RCEP recommendations concerned the administration and supervision of RWM. The first was that the responsibility for waste
should be unified and placed in the DoE rather than the DEn or the

UKAEA, and that a 'Nuclear Waste Management Advisory Committee' be established. This was agreed by the government in Cmnd. 6820. Later the title was changed to Radioactive Waste Management Advisory Committee (RWMAC) with a remit extending to non-energy wastes. The second was the creation of an independent Nuclear Waste Disposal Corporation, charged with the responsibility for developing and operating safe disposal facilities for all wastes arising from nuclear power operations. A decision on this was postponed by the government in Cmnd. 6820 pending review by the newly-created RWMAC. The RWMAC first Annual Report argued that a decision was not required until the specifics of waste storage/disposal policy had been determined after the current evaluatory research programme (RWMAC, 1980, p. 32).

However, in July, 1982, the government announced, within a White Paper on RWM (Cmnd. 8607, 1982), that having taken the advice of the RWMAC, it had concluded that a separate new body was not 'the most effective way of carrying out the tasks that lie immediately ahead' and that instead, a consortium made up of the UKAEA, BNFL, CEGB and the South of Scotland Electricity Board, and known as the Nuclear Industry Radioactive Waste Executive (NIREX) should be created. This executive is expected to use the private sector, wherever feasible, for the design of facilities and for disposal operations.

The RCEP discussion of waste management policy and possible disposal on land is also notable in that potential adverse public reaction is for the first time identified as a factor pertinent to repository site investigation. It is clear that until the mid-1970s, despite the early Forest of Dean case, the need to pursue all stages of the site-selection procedure for land disposal through the town and country planning process had not been seen as a constraint on achieving an orderly and punctual programme aimed at identification of sites and eventual facility construction. This oversight was acknowledged by the UKAEA in cross-examination at the public inquiries into proposed test drilling (Scottish Office, 1980, p. 33).

The RCEP's prescient observation is also interesting because the reference to public reaction was made in its discussion of the repository suitability of the extensive clay deposits of southern England. In considering salt deposits in Cheshire, Somerset and Yorkshire and hard rock disposal in which 'remote districts' of Scotland were mentioned, the obstacle of public reaction was not.

Whether or not this reflected the Commission's considered opinion on the relative levels of reaction expected to emerge in different areas, the response, both local and throughout Scotland, which followed the UKAEA's November, 1976 indication to Kyle and Carrick District Council that they were interested in preliminary investigations into the suitability of the Loch Doon/Carrick Forest area of the Southern Uplands, only 2 months after publication of the RCEP report, showed that public reaction was widespread and almost universally hostile.

## The Administration of Radioactive Waste Management

As noted, the Radioactive Substances Act, 1960, laid down the principle that the control of all aspects of radioactivity, including radioactive waste was to be the exclusive concern of central government. Radioactive waste disposal is therefore administered separately from all other waste types. These are controlled by the Control of Pollution Act, 1974, which makes most aspects of disposal a responsibility of the county councils. Authorisations under the 1960 Act usually specify the sites at which a waste is to be disposed of and if such a site is owned by a county council, then the authority is required to accept the waste. The DoE, under the 1960 Act, is required to notify local authorities if special precautions are likely to be needed for a waste but because the radioactive wastes usually disposed of onto public, or private licensed tips are only LLWs, the need for special precautions is rare. Some concern has been expressed that the DoE monitoring of radioactive waste disposal on such sites has not ensured that the disposal has been in accordance with the authorisation (ACC, 1982, p. 8). It is therefore only when planning proposals come forward for the development of disposal or storage sites that the local authorities are formally involved in any aspect of RWM.

Before 1977 the primary responsibility for RWM research work lay with the UKAEA, funded through the DEn and also in some research by EC money. Overall responsibility for the implementation of the 1960 Radioactive Substances Act lay with the DoE. However, the Ministry of Agriculture, Fisheries and Food (MAFF) had responsibility under the 1960 Act for the monitoring of radioactive discharges from UKAEA and licensed nuclear sites likely to contaminate agricultural products or fisheries and for licensing under the 1974 Dumping at Sea Act. As with all other matters, military wastes were and remain the responsibility of the Defence Ministry.

In its sixth report the RCEP made a very clear recommendation that the responsibility for RWM strategy should rest with a department responsible for environmental protection and not one concerned with promotion of nuclear power (RCEP, 1976, p. 162). This was accepted by government and responsibility was transferred in Cmnd. 6820 (1977) to the DoE. MAFF retained its regulatory and research responsibilities for agricultural and marine impacts while the NRPB continues to be the agency responsible for interpreting international regulations on radiation exposure. Because of this it has carried out extensive research on potential exposure pathways and effects from various disposal options (Hill and Grimwood, 1978; Hill et al., 1980; Hill and Lawson, 1980). DoE responsibility is contained within the department's Environmental Protection Group, as part of the Air, Noise and Wastes Directorate. There are two divisions involved in RWM work—administrative and scientific.

The separation of responsibility from the nuclear industry and its incorporation within the DoE was obviously designed to provide reassurance that review and regulation would primarily be motivated by the aim of environmental protection rather than easing the problems of the nuclear industry. This transfer of responsibility has in most respects been successful, especially in the drawing-up of detailed and coherent research programmes and in the identification of long-term R, D & D strategies (Duncan, 1981; DoE, 1981a).

Criticism has been made of two aspects of the arrangements. One has been that although there has been a separation of responsibility from the nuclear power industry, significant personnel involved in the DoE's RWM policy-making, regulatory and research activities have close contacts with the nuclear industry and are often former employees. This 'problem' is one which is not unique to RWM but confronts any organisation seeking experience which is recent, of high calibre and yet also transparently independent (Council for Science and Society, 1976).

The other criticism relates directly to the operation of the planning system. Because the Secretary of State for the Environment is responsible for determining appeals against refusal of planning permission or can, at his discretion, call in and determine significant applications, the DoE is, effectively, responsible for both the programme of RWM research and also for deciding on outcomes of particular aspects of that research. Of course, the divisions involved in the routine administration of the planning system and RWM are different but in the light of the strong statements of support for the test-drilling programme made by the Secretary of State (DoE, 1979b, 1980) it is almost inevitable that the suggestion should arise that the overlap of responsibilities is too great to permit the objective determination of planning appeals.

### The Radioactive Waste Management Advisory Committee

The Radioactive Waste Management Advisory Committee was set up in May, 1978, to advise principally the DoE on development and implementation of overall civil RWM policy.

Although the committee as constituted lacks the formal guarantee of longevity and does not have the direct research commissioning responsibility suggested by the RCEP, it has placed strong emphasis in its annual reports on the need for long-term perspectives. The RCEP also suggested the committee should have 'a strong environmental representation' but it could be argued that, with only one of the seventeen members holding a position which formally incorporates the term environment in his title, this has not been fully implemented in practice. The committee is composed of nine independent scientists, four representatives of the nuclear and electricity industries, three representatives of trades unions in these industries and has civil servants from MAFF, DEn, DoE, the Scottish and Welsh Offices, the Health and Safety Executive, NRPB and the Natural Environment Research Council attached as assessors to interpret technical information.

Unsurprisingly, in view of its origins, the committee began as one of its first tasks a review of the HLW research and management programme. The first and second Annual Reports of the committee indicate the evolution of its examination. The committee regards accurate public information on RW as of great importance and sees a role for itself in the provision of objective advice and a 'dispassionate perspective' on the subject to a wider audience than the government departments to whom it is formally required to provide advice. It would be difficult, however, to claim that so far the RWMAC has had a wide impact on public awareness of the issues involved in RWM.

The most significant early action of the committee related to the exploratory drilling programme was the sending of a letter to the Secretary of State for the Environment * stating that its remit could not be discharged until the information that the exploratory drilling programme would yield had been obtained. While noting that the committee did not 'seek to intervene in matters which must of course be dealt with through the appropriate planning procedures' the letter stated that it felt that local concern over test-drilling 'while understandable, is misplaced and is based on a fundamental misunderstanding of the purpose and nature of the research involved'. In this statement the committee sought to reinforce the official policy that there was no prejudgement of the preferred disposal/storage option and its letter was used in advancing the cases for drilling at the public inquiries into the proposed test-drilling.

The committee's first report does make clear that it recognised that disposal choices were dependent on public acceptability as well as technical feasibility but while seeing the provision of advice on public acceptability as one of its most important functions, it did not seek to advance a position on this until completion of the research programme. The thrust of the committee's position is, however, probably well indicated by the emphasis which it has placed, particularly in its second report, on the comparative analysis of risk of various energy source options, on the quantification of such risks and on the need for the public to understand the methods of risk assessment and the nature and level of risks from everyday activities as well as nuclear processes.

Comparison of the committee's annual reports also shows a shift in its thinking from an emphasis on the urgency of a staged programme moving from storage to disposal towards an increasingly favourable attitude over long-term storage of HLW in engineered repositories 'for decades or even centuries', with the final decision on the choice being unlikely 'before the beginning of the next century'. It has been noted that the disposal/storage distinction may have little significance for the choice of site for a storage/disposal facility.

The committee presented its reasoning on the storage/disposal choice in

* And for Scotland and Wales.

terms of a multifactor choice, involving cost considerations but also the extent to which the problem of HLW should be resolved in the present, as opposed to future resolution which involves passing on the responsibility for the choice to a future government and society. The committee argued that the early *disposal* of waste reduced the responsibility placed on future generations but that even when all the requisite information necessary for the storage/disposal option was available it was better not to advance immediately to irreversible decisions (i.e. disposal) but to leave to future generations the flexibility of choice on how and when to dispose of solidified waste.

Some type of overview committee, of which the RWMAC might be argued to be a form, has been seen by some commentators as a desirable ingredient of a 'rational' process of decision-making over complex technologies (Council for Science and Society, 1976). Such an overview body might be able to tackle the national policy framework which constrains local land-use planning aspects. The experience with the RWMAC since its inception suggests that it will be unlikely to provide this function in its present form. The cancellation of the test-drilling programme, apparently with little consultation of the committee, was obviously a blow to its integrity (one member resigned). It has been criticised by the Association of County Councils (1982) for having no local authority representation, an omission which does seem surprising. However, despite the claim of the Association, the committee *has* seen itself as having a role in providing public reassurance but it is open to question whether it has been successful in this.

## The Development of the British Programme of Research into the Feasibility of Geological Disposal of Radioactive Waste

### The Early Stages of Geological Research

Although there has been research on land-based LLW disposal since 1951, it was only in 1975 that the UKAEA, then responsible for RWM research, commissioned the Institute of Geological Sciences to study the criteria appropriate for geological disposal (Gray *et al.*, 1976) and to identify areas meeting this potential (IGS, 1976). It was then considered that many such areas would be found and the search was concentrated in north west England, close to the Windscale site and also on offshore islands all around the British coast (but not the Channel Islands or Northern Ireland) (Scottish Office, 1980; IGS, 1976). Offshore sites would have the dual advantages of potential ship-borne access from Windscale and potential marine dilution of groundwater leakages.

At this stage, the main thrust of research was into HLW disposal possibilities in crystalline rocks, because of the emphasis of the EC research programme in which the UK participated. There was, however, always an

TABLE 10.2 *The Selection Process for Areas for Test-drilling*

| *24 Crystalline Rock areas identified in 1979* | *Areas Selected for More Intensive Study* | *Areas Where Planning Permission Sought* |
|---|---|---|
| Rhum | Eskdale and Ennerdale * | Cheviot |
| St. Kilda | Cheviot | Loch Doon |
| Eskdale and Ennerdale | Loch Doon | Strath Halladale |
| Cheviot | Strath Halladale | Widmerpool Gulf |
| Loch Doon | Strath Ossian | Worcester Basin |
| Strath Halladale | Etive | Somerset Basin |
| Morven/Cabrach | entire Loch Laxford area | |
| Rogart | Loch Shin | |
| Peterhead | | |
| Hill of Fare/Benachie | *Argillaceous and* | |
| Strath Ossian | *Evaporitic Areas Added* | |
| Etive | North Wales | |
| Loch Laxford—Enard Bay | Widmerpool Gulf | |
| Loch Laxford—Cape Wrath | Worcester Basin | |
| S. Rona | S. Cumbria | |
| S. W. Lewis | Cheshire Basin | |
| N. Harris | Somerset Basin | |
| Scarp | Wessex Basin | |
| Taransay | | |
| Pabbay | *Additional Area* | |
| Loch Shin | Harwell | |
| Ben Armine | | |
| Jura | | |
| River Strathey | | |

* This area was included after the other areas had originally been identified.

intention to cover other rock types (UKAEA, 1980, 2, p. 35). Originally thirteen crystalline rock areas were selected for more detailed study but in late 1977 a further eleven areas were added. All these areas were chosen for reasons of ease of access through land ownership, as well as on purely geological criteria (CEC, 1978, p. 148). The selection of the additional eleven sites occurred alongside the broadening of concern with other disposal options and around the time that responsibility for the research programme was transferred from the UKAEA to the DoE in May, 1977. The 24 crystalline areas were subjected to a further process of sifting to produce a shortlist of eight areas, to which were added four argillaceous and three evaporitic rock areas (Table 10.2 and Figure 10.5).

### The 'Widening Remit' and its planning significance

The official evidence presented at the test-drilling inquiries and all other official statements have carefully pointed out that as from the late 1977 widening of the research programme remit, it altered from one concerned solely with identification of potential repository sites to one concerned with the wider evaluation of the entire option of geological disposal (UKAEA, 1980, 4. p. 3). Examination of this changing emphasis and its significance played an important part in the public inquiries held into test-drilling because establishing the precise nature of the research programme related strongly to an important planning consideration—that of 'subsequent developments' discussed below in the section on the land-use planning system.

### The Test-drilling Programme and the Land-use Planning System

#### *Introduction*

The first two parts of this chapter have set the context in which the relation between the land-use planning system and the development of radioactive waste management has been worked out. Some important characteristics of

radioactive waste which create management requirements, such as the location of potential containment repositories, that are particularly significant for land-use planning have been described and the overall national administrative and advisory framework in which RWM policy has developed has been outlined. The concluding part of the chapter examines the particular issues which the treatment of plans for test-drilling by the land-use planning system created or involved in widespread public examination. It then goes on to consider some lessons which have emerged from the sequence of events in the research programme on high-level waste containment, which, at least in the drilling research component, was brought to an abrupt halt by the December, 1981 decision to abandon the programme of test-drilling (see below).

### The Series of Planning Applications for Test-drilling

It is first necessary to outline the entire sequence of test-drilling events which began formally in January, 1980 with the application by the UKAEA for permission for test-drilling in the Loch Doon area of the Scottish Southern Uplands and ended formally with the December, 1981 announcement by the DoE that the test-drilling programme was being abandoned. However, as with all stories, there was a beginning before the beginning and the end is not really an end. There had been informal indications of the

FIG 10.5 *Distribution of Rock Types Considered to Meet the Selection Criteria for High-level Waste Containment and of Areas Selected for Feasibility Studies*

 Crystalline, igneous and metamorphic areas

 Argillaceous areas

Halitic and evaporitic areas

SITES
a.)  Crystalline rocks
1   Loch Doon Caledonian granitic intrusion
2   Cheviot granitic intrusion
3   Ossian granitic intrusion
4   Etive granitic intrusion
5   Strath Halladale granitic intrusion
6   Morven/Cabrach Caledonian basic intrusion
7   Moine metamorphosed arenaceous and argillaceous sediments
8   Lewisian basement gneisses, granite and pegmatite

b.)  Argillaceous and evaporitic rocks
9   North Wales Ordovician and Silurian argillaceous rocks
10  Widmerpool Gulf Lower Carboniferous mudstones, siltstones and limestones
11  Worcester Basin Triassic mudstones
12  Southern Cumbrian Silurian mudstones and greywackes
13  Cheshire Basin Permo-Triassic evaporites and mudstones
14  Somerset Basin Permo-Triassic evaporites and mudstones
15  Wessex Basin Permo-Triassic evaporites and mudstones

Source: modified from RWMAC (1981)

possibility of test-drilling from 1976 onwards at Loch Doon, while, as already noted, the programme of research on ILW will require some forms of test-drilling and it remains to be seen whether public concern in any areas which may be chosen will be allayed by the welter of assertions that ILW characteristics are very different from those of HLW. The Association of County Councils, for one, is somewhat doubtful about this (ACC, 1982, p. 9).

Between them, the seven planning applications and/or test drillings which were made under the HLW research programme (and the 'rogue' case at Harwell) represent virtually every procedure by which development proposals are handled by the British planning system. Space precludes detailed examination of all the characteristics of the various cases but they provide an intriguing set of occurrences for comparison. Both the Scottish and English planning and public inquiry procedures were involved. The introductory chapter to this book comments on the importance of the two-tier system of planning in Britain, with responsibility divided between district and county (in Scotland, regional) planning authorities. In the test-drilling cases, some fell to district authorities for determination while others were within the province of the county (regional) authorities. The Widmerpool Gulf and Worcester Basin cases involved two district authorities simultaneously, as two borehole sites were proposed, in different authorities. However, in each case, the two authorities worked in close harmony in formulating their responses to the planning applications.

County (regional) authorities became involved in determining the planning applications for different reasons. The Altnabreac case was considered by Highland Regional Council. It is the planning authority in all cases in its area; the sparse population of its constituent districts led to them being given no planning functions in the Scottish local government reorganisation. The Cheviot application in Northumberland was determined by the county because the two sites at which clusters of boreholes were proposed lay within a National Park and so any development had to be considered by the county through its National Park Committee. Finally, and most interestingly, the application for two test boreholes in Somerset became the province of the county initially because the proposals seemed possibly to involve waste disposal, were a departure from the development plan and therefore were considered a matter for county determination. Subsequently the justification for county involvement became that as the proposed investigation was into halitic rocks, these were a 'mineral' source and so a matter for the county to determine. The test-drilling carried out at Harwell, Oxfordshire, in February, 1981 did not come under the HLW research programme, being primarily related to possible ILW containment. No planning permission was anyway needed for it to be carried out because Harwell is one of the sites listed in the Town and County Planning (Atomic Energy Establishments Special Development) Order, 1954, which permits certain small-scale developments at nine UKAEA, AWRE and BNFL sites in England and Wales, without the need for planning permission. The passage of the various planning applications through the planning system also shows the great variety of outcomes possible in the British planning system. In only one case was planning permission straightforwardly granted by the planning authority—at Altnabreac, in Highland Region, Caithness district. In three cases, the Cheviot and Loch Doon granites and the Widmerpool Gulf, the competent authorities (Kyle and Carrick District Council, Northumberland County Council, Rushcliffe Borough Council and Charnwood Borough Council) all refused planning permission for the test-drilling proposals. The UKAEA or the IGS appealed against these refusals and there were public inquiries on the appeals. In the Cheviot and Loch Doon cases, the inquiry inspector (reporter) submitted a report to the DoE or Scottish Office. In both cases the inspector recommended that the minister should allow the appeals and the test-drillings should go ahead. In the Widmerpool Gulf case, the December, 1981 decision to forego test-drilling came before the inspector could submit his report, a purely factual document, in February 1982. In the Somerset case, the county decided not to determine the application, that is, not to take any action over it, but to make representations that a special form of inquiry under section 48 of the 1971 Town and Country Planning Act should be set up because of the national and regional significance of the proposals and their complex technical nature (Somerset County Council, 1981).

By refusing to determine the application, the county council left it open to the applicant (the IGS) to appeal against this inaction, which they duly did. However, before a public inquiry could be held the test-drilling programme was suspended and the appeal withdrawn.

Finally, in the Worcester Basin case, the local authorities had not had time to make their formal positions on the planning applications known before the December, 1981 decision was taken and the applications withdrawn early in 1982. However, the thrust of the local authorities' position was also that a special 'section 48' planning inquiry commission was appropriate in this case.

The overall impression of this account is of various pathways being taken to the same end of opposition to the test-drilling proposals, with the single exception of Altnabreac, although even here four out of 20 members of the planning committee voted against granting of planning permission. Against this, in the Widmerpool Gulf case, both councils' planning committees recommended approval of the application, only to have their views rejected by the elected members at full council meetings.

A small inter-authority dispute over test-drilling did arise between Kyle and Carrick District Council and Strathclyde Regional Council, which tried to 'call-in' the UKAEA test-drilling application for determination by itself as involving regional scale matters more appropriate for consideration by a regional authority. The district council resisted this and its view was upheld by the Secretary of State for Scotland. However, the basic positions of the district and regional authorities over the proposed test-drillings did not differ greatly.

The progress of the test-drilling applications for HLW research and the Harwell drilling through the British planning system is summarised in Table 10.3. For sake of completeness, mention should be made of another radioactive waste disposal situation which occurred during the period under review which, although it involved LLW, was instrumental in alerting the Association of County Councils to some of the problems of RW disposal, leading to the creation of a working party to review the entire procedure currently adopted for involvement of local authorities in the disposal authorisation process (Association of County Councils, 1982). Plans for disposal of spent catalyst containing depleted uranium and originating in Cleveland county were strongly opposed by Durham County Council, especially as sites in the originating county had declined to accept the waste. Under the 1980 Control of Pollution (Special Works) Regulation, the DoE could have directed such sites to take the waste but it decided not to do so.

The intention to investigate the Widmerpool, Somerset and Worcester Basin areas was originally announced by the DoE in January, 1980. The announcement also contained reference to a fourth area in Gwynned and Powys in North Wales. However, this intention was never followed through with a planning application. Opposition to test-drilling, while it existed in all areas, was particularly intense in North Wales and field staff working on preliminary exploration were subjected to some harassment. It is widely believed that the disruption of the research work and the fear of major public disquiet were the reasons that no planning application was ever made in this area.

### The Abandonment of High Level Waste Test-drilling

On December 16th, 1981, the Minister for Local Government and Environmental Services in the Department of the Environment, in reply to a Parliamentary question from an MP in one of the areas affected by test-drilling proposals, announced that a review had been completed of HLW research and that this had led to a re-orientation of the programme. The option of surface storage of vitrified HLW for at least 5 years was to become preferred policy. In justifying this, the government announcement placed a strong emphasis on the views of the RWMAC, contained in their second Annual Report. The government naturally made no reference to the letter expressing strong support for the HLW test-drilling programme contained in the *first* Annual Report of the committee. It was decided that there was no need to proceed with construction of a demonstration facility in

TABLE 10.3 *The Progress of Planning Applications for Test-drilling through the British Planning System 1978–1981*

| | | | | | | | |
|---|---|---|---|---|---|---|---|
| Area | Loch Doon | Cheviots | Altnabreac | Widmerpool Gulf | Somerset | Worcester Basin | Harwell |
| Date of Planning Application | Jan. 1978 | Feb. 1978 | May 1978 | Oct. 1980 | Oct. 1980 | Oct. 1981 | Not Applicable [1] |
| Rock Type | Caledonian Granite | Caledonian Granite | Migmatite | Mudstone and Siltstones | Halite/mudstone sequences | Mudstone and Siltstones | Oxford Clay |
| Determining Authority | Kyle and Carrick D.C. | Northumberland C.C. | Highland R.C. | Rushcliffe B.C. and Charnwood B.C. | Somerset C.C. | Wychavon D.C. and Tewkesbury B.C. | Not applicable |
| Outcome of Planning Application | Permission refused | Permission refused | Permission granted | Permission refused by both councils | C.C. declined to process application | No decision taken by time of programme abandonment | Not applicable |
| Subsequent events | Appeal submitted Apr. 1979 Public inquiry Feb. 1980 Inspector's report Dec. 1980 | Appeal submitted Dec. 1978 Public inquiry Oct. 1980 Inspector's report July 1981 | Drilling Nov. 1978 | Appeal submitted July 1981 Public inquiry Nov. 1981 Inspector's report without recommendations submitted Feb. 1982 | Appeal submitted July 1981 | | Drilling Feb. 1981 |

All development proposals withdrawn as result of government statement Dec. 1981

Notes:
[1] Under the Town and Country Planning (Atomic Energy Establishments Special Development) Order, 1954, certain developments at the Atomic Energy Establishment, Harwell and eight other sites, do not need planning permission. D.C.—district council, C.C.—county council, B.C.—borough council, R.C.—regional council.

Britain and that the proposals in other countries would, instead, be monitored for their applicability to Britain, as would the general geological work carried out abroad.

The appeal for planning permission in the Cheviots was dismissed (as was the Loch Doon appeal by the Secretary of State for Scotland) and all the other appeals and applications were withdrawn. No further field drilling on HLW containment was to proceed, although the statement emphasised that priority would henceforward be given towards 'the early *disposal* (our emphasis) of those wastes with a lower level of radioactivity for which there is no technical advantage in delaying disposal' (DoE, 1981c).

This decision meant that the immediate concerns of local authorities involved in the various procedures summarised in Table 10.3 were resolved instantly although those authorities in whose areas lie rock formations which may also be suitable for ILW containment noted the possible consequences of the change in emphasis.

The most noteworthy feature of the decision to dismiss the appeals and withdraw the outstanding appeals and applications was that it was firmly based on the perceived national *need* for the developments proposed, in terms of their relation to national policy on RWM. However, at the three public inquiries held into the test-drilling proposals, although the inspectors (reporter) allowed some discussion of these aspects, there was a strong emphasis placed on the decisions being made on the local planning consequences of the test-drilling proposals alone. This was strongly disputed by most of the objectors to the proposals at the inquiries and the justifications for the abandonment of the programme bear out their contentions.

The government statement of December, 1981 creates the impression that the storage option and the need to focus attention on ILW matters were relatively new considerations in RWM policy, whereas their significance had been established for several years and was raised at each of the public inquiries into the test-drilling proposals.

As a result of the decision to apply for individual local planning permissions in each of the areas concerned, three local public inquiries were held, two of them large-scale. Considerable work on the part of local authorities and other objectors was occasioned. The DoE and the Scottish Office estimated the costs of the three public inquiries to *themselves alone* as—

|  | £ |
|---|---|
| Loch Doon inquiry, Ayr | 19,700 |
| Cheviot inquiry, Newcastle | 21,169 |
| Widmerpool inquiry, Loughborough | 1,408 |
| (House of Commons Hansard, March 17th, 1982). | |

These are simply the direct costs and do not take into account the time of professional staff in preparing evidence, nor establishment costs which cannot be readily identified. These costs at least could therefore be set off against the costs of carrying out a specific public presentation of the entire field of RWM policy, including the storage option and the requirements for ILW treatment, under the section 48 arrangements of the 1971 Town and Country Planning Act, or some other arrangements.

*Test-drilling and 'subsequent developments'*

As well as the entire issue of how decision-making should proceed on a complex, national-policy-related, technical subject such as RWM, discussed in the previous section, the public inquiries into the test-drilling proposals also raised a number of specific planning considerations which are particular to test-drilling or are well illustrated by it.

A notable feature of the debate on land-use planning aspects of RWM which occupied considerable parts of the discussions at the public inquiries was whether it was appropriate to make a decision on the applications for test-drilling not on the characteristics of the test-drilling activity itself but on those of any subsequent development, especially a demonstration or operational repository for wastes, which might subsequently follow the carrying-out of the test drilling. This concern arose because in general the environmental impact and loss of amenity of the temporary, small-scale activity involved in the actual test-drilling was comparatively insignificant. In the Cheviot case, the Northumberland County Council National Park and Countryside Committee stated outright that it did not consider the proposal to relate to exploration purposes but to determine the feasibility of 'storage' of nuclear waste underground in the Cheviot Hills (DoE, 1981a, p. 3). The proposal therefore conflicted with the statutory purposes of the National Park and was viewed unfavourably. In the Loch Doon case the local authority was opposed to the test-drilling because of its association in the minds of the public, developers and investors with the possible disposal of nuclear waste' (Scottish Office, 1980).

The problem of the possible subsequent consequences of a particular development, especially the *exploitation* of a mineral, which might follow from allowing *exploration* for it, has frequently presented dilemmas to the land-use planning process. Clearly the general principle of considering the full flow of possibilities which might result from granting of planning permission is entirely rational. The apprehension that to allow the first stage of what may be a linked series of development stages will inevitably increase the chances of the same area being selected for subsequent developments is a natural concern of those who may oppose the consequences of such developments. However, the general principle has been that applications for permission to explore for minerals should be handled without reference to the consequences of mineral extraction. This principle was forcibly upheld in the report of the Committee on the Control of Mineral Working (the Stevens Committee) in 1976.

In the Cheviot case the inquiry inspector concluded that the test drilling proposals did not refer to 'the construction of a repository for the storage of nuclear waste' and, if approved, the planning proposals did not 'infer that a repository would be constructed' (DoE, 1981, p. 173). At Loch Doon the inquiry reporter (under Scottish law) endorsed the assertions of the UKAEA that the principle of geological containment had not been accepted by the government, that no criteria for site selection yet existed, that none of the possible areas for development of a repository had been ruled out and that the research was solely into the characteristics of various rock types (Scottish Office, 1980). For these reasons he rejected the inevitability and therefore the relevance of subsequent developments.

The importance of the 'widening remit' in allowing the inspectors to come to this decision was critical and if the planning inquiries had been directed towards evaluation of the original research plans with their rigid sequence of events moving from preliminary site characterisation to establishment of a test repository, the significance of subsequent developments would almost inevitably have influenced the inspectors' interpretations of the planning applications. The fact that a specific decision had not been taken to go for any further activity 'downstream' from the test-drilling itself enabled the UKAEA in the Cheviot case to argue that the rejection of planning permission for test-drilling proposed for evaluating the construction of a reservoir in Wales (the Dulas valley), did not relate to the Cheviot case because in the Welsh case the valley site had already been identified as *desirable* for a reservoir and the test-drilling was merely to confirm this whereas no such decision about the desirability of location of a repository in the Cheviot Hills had been taken.

It is difficult for the impartial observer to avoid the conclusion that the 'widening remit' of the UK research programme was distinctly underplayed at the time of its occurrence and subsequently, compared with the critical position it was held to represent at the public inquiries. A number of publications after 1977 continued to place a heavy emphasis on the land-based disposal option despite the 'opening-up' of the research programme. The sites selected in the EC-linked programme, developed before the widening of the research remit, were the same sites for which planning applications were made under the revised programme. Sites which were the prime focus of attention when a search was being made for detailed repository-suitability evaluation were the same sites said to offer the best information for a more general evaluation of rock types and environments.

Whether or not the 'evidence seems to suggest that the change (in the research emphasis, DRC) has been no more than cosmetic' and that it is 'totally misleading and untrue to say that the original process of selection has been abandoned' as alleged in the Cheviot case by counsel for Northumberland County Council (UKAEA, 1980, 15, p. 6, 7), it is clear that the reversal of a conventional process of movement from the general to the particular led to considerable confusion and suspicion over the exact status of the UK land-disposal research programme. In their own words the early UKAEA programme of site-specific investigation was 'naive' (UKAEA, 1980, 2, p. 39; 19, p. 16). The need to pursue the proposed test-drillings through the planning system, where the issue of subsequent developments and their relevance to the matter under immediate consideration was well-established, seems to have been overlooked.

Of course, in any research programme, new circumstances, aims, criteria and so on may occur which require the re-definition of the original schedule of research. A greater emphasis on the changing nature of the UK programme at the time it occurred would have helped to allay the suspicions of objectors to the proposed test-drilling that there was an element of *ex post facto* elaboration of the significance of the change of the programme's emphasis to help to defuse the concern about subsequent developments. This concern was the greater because of the site-specific way in which the planning examination of the test-drilling programme proceeded. If, in mid- to late 1979, before the public inquiry into the Loch Doon drilling proposals was held, there had been a national exposition of the entire programme of research, especially the circumstances surrounding on-land test-drilling, the assertions of the significance of the changing emphasis might have enjoyed greater credibility.

### Test-drilling, the Planning System and its Environmental Impacts

There was also discussion at the inquiries and subsequently, on whether test-drilling on the scale contemplated in the radioactive waste research programme constituted a 'development' within the accepted sense of the term. If it were held not to be a development, or were to be accorded special status as a permitted development, then any proposals for test-drilling would not have to be processed by the planning system in the conventional way. This debate, which is separate from the issue of developments which might follow after the carrying out of test-drilling, centres on the temporary nature of the activity and the comparatively small scale of the equipment and supporting facilities involved. The overall legal issues surrounding this question are discussed by Rowan-Robinson (undated, b.). It is important to note that if the test-drilling had not been classed as a development, then the public inquiries which followed those cases where the local authorities refused permission would not have occurred. Although there was dissatisfaction on the part of opposition groups even to the form of the public inquiries which did take place, largely on the grounds of their restricted terms of reference, it is likely that the level of agitation in the proposed test areas would have been even greater if the planning system had not offered the opportunity for public examination of the drilling proposals.

The Association of County Councils has suggested that test-drilling be treated as having deemed planning permission under the General Development Order of the 1971 Town and Country Planning Act (ACC, 1982). It argues that 'the application of the full planning process to exploratory drilling represents a considerable waste of administrative effort which would be better devoted to considering the implications for those sites believed to be feasible as a result of the exploratory operations' (p. 6). At the same time, however, the association called for the development of new machinery for public participation in decisions such as radioactive waste disposal and for a formal requirement that if a local authority consulted under the 1960 Act over radioactive waste disposal objected to the proposal, a local 'hearing' (seen as less formal than an inquiry) be constituted (p. 11). While apparently loosening the opportunities for public examination of stages in the waste management process on the one hand, the association has sought to strengthen this on a more general basis.

Although there was considerable discussion of the possible environmental impact of the test-drilling in the public inquiries into the Loch Doon and Cheviot cases, this was in part because they were the earlier cases and involved undoubtedly attractive, upland recreation areas. By the time the proposals for further areas were submitted, the affected planning authorities, mindful of opposing them, accepted that the actual environmental impacts of the drilling, in somewhat more mundane areas, including disused airfields and coal-ash stocking yards, were not sufficient reasons for opposition and sought other, more significant factors, especially the subsequent development possibility.

At both Cheviot and Loch Doon, the drilling was expected to last for around 2 years, with rigs about 15 metres high. Continuous operation was envisaged and this raised the question of noise intrusion, which together with visual intrusion were the two main environmental impacts examined. Arrangements were proposed to minimise surface water pollution from drilling slurry and to prevent erosion by access vehicles, with supervision of these by the Nature Conservancy Council and the relevant water authorities. In both cases, the inspector (reporter) concluded that environmental impact would not be major or injurious, from either noise or visual effect. In general, these conclusions and the administrative and overview arrangements proposed to substantiate them, aroused little controversy at the inquiries.

### Radioactive Waste Management and National Planning Guidelines

The identification of areas for possible containment facilities for high-level radioactive waste involved the sifting of national data on geological characteristics throughout the United Kingdom. Geomorphological data, especially related to natural hazard incidence were also important. It is also clear that at various stages in the selection process, constraints were introduced, involving land ownership and location of areas in relation to location of waste arisings, especially Windscale. It is not difficult to argue that, at this stage, it might also be appropriate to introduce other constraints which would stem from the adoption of certain national planning guidelines.

Such guidelines have not been formally adopted for England and Wales, although they have been adopted in Scotland. They would make assumptions about the desirability of certain developments, or any developments at all, in particular areas, such as recreation or scenic regions, and might also, as well as such negative assumptions, state positive preferences for the location of some developments in certain areas.

Not surprisingly, there was considerable discussion in the Cheviot case of whether the existing national park policy provided such a guideline and assumption against development, with the UKAEA pointing to anomalous developments such as test ranges which were accepted in the park because of their national importance and the opponents of test-drilling arguing that there were many other possible sites where test-drilling and repository siting could be carried out before it became necessary to go into a national park. Similar arguments were put forward over Loch Doon. Although there are no national park areas in Scotland, it was argued that if there were, then the Loch Doon area would be one beyond doubt.

Such arguments obviously intensified the 'anywhere but here', or 'horizontal shift' syndrome, whereby local authorities and other organisations in places identified as possible test areas sought to ensure that it was not *their* area which, because opposition was not total, strident and well-organised, ended up being the 'soft option'. National planning guidelines might help to provide a logical, coherent set of evaluational criteria to restrain such a pell-mell response by identifying areas on which a national consensus exists that there should be a presumption against development. More sophisticated guidelines might lay down some concepts of 'maximum tolerable collective environmental insult' for certain areas, whereby it was assumed that if a developer was proposing a development in a certain area, then he would also be expected to remove an existing environmentally intrusive development in the same, or a similar area.

The Commission on Energy and the Environment discussed the use of national planning guidelines in its study of the environmental impact of the use of coal (CENE, 1981, p. 200). It argued that their development would be much more complex in England and Wales than in Scotland and that guidelines issued by the Department of the Environment might prejudice the impartiality of the department in determining planning application appeals. Neither of these arguments seems particularly convincing and the development of a comprehensive national framework for location of RWM facilities, incorporating physical environmental, population density, transport network and emergency response capability considerations as well as geological and geomorphological factors would seem to be a particularly good case on which to try such an exercise. 'At risk' areas which might provoke particular concerns could be early identified by such a process. For example, given that the UK search initially concentrated on crystalline rock areas for RWM containment, it was inevitable that the search would come into conflict with amenity and recreation considerations which tend to be disproportionately located in the crystalline highland areas.

## Social Management Strategies for RWM

The level of public opposition to the HLW test-drilling programme was obviously something of a surprise to policy-makers, even though it is a phenomenon which has occurred in every country which has attempted to develop a RWM policy, even in France, which is generally felt to have a compliant population over nuclear power. Consequently the development of strategies to 'inform' and 'educate' the public over the nature of nuclear power in general and radwaste in particular has been identified as of considerable importance (Firebaugh, 1980). In 1982/83 the RWMAC identified public perception of risk as an area for particular attention by the committee (RWMAC, 1982, p. 45) and has also argued that there may be positive *advantages* to local communities from engaging in work related to the nuclear industry (RWMAC, 1982, p. 32).

Such an interpretation is probably based on the well-known phenomenon of considerable local support for existing facilities closer to the 'front-end' of the nuclear fuel cycle. It is not such an established phenomenon for *new* facilities, and it is likely to be a particularly difficult interpretation to 'seed' over RWM facilities in particular, perhaps with the exception of their location at existing nuclear sites (*'Financial Times'*, 1982b). RWM containment facilities will not be particularly large employers; their operation, as opposed to construction, is not likely to offer significant employment opportunities for the local populations in areas where they might be located. Waste facilities of *all* types are particularly undesired facilities and closely parallel nuclear power stations themselves in public hostility to their proximate location (Council on Environmental Quality, 1980).

Given that the natural soil for the seed of local public support for the development of RWM facilities is so poor, it is not surprising that the possibility of 'artificially fertilising' the ground should be considered. Already in France, Electricité de France has undertaken to pay a direct grant of 1 million FFr to the regional council at a site where a new nuclear plant is under construction, as well as to place $1.2 \times 10^9$ FFr of contracts with local firms (*'Energy Daily'*, 1982, p. 5). In the USA, the discussion about possible forms of local compensation has included federal tax rebates and the promise of additional local federal investment (Wilbanks, 1981a; OTA, 1982). There has even been discussion of holding some form of auction whereby authorities would be encouraged to bid for RWM facilities *and* some compensatory investment, with both going to the locality which fitted technical requirements *and* made the lowest compensation demand (Wilbanks, 1981b).

## Conclusions

This chapter has shown that, as in all other countries, RWM policy in the UK is in a state of rapid evolution. Its technical evolution has, however, been faster than that of the administrative arrangements necessary to integrate it unexceptionably into the multitude of goals set by groups in society for themselves. This has been shown up both *by* and *through* the planning system. The treatment of the gathering momentum of the high level waste research programme which has formed the focus of this chapter shows that confusion, delay and political expediency have characterised the unfolding of the events and that a major explanatory factor for this state of affairs has been the attempt to pursue what is demonstrably a national programme, with a multitude of ramifications, some environmental, others lying outside the conventional concerns of the planning system, piecemeal, on a site-by-site basis, through the local planning system. Among the dilemmas this created were undoubtedly the demands placed upon several local authority planning departments to develop technical expertise which might better have been handled by the research activity of a national overview inquiry.

Space has prevented the discussion of many other aspects of RWM and its links to the planning system. The spatial equity of disposal of waste in a way which affects disproportionately those who have had disproportionately little benefit from its production is one consideration which is central to the concerns of planners (Kasperson, 1980). The temporal aspects of the same equity problem may also be within the remit of planners, if it is accepted that they, as well as the state, can be legitimately regarded as custodians of the interests of future inhabitants of their areas (Maclean, 1980; Montefiore, 1981).

The role of non-official opposition to test-drilling and the part played by such groups in the planning process is also singularly interesting. More letters of opposition were received about the Loch Doon proposal than for any other planning application in Scotland to date (Miller, 1981). A local petition secured support from 117,000 out of around 200,000 of the local population.

The level of opposition in the Cheviots was equally intense, while the threat of direct action in North Wales and its part in the non-pursuit of research in that area has already been discussed. Opposition, while present, seems to have been more muted in the Widmerpool Gulf case. A comparison of the mainsprings of opposition must consider the question of public perception of waste management and the planning system, another area which has only been alluded to in this chapter.

For many of the scientific and technical staff involved in the RWM programme, the need to develop research that would be subject to public scrutiny and therefore would need to withstand the legal rigours of the planning system presented considerable dilemmas because it limited the powers of speculation and intuition on which a programme often can rely heavily. This subject is also worthy of further and more general study as part of the technical complexity dilemma discussed in the introduction to this book.

The chapter has not looked at the economics of RWM, about which there is very little hard information. Much of the literature argues that the costs, compared with other stages in the nuclear electricity generation cycle, are likely to be insignificant, but this is based on extremely limited experience of managing the back-end of the cycle. Also excluded from discussion has been the significance of the choice between AGR and PWR reactors for RWM policy, as well as the role of fast breeders. This is an extremely important issue and it can be said that PWRs increase the requirements for early development of ILW management facilities.

The issues of high-level waste management may have been suspended by the decision to opt for medium-term storage, but as this chapter has pointed out, the involvement of the planning system is equally, if not more, likely to be as great in the development of intermediate waste management. If a large number of sites, including existing hazardous non-radioactive waste sites, are under investigation for ILW disposal (*'Financial Times',* 1982a) then many authorities may feel potentially involved. The development of a rational evaluation of alternative transport options for ILW will inevitably require the identification of the alternative *sites* or at least areas, to which the waste will be moved. If a policy of on-site containment of wastes is preferred, this may come into conflict with existing or proposed arrangements between local authorities and nuclear site operators.

Successive governments have given assurances that they will take into account public concern in the development of RWM policy. The latest reiteration of this in the July, 1982, White Paper on *Radioactive Waste Management* (Cmnd. 8607) implies (p. 20) that in the case of intermediate waste, the opportunity for this will arise through the local planning inquiry into any proposal for a specific facility. The experience to date with high-level waste research does not support such an implication. Some form of wider-ranging investigation and alternative site evaluation is required, not necessarily a full-blown Planning Inquiry Commission as provided for by the 1971 Town and Country Planning Act, section 48, but perhaps on more informal lines, in keeping with the thinking of the Association of County Councils' working party (ACC, 1982) but with more than a purely local remit on one site at a time. There has been a tendency to resist such demands by referring to the review of RWM carried out by the Royal Commission on Environmental Pollution in its sixth report (1976). The information on which this report, excellent though it is, is based is nearly a decade old and there have been many developments in the field since then. The only guarantee that the unfortunate saga of the high-level waste programme will not be repeated by intermediate level waste developments is to incorporate such an inquiry into the planning system's response to the unique dilemmas which radioactive waste poses.

## References

ACC (Association of County Councils) (1982) *Radioactive Waste; report of an ACC working party*, May, Association of County Councils, London.

CEC (Commission of the European Communities) (1978) *Second Annual Progress Report on the Community's R & D Programme on Radio-active Waste Management and Storage*, EUR 6128 en, Commission of the European Communities, Brussels.

CENE (Commission on Energy and the Environment) (1981) *Coal and the Environment*, HMSO, London.

Cmnd. 884 (1959) The Control of Radioactive Wastes, November, HMSO, London.

Cmnd. 6820 (1977) Nuclear power and the environment; the government's response to the Sixth Report of the Royal Commission on Environmental Pollution (Cmnd. 6618), HMSO, London.

Cmnd. 8607 (1982) Radioactive Waste Management, July, HMSO, London.

Cottrell, A. (1981) *How Safe is Nuclear Energy?* Heinemann, London.

Council for Science and Society (1976) *Superstar Technologies*, Barry Rose, in association with the Council for Science and Society, London.

Council on Environmental Quality (1980) *Public Opinion on Environmental Issues, results of a national public opinion survey*, US Government Printing Office, Washington D.C., p. 31.

Department of Energy (UK) (1979) Press release on the government statement on the nuclear power station ordering programme, December.

DoE (Department of the Environment) (1979a) *A Review of Cmnd. 884 The Control of Radioactive Wastes*, a report by an expert group to the Radioactive Waste Management Committee, Department of the Environment, London.

DoE (Department of the Environment) (1979b) Press notice 309A 'Research into the disposal of high-level radioactive waste', 24 July.

DoE (Department of the Environment) (1980) Press notice 17 'Geological research into radioactive waste disposal' 17 January.

DoE (Department of the Environment) (1981a) Letter and enclosures giving details of the radioactive waste management research programme, 1982/83, 20 March, London.

DoE (Department of the Environment) (1981b) Section 36, Town and Country Planning Act 1971, Atomic Energy Act 1954 (as amended), Acquisition of Land (Authorisation Procedure) Act 1946, Northumberland County Council, Appeals by United Kingdom Atomic Energy Authority, Objections to Three Compulsory Purchase Orders, report of the Inspector, July.

DoE (Department of the Environment) (1981c) Press notice 489 on 'Test-drilling', 16 December.

Duncan, A. (1981) Strategy for development of a UK radioactive waste management system, in *Environmental Impact of Nuclear Power*, proceedings of a conference organised by the British Nuclear Energy Society, British Nuclear Energy Society, London, pp. 107–118.

Duncan, A. and Brown, S. (1982) Quantities of waste and a strategy for treatment and disposal, *Nuclear Energy*, **23**(3), 161–166, June.

Edwards, L. (1980) Orkney uranium—the planning issues, Discussion Paper 80-01, Department of Political Economy, University of Aberdeen.

*Energy Daily*, (1982) Issue of Monday, May 3rd, 'Cash solves nuclear plant siting problems in France', p. 5.

*Financial Times* (1982a) Article 'Difficulties of a decent burial for radioactive wastes', 10 August.

*Financial Times* (1982b) Letter from Mr. D. Kinnersley, Amersham, Bucks., 19 August.

Firebaugh M. (1980) Public attitudes and information on the nuclear option, Research Memorandum ORAU/IEA–80–6(M), Institute for Energy Analysis, Oak Ridge Associated Universities, Oak Ridge, Tennesssee.

General Accounting Office (1981) *Coal and Nuclear Wastes—Both Potential Contributors to Environmental and Health Problems,* EMD-81-132, September 21, General Accounting Office, Washington, D.C.

Gray, D., Greenwood, P., Bisson, G., Cratchley, C., Harrison, R., Mather, J., Ostle, D., Poole, E., Taylor, B. and Willmore, P. (1976) *Disposal of Highly-active, Solid Radioactive Wastes into Geological Formations—relevant geological criteria for the United Kingdom,* report 76/12, Institute of Geological Sciences, HMSO, London.

Haytinck, B. (1980) Conceptual design of radioactive waste repositories in geological formations, in *European Applied Research Reports—Nuclear Science and Technology,* 2(1), 179–215.

Hill, M. (ed.) (1980) Radioactive waste management in perspective, supplement to *Radiological Protection Bulletin,* 36, 6, 8, September.

Hill, M. and Grimwood, P. (1978) *Preliminary Assessment of the Radiological Protection Aspects of Disposal of High-Level Wastes in Geological Formations,* report NRPB-R69, January, National Radiological Protection Board, Harwell.

Hill, M. and Lawson, G. (1980) *An Assessment of the Radiological Consequences of Disposal of High-Level Waste in Coastal Geologic Formations,* report NRPB-R108, November, National Radiological Protection Board, Harwell.

Hill, M., White, I., and Fleishman, A. (1980) *The Effects of Actinide Separation on the Radiological Consequences of Geological Disposal of High-Level Waste,* report NRPB-R95, January, National Radiological Protection Board, Harwell.

House of Commons Hansard (1982) Written replies to questions asked of the Secretary of State for the Environment and the Secretary of State for Scotland, 17 March, by Mr. S. Chapman, M.P.

House of Commons Select Committee on Energy (1981) First Report Session 1980–81 *The Government's Statement on the New Nuclear Power Programme,* I (HC 114-I), Report and Minutes of Proceedings, HMSO, London.

IAEA (International Atomic Energy Authority) (1977) *Site Selection Factors for Repositories of Solid High-Level and Alpha-Bearing Wastes in Geological Formations,* Technical Reports series no. 177, International Atomic Energy Authority, Vienna.

IGS (Institute of Geological Sciences) (1976) *Selection of areas for the disposal of highly active, solid radioactive waste into geological formations in the United Kingdom,* report G/D6/103.

Inhaber, H. (1978) *Risks of Energy Production,* Report AECB-1119/Rev. −1, May, Atomic Energy Control Board of Canada, Ottawa.

Kasperson, R. (1980) The dark side of the radioactive waste problem, in O'Riordan, T. and Turner, K. (eds.) *Progress in Resource Management and Environmental Planning,* II, 133–163, Wiley, London.

Lee, B. (1981) Brighter future for nuclear wastes?, *New Scientist,* 23 April, 227–229.

Lewis, A. (1981) Management of commercially generated radioactive wastes, *Engineering and Mining Journal,* February, 104–109.

Lindblom, U. and Gnirk, P. *Nuclear Waste Disposal; can we rely on bedrock?,* Pergamon, Oxford.

Maclean, D. (1980) Benefit-cost analysis, future generations and energy policy: a survey of the moral issues, *Science, Technology and Human Values,* 5(31), 3–10 (Spring).

Miller, Mrs. K. (1981) Secretary of the Scottish Conservation Society, personal communication to the author.

Montefiore, H. (1981) Ethics and energy, *Interdisciplinary Science Reviews,* 6(2), 103–109.

National Radiological Protection Board (1981) *Living with Radiation,* HMSO, London.

OTA (Office of Technology Assessment) (1982) *Managing Commercial High-Level Radioactive Waste, Summary,* Congress of the United States, Office of Technology Assessment, Washington D.C.

Parker, Hon. Mr. Justice (1978) *The Windscale Inquiry,* I, HMSO, London.

Pearce, D., Edwards, L. and Beuret, G. (1979) *Decision Making for Energy Futures,* Macmillan, London.

Rowan-Robinson, J. (undated, a.) Orkney uranium and the planning process, Discussion Paper, Department of Land Economy, University of Aberdeen.
Rowan-Robinson, J. (undated, b) Test drilling—the legal framework, Discussion Paper, Department of Land Economy, University of Aberdeen.
Royal Commission on Environmental Pollution (1976) *Nuclear Power and the Environment*, Sixth report (Cmnd. 6618), HMSO, London.
RWMAC (Radioactive Waste Management Advisory Committee) (1980) *First Annual Report*, May, HMSO, London.
RWMAC (Radioactive Waste Management Advisory Committee) (1981) *Second Annual Report*, May, HMSO, London.
RWMAC (Radioactive Waste Management Advisory Committee) (1982) *Third Annual Report*, May, HMSO, London.
Saunders, P. (1981) The management of high-level waste and its environmental impact, in *Environmental Impact of Nuclear Power*, proceedings of a conference organised by the British Nuclear Energy Society, 187–214, British Nuclear Energy Society, London.
Scottish Office (1980) Town and Country Planning (Scotland) Act 1972, Kyle and Carrick District Council, Appeal by the United Kingdom Atomic Energy Authority against the refusal of planning permission for (a) the drilling of boreholes for the purposes of studying the properties and structure of the rocks and the movement of water within them and (b) the temporary siting of up to 6 small portable buildings or caravans at Carrick Forest, Strathclyde, Reporter's Report, December.
Somerset County Council (1981) Minutues of the Planning and Transportation Committee, 18th January.
Stott, M., and Taylor, P. (1980) *The Nuclear Controversy*, Town and Country Planning Association and Political Ecology Research Group, London.
TCPA (Town and Country Planning Association) (1978) *Planning and Plutonium*, Town and Country Planning Association, London.
UKAEA (United Kingdom Atomic Energy Authority) (1980) Town and Country Planning Act 1971, Appeal by the United Kingdom Atomic Energy Authority against refusal of planning application for drilling of boreholes in the Northumberland National Park (Cheviot Hills), Transcripts of the inquiry proceedings. (These are referenced with the first number referring to the day of the transcript and the second to the page).
Weinberg, A. (1972) Social institutions and nuclear energy, *Science*, **177** (7 July), 33.
Weinberg, A. (1977) Is nuclear energy acceptable?, *Bulletin of the Atomic Scientists*, April, **33**(4), 54–60.
Weinberg, A., and Blomeke, J. (1982) Nuclear energy's achilles heel? A review of Fred C. Shapiro's *Radwaste*, submitted for publication in *Across the Board*, obtainable from Institute for Energy Analysis, Oak Ridge Associated Universities, Oak Ridge, Tennessee.
Wilbanks, T. (1981a) Building a consensus about energy technologies, Oak Ridge National Laboratory, report ORNL 5784, September, Oak Ridge, Tennessee.
Wilbanks, T. (1981b) Personal communication to the author, October.
Williams, R. (1980) *The Nuclear Power Decisions*, Croom-Helm, London.

# Conclusion

DAVID R. COPE, PETER JAMES AND PETER HILLS

The preceding chapters have revealed the many problems which energy developments and issues have created for planners over the last decade, and outlined some of the solutions which have emerged. They have also demonstrated the range of levels at which energy and planning choices are debated—a range which was graphically illustrated at the Sizewell and Windscale public inquiries, whose proceedings veered between, at one extreme, their implications for the future of British and world society and, at the other, the effects of buildings on the local landscape.

Discussion of energy and planning problems has often been couched in terms which are familiar to political scientists. Existing policies and institutions are seen as unsatisfyingly incremental in nature, so that the duty of planners and the planning system is to adopt, and encourage in others, a synoptic vision. If only better procedural mechanisms were introduced, more information was available, actors were less motivated by self-interest—then, it often appears to be assumed—a consensus over energy matters would emerge, and the role of planners would once again be unproblematic.

Much of this search has rested on an implicit, but often unacknowledged, belief in 'rational decision-making'. One important source of such views is the organisational theorist, Herbert Simon. In 'Administrative Behaviour' (1976) Simon criticised the traditional ends-means approach to action (in which decisions are made on an incremental basis, and only a narrow range of options examined) and compared it with a 'behaviour alternative model'. This comprised:

1. The listing of all the alternative strategies.
2. The determination of all the consequences that follow upon each of these strategies.
3. The comparative evaluation of these sets of consequences.

Although Simon has since admitted the impossibility of achieving such a counsel of perfection—and the technocratic implications of his theories have been widely criticised—this model retains a widespread acceptance as an ideal to be aimed at wherever possible.

283

Simon's views, albeit unacknowledged, have been influential in the energy debates of most Western countries, perhaps most of all in the UK. Traditional ends-means approaches have appeared to be well-established in Whitehall, where policy seems set in a traditional and unquestioned mould determined by the influence of powerful vested interests—the nationalised energy industries, the nuclear lobby, the oil companies—with little attempt to evaluate alternative courses of action. Outside Whitehall, many have demanded that an approximation of the 'behaviour alternative model' be introduced. Time after time—at inquiries, energy debates, meeting halls across the land—critics have argued that alternatives were not being explored, the true costs and benefits of different options were not being properly analysed, decisions were being taken in irrational ways.

In most respects such critics clearly had right on their side. The large energy organisations have had an unhealthy degree of influence and much of what passed for energy policy in the 1970s was little more than an expensive and wasteful 'squaring of the circle'. Each of the main energy 'great powers' was too powerful to be denied its share of the cake, so that expectations were met by positing a high-demand future in which major contributions from each would be needed—a proposal already dubious in the late 1970s and rendered even more suspect by the post-1979 recession. It was also true that too little was being spent on the exploration of other alternatives, particularly conservation but also some forms of renewable energy.

Nevertheless, the many uncertainties of energy policies and the still little understood relationships between the different energy sectors make the achievement of the 'synoptic' vision which might produce solutions extremely difficult. This has been readily apparent in the case of central government but some have argued that land-use planning may be able to contribute what politicians and civil servants cannot. Understandably frustrated by the conservatism and intertia of British and other national politics, opponents of energy policy (and in other areas such as transport) have turned to the publicly accessible arenas of the planning system to continue the battles they have lost before the electorate or in 'smoke-filled rooms'. The problem is that the planning system is not, and cannot be, a mechanism for resolving fundamental political and social conflict. Where issues are controversial and large numbers of people and organisations are lined up on different sides, almost any outcome will inevitably leave many people more or less embittered, more or less hostile to the planning system which has worked against their interests. Clearly if such people are persistent losers, their frustration and bitterness grows and the situation becomes ever more contentious and fraught. In liberal democracies there is a tendency to 'buy off' or 'put off' trouble when numbers of such groups become large enough to be of political significance—but there is always the potential for bitterness to spill over into violence and illegal action, as has happened in several countries.

The rights and wrongs of such actions and the decisions of the planning system are beyond the scope of this book. The point is that the resolution and containment of conflict is a political process, which will primarily take place on the political stage. Planners and the planning system are in this drama only as supporting players, whose role is to clarify the nature of the available choices, provide a forum for views to be heard and to ensure that, once decisions are made, they are effectively implemented. Attempts to substitute the planning system for the political system obscure the real issue of the energy debate—the failure of critics of existing energy policies to influence governments in anything but marginal ways, or to convince electorates of the merits of their case, with all the questions which these facts raise about the nature of power in western societies. Such attempts place intolerable strains on institutions which are not, and cannot be, able to cope with them.

To argue thus is not to suggest that planning should be seen as an apolitical, technical activity; rather to posit that an abandonment of the more utopian perspectives which have influenced some planners in recent decades will reveal new roles and areas of influence which, although more limited, may give greater practical opportunities to determine energy and social futures.

Dissatisfaction with the somewhat sterile division between incremental and synoptic approaches has created interest in theories of critical decision-making. These are based on the assumption that:

> "no decision may be justified, so that any individual decision may be discovered to have been mistaken after it has been made. The rational way for an individual agent to proceed is therefore to make choices whose errors, if they exist, can be detected quickly or remedied rapidly and without unduly high cost . . . Making a social choice is not finding some reasonable compromise between the fixed values of the individuals concerned. On the contrary, disagreement is resolved by some of the people involved in the decision changing their views about what their interests are, realising that their original opinions about what the group should choose were mistaken . . . Thus *debate* and not *compromise* is the key to the making of social decisions' (Collingridge, 1982).

Although its applicability depends upon particular circumstances, the general tenets of critical decision-making may help to clarify the role of planners in energy matters.

One task is to clarify and elaborate the nature of available energy choices and their land-use and social implications. While a synoptic vision may be impossible, few would deny that planners and planning procedures have often had insufficient resources—of money, manpower and expertise—to properly fulfil this goal. Much of the controversy about public inquiries has centred on this very point, with critics arguing that (amongst other problems) objectors to such developments as the Sizewell PRW lack sufficient funds to present their case and should receive state funding, that the inability of inquiries to conduct their own research limits the information they can consider and that the simultaneous consideration of strategic and tactical issues limits the extent to which either can be thoroughly examined.

Theories of critical decision-making also view decisions as part of a process rather than a series of points. This coincides with a growing awareness amongst planners that their involvement with energy matters needs to be continuous rather than discrete in nature. As the various chapters in this book demonstrate, a particular energy development is part of a cycle of construction, operation, waste disposal and decommissioning which may last for decades or centuries and affect a wide geographical area. A particular development—such as a new coalfield or nuclear reactor—may be one of a series whose quantitative increase may produce qualitative changes in nature and effects, which will concern the planning system for many years. The ability of planners to influence energy demand by changes in land-use patterns will also be an accummulation of small, individually insignificant advances: a feature of their work which, as Susan Owens notes, emphasises the importance of an energy 'awareness' which extends over time. All this suggests a need for a much greater level of energy expertise within the planning system, mechanisms to ensure that such expertise is available at the times and in the places when it is most required, some degree of anticipatory planning and, as planners themselves have increasingly developed in recent years, adequate monitoring to ensure that past decisions are implemented and that outcomes can be used to correct errors and influence present decisions.

**Expertise**

One of the main problems affecting planners in their consideration of both simple and complex substantive issues is—as the evidence of many chapters in this book demonstrates—a lack of expertise, not least because of the complexity and sophistication of modern energy technologies. Their advanced nature is readily apparent in the case of nuclear power, gas and oil (especially with offshore recovery), but even with such an apparently well-established energy source as coal, the scale and technological content of new developments frequently makes past experience of little value. The same is true of various energy demand management options such as combined heat and power (CHP) or district heating.

The problem of assessing such sophisticated technologies was noted, in a UK context, by the Inspector at the North East Leicestershire (Belvoir) Coalfield inquiry who saw it as (Mann, 1981) 'a major problem for the local authority' and indeed for any party (sometimes including the developer) to a major energy-related proposal. A similar situation exists in other western countries. One difficult area is that of determining the truth of claims that technologies and practices are 'acceptable'. Even more problematic is the tendency, given the long-term nature of many energy developments, to base substantial parts of the case for a particular project or even an entire energy option on the expectation that 'technological fixes' to presently unsolved problems will be found in the future. This is best illustrated in the case of anticipated advances in vitrification, storage and disposal technology for nuclear waste but has also occurred in mining waste disposal, where current research could result in better methods of land restoration.

Such problems of technological competence are by no means limited to the local authorities responsible for the operation of local land-use planning but they are particularly acute for them. The Council for Science and Society, in considering the problems of monitoring complex technologies where technical competence is the preserve of a small number of institutions or individuals with common goals, has argued that adequate technical 'overview' competence requires several factors:

(a) access to appropriate information;
(b) technical expertise to interpret information;
(c) an interdisciplinary perspective in the interpretation;
(d) time to carry out an adequate assessment;
(e) total independence from interested parties;
(f) institutional authority, so that conclusions will be implemented
(Council for Science and Society, 1976, p. 28–29).

Of course, for many aspects of the impact of a facility on a surrounding area, the local planning authority will be the source of the most detailed information on site characteristics and other features of the locality, existing and potential, which may interact with the development. But problems may arise when data on the specific characteristics of a development or policy option are the preserve of the developer or some other agency, who are reluctant to reveal information which may give away commercial confidences or otherwise disadvantage them (as with information on the assumptions made on future wage rates, in the economic costing of a project or its product). While the widespread operation of various procedural options, such as pre-inquiry meetings and developer/regulator liaison (given goodwill on both sides), may go a long way towards resolving the information supply problem, there will remain a need for the systematic extraction and collation of information from wide-ranging sources if evaluatory and regulatory authorities are to discharge their activities adequately. This implies a high degree of foresight and technological awareness in identifying emerging and pertinent issues which potential projects or policy options may create within the areas for which the authorities have jurisdiction.

Such needs emphasise the importance of *interpretational* competence, compared with the simple need for adequate information. Often planning or other assessing agencies need to tackle a surfeit of information (illustrated by the mass of inquiry material prepared for the UK Sizewell nuclear reactor inquiry), from which they must extract the *critical* facts and opinions.

In developing this interpretational competence, local planning authorities face a number of options, each with advantages and disadvantages. Obviously, they can attempt to develop an 'in-house expertise' and, given the obvious constraints on resources, this may be the most satisfactory approach, especially if a particular problem is likely to be an enduring one within the authority's remit. As a number of chapters in this book illustrate, the record of local planning authorities in Britain and elsewhere has been quite impressive in this respect. Several Scottish authorities have developed quite sophisticated liaison schemes; Barrow-in-Furness District Council's contribution to the development of hazard assessment is well described in the chapter on gas, while the record of Leicestershire County Council over the assessment of the North East Leicestershire (Belvoir) Coalfield demonstrates the 'learning curve' which can arise from inter-authority co-operation.

Such co-operation is an obvious response to the resource and expertise constraints discussed above and may take several forms. *Ad hoc* working parties may be set up, as illustrated by power station siting in the South East of England, discussed in Chapter 5 by John Glasson. More enduring arrangements can be established, as with inter-authority co-operation over the impact of mining spoil and subsidence problems in the Yorkshire and Humberside region of the UK. In North West England planning authorities have worked together on the general problems of regional development, including the location of hazardous industries, which are often energy-related. These associations are often of great value in co-ordinating responses to particular problems or in developing general expertise. A recent example of the former has been the Association of Metropolitan Authorities' promotion of guidelines for opencast coal-mining in England and Wales, while in the USA there has been a notable contribution to the development of local energy management schemes, for orthodox and emergency circumstances, by numerous, county, state and regional inter-authority organisations. The professional organisations, such as the Royal Town Planning Institute, are another obvious mechanism for development and interchange of expertise (Royal Town Planning Institute, 1979).

The development of expertise through piloting and testing exercises is rarely possible for planners. It has to be replaced by the transfer of information and experience from sequential developments on the assumption that they share common features which make transfer of data from one to another a legitimate activity. Whie this can be done quite comprehensively when dealing with a large number of developments, as with opencast coal mining in the UK, many energy developments are large and limited in number, with many site-specific features. This problem is well illustrated in previous chapters.

Frequently, planning authorities will find their assessment tasks aided, at least in theory, by national regulatory or evaluational agencies. In the UK, the Nuclear Installations Inspectorate, the National Radiological Protection Board and the Radioactive Waste Management Advisory Committee can, or have the potential to, aid authorities nuclear waste planning decisions. In the USA the Nuclear Regulatory Commission has a broad-ranging but similar role. However, the interface between such agencies and local planning authorities can be disjointed, especially if the agency does not have the resources to adequately handle all the cases which planning authorities may bring to it. This has recently occurred in the UK, where the Health and Safety Executive has had difficulty in evaluating hazardous industrial installations. The work of permanent agencies in providing expertise and information to planners is sometimes extended by 'one-off' exercises to deal with particular sources of concern. Thus in the UK the Commission on Energy and the Environment's 'Coal Study' was concerned with 'the identification of matters that are of common concern to all features of coal production; and therefore . . . the extent to which planning enquiries (sic) can be streamlined' (Commission on Energy and the Environment, 1979).

Whatever the contribution of such external sources (and one-off studies in the field of energy and environment rapidly become outdated) there is an increasing desire by planning authorities to develop an in-house capacity for the competent technical evaluation of energy-related issues. This is especially true where the location of fossil fuel sources, or related conversion facilities, will result in an enduring impact on the authorities' localities. Moves in this direction will require people with a strong grounding in technical expertise, quantitative analysis and economic and other appraisal techniques, and a familiarity with the policy-making process in complex subject areas. These will extend the remit of their concern far beyond the traditional narrow limits of physical design oriented planning—a development which has also been recognised as necessary for other areas of planning (Amos, 1982). It is perhaps a condemnation of the dominant approach to planning education that so many of this 'new breed' of planners are likely to spring from outside its conventional founts.

**Anticipatory Planning**

One theme which runs through all discussions of the relation between energy developments and land-use planning and which is taken up, for their different purposes, by energy facility developers, opponents of particular developments or energy policies in general and those interested in the professional advancement of planning methods and processes, is the extent to which it is possible to develop *anticipatory* planning systems. Instead of reacting on an *ad hoc* basis to each development proposal as it is put forward—which is generally the case at present—anticipatory planning would operate according to a structured process of prevision.

A critical component of such a system, and one which is obviously of central concern for land-use planning, is the extent to which it is feasible to make an explicit and early identification of the *sites,* or more particularly, the alternative sites, which are implied by national, regional or local energy options. In the UK the Commission on Energy and the Environment has argued that 'wider public debate and understanding of national energy policy can only go so far without the translation of energy policy into possible requirements for sites' (1981, p. 198).

Developers wish to have a pre-determined 'pool' of sites, from which they can select as and when an individual project becomes necessary. Opponents of projects or entire energy options may wish to demonstrate that alternative locations for an individual development exist or, conversely, that siting constraints rule out a particular option. Land-use planners have a professional commitment to the production of ordered, anticipatory site allocations. They may also wish to be free of sudden surprises being sprung on them, and increasingly, of protracted periods of uncertainty while a proposal is evaluated by the planning system, which effectively sterilises decision-making about many policy areas.

Given these common interests, it might be thought that anticipatory site-identifying planning would be the unexceptionable norm and indeed there are examples of the development of such plans, such as the identification of sites for power stations in the Netherlands (see Chapter 8) and the procedures adopted in Scotland for oil-related developments (see Chapter 3). However, there are both difficulties of method and disbenefits which stem from advanced site identification and these, together with simple system inertia, explain why in the UK as a whole, and many other countries, anticipatory, site-identifying planning remains a matter to be urged rather than applied.

Strategic site identification is the final stage of a linked series of anticipatory planning steps. Obviously at first the *overall supply and demand configuration* must be established in terms of primary and secondary energy requirements for future dates. These data, which are themselves the subject of uncertainty and disagreement, must then be translated into estimates of the *type and number of facilities* required to meet them. Early formulations of energy plans were based on forecasts or relatively high rates of growth of energy demand. Many new facilities were needed to meet this predicted demand and the *overall land requirements* and *other locational features* (such as water requirements) rapidly emerged as constraints. *Changes in technological characteristics or operational requirements* of energy supply facilities may also alter the siting circumstances and must be taken into account.

For example, the need to fit flue gas desulphurisation units to coal-fired stations restricts the number of suitable sites. Conversely, development of an inherently safe nuclear reactor, such as the Swedish SECURE system, would release nuclear heat generation from its current locational restrictions (Openshaw, 1982).

Only after these stages have been developed and executed can the process of site identification begin. In some cases an intermediate stage may arise where particular geographical land-forms such as the estuarine sites identified by the Watt Committee on Energy (1979) or particular areas of a country (such as the need for electricity generation capacity in South West England, because of grid transmission capacity difficulties) may emerge before individual sites can be narrowly identified. However, the final outcome will almost always be the demarcation of individual localities. Often specific sites, as with fossil fuels, are determined by pre-existing geology, so that the only flexibility derives from the sequencing of 'prospects', as discussed for the UK coal industry by Peter Hills in Chapter 2.

Disbenefits can result from the identification of possible locations. Regular, updated indications of the order of magnitude of future requirements for major energy projects—as advocated by the Commission of Energy and the Environment—may, given current uncertainties over future primary energy demand levels and supply mixes, result in the 'on-off-on-off-on' type of situation known only too well to the residents of sites shortlisted for airport location, as at Stansted in the UK. Such intolerable uncertainty rapidly leads those adversely affected to oppose a development at all costs, in the hope that least resistance strategies will cause developers to drop the particular site from their list of options. Developers may also resist being required to state their inventories for fear of incurring liabilities for the supposed blighting effects that could arise. These may be considerable, given the increasing tendency to 'safeguard' not merely the immediate land required for a development but also various zones around it. In addition there may be additional costs incurred in anticipation of subsequent energy developments, such as soundproofing or subsidence-resistant construction.

Considerable doubt remains as to the extent to which developers, if pressed to engage in advanced site identification, can be expected to approach this task with discrimination rather than a blanket identification of all possible sites in which they might conceivably be interested. In the UK there have been some suggestions that the identification of potential sites for synthetic natural gas (SNG) production, which require the retention of existing but disused sites, has displayed this tendency.

With nuclear power it is possible to concentrate future developments on existing sites. This 'nuclear park' strategy is rapidly becoming a central feature of location policy, as illustrated by Antoine Janssen in Chapter 8 on the Netherlands, or the proposed development of the Sizewell 'B' reactor in the UK. As well as raising numerous locational equity issues, especially when introduced retrospectively, this policy undoubtedly exacerbates the determination to resist *new* developments in the nuclear cycle. Much of the local opposition to proposed nuclear waste facilities in Britain and other countries has arisen from fears that the site chosen for initial development would find itself the recipient of sequential developments.

Numerous other problems arise with advanced site identification such as the fact that, if an 'insurance policy' of deliberate over-provision of supply is adopted, some sites may be needlessly identified. While this may be acceptable (except to those directly affected) if only one option for energy supply has such principles applied, the impact can rapidly escalate if it applies in all sectors.

For these reasons alone, the identification of sites in a system of anticipatory planning is unlikely to resolve some of the difficulties of energy development planning and will inevitably create some dilemmas of its own. As an intermediate stage, it may be possible to identify *dominant siting constraints* earlier in the planning process and to imbue these with a greater resilience than seems to be the case at present. For example, an overriding presumption may be made that agricultural self-sufficiency should have precedence over energy self-sufficiency or that developments of all forms would be vetoed in areas of special landscape value. However, as numerous cases illustrate, including the decision to carry out nuclear waste test-drilling in national park areas, specific energy-related exigencies may overrule even widely-supported guidelines.

### Regionalism and Energy

The question of anticipatory planning and advanced site identification is often closely related, because of the frequent geographical concentration of sites and their effects, with problems of regional equity and local sectionalism. A particularly striking example of this is provided by the development of Scottish oil and gas resources where, as Mackay notes in Chapter 3, many local areas have paid a high price for national or regional gains. Here, as in many other cases, tensions over the inequitable distribution of economic, social and environmental costs and benefits has exacerbated pre-existing tensions between the individual areas of Scotland, and between Scotland and the UK as a whole. Elsewhere, however, disputes related to energy development have created completely new conflicts (Corrigan and Stanfield, 1980). One response to these problems has been increased interest in the development of regional and local-scale energy economies, which have probably been explored to the greatest degree in the USA and Sweden. Advances in energy supply technologies, particularly greater use of renewable sources and district heating, together with fears about the strategic vulnerability of centralised systems and a preference amongst many of the rising generation for 'small is beautiful' philosophies will probably further encourage this trend (Wilbanks, 1981a, b). This is one area where land-use planning could be extremely influential and effective in coming decades.

### Planning and Energy: The Future

The evidence of the chapters collected here suggests that there is much that the planning system can do to help western societies adapt to the changed energy environment of coming decades and to ensure the optimum development of available energy resources. However, the lesson of many of the chapters—including this conclusion—is that, in order to operate more effectively, planners may need to cast off some of the more utopian aspirations which have surfaced during the anguished debates of recent years. The planning system is not a substitute for the political system, nor can it always proceed on a wholly 'rational' basis. Real conflicts, representing the clash of more or less powerful social groups, cannot be resolved by procedural reforms—although, of course, such reforms may be necessary in order to allow the nature of such conflicts to emerge, to be more clearly analysed and to allow the groups concerned to put their own views forward more effectively.

One opportunity is that of improving procedures for predicting the impacts of energy and related developments, and monitoring their eventual outcome over a number of years. As the chapters on Scottish oil, UK gas and Canada, among others, demonstrated, environmental impact assessment has an important role to play in this particular context, although its benefits have sometimes been exaggerated. Associated with this, but also related to other areas, is the need to develop greater technical competence within the planning system. Energy is a complex subject and developers have often taken advantage of their monopoly of expertise to limit the influence of planners on their activities. In addition to changes in planning education, there is a great deal of scope for co-operation between planning authorities, possibly including the establishment of jointly-funded bodies to provide expert help in particular fields. This already occurs to an increasing extent on an informal basis but there are certainly benefits to be derived from extending such arrangements.

Improved technical competence would also be of great value in helping planners determine the key aspects of energy developments and issues. Mackay's analysis of oil developments demonstrates the importance of such factors as skilled labour requirements, control of the construction process and taxation policies to eventual outcomes. A clearer knowledge of such key issues would maximise the opportunities available to planners to influence the eventual outcome of energy-related proposals.

Finally, planners may have the opportunity to establish a new role with the change in emphasis from a narrow focus on either energy supply *or* energy demand considerations to the systematic evaluation of complete energy systems. The ability of planners to influence all aspects of large-scale energy supply developments will always be limited. Their contribution to energy demand management, while currently under-realised, as explored in Chapter 9 by Susan Owens, must be developed with the acceptance that many aspects of this side of the energy balance, such as equipment and construction standards, will also remain outside their realm of direct concern. It is in the *integration* of supply and demand to maximise benefits that planners can make their most significant contribution. This is already being recognised by countries such as Sweden, which are now giving planners and local government an important role in achieving the goals of national energy policies and the trend can be expected to continue in the future. It should be given further impetus by continued interest in the development of more self-sufficient regional and local energy economies.

Land-planning seems assured of a central role in the evolution of energy supply and demand management in all the countries covered in this book. There is very considerable evidence that planners have coped well with the pressures which energy developments and their associated problems have placed on them in the last decade. The experience and achievements of those regional, county and local planning organisations whose exposure to such pressures are discussed in the preceding chapters provide a firm basis on which the future pattern of the relationship between land-use planning and energy can be developed.

## References

Amos, J. (1982) Few jobs, few top women, *Planning*, July, **9**, 8–9.

Collingridge, D. (1982) *Critical Decision-Making*, Frances Pinter, London.

Commission on Energy and the Environment (1979) Coal Study: Organisation and Structure. Note by the Secretariat, CENE (78) 21, Amended, Feb. 1979.

Commission on Energy and the Environment (1981) *Coal and the Environment*, HMSO, London.

Corrigan, R. and Stanfield, R. L. (1980) Rising energy prices, *National Journal*, 22 March, 468–473.

Council for Science and Society (1976) *Superstar Technologies*, Barry Rose, London.

Mann, M. (1981) Problems of the local planning inquiry, in *Planning Law for Industry*, proceedings of a seminar organised by the Committee on Environmental Law of the International Bar Association, Cambridge, March 29–April 2, International Bar Association, London.

Openshaw, S. (1982) The siting of nuclear power stations and public safety in the UK, *Regional Studies* **16**(3), 183–198.

Royal Town Planning Institute (1979) *Coal and the Environment*, Evidence submitted to the Commission on Energy and the Environment, Royal Town Planning Institute, London.

Simon, H. (1976) *Administrative Behaviour*, Free Press, New York.

Watt Committee (1979) *Energy and Land-use in the UK*, Report no. 4, Watt Committee on Energy, London.

Wilbanks, T. J. (1981a) *Solving our national energy problem through local planning: Keynote Address, Tennessee Chapter of the American Planning Association*, Gatlinburg, Tennessee.

Wilbanks, T. J. (1981b) Energy Self-sufficiency as an issue in regional and local development, in Lakshmanan, T. R. (ed.) *Energy and Regional Growth*.

# Author Index

# Subject Index

## Other Titles in the Series

The terms of our inspection copy service apply to all the above books. A complete catalogue of all books in the Pergamon International Library is available on request. The Publisher will be pleased to consider suggestions for revised editions and new titles.